ZAGAT®

Paris
Restaurants
2008/09

LOCAL EDITORS
Alexander Lobrano, assisted by Amy Serafin
LOCAL COORDINATORS
Mary Deschamps and Claire Fitzpatrick-Quimbrot
STAFF EDITOR
Troy Segal

Published and distributed by
Zagat Survey, LLC
4 Columbus Circle
New York, NY 10019
T: 212.977.6000
E: paris@zagat.com
www.zagat.com

ACKNOWLEDGMENTS

We thank Axel Baum, Patrick and Sabine Brassart, Gilbert Brownstone, Erin Emmett, Bertin Leblanc, Anne and Gérard Mazet, Bruno Midavaine, Denis Quimbrot, Steven Shukow, Boi Skoi and François de la Tour d'Auvergne, as well as the following members of our staff: Josh Rogers (associate editor), Sean Beachell, Maryanne Bertollo, Sandy Cheng, Reni Chin, Larry Cohn, Alison Flick, Jeff Freier, Roy Jacob, Natalie Lebert, Mike Liao, Dave Makulec, Chris Miragliotta, Andre Pilette, Kimberly Rosado, Becky Ruthenburg, Sharon Yates, Anna Zappia and Kyle Zolner.

Contents

Ratings & Symbols

Zagat Top Spot	Name	Symbols	Cuisine	Zagat Ratings			
				FOOD	DECOR	SERVICE	COST

Area, Address, Métro Stop & Contact*   **Z Tim & Nina's ❍** *French/Thai*   ▽ 23 | 9 | 13 | €15
6ᵉ | 604, rue de Buci (Odéon) | 01 23 45 54 32 | fax 23 44 55 66 | www.zagat.com

Review, surveyor comments in quotes

Jamais fermé, this "crowded" 6th-arrondissement cafe started the "French-Thai craze" (e.g. foie gras in pad Thai or lychee bouillabaisse); though it looks like a "garage" and T & N "never heard of credit cards or reservations" – yours in particular – the "*merveilleuse* Bangkok-Brest cuisine" draws delighted diners due to downmarket tabs.

Ratings   **Food, Decor** and **Service** are rated on the Zagat 0 to 30 scale.

0	– 9	poor to fair
10	– 15	fair to good
16	– 19	good to very good
20	– 25	very good to excellent
26	– 30	extraordinary to perfection
	▽	low response | less reliable

Cost reflects our surveyors' average estimate of the price of a dinner with one drink and tip and is a benchmark only. Lunch is usually 25% less.

For **newcomers** or survey **write-ins** listed without ratings, the price range is indicated as follows:

I	30€ and below
M	31€ to 50€
E	51€ to 80€
VE	81€ or more

Symbols

Z	Zagat Top Spot (highest ratings, popularity and importance)
❍	serves after 11 PM
S	closed on Sunday
M	closed on Monday
⊘	no credit cards accepted

* When calling from outside France, dial the country code +33, then omit the first zero of the number listed.

About This Survey

Here are the results of our **2008/09 Paris Restaurants Survey,** covering 1,000 eateries in Paris and its immediate suburbs. Like all of our guides, this one is based on the collective opinions of thousands of local consumers who have been there before you. Ratings have been updated throughout, and reviews have been rewritten as needed to reflect significant changes since our last survey.

WHO PARTICIPATED: Input from 5,487 frequent diners forms the basis for the ratings and reviews in this guide (their comments are shown in quotation marks within the reviews). Of these surveyors, 40% are women, 60% men; the breakdown by age is 6% in their 20s; 20%, 30s; 21%, 40s; 26%, 50s; and 27%, 60s or above. Collectively they bring roughly 930,000 annual meals worth of experience to this Survey. We sincerely thank each of these participants – this book is really "theirs."

HELPFUL LISTS: Whatever you're looking for, our top lists and indexes can help you find exactly the right place. See Key Newcomers (page 7), Most Popular (page 9), Top Ratings (pages 10–16) and Best Buys (page 17). We've also provided 43 handy indexes.

OUR EDITORS: Special thanks go to our local editors, Alexander Lobrano, European correspondent for *Gourmet* and a food and travel writer based in Paris, and Amy Serafin, an American journalist who has lived in Paris for the past 15 years. Our thanks go as well to our local coordinators Mary Deschamps and Claire Fitzpatrick-Quimbrot.

ABOUT ZAGAT: This marks our 29th year reporting on the shared experiences of consumers like you. What started in 1979 as a hobby involving 200 of our friends has come a long way. Today we have well over 300,000 surveyors and now cover dining, entertaining, golf, hotels, movies, music, nightlife, resorts, shopping, spas, theater and tourist attractions worldwide.

SHARE YOUR OPINION: We invite you to join any of our upcoming surveys – just register at **ZAGAT.com,** where you can rate and review establishments year-round. Each participant will receive a free copy of the resulting guide when published.

AVAILABILITY: Zagat guides are available in all major bookstores, by subscription at **ZAGAT.com** and for use on web-enabled mobile devices via **ZAGAT TO GO** or **ZAGAT.mobi.** The latter two products allow you to contact any establishment by phone with just one click.

FEEDBACK: There is always room for improvement, thus we invite your comments and suggestions about any aspect of our performance. Is there something more you would like us to include in our guides? Just contact us at **paris@zagat.com.**

New York, NY
May 14, 2008

Nina and Tim Zagat

What's New

(SMOKE) FREE AT LAST: On January 2nd, smoking was outlawed in all Parisian restaurants – doubtless to the delight of Zagat surveyors, 83% of whom support the ban. But, be warned: lighting up is still permitted on terraces.

SCENE-STEALING SETTINGS: Starting with the success of Georges, the striking venue atop the Centre Pompidou, an obsession with interiors has been building in the restaurant world. Now almost all owners seem convinced that, budget permitting, you need a designer label on your new or renovated establishment. Recent high-profile – and highly publicized – style statements include Patrick Jouin's futuristic revamp of Jules Verne, Philippe Starck's slightly surreal, tented decor for Le Dali in the Hôtel Meurice, Philippe Boisselier's monochromatic scheme for Le Saut du Loup and the Fornasetti art- and artifact-adorned L'Eclaireur. Their efforts should prove profitable, since nearly 40% of our surveyors say they'd patronize a place just for its decor or ambiance.

SIMPLICITY RULES: But if the restaurateurs are thinking big, many of the chefs are thinking small – or at least smaller. After leaving her Haute Cuisine establishment a few years ago, Ghislaine Arabian has returned with a modest bistro, Les Petites Sorcières; Christian Constant (Le Violon d'Ingres) keeps things casual at Les Cocottes, his new counter-service site; and Hélène Darroze's latest spin on Southwestern fare takes place at the informal Le Toustem. In terms of the cuisine itself, simplicity also rules. For example, Le Grand Pan is one of the town's newest hits with a menu that consists mainly of straightforward grills.

NEW VINTAGE WINE BARS: Another trend has been the comeback of the *bar à vins* and *bistrot à vins*, a movement appreciated by the 79% of surveyors who typically order a bottle of wine when dining out (this is France, after all). Members of the new generation like La Crémerie, Les Fines Gueules and Les Racines accompany their pours with cheese and charcuterie, and a few cooked dishes – but unlike the generic pub grub of yore, these edibles are high-grade goods.

GREEN IS THE NEW BLACK: The French have been a bit late to jump on the *"bio"* bandwagon. But now 56% of our surveyors say they're willing to pay more for sustainably raised or organic food, and 72% feel trans fats should be banned.

ELEVATED EATS: Willing or not, respondents are paying more in Paris. Since 2006, the average cost per meal rose 2.9% annually, to 55.43€, or $85.89. But nearly half state they're eating out just as often as they did two years ago – and 30% say they're patronizing restaurants even more. The favorite neighborhood remains the 8th arrondissement, home to such stalwarts as Taillevent and Alain Ducasse – and to popular new lights like Mini Palais, Le Mood and SYDR.

Paris
May 14, 2008

Alexander Lobrano

subscribe to ZAGAT.com

Key Newcomers

Our editors' take on the most notable new arrivals of the past year. For a full list, see the index on page 241.

Afaria | *New French/Southwest*	Il Vino | *Classic French/Mediterranean*
Agassin | *Classic/New French*	Karl et Erich | *New French*
Breizh Café | *Brittany*	Lup | *Eclectic*
Chéri Bibi | *Bistro*	M Comme Martine | *Bistro*
Christophe | *Bistro*	Mini Palais | *New French*
Cocottes | *New French*	P'tit Casier | *Seafood*
Cristal de Sel | *New French*	Saut du Loup | *New French*
Epigramme | *Bistro*	SYDR | *Southwest*
Fines Gueules | *Wine Bar/Bistro*	Toustem | *Southwest*
Grand Pan | *Bistro*	Urbane | *Bistro*

Other *arrivistes* are actually revivals that have been rejuvenated by a fresh address or fresh management. After delighting devotees for a decade with its combination of Classic and New French cuisine in the 6th, **Au Gourmand** took a year off, then resurfaced in the 1st. Vincent Cozzoli, one of the town's top-ranking Italian toques, moved his **Chez Vincent** to a pretty Parc des Buttes Chaumont locale. Talented chef-owner Eric Chauvet, whose pedigree includes La Tour d'Argent, is transforming typical neighborhood bistro **Le Triporteur** in the 15th. A new regime is also in place at **Natacha,** hoping to restore the star power of this former celebrity-studded Classic French in the 14th.

In the year to come, **Altitude 95,** the more casual eatery in the Eiffel Tower, rises afresh under the aegis of chef-restaurateur Alain Ducasse, who just transformed sibling **Jules Verne;** British super-chef Gordon Ramsay makes his Paris debut, taking over the kitchen at the **Trianon Palace** hotel in Versailles; luxury grocer **Fauchon** reopens its restaurant with black, pink, white and silver decor by designer Christian Biecher; the legendary **Le Palace,** the city's reigning disco of the 1970s and '80s, returns as a restaurant with a former sous-chef of Pierre Gagnaire at the helm; the **Royal Monceau** hotel unveils a fresh look by the omnipresent Philippe Starck throughout its premises, including its two new Italian and French eateries; chef Yannick Alléno (Le Meurice) is the likely culinary consultant for a new 21st-century brasserie to open in the back of the Opéra Garnier; **L'Arbuci,** the mythic Saint-Germain brasserie, comes back with new decor by international designer India Mahdavi and with Thierry Costes, who's made the Hôtel Amour such a hit, as director; and – speaking of the indefatigable Costes family – its Napoleonic march on the Paris restaurant scene continues with three projects: a relaunch of **L'Appart',** a restaurant with a view at the Printemps department store and a new place in the Parc Vincennes.

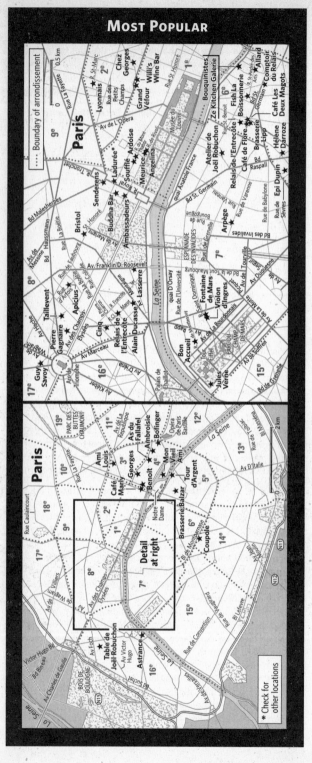

Most Popular

1. Taillevent | *Haute*
2. Atelier Joël Robuchon | *Haute*
3. Grand Véfour | *Haute*
4. Alain Ducasse | *Haute*
5. Tour d'Argent | *Haute*
6. Cinq (Le) | *Haute*
7. Guy Savoy | *Haute*
8. Ladurée | *Classic French/Tea*
9. Jules Verne | *Classic French*
10. Bofinger | *Brasserie*
11. Pierre Gagnaire | *Haute*
12. Ami Louis | *Bistro*
13. Relais/l'Entrecôte | *Steak*
14. Epi Dupin | *Bistro*
15. Brass. Lipp | *Brasserie*
16. Benoît | *Lyon*
17. Lasserre* | *Haute*
18. Meurice | *Haute*
19. Comptoir/Relais | *Bistró/Brass.*
20. Ambassadeurs | *Haute/New Fr.*
21. Table de Joël Robuchon | *Haute*
22. Angelina | *Tearoom*
23. Ambroisie | *Haute*
24. Café/Deux Magots | *Classic Fr.*
25. Bouquinistes | *New French*
26. Coupole | *Brasserie*
27. Ze Kitchen Galerie* | *Eclectic*
28. Bristol | *Haute*
29. Hélène Darroze* | *New Fr./SW*
30. Senderens* | *Brass./New French*
31. Soufflé | *Classic French*
32. Allard | *Bistro*
33. Astrance | *New French*
34. Bon Accueil | *Bistro*
35. Arpège | *Haute*
36. Chez Georges* | *Bistro*
37. Café de Flore | *Classic French*
38. Lyonnais* | *Lyon*
39. Brass. Balzar | *Brasserie*
40. Georges | *Eclectic*
41. Fish La Boissonnerie | *Provence*
42. Ardoise | *Bistro*
43. Buddha Bar* | *Asian*
44. As du Fallafel | *Israeli*
45. Apicius | *Haute*
46. Café Marly* | *Classic/New Fr.*
47. Fontaine de Mars* | *Southwest*
48. Willi's | *Wine Bar/Bistro*
49. Violon d'Ingres | *Bistro*
50. Mon Vieil Ami | *Bistro*

It's obvious that many of the above restaurants are among Paris' most expensive, but if popularity were calibrated to price, we suspect that a number of other restaurants would join their ranks. Thus, we have added a list of 80 Best Buys on page 17. These are restaurants that give real quality at extremely reasonable prices.

Top Food Ratings

Excludes places with low votes, unless indicated by a ▽.

28	Taillevent	Haute	
	Cinq (Le)	Haute	
	Guy Savoy	Haute	
	Astrance	New French	
	Pierre Gagnaire	Haute	
	Ambroisie	Haute	
	Alain Ducasse	Haute	
	Atelier Joël Robuchon	Haute	
	Grand Véfour	Haute	
	Ambassadeurs	New French	
27	Lasserre	Haute	
	Michel Rostang	Classic French	
	Braisière	Gascony	
	Bristol	Haute	
	Dominique Bouchet	Haute	
	Meurice*	Haute	
	Pré Catelan	Haute	
	Relais d'Auteuil	Haute	
26	Apicius	Haute	
	Trou Gascon	Southwest	
	Hiramatsu	Haute	
	Carré des Feuillants	Haute	
	Table de Joël Robuchon	Haute	
	Arpège	Haute	
	Espadon (L')	Classic French	

	Pavillon Ledoyen	Haute
	Villaret	Bistro
	Jacques Cagna	Haute
	Comptoir/Relais	Bistro/Brass.
	Senderens	Brass./New French
	Bistrot de l'Oulette	Southwest
	Vin sur Vin	New French
	Passiflore	Asian/Classic French
	Stella Maris	Classic French
25	Os à Moëlle	Classic French
	Gérard Besson	Classic French
	Régalade*	Basque/Bistro
	144 Petrossian	Seafood
	Pavillon/Gr. Cascade*	Haute
	Ami Louis	Bistro
	Tour d'Argent	Haute
	Relais Louis XIII	Haute
	Hélène Darroze	New Fr./SW
	Cagouille	Seafood
	Isami*	Japanese
	Temps au Temps	Bistro
	Caviar Kaspia	Russian
	Marius et Janette	Seafood
	Violon d'Ingres*	Bistro
	Ze Kitchen Galerie	Eclectic

BY CUISINE (FRENCH)

BISTRO (CONTEMP.)

26	Villaret
	Comptoir du Relais
25	Temps au Temps
	Violon d'Ingres
24	Timbre

BISTRO (TRAD.)

25	Régalade
	Ami Louis
	D'Chez Eux
24	Bon Accueil
	Voltaire

BRASSERIE

23	Relais Plaza
	Chez Les Anges
22	Garnier
20	Stella
19	Coupole

CLASSIC

27	Michel Rostang
26	Espadon (L')
	Passiflore
	Stella Maris
	Os à Moëlle

CONTEMPORARY

28	Astrance
	Ambassadeurs
26	Hiramatsu
	Senderens
	Vin sur Vin

HAUTE CUISINE

28	Taillevent
	Cinq (Le)
	Guy Savoy
	Pierre Gagnaire
	Ambroisie

LYON	**SHELLFISH**

LYON

- 24 Benoît
- 21 Chez René
- Lyonnais
- Vieux Bistro
- 20 Aub. Pyrénées Cévennes

OTHER REGIONS

- 27 Braisière | *Gascony*
- 24 Chez Michel | *Brittany*
- Chez L'Ami Jean | *Basque*
- Troquet | *Basque*
- 23 Pamphlet | *Basque*

PROVENCE

- 24 Casa Olympe
- 23 Chez Janou
- 22 Bastide Odéon
- Fish La Boissonnerie
- 18 Bistro de l'Olivier

SEAFOOD

- 25 144 Petrossian
- Cagouille
- Marius et Janette
- 24 Fables de La Fontaine
- Divellec

SHELLFISH

- 25 Marius et Janette
- 22 Dôme
- Garnier
- 20 Huîtrier
- Stella

SOUTHWEST

- 26 Trou Gascon
- Bistrot de l'Oulette
- 25 Hélène Darroze
- D'Chez Eux
- 23 Pamphlet

STEAK

- 24 Relais de Venise
- 22 Relais/l'Entrecôte
- 20 Severo
- 18 Ribouldingue
- 17 Gavroche

WINE BARS/BISTROS

- 23 Bourguignon du Marais
- 22 Cave de l'Os à Moëlle
- 20 Bouchons/Fr. Clerc
- Enoteca
- Willi's Wine Bar

BY CUISINE (OTHER)

CHINESE/ASIAN

- 21 Diep
- Chez Vong
- 20 Mirama
- Passy Mandarin
- 18 Davé

ECLECTIC

- 25 Ze Kitchen Galerie
- 23 Relais Plaza
- 22 Spoon, Food & Wine
- Market
- Comptoir

GREEK/MED.

- 22 Pasco
- 21 Sept Quinze∇
- 19 Mavrommatis
- 15 7ème Sud

ITALIAN

- 23 Sormani
- Il Cortile
- 22 Ostéria (L')
- Stresa
- 21 Casa Bini

JAPANESE

- 25 Isami
- 23 Kinugawa/Hanawa
- 20 Yen
- 18 Inagiku
- Orient-Extrême

MIDDLE EASTERN

- 24 As du Fallafel
- Liza
- 21 Al Dar
- Al Diwan
- 19 Noura

MOROCCAN

- 22 404
- Mansouria
- 21 Comptoir
- Chez Omar
- 20 Atlas

SPANISH/LATIN AMER.

- 21 Anahuacalli
- Fogón
- 19 Bellota-Bellota∇
- Anahï
- El Palenque

THAI

21	Thiou/Petit Thiou
20	Baan-Boran
	Blue Elephant
19	Banyan
17	Erawan

VIETNAMESE

23	Tan Dinh
22	Coin/Gourmets
20	Lac-Hong∇
18	Davé
	Palanquin

BY SPECIAL FEATURE

BRUNCH

24	Liza
22	404
	Market
	Jardin des Cygnes
21	Mariage Frères

HOTEL DINING

28	Cinq (Le)
	(Four Seasons George V)
	Pierre Gagnaire
	(Hôtel Balzac)
	Alain Ducasse
	(Plaza Athénée)
	Atelier Joël Robuchon
	(Hôtel Pont Royal)
	Ambassadeurs
	(Hôtel de Crillon)

LATE DINING

28	Atelier Joël Robuchon
26	Villaret
	Bistrot de l'Oulette
25	Os à Moëlle
	Caviar Kaspia

LIVE ENTERTAINMENT

27	Lasserre
23	Relais Plaza
	Bar Vendôme
22	Café Faubourg
20	Djakarta

SLEEPERS∇

26	Restaurant (Le)
25	Grand Venise
	Cave Gourmande/Mark Singer
	Magnolias*
	Cuisine (7e)

SUNDAY DINING

28	Cinq (Le)
	Atelier Joël Robuchon
	Ambassadeurs
27	Bristol
26	Table de Joël Robuchon

TEA & DESSERTS

24	Jean-Paul Hévin
23	Ladurée
	Dalloyau
22	Table d'Hédiard
21	Mariage Frères

TRENDY

26	Comptoir du Relais
25	Ze Kitchen Galerie
24	Sensing
23	Aida∇
22	Chateaubriand

WINNING WINE LISTS

28	Taillevent
	Ambroisie
26	Vin sur Vin
25	Tour d'Argent
23	Macéo

BY ARRONDISSMENT

1ST

28	Grand Véfour
27	Meurice
26	Carré des Feuillants
	Espadon (L')
25	Gérard Besson

2ND

24	Liza
	Chez Georges

22	Fontaine Gaillon
	Drouant
21	Lyonnais

3RD

25	Ami Louis
23	Pamphlet
	Chez Janou
22	404
	Petit Marché

subscribe to ZAGAT.com

4TH

- 28 Ambroisie
- 26 Bistrot de l'Oulette
- 25 Isami
- 24 As du Fallafel
- Benoît

5TH

- 25 Tour d'Argent
- 23 Truffière
- Papilles
- Coupe-Chou
- Rôtiss. du Beaujolais

6TH

- 26 Jacques Cagna
- Comptoir du Relais
- 25 Relais Louis XIII
- Hélène Darroze
- Ze Kitchen Galerie

7TH

- 28 Atelier Joël Robuchon
- 26 Arpège
- Vin sur Vin
- 25 144 Petrossian
- Violon d'Ingres

8TH

- 28 Taillevent
- Cinq (Le)
- Pierre Gagnaire
- Alain Ducasse
- Ambassadeurs

9TH

- 24 Casa Olympe
- 23 Ladurée
- Spring
- 19 Jean
- BE Boulangépicier

10TH

- 24 Chez Michel
- 19 Brass. Julien
- 18 Deux Canards
- Brass. Flo
- 17 Chez Papa

11TH

- 26 Villaret
- 25 Temps au Temps
- 23 Bistrot Paul Bert
- 22 Chateaubriand
- Mansouria*

12TH

- 26 Trou Gascon
- 20 Biche au Bois
- 19 Oulette
- Train Bleu
- 16 Lina's

13TH

- 24 Ourcine
- 23 Avant Goût
- 21 Petit Marguery
- 16 Chez Paul
- 10 Buffalo Grill

14TH

- 25 Régalade
- Cagouille
- 23 Duc (Le)
- 22 Dôme
- Crêperie de Josselin

15TH

- 25 Os à Moëlle
- 24 Troquet
- 22 Cave de l'Os à Moëlle
- 21 Fellini
- 20 Villa Corse

16TH

- 28 Astrance
- 27 Pré Catelan
- Relais d'Auteuil
- 26 Hiramatsu
- Table de Joël Robuchon

17TH

- 28 Guy Savoy
- 27 Michel Rostang
- Braisière
- 24 Relais de Venise
- 23 Sormani

18TH, 19TH & 20TH

- 20 A. Beauvilliers
- 19 Famille
- 16 Boeuf Couronné
- Baratin
- 15 Lao Siam

OUTSIDE PARIS

- 23 Dalloyau
- 22 Cazaudehore
- 21 Bistrot d'à Côté
- 20 Camélia
- 19 Potager du Roy

Top Decor Ratings

29 Cinq (Le)
Pavillon/Gr. Cascade
Grand Véfour
Ambassadeurs

28 Pré Catelan
Lasserre
Meurice
Tour d'Argent
Bristol
Taillevent
Cristal Room

27 Alain Ducasse
Train Bleu
Ombres (Les)
1728
Espadon (L')
Ambroisie
Lapérouse

26 Jules Verne
Laurent
Apicius
Pavillon Ledoyen
Bar Vendôme
Brass. Julien

25 Buddha Bar

Georges
Costes
Guy Savoy
Bouillon Racine
Kong
Maxim's
Coupe-Chou
404
Pierre Gagnaire
Hiramatsu

24 Chalet des Iles
Fermette Marbeuf
Relais Louis XIII
Liza
Elysées (Les)
Maison Blanche
Michel Rostang
Grand Colbert
Bofinger
Café Marly
Ladurée
Atelier Joël Robuchon
Arpège

23 Jacques Cagna
Rest. du Musée d'Orsay

HISTORIC SPACES

Ambassadeurs
Angelina
Aub. Nicolas Flamel
Bofinger
Café Les Deux Magots
Charpentiers
1728
Espadon (L')
Grand Véfour
Jules Verne

Lapérouse
Lasserre
Laurent
Maxim's
Pavillon/Gr. Cascade
Pavillon Ledoyen
Pré Catelan
Relais Louis XIII
Tour d'Argent
Train Bleu

OUTDOORS

Absinthe
Bar Vendôme
Bristol
Café Lenôtre
Chez Gégène
Closerie des Lilas
Fables de La Fontaine
Jardin des Cygnes
Jardins de Bagatelle
Maison de l'Amer. Latine

Méditerranée
Pavillon/Gr. Cascade
Pavillon Montsouris
Petite Cour
Point Bar
Pré Catelan
Rest. du Palais Royal
Romantica
Saut du Loup
Terrasse Mirabeau

ROMANCE

Alain Ducasse
Ambassadeurs
Ambroisie
Astrance
Bristol
Caviar Kaspia
Coupe-Chou
Espadon (L')
Grand Véfour
Guy Savoy
Joséphine/Dumonet
Lapérouse
Lasserre
Meurice
Orangerie
Pavillon/Gr. Cascade
Pavillon Ledoyen
Pré Catelan
Restaurant (Le)
Tour d'Argent

ROOMS

Ambassadeurs
Ambroisie
Blue Elephant
Brass. Mollard
Brass. Printemps
Cristal Room
Dali
1728
Ladurée (16, rue Royale)
Lapérouse
Liza
Maison Blanche
Market
Mini Palais
Mori Venice Bar
Nouvelle Athenes
Ozu
Pré Catelan
Saut du Loup
Senderens
Tokyo Eat
Train Bleu

VIEWS

Bar Vendôme
Bon Accueil
Bouquinistes
Caviar Kaspia
Cinq (Le)
Espadon (L')
Fontaine de Mars
Fontaine Gaillon
Georges
Grand Véfour
Il Cortile
Isami
Jules Verne
Lapérouse
Lasserre
Maison Blanche
Méditerranée
Pavillon/Gr. Cascade
Pavillon Ledoyen
Petite Cour
Quai
Tour d'Argent

Top Service Ratings

28 Cinq (Le)
    Ambassadeurs
    Taillevent
    Lasserre
    Grand Véfour
    Espadon (L')

27 Pierre Gagnaire
    Guy Savoy
    Meurice
    Alain Ducasse
    Bristol
    Astrance
    Michel Rostang

26 Ambroisie
    Pavillon/Gr. Cascade
    Pré Catelan
    Apicius
    Tour d'Argent
    Hiramatsu
    Florimond
    Pavillon Ledoyen
    Relais d'Auteuil

25 Jacques Cagna
    Carré des Feuillants
    Bar Vendôme

D'Chez Eux
Temps au Temps
Table de Joël Robuchon
Arpège
Elysées (Les)
Relais Louis XIII
Maupertu

24 Gérard Besson
    Lapérouse
    Angle du Faubourg
    Atelier Joël Robuchon
    Dominique Bouchet
    Timbre*
    Jules Verne
    Trou Gascon

23 Laurent
    Braisière
    Ferme St-Simon
    Villaret
    Goumard
    Table du Lancaster
    Truffière
    Maison du Jardin
    Poule au Pot
    Violon d'Ingres*

Best Buys

1. As du Fallafel
2. Cosi
3. Crêperie de Josselin
4. Breakfast in America
5. Lina's
6. A Priori Thé
7. Jean-Paul Hévin
8. Mariage Frères
9. Angelina
10. Chartier
11. BE Boulangépicier
12. Chez Marianne
13. Boulangerie Éric Kayser
14. Chez Papa
15. Ladurée
16. Loir dans la Théière
17. Dalloyau
18. Flore en l'Ile
19. Temps au Temps
20. Cave de l'Os à Moëlle
21. Chez Janou
22. Rest. du Musée d'Orsay
23. Gamin de Paris
24. Chez Omar
25. Higuma
26. Bistrot d'Henri
27. Verre Volé
28. Paradis du Fruit
29. Polidor
30. Relais de Venise
31. Coin/Gourmets
32. Café Charbon
33. 404
34. Dame Tartine
35. Trumilou
36. Bistrot de l'Oulette
37. P'tit Troquet
38. Timbre
39. Bouillon Racine
40. Maison du Jardin

OTHER GOOD VALUES

Accolade
Afaria
Agassin
Allobroges
AOC
Astier
Bascou
Bon Saint Pourçain
Breizh Café
Buisson Ardent
Café Constant
Carte Blanche
Chantairelle
Chateaubriand
Chéri Bibi
Chez L'Ami Jean
Chez Marcel
Chez Ramulaud
Christophe
Comptoir du Relais

Duc de Richelieu
Ecailler du Bistrot
Entredgeu
Epi Dupin
Epigramme
Fines Gueules
Hier & Aujourd'hui
Huîtrerie Régis
Mesturet
Pré Verre
Pure Café
Racines
Reuan Thai
Sot l'y Laisse
Temps des Cerises
Tricotin
Uitr
Vieux Chêne
Vivres
Winch

RESTAURANT
DIRECTORY

	FOOD	DECOR	SERVICE	COST

Abadache (L') 🗷 *Bistro* — | - | - | - | M

17ᵉ | 89, rue Lemercier (Brochant/Place de Clichy) | 01 42 26 37 33 |
fax 01 42 26 37 33

The name is a play on 'haberdasher', English for *le mercier,* the street
where a Franco-British couple runs this "small" Batignolles bistro –
a cheap and "charming" place that hits the spot with traditional
French flavors (and some English touches) that "dance in your
mouth like fireworks"; the slapdash decor "is of no importance", but
the staff makes you "feel like you belong to a family."

A. Beauvilliers 🗷Ⓜ *Classic French* — 20 | 21 | 18 | €76

18ᵉ | 52, rue Lamarck (Lamarck-Caulaincourt) | 01 42 55 05 42 |
fax 01 42 55 05 87 | www.abeauvilliers.com

Young chef-owner "Yohan Paran has resurrected" this three-
decade-old Montmartre institution named for Marie-Antoinette's
chef; his "imaginative" take on Classic French dishes has "surprising
and harmonious" results, while the updated decor still breathes
"old-world romance" with "individual, intimate rooms" – and though
the "plethora of fresh flowers is no more", there's still a shady plant-
filled terrace in summer.

Absinthe (L') 🗷 *Bistro* — 20 | 18 | 18 | €50

1ᵉʳ | 24, pl du Marché St-Honoré (Pyramides/Tuilleries) | 01 49 26 90 04 |
fax 01 49 26 08 64 | www.michelrostang.com

Now "under the direction of Caroline Rostang", Michel's daughter,
this "stylish" place "decorated like a NYC loft" with exposed-brick
walls and a big clock face overlooks "one of the trendiest addresses
in Paris today" – the Marché Saint-Honoré, which makes it "a must,
even if the food is mediocre", as some snap; others, however, applaud the bistro cooking for its "inventive touch"; service is
"friendly", if "spotty", prices are "relatively reasonable" and there's
a "great terrace" to grab early.

Accolade (L') 🗷Ⓜ *Bistro* — | - | - | - | M

17ᵉ | 23, rue Guillaume Tell (Perreire) | 01 42 67 12 67 | fax 01 42 67 12 67 |
www.laccolade.com

A former butcher shop has been transformed into an "intimate
neighborhood bistro" by a young couple – he's in the kitchen, turning out "good" contemporary French cuisine (after training under
chef Michel Rostang), and she's in the dining area, two "appealing"
rooms simply decorated with wood tables and brightly painted
walls; while still a sleeper, this *bonne adresse* is gradually garnering
plaudits from Porte de Champerret locals.

A et M, Restaurant 🗷 *Classic French* — ▽ 21 | 14 | 19 | €45

16ᵉ | 136, bd Murat (Porte de St-Cloud) | 01 45 27 39 60 |
fax 01 45 27 69 71

This venue is one of several Parisian places where a Japanese chef
nails Classic French cuisine – though its "out-of-the-way" location
near the Porte de Saint-Cloud may feel halfway to Tokyo; fortunately,
the dishes are "consistently" "well executed", the service is "pleasant" and even if the modern decor is just "average", this "great-

value" restaurant co-owned by chefs Jean-Pierre Vigato (Apicius) and François Grandjean (Marius) is "a place to go back to."

NEW Afaria ☒ *New French/Southwest* — — — M
15e | 15, rue Desnouettes (Convention) | 01 48 56 15 36
On a quiet street in the 15th, young chef-owner Julien Duboué has created a stir with this funky new bistro that serves up some innovative spins on Southwestern French fare (apple-infused blood sausage, grilled duck in balsamic vinegar), along with tapas for grazing types; the casual brown-and-white dining room is decked out in country Basque fashion, with bare wood floors and red-glass lighting fixtures to lure a lively local crowd.

Affriolé (L') ☒Ⓜ *Bistro* 22 15 19 €48
7e | 17, rue Malar (Invalides/La Tour-Maubourg) | 01 44 18 31 33
Tucked away in a "quiet street in the 7th" is this "gastronomic pearl with low prices" – that is, relative to the "excellent" bistro menu that is "modern without being too trendy" and "changes often"; "young professionals who look as good as the chef's offerings" dine in the "hip, small" surrounds, distinguished mainly by the "gorgeous mosaic-topped tables"; "service is frenetic, if affable", and overall, this "tiny little place packs a delightful punch."

NEW Agassin (L') ☒ *Classic/New French* — — — M
7e | 8, rue Malar (Invalides/La Tour-Maubourg) | 01 47 05 18 18
After a distinguished career that's included La Tour d'Argent and the old Anacréon, chef-owner André Le Letty beckons to the business types of the 7th with this intimate establishment, whose tasteful beige-and-burgundy decor is enlivened with photos of his native Brittany; though grounded in the classics – veal kidneys in mustard, sautéed scallops in rosemary *jus* – the French menu also has its innovative moments, especially with desserts.

Aida ☒Ⓜ *Japanese* ▽ 23 15 19 €105
7e | 1, rue Pierre Leroux (Duroc/Vanneau) | 01 43 06 14 18 | fax 01 43 06 14 18 | www.aidaparis.com
As "trendy" as a sake cocktail, this "memorable" Asian near the Bon Marché serves "interesting, delectable" Japanese dishes to a select crowd of 20 well-heeled diners (with or without their heels); the "minimally decorated", Kyoto-inspired interior allows clients "to focus on the Japanese food" (prix fixe or tasting menus) and the Burgundy list; men are requested to wear jackets, the pockets preferably stuffed with yen.

Aiguière (L') ☒ *Classic French* — — — E
11e | 37 bis, rue de Montreuil (Faidherbe-Chaligny) | 01 43 72 42 32 | fax 01 43 72 96 36 | www.l-aiguiere.com
In a former roadhouse for Louis XIII's musketeers, this Classic French "on the eastern reaches" of the 11th might feel like "a trek" if you're not on horseback, but adventurers say it's "worth it" for "seamless service" and cooking that's a "wonderful treat for the taste buds", washed down by a bottle from the "very fine cellar"; the

| | FOOD | DECOR | SERVICE | COST |

Gustavian-style "rustic country" decor – pale yellow with blue checked curtains – is "cheerful."

Aimant du Sud (L') ●⌾ *Classic French* — | — | — | M

13ᵉ | 40, bd Arago (Les Gobelins) | 01 47 07 33 57 | fax 01 44 24 24 84
With a name that means 'lover of the south', it's no surprise there's much Midi on the menu of this Classic French, "one of the better little bistros in the 13th"; service is "friendly but irregular", and if the kitchen "occasionally misses", the "good Basque wine list" restores a sunny disposition.

Alain Bourgade ⌾Ⓜ≠ *New French* — | — | — | VE

16ᵉ | 25, rue de Boulainvilliers (La Muette/Ranelagh) | 01 45 56 10 41
For those who prefer to eat out surrounded by friends rather than strangers, chef Alain Bourgade, who formerly ran the acclaimed La Poêle d'Or, offers "private dinners" for small groups (14 folks, max) "at his home", a stunning mansion and garden in the 16th; clients tuck into a New French menu they've prearranged with the master, at least two weeks in advance.

ⓩ Alain Ducasse 28 | 27 | 27 | €187
au Plaza Athénée ⌾ *Haute Cuisine*

8ᵉ | Plaza-Athénée | 25, av Montaigne (Alma Marceau/ Franklin D. Roosevelt) | 01 53 67 65 00 | fax 01 53 67 65 12 | www.alain-ducasse.com

The legendary Alain Ducasse serves up "a meal of a lifetime" at his Paris flagship, an "*ancien régime* meets high-tech" setting in the Plaza-Athénée; "from the amuse-bouches to the delightful candy cart" and tea made from "live herbs snipped by white-gloved waiters", the Haute Cuisine is "probably similar to what the angels are eating", while "exceptional" service "without the starch" makes each diner feel like "the most important client in the world"; it's all "divine", but if the bill seems "hellish", consider it "tuition toward [learning] the art of eating."

Alcazar ● *New French* 19 | 22 | 19 | €56

6ᵉ | 62, rue Mazarine (Odéon) | 01 53 10 19 99 | fax 01 53 10 23 23 | www.alcazar.fr

Perhaps it's "not quite as trendy as it used to be" ("what once seemed fresh and modern now seems just big and brash"), but still it's "always interesting" to "take in the scene" at Terence Conran's Saint-Germain brasserie – and what a scene it is, with seats for 200 under a skylight roof; the New French "food is not up to the panache of the place", but it's "pleasant" and "light" – and there's always the "buzzy bar", which compensates for the oft-"inattentive" service.

Al Dar ● *Lebanese* 21 | 13 | 18 | €40

5ᵉ | 8, rue Frédéric Sauton (Maubert-Mutualité) | 01 43 25 17 15 | fax 01 45 01 61 67 ⌾
16ᵉ | 93, av Raymond Poincaré (Victor Hugo) | 01 45 00 96 64 | fax 01 45 01 61 67

"Excellent, authentic" – if comparatively "expensive" – Lebanese food (including "the best baklava" in Paris) is the draw at these pop-

ular twins in the 5th and 16th; the "less-than-convincing atmosphere" makes some believe it's "better to get the same dishes at the take-out counter"; still, the servers "are always smiling" and so this pair's assiduously frequented by expats and others ("we eat there so often the maitre d' asked if we owned a kitchen").

Al Diwan ● Lebanese
21 | 14 | 20 | €49

8ᵉ | 30, av George V (Alma Marceau/George V) | 01 47 23 45 45 | fax 01 47 23 60 98

Homesick Lebanese and other mezeholics find "a bit of old Beirut" at this "comfortable", "high-end" Middle Easterner in "a central location" on the posh Avenue George V; most find the "feel and the food authentic and addictive", and those who deem the wood-paneled decor and prices a little too "fancy" head next door for "reasonably priced" "great takeaway."

NEW Alfred ⊠ Bistro
- | - | - | M

1ᵉʳ | 8, rue de Montpensier (Palais Royale/Pyramide) | 01 42 97 54 40

Overlooking the Palais-Royal, this tiny new dining room has quickly become a clubby insider's address for employees of the Ministry of Culture and performers from the Comédie Française; what attracts them is the cozy atmosphere, professional service and sincere, classic bistro cooking by a politician-turned-chef.

Alivi (L') Corsica
16 | 15 | 15 | €44

4ᵉ | 27, rue du Roi de Sicile (Hôtel-de-Ville/St-Paul) | 01 48 87 90 20 | www.restaurant-alivi.com

"Corsican cuisine, Corsican ambiance, Corsican waiters" characterizes the scene at this small spot "on a little lane" in the Marais; there's debate whether the fare is "original" or "uninspiring" (it may depend on whether you "skip the formula menu, strictly for tourists, and order à la carte"); but all agree the "staff's friendly" and the prices fair.

Z Allard ⊠ Bistro
21 | 16 | 19 | €58

6ᵉ | 41, rue St-André-des-Arts (Odéon) | 01 43 26 48 23 | fax 01 46 33 04 02 | www.restaurant-allard.com

"As traditional as tradition gets", this seventysomething Saint-Germain "institution" serves "rich, copious" bistro fare – including a signature duck with olives that "has no challenger" – amid a setting from "bygone times" that's so "cozy" you have to "climb over each other to get to your table"; the "old-time waiters" somehow manage to be both "amiable" and "grumpy", and overall the place oozes a "Gallic charm" only slightly diluted by the clientele: "if I wanted to eat with so many Americans, I could've stayed home."

Allobroges (Les) Ⓜ Classic French
∇ 22 | 18 | 21 | €37

20ᵉ | 71, rue des Grands-Champs (Buzenval/Maraîchers) | 01 43 73 40 00 | fax 01 40 09 23 22

Those who have journeyed to this "out-of-the-way gem" "tucked away in the 20th" "highly recommend" its "delicious", "carefully prepared" seasonal Classic French dishes at "great-value" prices, "soft lighting in a contemporary atmosphere" and "exceptional ser-

vice" (even to the extent of "providing a chef's jacket to a rain-soaked customer"); best of all, the "trek from central Paris" tends to make it "non-touristy."

Al Mounia ☒ *Moroccan*

FOOD	DECOR	SERVICE	COST
17	16	14	€46

16ᵉ | 16, rue de Magdebourg (Trocadéro) | 01 47 27 57 28 | fax 01 47 27 39 63 | www.al-mounia.com

At this 16th-arrondissement Moroccan, the "absolutely stunning atmosphere instantly transports you to North Africa" (as, alas, do the "slow service" and "low seats"); though many find it "a little expensive", it's "reliable" for a "quality meal" à la Marrakech.

Alsace (L') ◑ *Alsace*

FOOD	DECOR	SERVICE	COST
18	19	15	€46

8ᵉ | 39, av des Champs-Elysées (Franklin D. Roosevelt) | 01 53 93 97 00 | fax 01 53 93 97 09 | www.restaurantalsace.com

Though it's a "tourist factory" on the Champs-Elysées, this "traditional brasserie" manages to turn out "edible, if not memorable" Alsatian food, including shellfish platters and "choucroute by the ton"; and while "the service can go both ways", warm-weather visitors enjoy "people-watching from the outdoor seating (so very Parisian)", while nocturnal noshers find the 24/7 opening "hours ideal."

Alsaco (L') ☒ *Alsace*

FOOD	DECOR	SERVICE	COST
-	-	-	M

9ᵉ | 10, rue Condorcet (Gare du Nord/Poissonnière) | 01 45 26 44 31

"Without a doubt the best *weinstube* west of Alsace", this "warm and homey (in a Germanic sort of way)" wood-paneled den on a quiet side street in the 9th seduces with "succulent" food, "a charming owner" who "makes his own choucroute" and a "sumptuous" selection of schnapps, eaux de vie and regional wines – all for "wonderfully low prices."

Ambassade d'Auvergne *Auvergne*

FOOD	DECOR	SERVICE	COST
20	18	20	€47

3ᵉ | 22, rue du Grenier St-Lazare (Rambuteau) | 01 42 72 31 22 | www.ambassade-auvergne.com

"Come hungry" to this "cozy", country-style table in the 3rd, a "satisfying, belt-loosening experience" whose "rustic food" "at reasonable prices" is not only "good" but offers a snapshot of the "hearty", "salty" kitchens of the Auvergne; the "friendly service borders on the paternal", urging you to finish all the signature *aligot* (potatoes whipped with cheese curds and garlic), before diving into dessert.

🄩 Ambassadeurs (Les) Ⓜ *Haute Cuisine/New French*

FOOD	DECOR	SERVICE	COST
28	29	28	€174

8ᵉ | Hôtel de Crillon | 10, pl de la Concorde (Concorde) | 01 44 71 16 16 | fax 01 44 71 15 03 | www.crillon.com

The "sumptuous" "gold and marble" surroundings of the Crillon hotel are "like being inside a jewel box", a "perfect showplace" for the "incredibly inventive" New French Haute Cuisine of chef Jean-François Piège (who has "enchanted" "serious foodies" ever since he was at Alain Ducasse); the 1,100-label wine list is "*extraordinaire*", the service is "choreographed to perfection" while remaining "refreshingly friendly" and though the experience may "relieve you

of many euros", "you get a lot for the price"; P.S. "the lunch menu at 75€ is a delight" – and a relative deal.

Z Ambroisie (L') 🅱️🅼 *Haute Cuisine* | 28 | 27 | 26 | €158 |

4e | 9, pl des Vosges (Bastille/St-Paul) | 01 42 78 51 45 | www.ambrosie-placedesvosges.com

It's like "dining in a nobleman's home" at this "smoothly run", "aptly named" Haute Cuisine haven "serving food of the gods" along with a "top flight wine list" that helps to "rationalize" the "damage the bill inflicts"; "the most intimate of Paris' grand restaurants" (only 40 seats), it's also possibly the "toughest table in town" – and beware of "being exiled to the back room" – but "who wouldn't want to be king of the Place des Vosges, even just for a few hours?"

Amici Miei 🅱️🅼 *Italian* | 19 | 13 | 13 | €33 |

11e | 44, rue Saint-Sabin (Bréguet-Sabin/Chemin-Vert) | 01 42 71 82 62 | fax 01 43 57 07 71 | www.amici-miei.net

Many fans of the "really good pizzas" thrown at this tiny place regret its move to larger digs in the 11th, saying the "charm got lost" – but the "high-strung service" stayed ("where's the warmth of Italy?"); still, those pining for pie pant it's a decent enough "neighborhood address."

Z Ami Louis (L') 🅼 *Bistro* | 25 | 16 | 18 | €109 |

3e | 32, rue du Vertbois (Arts et Métiers/Temple) | 01 48 87 77 48

"Don't eat beforehand", as the "Pantagruelian portions" at this classic bistro make it "a scene from a classic food orgy", starring "superb foie gras", "orgasmic fries" and the world's "priciest", most "renowned" roast chicken; over the decades regulars, tourists and "many a VIP" have made this 3rd-arrondissement vet "a favorite", and if foes find it "a bit *fatigué*", scores support those who see it as "blessedly unchanged", from the "shabby" interior to the "cranky French" service ("the waiters still toss your coat onto the overhead racks").

Ami Marcel (L') 🅱️🅼 *Bistro* | ∇ 17 | 14 | 16 | €48 |

15e | 33, rue Georges Pitard (Convention/Plaisance) | 01 48 56 62 06 | fax 01 48 56 62 06 | www.lamimarcel.com

Intrepid gourmands willing to travel deep into the 15th have discovered this "pleasant", '70s-style chocolate-and-caramel-toned bistro with a "small but inventive menu" and "fairly extensive wine list" that's "not heavily inflated"; however, a few have felt "disappointed" since a new owner took over in March 2007.

Ami Pierre (A l') ◑🅱️🅼 *Southwest* | 17 | 15 | 16 | €37 |

11e | 5, rue de la Main-d'Or (Ledru-Rollin) | 01 47 00 17 35

Not much bigger than a cork, this "small, noisy" *bistrot à vins* near the Bastille claims a devoted following of vinophiles who, in between sips, soak up the "good, simple" Southwest cooking under the watchful eye of the "charming" owner.

Ampère (L') 🅱️ *Bistro/Eclectic* | - | - | - | M |

17e | 1, rue Ampère (Wagram) | 01 47 63 72 05 | fax 01 47 63 37 33

Followers of chef-owner Philippe Detourbe, who disappeared for a few years after running an acclaimed restaurant in the 15th, "wel-

come" him back at this place north of the Parc Monceau, where he whips up an Eclectic array of "great bistro food" on "varied, highly creative menus"; clients commend "friendly service", the "nice surroundings and reasonable prices" – in short, "what's not to like?"

Amuse Bouche (L') ⊠Ⓜ New French

FOOD	DECOR	SERVICE	COST
17	13	15	€44

14e | 186, rue du Château (Gaîté/Mouton-Duvernet) | 01 43 35 31 61
This "charming, small" amuse-bouche "off the Avenue du Maine" in the 14th may be "a little out of the way" but its "original" New French menu has many murmuring "yum, yum" within the "*très fun*" environs; prices are judged "correct" and service "considerate", and the owner uses family photos and copper pots to create a "cozy" feel.

Anahï ◗ Argentinean

FOOD	DECOR	SERVICE	COST
19	15	15	€49

3e | 49, rue Volta (Arts et Métiers/Temple) | 01 48 87 88 24 | fax 01 48 87 93 04
"Chichi" carnivores from the fashion crowd congregate at this Latin American, a former *boucherie* in the 3rd, where "meat meat meat" is the name of the game, notably "choice Argentine steak"; though some find the "butcher-chic" decor a bit "creepy", this "high-volume" "hangout" is so much "fun" that nobody even beefs about the "expensive" bill.

Anahuacalli Mexican

FOOD	DECOR	SERVICE	COST
21	14	19	€41

5e | 30, rue des Bernardins (Maubert-Mutualité) | 01 43 26 10 20
Adoring amigos attest that this Latin Quarter cantina – "Margaritaville in the City of Lights" – is "the only good Mexican" in Paris, with "genuine", "expertly prepared" south-of-the-border eats ("come early for the chiles rellenos, before they run out") and "a warm welcome" from the staff; some feel "the prices are high", given the "cramped" digs, "but a pitcher or two of margaritas will help you forget" all that.

Andy Wahloo ◗⊠ Moroccan

FOOD	DECOR	SERVICE	COST
▽ 14	22	12	€36

3e | 69, rue des Gravilliers (Arts et Métiers) | 01 42 71 20 38 | fax 01 42 74 03 41
The name of this "lively bar" in the Marais, adjacent to 404, means "I have nothing" in Arabic (perhaps the mantra for the "really bad" service), but it also channels the spirit of that other Andy and his Factory with its North African Pop Art decor, "good music", "exotic" cocktails and "simple" Moroccan mezes that clients nibble while sitting on paint-can stools; it's the "perfect place to start an evening quietly with friends or to finish it, madly dancing."

Ⓩ Angelina ⊠ Tearoom

FOOD	DECOR	SERVICE	COST
20	20	15	€28

1er | 226, rue de Rivoli (Concorde/Tuileries) | 01 42 60 82 00 | fax 01 42 86 98 97 | www.groupe-bertrand.com
"You can go for brunch if you want", but most "skip the food" at this "legendary" tea salon and go straight to the "otherworldly" African hot chocolate so thick "your spoon almost stands up in the cup", plus "decadently dense whipped chantilly" and the "famous Mont Blanc" for an added sugar rush; despite "surly service" and "long lines", this belle epoque address across from the Tuileries is eter-

| | FOOD | DECOR | SERVICE | COST |

nally "crowded", mainly with tourists, who swear that once you've consumed their *chocolat chaud*, "everything else is just a beverage"; N.B. the Decor score doesn't reflect a post-Survey refresh.

Angle du Faubourg (L') ⊠ *New French*   24 | 21 | 24 | €75

8ᵉ | 195, rue du Faubourg St-Honoré (Charles de Gaulle-Etoile/ Ternes) | 01 40 74 20 20 | fax 01 40 74 20 21 | www.taillevent.com
The Vrinat family's "stylish" New French in the 8th is a "budget alternative" to their "celebrated Taillevent", and yet there's "nothing second-rate" about the "edgy", "inspired" dishes in a "refreshingly different" "contemporary setting", with "excellent wines" by the bottle or glass and "well-paced service"; lunch hour sees a corporate crowd while evenings are more "serene", but day or night, the "nicely spaced tables" make this "great for business and/or romance."

Angl'Opéra ⊠ *New French*   19 | 17 | 17 | €55

2ᵉ | Hôtel Edouard VII | 39, av de l'Opéra (Opéra/Pyramides/ Quatre-Septembre) | 01 42 61 86 25 | fax 01 42 61 47 73 | www.anglopera.com
A citrus-colored, modern room within earshot of the Opéra Garnier sets the stage for chef Gilles Choukroun's New French fusion fare that's "wildly inventive, surprising and full of flavors you can't always identify"; but while fans sing the praises of this "exciting adventure on the plate", critics decry "outrageously complicated" dishes at "excessive" prices; and some snap the staff, while generally "correct", can be as "haughty" as prima donnas.

Annapurna ●⊠ *Indian*   ∇ 18 | 17 | 19 | €37

8ᵉ | 32, rue de Berri (George V/St-Philippe-du-Roule) | 01 45 63 91 62
While it "caters to French taste buds by extinguishing the heat and more complicated flavors", the refined curries and tandooris "certainly satisfy" at this upscale Indian – Paris' oldest – off the Champs; those in-the-know spend a bit more and "book the little 'Punjab' salon" where low tables are surrounded by tapestries and diners eat to the melodious accompaniment of a sitar player.

AOC (L') ⊠Ⓜ *Bistro*   18 | 14 | 16 | €40

5ᵉ | 14, rue des Fossés St-Bernard (Cardinal Lemoine/Jussieu) | 01 43 54 22 52 | www.restoaoc.com
This Latin Quarter bistro run by a "lovely couple" is a "fantastic place to irritate your vegetarian friends" with "copious amounts" of "traditional" "country French cuisine" made with "top-notch meat" and other "fresh ingredients" (a mark of quality, 'AOC' indicates adherence to government standards); while the decor is, at best, "not bad", at least the staffers are "pros who never lose their smile."

🅩 Apicius ⊠ *Haute Cuisine*   26 | 26 | 26 | €135

8ᵉ | 20, rue d'Artois (George V/St-Philippe-du-Roule) | 01 43 80 19 66 | fax 01 44 40 09 57 | www.restaurant-apicius.com
It's easy to "fall in love" with "movie-star-handsome" chef-owner Jean-Pierre Vigato and his Haute Cuisine establishment, a "stunning" mansion in the centrally located 8th with "spectacular decor" and a "hidden garden", plus "welcoming service" that's "close to

vote at ZAGAT.com   27

perfection"; "but the food trumps all", "combining the very best of the French classics with creative modern influences"; in short, supporters swear this place "outshines" the rest, though "alas, it's impossible to get a reservation."

Apollo *Eclectic*

-	-	-	M

14e | 3, pl Denfert-Rochereau (Denfert-Rochereau) | 01 45 38 76 77 | fax 01 43 22 02 15 | www.restaurant-apollo.com

The "fantastic terrace" on the street-level concourse of a métro station in the 14th may be "super-nice in summer", but otherwise this Eclectic with "kitschy" "retro"-'70s decor fails to inspire: "Apollo was the god of prophesy – I wish that someone had prophesized that this place serves totally forgettable food."

A Priori Thé *Tearoom*

16	19	15	€24

2e | 35, Galerie Vivienne (Bourse/Palais Royal-Musée du Louvre) | 01 42 97 48 75

"Deliciously fresh and creatively prepared" cakes, scones and savories (including many meat-free, "great-for-vegetarians" varieties) make this "adorable" little tearoom with a "gorgeous" skylight in the "sparkling" Galerie Vivienne a perennial favorite – even, dare we say, a priority – "between two shopping sessions" in the 2nd; "owned by a cheery American expat", Peggy Hancock, for 28 years, it also does "a nice Sunday brunch."

☑ Ardoise (L') Ⓜ *Bistro*

24	13	19	€41

1er | 28, rue du Mont-Thabor (Concorde/Tuileries) | 01 42 96 28 18 | www.lardoise-paris.com

In a high-rent district steps near the Place de la Concorde, "an abundance of Americans" crowds into the "hole-in-the-wall" digs of this "perfect neighborhood bistro" for "marvelous, inventive" French food that "does not require a chemistry degree and six hours to appreciate", delivered by "friendly, bilingual" servers at an "unbelievable price"; the "minimal" decor is easy to ignore, but avoid the "basement hinterland."

Arome (L') ☒ *Classic/New French*

-	-	-	M

8e | 3, rue St-Philippe-du-Roule (St-Philippe-du-Roule) | 01 42 25 55 98 | fax 01 42 25 55 97

Following up on the success of L'Ami Marcel, owner Eric Martins has moved on to this chic location in the 8th, which has an eye-pleasing decor of arched doorways, Murano lamps and chestnut tablecloths and a new chef, Thomas Boullault (ex Le Cinq), whose French cuisine surfs from Classic to contemporary; the prix fixe lunch has made regulars of local business types, while a valet service is the icing on the cake in the evenings.

☑ Arpège (L') ☒ *Haute Cuisine*

26	24	25	€187

7e | 84, rue de Varenne (Varenne) | 01 47 05 09 06 | fax 01 44 18 98 39 | www.alain-passard.com

It's like "tasting such fundamental products as tomatoes, lobster, potatoes for the first time" aver acolytes of the "astonishingly intense experience" provided by this Haute Cuisine temple in the 7th,

where chef-owner Alain Passard has a "genius" for turning even "simple vegetables" and seafood (no red meat) into a "religious experience"; the "elegant" Lalique-paneled setting may seem "spare" ("beware the downstairs dining room"), "the service stiffly correct" and the bill the "most expensive" you've ever seen (after all, "an onion is just an onion") – unless, as many do, you think of the "food as art."

Z As du Fallafel (L') ● _Israeli_ — 24 | 7 | 14 | €13

4ᵉ | 34, rue des Rosiers (St-Paul) | 01 48 87 63 60

"Long lines" help you locate this "go-to location" for "fantastic falafels" "brimming with all the fixings" (including "transcendent" fried eggplant) and other Israeli eats, to be consumed "while traipsing in the Marais" or else sitting "shoehorned" inside; "service would have to improve to be indifferent and the place looks like a dump, but who cares" when you're noshing on "one of the most delicious inexpensive meals in Paris" – its Best Buy, in fact.

Asian ● _Asian_ — 16 | 18 | 15 | €49

8ᵉ | 30, av George V (Alma Marceau/George V) | 01 56 89 11 00 | fax 01 56 89 11 01 | www.asian.fr

"Grandiose", "dark"-lit Asiatic decor remains the main, if not "the only reason to visit" this once "trendy", now "touristy" bar/restaurant that's "quite expensive, as it's in the Champs-Elysées" area; though "they try hard", the Pan-Asian cuisine – "20% Thai, 20% sushi, 20% Chinese and the rest, indeterminate" – "just doesn't measure up", except possibly "for Sunday brunch", and the service could "drive even the Dalai Lama to drink."

Assiette (L') Ⓜ _Bistro_ — - | - | - | E

14ᵉ | 181, rue du Château (Gaîté/Mouton-Duvernet) | 01 43 22 64 86 | www.chezlulu.fr

"Mitterrand made it famous, but he is gone and so is the buzz", which may account for the low-vote count of this veteran Montparnasse bistro; nevertheless, the simple Southwestern cooking by the chef-owner known as Lulu still thrills, and the "informal" 1930s butcher shop setting feels "fresh and stylish", though the four-course, daily changing prix fixe is not for cash-strapped socialists.

Astier _Bistro_ — 21 | 15 | 18 | €41

11ᵉ | 44, rue J.P. Timbaud (Oberkampf/Parmentier) | 01 43 57 16 35

The "familial feel" of this "delightful" neighborhood bistro near the funky Rue Oberkampf owes as much to the "tightly packed" tables as to the "gargantuan cheese tray" "shared by all" – the culmination of a "consistently good" three-course meal of Classic French fare, from "fresh seafood" to "forgotten dishes" featuring offal, on a fixed-price menu that surveyors call "a steal."

Astor (L') Ⓩ Ⓜ _Haute Cuisine_ — 16 | 16 | 16 | €64

8ᵉ | Hôtel Astor | 11, rue d'Astorg (St-Augustin) | 01 53 05 05 20 | fax 01 53 05 05 30 | www.hotel-astor.net

Hotel guests and businesspeople frequent this "classy" '30s-style room in the corporate 8th for "attentive" service and Haute

Cuisine that's "satisfying" if "not terribly original"; still, the "well-spaced tables allow for conversation", the prices, while still "dear", have actually dropped and it always helps that "they can make a good martini."

☑ Astrance (L') ⑤ Ⓜ *New French* 　　28 | 22 | 27 | €154

16ᵉ | 4, rue Beethoven (Passy) | 01 40 50 84 40

"Young, passionate" chef/co-owner Pascal Barbot "manages to wow the most blasé palates" with "inventive" New French cuisine that's "otherworldly", "intellectual" and always "surprising" (especially at dinner, when the "no-choice" tasting menu is the only option) at this "hard-to-get-into" table in the 16th, where a near-"flawless" staff with a "personal touch" services the small, "sophisticated" room; aesthetes argue "they could rethink the decor, but with bookings two months in advance, why – and when?"

Atelier Berger (L') ⑤ *New French* 　　21 | 17 | 17 | €48

1ᵉʳ | 49, rue Berger (Louvre-Rivoli) | 01 40 28 00 00 | fax 01 40 28 10 65 | www.restaurant-atelierberger.com

A Scandinavian chef-owner comes up with some "really fascinating combinations, like tuna tartare with black squid-ink sorbet" on the New French–with-Norwegian-notes menu at this duplex on the edge of Les Halles; sometimes the service and "surrealist" cuisine are "uneven", but overall, this "original" offers "good value for the money"; N.B. a recent redo has lightened up the digs, elevating the Decor score.

☑ Atelier de
Joël Robuchon (L') ● *Haute Cuisine* 　　28 | 24 | 24 | €100

7ᵉ | Hôtel Pont Royal | 5, rue de Montalembert (Rue du Bac) | 01 42 22 56 56 | fax 01 42 22 97 91 | www.joel-robuchon.com

In the tony 7th, the idolized chef's "Asian-sleek" "canteen for the rich" has them queuing at the door, then sitting "on a stool at a counter" ("singles welcomed") and watching the kitchen turn out "sublime", "cutting-edge" Haute Cuisine; tapas-size portions offer "a great way to sample the offerings" from the Robuchon repertoire, though the "hearty of appetite" must be "prepared to pay a fortune"; cynics snap the staff, while "attentive", displays "typical French insouciance", but the only really "irksome" item is the no-reservations policy (except for very early and very late).

Atelier Maître Albert (L') ● *Bistro* 　　21 | 22 | 21 | €62

5ᵉ | 1, rue Maître-Albert (Maubert-Mutualité) | 01 56 81 30 01 | fax 01 53 10 83 23 | www.ateliermaitrealbert.com

"Redone nicely" since it became a Guy Savoy–run rotisserie a while back, this Latin Quarter site juxtaposes "traditional French" bistro cooking – it's "amazing how tasty roast chicken and mashed potatoes can be" – with an "edgy contemporary look and beautiful fireplace" to create a "dark", "smart atmosphere"; a few antagonists gripe about "the limited menu" and the "painful" bill, but most appreciate the "thoughtful food and glitzy crowd" ("even the servers look hip").

	FOOD	DECOR	SERVICE	COST

Atlas (L') Ⓜ *Moroccan*

| 20 | 16 | 19 | €42 |

5ᵉ | 12, bd St-Germain (Maubert-Mutualité) | 01 46 33 86 98 |
fax 01 40 46 06 56

"On a cold winter night", this "brief stop in Morocco" with its "border-
line kitsch" decor warms travelers with "homey choices" from the
land of "sweet and tangy"; in fine weather "eat outside and watch
the crowd" of the *Quartier Latin*.

Auberge Aveyronnaise ⓿ *Aveyron*

| - | - | - | M |

12ᵉ | 40, rue Gabriel Lamé (Cour St-Emilion) | 01 43 40 12 24 |
fax 01 43 40 12 15

"If you're really hungry, this is the place to go for hearty fare" attest
aficionados of the Auvergne area – e.g. *aligot* (cheesy whipped potatoes), blood sausage and Aubrac beef that's "better" than most; it
may be in the modern Bercy district, but in between the decor
(checkered tablecloths, huge fireplace) and "reasonable prices", it
feels like it's smack-dab in the provinces.

Auberge Bressane (L') ⓧ *Classic French*

| 20 | 16 | 19 | €47 |

7ᵉ | 16, av de la Motte-Picquet (Ecole Militaire/La Tour-Maubourg) |
01 47 05 98 37 | fax 01 47 05 92 21 | www.auberge-bressane.com

A "loyal" clientele of "trendy people during the week and families on
weekends" makes pilgrimage to this "authentic" provincial bistro for
"heartwarmingly" Classic French dishes that are almost extinct in this
"well-heeled" area near Ecole Militaire; with its "friendly", "relaxed
vibe" and 1950s/Gothic château decor, it's "a great place to beat those
Sunday-night blues"; P.S. "don't forget to preorder your soufflé."

Auberge Dab (L') ⓿ⓧ *Brasserie*

| 16 | 14 | 15 | €56 |

16ᵉ | 161, av de Malakoff (Porte Maillot) | 01 45 00 32 22 |
fax 01 45 00 58 50 | www.rest-gj.com

Come to this "honest", "practical" "neighborhood brasserie" for a
"fresh" shellfish fix or some "consistent" classic dishes, served nonstop till 2 AM; fans find the well-heeled crowd from the surrounding
16th adds to the "old-fashioned charm" of the "typical decor"; but
foes fume the place is "pretentious" and "overpriced for what it is."

Auberge de la
Reine Blanche *Classic/New French*

| 19 | 18 | 19 | €39 |

4ᵉ | 30, rue St-Louis-en-l'Ile (Pont-Marie/St-Paul) | 01 46 33 07 87

"Cozy and charming", just like the Ile Saint-Louis where it's located,
this "warm" little bistro is perfect for a low-key lunch or "casual dinner" of carefully cooked Classic and New French fare, served by an
"inviting" staff; views vary as to whether the tight tables are "romantic" or "so small you risk eating your neighbors' dish", but prices
are "very reasonable", given the "generous portions."

Auberge du Champ
de Mars ⓧ *Classic French*

| 17 | 16 | 19 | €40 |

7ᵉ | 18, rue de l'Exposition (Ecole Militaire) | 01 45 51 78 08

"Gracious hosts", a husband-and-wife team, attract American "visitors and loyal regulars" to this "homey" and enviably situated "little

restaurant" near the Eiffel Tower; *hélas,* sliding scores support opponents who opine the "simple" Classic French fare is "ordinary" and the "wine list almost nonexistent."

Auberge du Clou (L') *Classic French*

16 | 12 | 14 | €53

9e | 30, av Trudaine (Anvers/Pigalle) | 01 48 78 22 48 | fax 01 48 78 30 08 | www.aubergeduclou.fr

Relatively new owners, and an even newer chef, have been working hard to dust off this 120-year-old auberge in the 9th, named for the nails on which artists left paintings to pay for their meals; "good quality, traditional French [cuisine] with some interesting 'world' dishes" is served amid "old-fashioned" decor with fireplace and wood beams – but the trump card is the terrace that's heated in winter.

Auberge Etchégorry 🗷 🅼 *Southwest*

– | – | – | M

13e | 41, rue Croulebarbe (Corvisart/Les Gobelins) | 01 44 08 83 51 | fax 01 44 08 83 69 | www.etchegorry.com

Cured hams and garlic braids hang from the ceiling of this bastion of Basque cooking, "worth a try" for "quality" Southwestern specialties such as *piperade* (a sweet pepper, onion and tomato sauté) or stuffed squid, all dished out with an equally sunny dose of hospitality; it occupies a "quiet" street in the 13th.

Auberge Nicolas Flamel 🗷 *Classic French*

▽ 23 | 23 | 25 | €54

3e | 51, rue de Montmorency (Arts et Métiers/Rambuteau) | 01 42 71 77 78 | fax 01 42 77 12 78

The "distant past" seems like yesterday at this "historic" home – the city's oldest – built by an alchemist in the upper Marais in 1407; but medieval meanderings aren't the only reason for a pilgrimage to this "romantic treasure": new young chef-owner Alain Al Geaam has refreshed the decor, brought in an "intelligent" new staff and prepares "excellent" Med-accented French classics; best of all, clients won't have to turn lead into gold to pay for it all.

Auberge Pyrénées Cévennes (L') 🗷 *Southwest*

20 | 13 | 21 | €46

11e | 106, rue de la Folie-Méricourt (République) | 01 43 57 33 78

"Its cassoulet could be the best in the world – but all else is pretty good too" at this "honest neighborhood table" near the Place de la République; a "hoot of an owner" reigns amid an "atmospheric" aubergelike decor as "friendly servers" set down "generous portions" of Lyonnais and Southwest dishes; prices are rising, but most still find them "reasonable", and the overall vibe "simply marvelous."

Auguste 🗷 *Classic French*

▽ 25 | 24 | 23 | €80

7e | 54, rue de Bourgogne (Varenne) | 01 45 51 61 09 | fax 01 45 51 27 34 | www.restaurantauguste.fr

It's been an august period for this "young", "chic" table in the 7th run by chef Gaël Orieux, ex-second at the Hôtel Meurice; politicians and the beau monde quickly fill the 30 coveted seats in a "modern", "elegant" room with a poppy-red wall and gray wood floor, and consult the "delightful", "varying" menu of "creative" Classic French

cuisine and mostly (if "not always consistently") "good service"; insiders insist "enjoy it before it becomes more of a celebrity", and while prices are still "reasonable" for this caliber of cooking.

Autobus Imperial (L') Ⓢ *Classic French*

FOOD	DECOR	SERVICE	COST
-	-	-	M

1er | 14, rue Mondétour (Etienne Marcel/Les Halles) | 01 42 36 00 18 | www.autobus-imperial.fr

You don't need a ticket to ride what some contented commuters call "the best bang for your euro in Paris", a vast restaurant/lounge with an "original art nouveau interior" under a soaring ceiling with skylight; "one of the rare good addresses near Les Halles", it offers "traditional French fare, jazzed up by the youthful culinary staff"; sweet tooths should be sure to stop off at the tea salon, with its "desserts to die for."

Autour du Mont ⓈⓂ *Seafood*

FOOD	DECOR	SERVICE	COST
-	-	-	M

15e | 58, rue Vasco de Gama (Lourmel) | 01 42 50 55 63 | fax 01 42 50 55 63

Near the Porte de Versailles, this cozy, "good seafooder" pulls a media crowd at noon – there are several TV studios nearby – and young working couples at night with an imaginatively prepared catch-of-the-day menu and a relaxed atmosphere; the marine-themed decor may be "a bit tacky", but the moderate prices have made it popular.

Autour du Saumon Ⓢ *Seafood*

FOOD	DECOR	SERVICE	COST
17	11	14	€39

4e | 60, rue François Miron (St-Paul) | 01 42 77 23 08 | fax 01 42 77 44 75
15e | 116, rue de la Convention (Boucicaut) | 01 45 54 31 16 | fax 01 45 54 49 68
17e | 3, av de Villiers (Villiers) | 01 40 53 89 00 | fax 01 40 53 89 89
www.autourdusaumon.eu

This salmon-seller has spawned three addresses in Paris that present a "pricey" but "good selection of smoked fish", plus other seafood specialties, in a "bright, uncluttered" nautical setting, almost "like being in a fishbowl" (but with better food); while service is "efficient", those in a hurry can migrate to the adjoining boutique for products to go.

Avant Goût (L') ⓈⓂ *New French*

FOOD	DECOR	SERVICE	COST
23	16	21	€43

13e | 26, rue Bobillot (Place d'Italie) | 01 53 80 24 00 | fax 01 53 80 00 77 | www.lavantgout.com

"If you're willing to make the trip to the 13th, this bustling bistro will never disappoint – and sometimes it'll stun" say supporters; the New French cuisine is "original", even "surprising" ("where else would we have been inspired to try a pig pot-au-feu?"), and "for a heck of a price" too; while the "minimally decorated" dining room has been redone, still "the tables are mighty close together" and service swings from "smiling" to "surly."

Avenue (L') ◐ *New French*

FOOD	DECOR	SERVICE	COST
18	19	16	€64

8e | 41, av Montaigne (Franklin D. Roosevelt) | 01 40 70 14 91 | fax 01 40 70 91 97 | www.restaurant-avenue.fr

"Extreme style" sums up this "place to see-and-be-seen in the heart of fashionland", aka the Avenue Montaigne; Jacques Garcia's "cool"

baroque decor is backdrop to the "up-to-the-minute-trendy" New French menu, and while "always good" – if "sooo nouveau riche" in price – "it's secondary to the people-watching"; "if you're not famous, getting the attention of the waitresses (all apparently models waiting to be spotted) can be tedious"; P.S. try to sit in the "lovely" "sidewalk-window area."

Azabu Ⓜ Japanese

∇ 24 | 17 | 17 | €52

6ᵉ | 3, rue André Mazet (Odéon) | 01 46 33 72 05

"For those who want to discover Japanese cuisine that goes beyond the clichés", this "rare find" in Saint-Germain offers "one of Paris' best teppanyaki" grills, manned by a chef who "cooks in front of you with great calm"; the "original" dishes include "melt-in-your-mouth fish" and a "surprising" foie gras, in a room decorated with Zen sobriety.

Baan-Boran ◑⊠ Thai

20 | 14 | 17 | €39

1ᵉʳ | 43, rue de Montpensier (Palais Royal-Musée du Louvre) | 01 40 15 90 45 | fax 01 40 15 90 45 | www.baan-boran.com

"Thai food with a delicate touch" – including "typical dishes from different regions" – distinguishes this "authentic" Siamese standby in the 1st; amid a "nice, bright" – some say "sterile" – setting, patrons also praise the "non-pompous" servers; pity that the "portions seem kind of small."

Bacchantes (Les) ◑⊠ Wine Bar/Bistro

- | - | - | M

9ᵉ | 21, rue de Caumartin (Havre-Caumartin/Opéra) | 01 42 65 25 35 | fax 01 47 42 65 87 | www.lesbacchantes.fr

Habitués "go back over and over again" to this "down-to-earth" wine bar/bistro conveniently located by the Opéra Garnier that serves late for a post-ballet bacchanalia; the "traditional French food" – "especially meat" – is washed down with a good selection of wines by the glass or bottle, amid rustic, low-key decor.

Ballon des Ternes (Le) ◑ Brasserie

15 | 13 | 14 | €54

17ᵉ | 103, av des Ternes (Porte Maillot) | 01 45 74 17 98 | fax 01 45 72 18 84

Located near the Porte Maillot, this "traditional brasserie" is a "convivial", if "slightly noisy" destination for "excellent shellfish" and other "respectable" French classics; however, most foes find the fare "costly for what it is", the service "middling" and even the "retro" belle epoque decor, consisting of wood paneling, glass partitions, moleskin banquettes and bric-a-brac, "uninteresting."

Ballon et Coquillages ◑ Seafood

- | - | - | M

17ᵉ | 71, bd Gouvion-St-Cyr (Porte Maillot) | 01 45 74 17 98 | fax 01 45 72 18 84

Near Porte Maillot, this pearl of an annex of the Ballon des Ternes consists of a curved mosaic counter with only 14 stools (and no reservations) where clients perch and partake of "magnificent seafood" and other briny treats, ordered à la carte or by the platter; strangers quickly become friends thanks to the "convivial" ambiance – though "you need to speak French to fit in."

	FOOD	DECOR	SERVICE	COST

Bamboche (Le) *New French* | 19 | 18 | 19 | €66 |

7ᵉ | 15, rue de Babylone (Sèvres-Babylone) | 01 45 49 14 40 |
fax 01 45 49 14 44

The pair of chefs who took over this "small, romantic" New French "away from the crowds, despite its [proximity] to the Bon Marché" emporium, have hit cruising speed, and a bevy of fans praise their "inventive flavors" and servers whose "suggestions are right on the mark"; still, not all are convinced the place is worth "the relatively high prices."

Banyan ● *Thai* | 19 | 12 | 16 | €38 |

15ᵉ | 24, pl Etienne Pernet (Félix Faure) | 01 40 60 09 31

This "little corner in the 15th" might be an "unexpected location" for a "culinary adventure", especially given the "plain" surroundings; but epicurean explorers know they'll find "a large variety" of "succulent", "original" Thai dishes prepared with "a bit of flair" by an alumnus of the Blue Elephant; the service is "serene" and the ambiance "relaxing", though some do get hot and bothered by the "expensive" cost for "derisory portions."

Baptiste ☒Ⓜ *New French* | - | - | - | M |

17ᵉ | 51, rue Jouffroy d'Abbans (Malesherbes/Wagram) | 01 42 27 20 18 |
fax 01 43 80 68 09

Traditionalists who yearn for a "well-run, truly Parisian neighborhood restaurant" hit pay dirt at this "charming" "insider's place" in the 17th with "satisfying" New French food, "cozy 1930s decor" (including an art deco tile floor) and "personal" yet refreshingly "formal service" – elements that make it "perfect for a second-round business lunch"; and though it's "near nothing of touristic interest" – hence "not often frequented by Americans" – the owner still "speaks very good English."

Bar à Huîtres (Le) ● *Seafood* | 17 | 14 | 14 | €41 |

3ᵉ | 33, bd Beaumarchais (Bastille) | 01 48 87 98 92 | fax 01 48 87 04 42
5ᵉ | 33, rue St-Jacques (Cluny La Sorbonne) | 01 44 07 27 37 |
fax 01 43 26 71 62
14ᵉ | 112, bd du Montparnasse (Raspail/Vavin) | 01 43 20 71 01 |
fax 01 43 20 52 04
www.lebarahuitres.com

The "eponymous [oyster] is the best thing" at this trio of seafooders "with kitschy, shells-plastered-all-over-the-walls" decor by Jacques Garcia; they're a tad "touristy" and "factorylike" (while "cordial", the staff's "happy to have you finish fast"), but they're "reliable for a quick, late supper"; do stick to playing the shell game, however, as "they don't know how to cook fish."

Baratin (Le) ●☒Ⓜ *Wine Bar/Bistro* | 16 | 11 | 12 | €33 |

20ᵉ | 3, rue Jouye-Rouve (Belleville) | 01 43 49 39 70

This "good little" Belleville *bistrot à vins* packs them in with "an original, reasonably priced wine list" and a short daily menu of "market-fresh", "copious", "original" French dishes; but the real appeal of this "unpretentious" hole-in-the-wall is its "remarkable ambiance for

an evening among friends" – even if some sense "the owner saves his smile for the regulars."

Bar des Théâtres ❶ *Bistro*

15	10	15	€44

8ᵉ | 6, av Montaigne (Alma Marceau) | 01 47 23 34 63 | fax 01 45 62 04 93

For 50 years, this "classic" bistro "facing the Théâtre des Champs-Elysées" has been "a rendezvous before or after the theater", "a place to stop if shopping on the Avenue Montaigne" or a "great perch for people-watching" the performers who often patronize it; if the "steak tartare is *magnifique,* the rest" of the menu is barely "adequate" – as is the service – and even the aura's "not what it was" since this vet "lost most of its dining rooms" to construction.

Barlotti ❶ *Italian*

15	22	15	€50

1ᵉʳ | 35, pl du Marché St-Honoré (Pyramides/Tuilleries) | 01 44 86 97 97 | fax 01 44 86 97 98 | www.buddhabar.com

"It's all about the decor" at this "modern Italian" in the midst of the furiously "trendy" Place du Marché Saint-Honoré – and yes, the setting's "superb", a two-story atrium with soaring glass windows, parquet floors and jewel-toned seats; but the "disappointed" declare if you're looking for "authentic cuisine" that's not "overpriced", you should walk right on past; as for the staffers, they're quite "caring . . . about their tip."

Baron Rouge (Le) Ⓜ *Wine Bar/Bistro*

-	-	-	M

12ᵉ | 1, rue Théophile Roussel (Ledru-Rollin) | 01 43 43 14 32

"Just off the Marché d'Aligre", this "really pleasant" *bar à vins* – a neighborhood "institution" – is a must for "amazing oysters" (a Sunday tradition) or "good cheese and sausage plates"; but of course, "it's mostly about the wine", which you can consume "standing up" *sur place* or bring home, in "decanters filled right from the barrel."

Barrio Latino ❶ *Pan-Latin*

▽ 12	21	14	€39

12ᵉ | 46-48, rue du Faubourg St-Antoine (Bastille) | 01 55 78 84 75 | fax 01 55 78 85 30 | www.buddhabar.com

Salsaholics "head downstairs to work off dinner with a little Latin dance" in this four-story nightclub near the Bastille that's "always crowded, always a scene" with "pulsing music" making temperatures rise around the Gustave Eiffel–designed staircase and "great" Hispanic decor; though the kitchen seems like an afterthought with its "bland" Pan-Latin cuisine, it doesn't much matter, for the fiesta is "so much fun."

Barroco ❶ *Brazilian*

-	-	-	M

6ᵉ | 23, rue Mazarine (Odéon/St-Germain-des-Prés) | 01 43 26 40 24 | fax 01 55 04 86 19 | www.restaurant-latino.com

The strains of "live" bossa nova lure passersby into this exotic, "enjoyable" Saint-Germain Latin where they settle into velvet banquettes, order "tapas and a bottle of wine", and admire the "great decor" reminiscent of a grand South American mansion; if the Brazilian fare is "somewhat patchy", the "friendly staff" and "good" musicians import the warmth of the tropics.

Bartolo ⊠Ⓜ⇗ *Italian*

	FOOD	DECOR	SERVICE	COST
	17	11	12	€40

6ᵉ | 7, rue des Canettes (St-Germain-des-Prés) | 01 43 26 27 08
What' s "probably the best pizza in town – the way they do it in Naples", baked in a wood-burning beehive-shaped oven – has kept 'em coming for over 50 years to this Italian in Saint-Germain; however, its notoriously "nasty" service, tacky 1950s-vintage decor (complete with Bay of Naples vistas) and "pricey" tabs that you "must pay with cash" cause many to murmur it's "for masochists" only.

Bar Vendôme ● *Classic French*

	FOOD	DECOR	SERVICE	COST
	23	26	25	€71

1ᵉʳ | Hôtel Ritz | 15, pl Vendôme (Concorde/Opéra) | 01 43 16 33 63 | fax 01 43 16 33 75 | www.ritzparis.com
"Drop your Hermès purse by your Manolo-clad feet nestled by all those shopping bags" and enjoy a "great glass of champagne" while celebrity-spotting at this "chic, sophisticated" bar at the Ritz; it's always "a good refuge" for a Classic French "light lunch", tea or happy-hour drinks, whether in the "elaborate" interior or in "the peaceful garden, with birds chirping"; and if you squawk "ouch after you see the bill" – well, just "charge it to the room."

Bascou (Au) ⊠ *Basque*

	FOOD	DECOR	SERVICE	COST
	20	14	20	€43

3ᵉ | 38, rue Réaumur (Arts et Métiers) | 01 42 72 69 25 | fax 01 55 90 99 77
"A touch of French Basque country right at the center of Paris" flourishes at this cracked-tile "hole-in-the-wall" in the 3rd; a Lucas Carton alum, the "new chef-owner is just as talented as the old one in preparing Southwestern cuisine", supplemented by a "good selection of regional wines"; "this is the kind of place you tell no one about, so it remains uncrowded" – and its prices "fair."

Basilic (Le) *Basque*

	FOOD	DECOR	SERVICE	COST
	15	13	16	€50

7ᵉ | 2, rue Casimir Périer (Invalides/Solférino) | 01 44 18 94 64 | fax 01 44 18 33 97
Possessing a "lovely terrace" "away from traffic and overlooking the park" that surrounds the Basilique Sainte-Clothilde ("hence, the play on basilica" in the name), this establishment in the silk-stocking 7th can be "charming for a Sunday evening" admirers attest; however, some sermonize that the Basque–Classic French cooking is "pleasant without prompting any gastronomic emotion" – even the signature leg of lamb is "uninteresting" – and there's almost "no service to speak of."

Bastide Odéon (La) ⊠Ⓜ *Provence*

	FOOD	DECOR	SERVICE	COST
	22	18	20	€55

6ᵉ | 7, rue Corneille (Odéon) | 01 43 26 03 65 | fax 01 44 07 28 93 | www.bastide-odeon.com
This "contemporary" bistro in Saint-Germain is popular with Americans in-the-know – so much so, they "tend to be seated together; some say it's to ensure we have an English-speaking server, while a cynic might surmise we're being hidden from the locals"; tables aside, surveyors split over this Southern French specialist: fans find the cuisine and "pleasant atmosphere" in the red-and-yellow rooms make it "almost as good as a trip to Provence", but others shrug it's "a standby, not a destination."

	FOOD	DECOR	SERVICE	COST

Bath's 🈂 *Auvergne/New French*   20 | 19 | 19 | €56

17ᵉ | 25, rue Bayen (Etoile) | 01 45 74 74 74 | fax 01 45 74 71 15 | www.baths.fr

Everybody's back into the bath after the "elegant launching" of this father/son-run table, moved from the exclusive 8th to the more egalitarian 17th and offering a younger, more "relaxed" (and less expensive) experience; there's still "delicious" Auvergnat cuisine "with Spanish-inflected dishes", wine recommendations from the lengthy list that are "spot on" and "warm service"; in short, "a real jewel."

Beaujolais d'Auteuil (Le) *Classic French*   17 | 14 | 14 | €44

16ᵉ | 99, bd de Montmorency (Porte d'Auteuil) | 01 47 43 03 56 | fax 01 46 51 27 81

Open seven days a week, this "classic at the edge of the 16th" "holds no surprises", which explains its "elbow-to-elbow" occupancy – regulars know they can count on the "bistro ambiance", "friendly enough" service and "quality", "typical French food" delivered in "sufficient quantity"; while "prices have increased", they're "still honest."

BE Boulangépicier 🈂 *Sandwiches*   19 | 11 | 14 | €23

8ᵉ | 73, bd de Courcelles (Courcelles/Ternes) | 01 46 22 20 20 | fax 01 46 22 20 21
9ᵉ | Printemps | 64, bd Haussmann, 3rd fl. (Havre-Caumartin) | 01 42 82 67 17
www.boulangepicier.com

"Eating on the run" becomes a gastronomic experience at this "new concept" bakery with branches in the 8th and 9th, owned by superstar chef Alain Ducasse; the "best baguettes ever" envelop haute sandwiches, alongside "excellent soups and salads", and though some find it "really overpriced", "only in Paris would you find food this extraordinary in a setting so completely ordinary."

Bel Canto *Italian*   13 | 15 | 17 | €56

4ᵉ | 72, quai de l'Hôtel de Ville (Hôtel-de-Ville/Pont-Marie) | 01 42 78 30 18 | fax 01 42 78 30 28
Neuilly-sur-Seine | 6, rue du Commandant Pilot (Les Sablons) | 01 47 47 19 94 | fax 01 47 38 60 49 🈂 Ⓜ
www.lebelcanto.com

The staff literally hits the high note of this "original" duo in the 4th and Neuilly – opera *artistes* all, they deliver arias along with traditional dishes from the land of Puccini, and their "talented singing more than makes up for any serving faux pas"; culinary critics pan the meals as "mediocre", especially given how "expensive" they are – though no more so than two on the aisle at the Opéra Bastille.

Bellini 🈂 *Italian*   ▽ 24 | 21 | 23 | €56

16ᵉ | 28, rue Le Sueur (Argentine) | 01 45 00 54 20 | www.restaurantbellini.com

There's something "about pasta and cheese that's very comforting" sigh surveyors about this "cozy" Italian near L'Etoile, whose "wonderful" noodles include tagliatelle in a flambéed Parmesan wheel;

paesanis also praise the "relaxed, yet formal service" and "tranquil ambiance" of the terra-cotta-colored room.

Bellota-Bellota 🍴Ⓜ *Spanish*　　▽ 19 | 15 | 19 | €50

7ᵉ | 18, rue Jean-Nicot (La Tour-Maubourg) | 01 53 59 96 96 | fax 01 53 59 70 44

"If there were a Nobel prize for ham", they'd win it at this *jamon*-and-wine bar in the 7th, which attracts with an "awesome" array of the cured pork, plus Spanish cheeses, wines and bread from the bakery next door; "amiable service" and modest but "pretty decor" of azulejo tiles explain why the place is so "popular with the locals", though even they lament the "expensive" cost of hamming it up.

Benkay *Japanese*　　▽ 24 | 21 | 19 | €94

15ᵉ | Hôtel Novotel Tour Eiffel | 61, quai de Grenelle (Bir-Hakeim/ Charles Michels) | 01 40 58 21 26 | fax 01 40 58 21 30 | www.novotel.com

Political bigwigs are often spotted at Seine-side tables with a "great view" that only adds to the "high-end" experience of this hotel eatery many call the city's "best" for "authentic" Japanese cuisine; patrons choose between the teppanyaki grill with its accompanying spectacle and classic plates, including sushi and sashimi, served by an "attentive", kimono-clad staff; be advised, though, that "you pay for what you get" (a lunchtime prix fixe diminishes the damage).

🅉 Benoît *Lyon*　　24 | 21 | 22 | €77

4ᵉ | Hôtel de Ville | 20, rue St-Martin (Châtelet-Les Halles/Hôtel de Ville) | 01 42 72 25 76 | fax 01 42 72 45 68 | www.alain-ducasse.com

"Step into 1912" at this "elegant" "Paris classic" in the 4th that has "kept its charm" after being "dusted off" by chef-restaurateurs Alain Ducasse and Thierry de la Brosse; while "prices have gone up", the "authentic" "high-quality Lyonnais bistro food" "tastes as good as it looks", and "the service is friendly, if variable"; really, "the only negative is the number of tourists", even if they're often "shunted" to "English-speakers' Siberia in the back room."

Berkeley (Le) ⚫ *Eclectic*　　14 | 16 | 14 | €60

8ᵉ | 7, av Matignon (Champs-Elysées-Clémenceau/Franklin D. Roosevelt) | 01 42 25 72 25 | fax 01 45 63 30 06 | www.leberkeley.com

It may have "a great location" just off the Champs-Elysées, but the "indifferent", "expensive-for-what-you-get" Classic French–Eclectic eats and "cool - make that frozen - service" at this *brasserie de luxe* leave most surveyors cold; still, some supporters smile at the striped-tented ceiling, the most noticeable feature of the decor, and "the great terrace out front", "a fantastic spot to see everyone who's anyone pass by."

Beurre Noisette (Le) 🍴Ⓜ *Bistro*　　▽ 23 | 13 | 19 | €44

15ᵉ | 68, rue Vasco de Gama (Lourmel/Porte de Versailles) | 01 48 56 82 49

Easy to overlook, this "neighborhood bistro" in the faraway 15th has a following among food lovers and off-duty chefs, thanks to chef-owner Thierry Blanqui's "refined", "inventive" French cuisine that's especially "great for the price", plus an equally "approachable wine

list"; the "laid-back but professional service" helps make for "a lovely, relaxed" experience, one "good for rubbing elbows with the locals (because there isn't much room!)."

Biche au Bois (A la) 🅑 *Bistro*

| 20 | 12 | 17 | €42 |

12ᵉ | 45, av Ledru-Rollin (Gare de Lyon) | 01 43 43 34 38

Lovers of wildlife – on their plate – hunt no further than this "convivial" bistro near the Gare de Lyon that's known for "excellent" game in autumn, and "massive portions" of "succulent" French "home cooking" (followed by an "awesome cheese plate") the rest of the year, all "smilingly" served in an "old-fashioned" brown-hued interior that reminds some of the forest; "no-stress" prices ensure the place is always "hopping."

BIOArt 🅑 *New French*

| - | - | - | M |

13ᵉ | 3, quai François Mauriac (Bibliothèque François Mitterrand/Quai de la Gare) | 01 45 85 66 88 | fax 01 45 85 04 24 | www.bioart.fr

Resetting the clock on 1960s hippie-ish health food, this spacious, contemporary dining room – self-styled as the largest organic restaurant in Paris – uses "excellent quality produce" to create "light, refined" New French dishes (bass with steamed veggies, chocolate-orange terrine); the "hinting toward the healthy" orientation extends to the environs, an ecological building with glass-wall views of the Seine and the area around the Bibliothèque François Mitterrand.

Bis du Severo (Le) *Bistro*

| - | - | - | M |

14ᵉ | 16, rue des Plantes (Mouton-Duvenet/Pernetty) | 01 40 44 73 09

When the popular Le Severo "is bursting at the seams", the Montparnasse "neighborhood crowd" heads down the street to its "relaxed" annex with a Japanese chef and a "good *quartier* vibe"; like its big brother, it has a meat-heavy traditional French menu – though they serve fish too – and connoisseurs claim the "quality of the food is exactly the same"; the wine list is heavy on organic labels.

Bistral (Le) 🅑 🅜 *Bistro*

| 19 | 10 | 15 | €48 |

17ᵉ | 80, rue Lemercier (Brochant/La Fourche) | 01 42 63 59 61

Boosters believe this Batignolles bastion of the 'bistronomic' scene (young chefs serving "serious gourmet" fare in a "bistro setting") is "worth the trek" for "ambitious", "highly creative cuisine paired with great organic wines", even if the "small" room's slightly "banal" decor "is not its strong point"; but some sigh that "prices – particularly of the wine – are creeping up."

Bistro 121 *Bistro*

| - | - | - | M |

15ᵉ | 121, rue de la Convention (Boucicaut) | 01 45 57 52 90 | fax 01 45 57 14 69

The "exceptionally warm welcome" at this long-standing neighborhood bistro in the 15th reminds surveyors why they "love the French"; and this place with its 1970s-era decor has built up a loyal clientele with its time-honored, "classic cooking" that keeps it "crowded and noisy" seven days a week.

	FOOD	DECOR	SERVICE	COST

Bistro de Breteuil (Le) *Bistro*
16 | 16 | 15 | €40

7e | 3, pl de Breteuil (Duroc) | 01 45 67 07 27 | fax 01 42 73 11 08 | www.bistrocie.fr

"A real bargain of a prix fixe that includes three courses and a bottle of wine" keeps this "stuff-yourself" bistro "popular with the locals" of the 7th; admittedly, the Classic French fare "ain't no Haute Cuisine" and the pace makes for rather "mechanical service", but "there's plenty to choose from on the regularly changing menu", "tables are decently spaced" and there's a "great terrace in summer", so why carp?

Bistro de l'Olivier (Le) 🔀 *Provence*
18 | 14 | 17 | €43

8e | 13, rue Quentin-Bauchart (George V) | 01 47 20 78 63 | fax 01 47 20 74 58

Parisians dreaming of Provence get "a whiff of vacation" at this "typically southern" French table that's a "reasonably priced", "welcome find" in the business-oriented 8th; diners taste "a bit of sunshine" in the "fresh and flavorful" dishes, soak in the "warmth" of the "simple" setting with olive trees and appreciate the "charming service" – though its "slow" rhythm is also "authentic" of the rush-free region.

Bistro des Deux Théâtres (Le) ◗🔀 *Bistro*
14 | 14 | 13 | €41

9e | 18, rue Blanche (Trinité) | 01 45 26 41 43 | fax 01 48 74 08 92 | www.bistrocie.fr

Featuring "three courses and a bottle of wine", "the prix fixe is a fabulous value" at this veteran in the 9th that's part of the "same chain as Bistro Melrose"; however, it's clearly the cheap eats that keep this production running, since most "find it average" foodwise, and the "theatrical, red-curtained" decor is "aging"; but at least the "hurried service" makes it "good for [pre- and] post-theater meals."

Bistro d'Hubert (Le) 🔀 *Classic/New French*
∇ 22 | 19 | 21 | €47

15e | 41, bd Pasteur (Pasteur) | 01 47 34 15 50 | fax 01 45 67 03 09 | www.bistrodhubert.com

Surveyors say you'll feel "more like a relative than a client" at this "homey", "unpretentious" Montparnasse bistro, whose "country-style" look belies a menu that "takes traditional French cuisine to a new level" with "unusual spicing" from various corners of the globe and "good Basque" wines; add in "affordable" prices and a "delightful staff" and it's a "pleasant place" all around.

Bistro du 17ème (Le) *Bistro*
18 | 16 | 16 | €36

17e | 108, av de Villiers (Péreire) | 01 47 63 32 77 | fax 01 42 27 67 66 | www.bistrocie.fr

This "neighborhood crowd-pleaser", part of Willy Dorr's Bistro & Cie group of low-priced places, ensures that residents of the 17th are well-fed with a "solid bargain" prix fixe of Classic French fare (including wine) that's "not overly imaginative" but "always a little better than you expect"; though "slow", the staff's "kind to kids", and the "convivial setting" is particularly appealing during "summer-terrace season."

	FOOD	DECOR	SERVICE	COST

Bistro Melrose ●🏿 *Bistro* — | - | - | M

17ᵉ | 5, pl de Clichy (Place de Clichy) | 01 42 93 61 34 | fax 01 44 70 99 19 | www.bistrocie.fr

This Place de Clichy standby, part of the Willy Dorr group of budget-friendly bistros, is "always crowded" with locals who can't resist what they call "the best buy in Paris", a fixed-price menu of service-able French faves comprising two or three courses, wine and *café*, served until midnight; the typically Parisian interior features red banquettes and a ceiling cupola.

Bistro Poulbot 🏿Ⓜ *Bistro* — | - | - | M
(fka Poulbot Gourmet)

18ᵉ | 39, rue Lamarck (Lamarck-Caulaincourt) | 01 46 06 86 00 | fax 01 46 06 63 14

Up in a quiet corner of Montmartre, this twentysomething bistro now boasts "new management and chef" (acclaimed French Polynesian toque Véronique Melloul), but the cuisine remains "as always – classic with sly innovations"; in fact, the entire scene is "su-perb", from the "helpful service" to the "non-touristy" clientele to the cozy dining room decorated with prints by illustrator Francisque Poulbot, who once lived on this street.

Bistro St. Ferdinand ● *Bistro* 14 | 12 | 13 | €36
17ᵉ | 275, bd Péreire (Porte Maillot) | 01 45 74 33 32 | fax 01 45 74 33 12 | www.bistrocie.fr

This Porte Maillot bistro is a lifesaver for locals when they just "don't feel like cooking", since the "all-inclusive" prix fixe menu might be "unoriginal" – even a tad "industrial" – but it's "good enough", and there are "no disagreeable surprises" when the bill comes; the new, "modern" decor with its varying rooms leaves most diners indifferent, though the courtyard remains a favorite when the weather's fine.

Bistrot à Vins Mélac 🏿Ⓜ *Wine Bar/Bistro* 14 | 12 | 13 | €34
11ᵉ | 42, rue Léon Frot (Charonne) | 01 43 70 59 27 | fax 01 43 70 73 10 | www.melac.fr

"The principal attraction is the wine" at this "cheap and cheerful" 11th-arrondissement *bistrot à vins* where the "quality and large choice" of vintages, especially from the Languedoc, make up for the limited menu of Auvergnat "dishes like *grand-mère* made"; the mus-tachioed Monsieur Mélac is a "character" who reigns over the "con-vivial ambiance", but the staffers can be "brusque" – especially "if you ask for water."

Bistrot d'à Côté 🏿 *Bistro* 21 | 16 | 18 | €51
17ᵉ | 10, rue Gustave Flaubert (Péreire/Ternes) | 01 42 67 05 81 | fax 01 47 63 82 75
17ᵉ | 16, av de Villiers (Villiers) | 01 47 63 25 61 | fax 01 48 88 92 42
Neuilly-sur-Seine | 4, rue Boutard (Pont-de-Neuilly) | 01 47 45 34 55 | fax 01 47 45 15 08
www.michelrostang.com

"Favorites with the bustling advertising and PR crowd", chef-owner Michel Rostang's "intimate" baby bistros serve "solid", "simple"

Classic French cuisine that seems "always the same" – that is, "consistently delicious"; "service is variable" – "friendly" vs. "snotty" – and the fare can be "too expensive for what you get"; "but with excellent ingredients and attentive preparation", "the quality is there"; P.S. "the old-grocery decor is nice" in the Rue Gustave Flaubert branch.

Bistrot d'André (Le) ⍉ *Bistro*

–	–	–	I

15ᵉ | 232, rue St-Charles (Balard) | 01 45 57 89 14 | fax 01 45 57 97 15

With an "atmosphere reflecting the long-gone Citroën factory" across the street, this bistro named for the carmaker coasts on the memory of the 1920s when it was a company canteen; the kitchen still turns out dishes workers might have eaten, "traditional French cuisine that's unexceptional but fine", and modern motorists appreciate the "inexpensive" prices.

Bistrot de l'Etoile Lauriston ⍉ *Bistro*

–	–	–	M

16ᵉ | 19, rue Lauriston (Kléber) | 01 40 67 11 16

"A great buy for the money", this bistro near the namesake Etoile is "a friendly favorite for the smart business traveler" or anyone who wants to be "away from the tourist hustle and bustle"; the menu is "reliably" "inventive but appealing", and the "service is personal"; the only weak spot is "the room that aspires to minimalist elegance", but is defeated by *Bonjour Tristesse*–type decor.

⍜ Bistrot de l'Oulette ◐◑⍉ *Southwest* (fka Bistrot Baracane)

26	16	21	€40

4ᵉ | 38, rue des Tournelles (Bastille) | 01 42 71 43 33 | fax 01 40 02 04 77 | www.l-oulette.com

This "intimate" favorite near the Bastille "has a new name", a different chef and updated decor, but the "same ownership" – and, most important, the "satisfying experience" hasn't changed, to the relief of those (including "many tourists") who call it a must; its "wonderful" menu of "serious Southwestern cooking" now has a few more "inventive twists", but the price is still "terrific" and the service "just super."

Bistrot de l'Université ⍉ *Bistro*

▽ 18	13	16	€34

7ᵉ | 40, rue de l'Université (Rue du Bac) | 01 42 61 26 64 | fax 01 42 61 26 64

That "simple" "little bistro you've been looking for" may reside in this "local spot" in the 7th; perhaps the cuisine's "nothing to write home about", but given the relatively "inexpensive" prices, patrons "have yet to find a *plat* that will not please"; if the service can be "frustratingly slow", "this place is so sincerely Parisian, you forget the clock."

Bistrot de Marius (Le) *Seafood*

21	14	16	€51

8ᵉ | 6, av George V (Alma Marceau) | 01 40 70 11 76 | fax 01 40 70 17 08

The "ultra-high-rent district known as the Triangle d'Or" can be a Bermuda Triangle for the wallet, so cost-conscious consumers set

The column headers at top right: FOOD, DECOR, SERVICE, COST.

sail for this "bustling" seafooder that serves "well-prepared" "fresh fish" at "lower prices" than the "mother ship, Marius et Janette, next door"; clients are "squeezed together" like sardines in the "cramped interior", so if possible, "eat outside and enjoy people-watching on Avenue George V."

Bistrot de Paris (Le) ◐⑤Ⓜ *Bistro* | 16 | 16 | 16 | €42 |

7e | 33, rue de Lille (Rue du Bac/St-Germain-des-Prés) | 01 42 61 16 83 | fax 01 49 27 06 09

Those "nostalgic for Paris of the [early] 1900s" time travel in this 100-year-old institution with an "authentic" "old" bistro interior that formerly welcomed André Gide and now draws a "busy lunch crowd including members of the French Senate" nearby; the "traditional dishes" are admittedly "unoriginal", but they're of "good quality", and besides, "at these prices you can't expect the moon."

Bistrot des Dames (Le) ⑤ *Bistro* ∇ | 14 | 17 | 14 | €30 |

17e | Hôtel El Dorado | 18, rue des Dames (Place de Clichy) | 01 45 22 13 42 | fax 01 43 87 25 97 | www.eldoradohotel.fr

"Go in summer for the garden" and "wonderful terrace" at this edgy, stylish little bistro in the ever-trendier Batignolles neighborhood; the "menu's unchanging, but suitable, and it's a "great place for friends and drinks", especially when the prices are as easygoing as the crowd.

Bistrot des Vignes (Le) *Bistro* ∇ | 17 | 13 | 20 | €37 |

16e | 1, rue Jean-de-Bologne (La Muette/Passy) | 01 45 27 76 64 | fax 01 45 27 76 64 | www.bistrotdesvignes.fr

"When you're looking for a casual, comfortable meal without spending too much" (after your shopping jag on the Rue de Passy nearby), this "atmospheric" yet "unpretentious little neighborhood bistro" open seven days a week is "appreciated by tourists and locals alike" for its "attentive" service, "very good" basic French cuisine, children's menu and "simple" decor recently repainted in cheery colors.

Bistrot d'Henri (Le) ◐ *Bistro* | 20 | 15 | 21 | €35 |

6e | 16, rue Princesse (Mabillon/St-Germain-des-Prés) | 01 46 33 51 12 | www.bistro-dhenri.com

"You won't go wrong" at this "busy, bustling and atmospheric" Saint-Germain spot, which is why it's been going strong for over 25 years; the "service is friendly" and "prices are terrific" for "large portions" of "excellent" "authentic" bistro cuisine ("oh, those potatoes!"); and though the "tables are so close you can eat from your neighbor's plate", habitués claim they "wouldn't want it any other way."

Bistrot du Cap (Le) *Seafood* | - | - | - | M |

15e | 30, rue Peclet (Convention/Vaugirard) | 01 40 43 02 18 | fax 01 40 43 02 18

Residents of this low-key corner of the 15th dock at this family-run bistro "for the owner's smile, the tranquility of the site" and especially "for the [teak] terrace in the summer"; but though the inexpensive prix fixe of mostly (but not all) fish dishes is "good for the 'hood", it's probably "not worth a trip" across town.

	FOOD	DECOR	SERVICE	COST

Bistrot du Dôme (Le) *Seafood* — 21 | 19 | 20 | €47
14ᵉ | 1, rue Delambre (Vavin) | 01 43 35 32 00

Dôme Bastille (Le) *Seafood*
4ᵉ | 2, rue de la Bastille (Bastille) | 01 48 04 88 44 | fax 01 48 04 00 59
"Simpler and less expensive than their parent, Le Dôme", these seafood siblings at Bastille and Montparnasse offer "oysters and more
oysters", plus a "wide variety" of *poissons* ("meat eaters should look
elsewhere" for sustenance); though the "fish are smaller [here],
they're just as tasty" and "wonderfully fresh", and served "without
any fuss" amid a "homey atmosphere."

Bistrot du Peintre (Le) ● *Bistro* — ▽ 18 | 18 | 18 | €46
11ᵉ | 116, av Ledru-Rollin (Bastille/Ledru-Rollin) | 01 47 00 34 39
This "hip" Bastille bistro is "where the bobos go" for a "seriously
funky", art nouveau–styled scene; the "standard fare" comes in
"generous portions", but the real reason people "love it" is because
it's a "friendly", "lovely place to dine on the sidewalk and watch the
world go by."

Bistrot du Sommelier ⊠ *Wine Bar/Bistro* — 18 | 16 | 19 | €58
8ᵉ | 97, bd Haussmann (St-Augustin) | 01 42 65 24 85 | fax 01 53 75 23 23 |
www.bistrotdusommelier.com
"A charming sommelier encourages you to guess the wine before he
identifies it" at this bacchanalian bistro known for "selected pairings
with each course" of "succulent", "inventive" fare; situated in a well-
heeled business quarter of the 8th, it can get "very dear", but "sometimes you just have to offer yourself a good time."

Bistrot Niel ⊠ *Bistro* — - | - | - | M
(fka Bistrot de l'Etoile Niel)
17ᵉ | 75, av Niel (Péreire) | 01 42 27 88 44 | fax 01 42 27 32 12
The decor, staff and "ownership recently changed" at this "comfortable" contemporary bistro with a prestigious location near the
Etoile; surveyors seem pleased by the exotic touches added to the
"comfortable" interior, and the "surprisingly good" New French food
by a chef who worked with Alain Dutournier; the sidewalk terrace
has always been a hit.

Bistrot Papillon (Le) ⊠ *Bistro* — 14 | 13 | 17 | €44
9ᵉ | 6, rue Papillon (Cadet/Poissonnière) | 01 47 70 90 03 |
fax 01 48 24 05 59
Natives of the 9th "feel at home" in this "neighborhood" hangout
with its "smiling personnel", "bustling" interior and "solid" bistro
food that, if "uninspired", remains "consistently above average";
what's more, it's "affordable."

Bistrot Paul Bert (Le) ⊠Ⓜ *Bistro* — 23 | 14 | 17 | €41
11ᵉ | 18, rue Paul Bert (Faidherbe-Chaligny) | 01 43 72 24 01
Just thinking of the "cozy atmosphere and excellent steak frites"
makes lovers of this "good-value" bistro "feel all warm and fuzzy inside", and the flush spreads further when they add in the "extraordinary wine list"; it's "off the beaten path" in the 11th but "reservations

are a must", since, even after a recent expansion, tables are tight – but "be squished and be happy" knowing this place offers "one of the best evenings out."

Bistrot Vivienne ☒ *Bistro* | 18 | 17 | 16 | €40 |

2ᵉ | 4, rue des Petits-Champs (Bourse/Palais Royal-Musée du Louvre) | 01 49 27 00 50 | fax 01 49 27 00 40

"Best for a quick lunch" with friends decrees the "young crowd" that frequents this "well-located" "little bistro"; it's got "average food, but great ambiance", especially if you "obtain a table" outside "in the fabulous Galerie Vivienne."

Black Calavados ●☒Ⓜ *Eclectic* | - | - | - | E |

8ᵉ | 40, av Pierre 1er de Serbie (George V) | 01 47 20 77 77 | fax 01 47 20 77 01 | www.bc-paris.fr

"If you can get in" to this *très* "exclusive" joint co-owned by rocker Chris Cornell and frequented by "Euro hipsters" (both "aging" and not), you'll find it lives up to its name, an "all-black lacquered box" that "can be fun" when it's not "claustrophobic"; as for the Eclectic menu, it's always "pricey" and sometimes "less than average", but patrons point out this is "more like a nightclub" anyway, a "great place to see and be seen . . . after you dine somewhere else."

Blue Elephant ● *Thai* | 20 | 22 | 19 | €51 |

11ᵉ | 43-45, rue de la Roquette (Bastille/Voltaire) | 01 47 00 42 00 | fax 01 47 00 45 44 | www.blueelephant.com

While it's "more theme park than restaurant, with jungle sounds, waterfalls and bamboo thickets", the "whimsical" food is a "pleasant surprise" at what the "transported" term one of the "top Thais" in town; "service is friendly although a bit automated", and "on nights with lots of groups" the place is "like a Dantesque version of Trader Vic's" – and it's "overpriced" ("you mainly pay for the decor"); still, most esteem this "Bangkok escapade" close to Bastille.

Bocconi ☒ *Italian* | 20 | 11 | 17 | €43 |

8ᵉ | 10 bis, rue d'Artois (St-Philippe-du-Roule) | 01 53 76 44 44 | fax 01 45 61 10 08 | www.trattoria-bocconi.fr

You might see actress Monica Bellucci tucking into "excellent" pasta at this "business-district" venue in this 8th that serves "true Italian food" from various regions and "seasonal specialties" with the "good humor" typical of The Boot; Neapolitan chef-owner Ciro Polge used to work at Il Cortile, and though some "might find the bill high" for a trattoria, they also note many "nice surprises" on the menu.

Boeuf Couronné (Au) ● *Classic French* | 16 | 13 | 12 | €49 |

19ᵉ | 188, av Jean Jaurès (Porte de Pantin) | 01 42 39 44 44 | fax 01 42 39 17 30 | www.rest-gj.com

"The French answer to American steakhouses", this "old-fashioned" carnivores' cave in a distant corner of the 19th (where the city's slaughterhouses once were) specializes in "excellent meat"; the remainder of the menu's "nothing exceptional", but patrons applaud the "patient staff", and the once-"dated" decor has recently gotten a refurb (not reflected in the Decor score).

	FOOD	DECOR	SERVICE	COST

Boeuf sur le Toit (Le) ●🗷 *Brasserie* | 18 | 19 | 18 | €56 |

8ᵉ | 34, rue du Colisée (Franklin D. Roosevelt/St-Philippe-du-Roule) | 01 53 93 65 55 | fax 01 53 96 02 32 | www.boeufsurletoit.com

"Seafood brimming over crates of ice" marks the entrance of this art deco "landmark" off the Champs that attracts herds of customers for "average" but "acceptable" brasserie fare ("best to go for the *fruits de mer*, which they can't ruin"); "the waiters are attentive but harried" and "the bar area can get festive", but that "craziness" is what makes it "great for last-minute, late-night, large-group dining."

🗹 Bofinger ● *Brasserie* | 20 | 24 | 19 | €54 |

4ᵉ | 5, rue de la Bastille (Bastille) | 01 42 72 87 82 | fax 01 42 72 97 68 | www.bofingerparis.com

This "old standby" at the Bastille offers a "perfect last act to the opera" (especially when "the tenor is at the next table"), with a "lively crowd" and a "sumptuous fin de siècle setting" featuring a "glorious glass dome"; but if the decor's "a feast for the eyes", the "standard" Alsatian-accented brasserie fare is somewhat less "exciting" (aside from the "reliable" "shellfish extravaganza"); also, the "still-authentic" ambiance suffers slightly when the "neighboring accents come from Brooklyn and Battersea" as often as Bretagne.

Bon *New French* | 15 | 21 | 13 | €64 |

16ᵉ | 25, rue de la Pompe (La Muette) | 01 40 72 70 00 | fax 01 40 72 68 30 | www.restaurantbon.fr

If this spot in the 16th "lives up to its name", it's thanks to Philippe Starck's simultaneously "trendy and romantic" decor, especially the "fabulous bar with its rotating candelabra"; alas, while the New French fare is "inventive", "at these prices" it is not *bon* enough, and the "slightly snide" attitude of a staff that's as "gorgeous" as the surroundings leads diners to suspect aesthetics are the "number one priority" here; N.B. scores don't reflect a post-Survey refresh, also by Starck.

🗹 Bon Accueil (Au) 🗷 *Bistro* | 24 | 19 | 22 | €56 |

7ᵉ | 14, rue de Monttessuy (Alma Marceau/Ecole Militaire) | 01 47 05 46 11 | fax 01 45 56 15 80

"At the base of the Eiffel Tower" (and boasting a "sensational" sidewalk view of same), this veteran bistro delights visitors who depend on its "terrific" Classic French cuisine, based on what's "seasonally available" and "prepared with panache"; "stylish service" adds to the *acceuil* ('welcome'), and while it's "no longer the amazing bargain it used to be", it "continues to be wonderful."

Bon Saint Pourçain (Le) 🗷⌿ *Classic French* | 18 | 14 | 20 | €43 |

6ᵉ | 10 bis, rue Servandoni (Odéon/St-Sulpice) | 01 43 54 93 63

"In the shadow of Saint-Sulpice", this "idiosyncratic" bistro makes you "feel like you've come home, even though you've never lived in France", with "friendly atmosphere" provided by its father-and-daughter team; the "small" menu offers "simple French fare prepared by Papa", who shares his "thoughts on everything"; and while the Vieux Paris decor is somewhat "bereft", it doesn't make this place any less "beloved by tourists."

	FOOD	DECOR	SERVICE	COST

Bons Crus (Aux) ⓩ *Wine Bar/Bistro* — | — | — | M

1er | 7, rue des Petits-Champs (Bourse/Palais Royal-Musée du Louvre) | 01 42 60 06 45 | fax 01 42 33 62 83

More than one bon vivant has been known to "pleasantly lose an afternoon" at this "delightful" 100-year-old wine bar behind the Palais-Royal; "perfect for a cold day" with some "filling" bistro dishes, cheese and charcuterie, it's "very French and very warm", especially after a few glasses of red.

Boucherie Roulière ❶Ⓜ *Bistro* — | — | — | M

6e | 24, rue des Canettes (St-Sulpice) | 01 43 26 25 70

Meat lovers steak out a table and sit "elbow-to-elbow" in the long, skinny, simply decorated room of this "tiny" eatery near Saint-Sulpice, co-owned by a butcher and a native of the Auvergne, home of the famous Salers cattle; grilled "huge steaks" are the main attraction here, though the beef-averse will also find alternate bistro options, "reasonably priced" for dependably "copious" portions.

Bouchons de François Clerc (Les) ⓩ *Classic French* 20 | 17 | 20 | €52

8e | 7, rue du Boccador (Alma Marceau) | 01 47 23 57 80 | fax 01 47 23 74 54

P'tit Bouchon (Le) ⓩ *Classic French*

8e | 13 rue de la Tremoille (Alma Marceau/Franklin D. Roosevelt) | 01 47 20 81 18

www.bouchonsdefrancoisclerc.com

A "dazzling wine list" at "near wholesale" prices makes this "old-fashioned"–looking bistro off the Avenue George V an oenophiles' "heaven"; regulars recommend booking the second dinner seating "so you will not be rushed" drinking and consuming the "creative" Classic French dishes and "the best cheese plate ever offered"; N.B. its nearby adjunct, Le P'tit Bouchon, does light breakfast and lunch for fashion-industry femmes.

Bouillon Racine ⓩ *Brasserie* 16 | 25 | 19 | €39

6e | 3, rue Racine (Cluny La Sorbonne/Odéon) | 01 44 32 15 60 | fax 01 44 32 15 61 | www.bouillonracine.com

The "remarkable" "mirrored art nouveau room" is "the principal reason to dine" at this brasserie near the Sorbonne; supplemented by "excellent Belgian beers", the "cooking's not noted for its finesse", but at least it's "a solid meal, not one that looks like plate decoration", and the staff has actually become "accommodating."

Boulangerie (La) ⓩ *Bistro* ▽ 23 | 17 | 20 | €32

20e | 15, rue des Panoyaux (Ménilmontant) | 01 43 58 45 45 | fax 01 43 58 45 46

There's nothing half-baked about this "darn good" bistro in a former bakery in the funky, multiethnic Ménilmontant neighborhood; the kitchen turns out traditional dishes with a "touch of modernity" and "consistent" quality, the wine list is "excellent" and the "pleasant surprise" only gets better with the bill – a "great bang for your euro."

	FOOD	DECOR	SERVICE	COST

Boulangerie
Eric Kayser ⊠ *Bakery/Sandwiches*   16 | 12 | 12 | €22

8^e | 85, bd Malesherbes (St-Augustin) | 01 45 22 70 30 |
www.maison-kayser.com

Master baker Eric Kayser's *boulangeries* "set a new standard for bread"
and pastries all over town, but this is the only freestanding shop that
is "also a restaurant" (albeit a pretty casual one) where a "*speedé*"
staff slings "beautiful, freshly prepared salads, pretty sandwiches"
and "star tarts" to the morning and midday crowds; a few "expected
better of the decor, given the location" in the elegant 8th, and it's "a
little dear for a lunch break – but you can't put a price on quality."

Boule Rouge (La) ◑⊠ *African*   - | - | - | M

9^e | 1, rue de la Boule-Rouge (Grands Boulevards) | 01 47 70 43 90 |
fax 01 42 46 99 57

Few surveyors know this large North African in the 9th, but those
who do commend the couscous (especially the "excellent" Friday
special with spinach); prices are as easygoing as the warm service,
and the atmosphere is nostalgic, since the decor reminds expats of
the Tunisian eateries they left for the City of Light.

Bound ◑ *Japanese/New French*   - | - | - | E

8^e | 49-51, av Georges V (George V) | 01 53 67 84 60 | fax 01 53 67 84 67 |
www.buddhabar.com

Golden Triangle–bound hipsters know this address as the old Barfly,
now revamped with "complicated" pink decor – an eye-popping
megabar, plasma screens, glossy mock-croc chairs and lighting
effects – while a DJ plays "loud music" nightly; as expected, it's "not
cheap", but the Japanese–New French food's "a cut above" what one
finds in such "cool-vibe" venues; the same goes for the "efficient" staff.

Ⓩ Bouquinistes (Les) ⊠ *New French*   23 | 19 | 21 | €62

6^e | 53, quai des Grands-Augustins (St-Michel) | 01 43 25 45 94 |
www.lesbouquinistes.com

"After all these years", this "casually sophisticated" baby bistro from
Guy Savoy is still "consistently excellent" (though much "pricier"),
offering New French flavors that "excite the tongue" in a "modern,
somewhat cool setting" with quayside "views of the Seine"; the
crowd combines the Left Bank "literary set" with a "heavy tourist"
contingent, and the servers are "professional" (despite a tendency
to "rush you through your meal"); in sum, "a great second choice, for
those who can't afford the full-blown Savoy restaurant experience."

Bourguignon
du Marais (Au) ⊠ *Wine Bar/Bistro*   23 | 18 | 20 | €51

4^e | 52, rue François Miron (Pont-Marie/St-Paul) | 01 48 87 15 40 |
fax 01 48 87 17 49

"Modern but cozy, with a warm French feel", this Marais *bistrot à
vins* offers "quite good food" that "pairs really well with the wines"
("if you love Burgundies, this is the place"); though it can be "one of
the best deals in Paris", beware – "the bill has a way of zipping upward" with all those "delicious" vinos by the glass.

	FOOD	DECOR	SERVICE	COST

Z Braisière (La) Z *Gascony* — 27 | 19 | 23 | €70

17e | 54, rue Cardinet (Malesherbes) | 01 47 63 40 37 | fax 01 47 63 04 76

The "quiet contented murmurings" attest to the "masterful" cuisine found in this "hidden gem" for "imaginative" Gascon gastronomy in the 17th, with connoisseurs claiming it offers "more value for the money than the better-knowns"; the "neutral" decor was recently redone, but the ambiance is still "cozy" and "down-to-earth", while the "relaxed service encourages you to linger over your meal and savor every bite."

Z Brasserie Balzar ● *Brasserie* — 19 | 20 | 19 | €44

5e | 49, rue des Ecoles (Cluny La Sorbonne/St-Michel) | 01 43 54 13 67 | fax 01 44 07 14 91 | www.brasseriebalzar.com

"A traditional haunt" for tourists, late-nighters and "Left Bank intellectuals" from the nearby Sorbonne, this "quintessential brasserie" "oozes charm" with its "glorious fin de siècle ambiance", "tasty, simple" classic fare and "very French waiters" (right down to "the gentleman with handlebar moustache"); while some old-timers are "wistful for the pre-Groupe Flo days", non-nostalgists claim "nothing's changed" – it may "feel like a cliché, but it's authentic."

Brasserie de l'Ile St. Louis ● *Brasserie* — 17 | 16 | 17 | €37

4e | 55, quai de Bourbon (Cité/Pont-Marie) | 01 43 54 02 59

"An institution on the Ile Saint-Louis" "facing Notre Dame", this "atmospheric" brasserie is blessed with decor of "1890s-vintage advertising posters" on dark-wood walls – a "tavernlike" setting for "solid Alsatian" eats, served by "slightly wry waiters"; and if a Food score drop supports skeptics who say "yes, Virginia, you can get a bad meal in Paris", at least the place is "not part of a chain."

Brasserie du Louvre *Brasserie* — 16 | 17 | 16 | €42

1er | Hôtel du Louvre | Place André Malraux (Palais Royal-Musée du Louvre) | 01 42 96 27 98 | fax 01 44 58 38 01 | www.hoteldulouvre.com

"Across the street from the Louvre in the hotel of the same name", this wood-banqueted brasserie offers "great people-watching" from an outdoor terrace, "dependable" if "ordinary" fare and a staff that's "attentive if somewhat cold"; it's "been better in the past", but the "sublime" location means "this place can be forgiven a lot of sins"; N.B. a new chef arrived mid-Survey, with plans to move the cuisine from traditional to trendy.

Brasserie Flo ● *Brasserie* — 18 | 20 | 18 | €54

10e | 7, cour des Petites-Ecuries (Château d'Eau) | 01 47 70 13 59 | fax 01 42 47 00 80 | www.flobrasseries.com

It may be a bit "grimy" in this patch of the 10th, but the decor of sinuous molding and mirrors "speaks of the Belle Epoque" at this brasserie that's "part of the Groupe Flo"; possessing the "noisy", "fun" "feeling of a Toulouse-Lautrec painting", it's a fine place "to take tourists", but with the food no more than "acceptable", most suggest you "keep to the conservative side of the menu and chew on the ambiance."

Brasserie Julien ◐ *Brasserie*

19 | 26 | 19 | €59

10ᵉ | 16, rue du Faubourg St-Denis (Strasbourg-St-Denis) | 01 47 70 12 06 | fax 01 42 47 00 65 | www.flobrasseries.com

This "art nouveau gem" glitters "in a seedy neighborhood" in the 10th, where clients "step off of one of Paris' least attractive streets" and into a "magical" setting with wood and mirrors, "waiters in long white aprons" and "large parties" who create the "pleasantly noisy" "action" within; it serves "typical", "reliable" brasserie food seven days a week until 1 AM, but no matter what time you arrive, "don't miss the profiteroles" with a "teapot full of chocolate sauce."

Brasserie La Lorraine ◐ *Brasserie*

17 | 17 | 16 | €63

8ᵉ | 2, pl des Ternes (Ternes) | 01 56 21 22 00 | fax 01 56 21 22 09 | www.brasserielalorraine.com

Though it was overhauled in 2004, many find the "makeover disappointing" at this "typical large brasserie" in the 8th; "the place looks brighter", but it's "a bit too Vegas" now, the formalized service "has become chilly" and while the food's "good" ("of course you must order the quiche"), "the prices, always high, have skyrocketed"; still, this "neighborhood standby" "definitely has an upbeat atmosphere"; N.B. don't ignore the *voiturier,* or you may be mysteriously towed away in the night.

Brasserie L'Européen ◐ *Brasserie*

- | - | - | M

12ᵉ | 21 bis, bd Diderot (Gare de Lyon) | 01 43 43 99 70 | fax 01 43 07 26 51 | www.brasserie-leuropeen.fr

One of the city's last independent brasseries, this veteran near the Gare de Lyon joined the Joulie group in 2006, which may be why foes feel the fare "has become very common" of late – though stalwarts insist the seafood choucroute continues to be among the "best in Paris"; the '70s Slavik decor is charmingly retro with mirrors and Chesterfield banquettes, but if you have a train to catch be forewarned: the clock runs backwards.

☒ Brasserie Lipp ◐☒ *Brasserie*

17 | 20 | 16 | €51

6ᵉ | 151, bd St-Germain (St-Germain-des-Prés) | 01 45 48 53 91 | fax 01 45 44 33 20 | www.brasserie-lipp.fr

"Parisian and international celebrities greet each other warmly" at this "stalwart" in Saint-Germain, a brasserie frequented by so many regulars "it's like a club", and where insiders say it's "imperative to be seated on the ground floor" for "priceless people-watching" amid art nouveau decor (upstairs is "where they stick the American rubes"); "the food isn't as interesting as the clientele" – keep to the "good old classics" – and since the service "depends on who you are", know that many "pay to be sneered at or ignored."

Brasserie Lutétia ☒ *Brasserie*

18 | 19 | 18 | €58

6ᵉ | Hôtel Lutétia | 23, rue de Sèvres (Sèvres-Babylone) | 01 49 54 46 76 | fax 01 49 54 46 00 | www.lutetia-paris.com

"Not bad for a hotel restaurant", this "plush and stylish" brasserie with art deco–style decor by Sonia Rykiel is "perfect" for "lunch while shopping" (though "service is slow" sometimes); it's a "lovely

place for a seafood platter", but otherwise there are "no real surprises here", including the 6th-arrondissement-"expensive" bills.

Brasserie Mollard ● ⊠ *Brasserie* ▽ 19 | 24 | 16 | €47

8ᵉ | 115, rue St-Lazare (St-Lazare) | 01 43 87 50 22 | fax 01 43 87 84 17 | www.mollard.fr

The mosaic "tiles alone are worth a visit" to this classified historic monument with its "extraordinary" art nouveau interior near the Gare Saint-Lazare; but while "the decor is always nice, the bill is hefty for traditional brasserie food" wallet-watchers wail (aside from the "succulent" seafood selection).

Brasserie Printemps *Classic French* 11 | 15 | 10 | €32

9ᵉ | Printemps | 64, bd Haussmann (Auber/Havre-Caumartin) | 01 42 82 58 84 | fax 01 45 26 31 24 | www.printemps.com

"One never tires of looking at the cupola" overhead, like a 1923 "gigantic stained-glass globe" – the highlight of the "hip" interior of the packed canteen of the "legendary department store" Printemps; *hélas*, the Classic French menu "doesn't shine" like the decor, even if shoppers say it's "passable quality for a quick lunch" – or perhaps a slow one, since patrons must put up with "long waits" for everything from "being seated to paying"; N.B. dinner Thursdays only.

Breakfast in America *American* 15 | 17 | 19 | €18

4ᵉ | 4, rue Mahler (St-Paul) | 01 42 72 40 21
5ᵉ | 17, rue des Écoles (Cardinal Lemoine/Jussieu) | 01 43 54 50 28
www.breakfast-in-america.com

From "those round red twirly stools at the soda counter" to the "burgers, omelets, fries" and shakes on the menu, "this diner could be from an episode of *Happy Days*"; with branches in the Latin Quarter and the Marais, it's "a perfect remedy" for "homesick Americans" on either side of the Seine (and there are many, judging by the "interminable weekend waits"), who confess "it's a crazy thing to do in Paris" – but it's authentic "down to the bad coffee."

NEW Breizh Café Ⓜ *Brittany* - | - | - | I

3ᵉ | 109, rue Vieille du Temple (Filles du Calvaire/St-Paul) | 01 42 72 13 77 | www.breizhcafe.com

An offshoot of a crêperie in Brittany and Tokyo, this "chic" new place in the upper Marais offers some "surprising" menu items, including organic buckwheat galettes with smoked herring, dessert crêpes with salted butter caramel and rare Tzarskaya oysters from the Bay of Cancal ("an exceptional treat"); wash it all down with 20 kinds of cider.

Ⓩ Bristol (Le) *Haute Cuisine* 27 | 28 | 27 | €145

8ᵉ | Hôtel Le Bristol | 112, rue du Faubourg St-Honoré (Miromesnil) | 01 53 43 43 40 | fax 01 53 43 43 01 | www.lebristolparis.com

When an "extravagant experience" is in order, this "special-night-out kind of place" in the 8th is "close to perfect", with "two separate dining rooms, depending upon the season": an oak-paneled, "sumptuous circular room" in winter and an "exquisite" garden in summertime; chef Eric Frechon's "phenomenal", "cutting-edge" Haute Cuisine is worth the "ooh-la-la" prices, "particularly for those who like strong

tastes in original combinations", while the "exceptional" service extends to "a silver tray of cleaning items" in case a customer should splash gravy on his recommended jacket.

☑ Buddha Bar ◐ *Asian*

| 16 | 25 | 15 | €67 |

8ᵉ | 8, rue Boissy-d'Anglas (Concorde) | 01 53 05 90 00 | fax 01 53 05 90 09 | www.buddhabar.com

This "legendary" "flashy-trashy-fabulous" nightclub/eatery is still "a scene" where the Buddha statue–dominated "digs are cool and the music is bumping", the "lychee martinis are to die for" and the Asian cuisine is "surprisingly good for a trendy bar" – even if the monastic portions amount to "finger foods at fistful prices"; protesting it's "past its heyday", nonbelievers call it "understaffed" and "overrun with tourists" (expect a "very long wait for a table"), but for fervent followers this "sexy" spot remains nirvana.

Buffalo Grill *Steak*

| 10 | 10 | 13 | €30 |

3ᵉ | 15, pl de la République (République) | 01 40 29 94 98
5ᵉ | 1, bd St-Germain (Jussieu) | 01 56 24 34 49
9ᵉ | 3, pl Blanche (Blanche) | 01 40 16 42 51
10ᵉ | 9, bd Denain (Gare du Nord) | 01 40 16 47 81
13ᵉ | 2, rue Raymond Aron (Quai de la Gare) | 01 45 86 76 71
14ᵉ | 117, av du Général Leclerc (Porte d'Orléans) | 01 45 40 09 72
15ᵉ | 154, rue St-Charles (Javel) | 01 40 60 97 48 | fax 01 40 60 17 48
17ᵉ | 6, pl du Maréchal Juin (Péreire) | 01 40 54 73 75
19ᵉ | 29, av Corentin Cariou (Porte de la Villette) | 01 40 36 21 41 | fax 01 53 26 88 17
www.buffalo-grill.fr

Like a "surreal take on an American steakhouse", this "popular faux-cowboy chain" serves up a mishmash of Yank eats (ribs, beef, Buffalo wings) in an "imitation Wild West" setting, complete with "Indian statues standing guard at the swinging saloon doors"; foes gun it down, calling "the pictures on the menu more appetizing than the food" itself and the "cowgirl"-clad staff "disagreeable"; "the only reason to go – they're kid-friendly", and the "affordable" eats are "better than a gas station's."

Buisson Ardent (Le) ☒ *Bistro*

| 19 | 16 | 17 | €38 |

5ᵉ | 25, rue Jussieu (Jussieu) | 01 43 54 93 02 | fax 01 46 33 34 77 | www.lebuissonardent.fr

A clientele of 5th-arrondissement academics creates a "calm" ambiance in this neighborhood "staple", giving high marks to the "frequently changing", "good-value" prix fixe menu; the young chef, formerly at Michel Rostang, makes "generous portions" of bistro cooking with a few "innovative" touches; the interior includes a "retro"-looking area with 1925 frescos and "lots of old wood."

Butte Chaillot (La) ☒ *Bistro*

| 21 | 19 | 20 | €54 |

16ᵉ | 110 bis, av Kléber (Trocadéro) | 01 47 27 88 88 | fax 01 47 27 41 46 | www.guysavoy.com

"Always pleasant for a simple business lunch" or "Sunday night supper", this "modern" bistro "under the auspices of Guy Savoy" has become a "classic" by offering "dependable food at reasonable

prices"; the handy location near Trocadéro is almost as much of a crowd-pleaser as what may be "the best roast chicken and mashed potatoes in the world", "well and quickly served."

Ca d'Oro *Italian*   ∇ 18 | 16 | 17 | €43

1ᵉʳ | 54, rue de l'Arbre-Sec (Louvre-Rivoli) | 01 40 20 97 79
A "favorite nobody-goes-there restaurant", this little location "overlooking the Louvre" offers "consistently good" "light Northern Italian food", plus some mighty "prime pasta"; "friendly waiters" add to the "relaxing atmosphere" of the place.

Café Beaubourg ● *Classic French*   16 | 20 | 15 | €34

4ᵉ | 100, rue St-Martin (Châtelet-Les Halles/Rambuteau) | 01 48 87 63 96 | fax 01 48 87 81 25
"The beautiful people are still, well, beautiful" at this "aging" but "hip cafe run by the Costes brothers" that "sits right in the face of the Centre Pompidou"; such a "great location" "makes it a good spot to meet friends" and offers some of the "best people-watching in Paris", within or without the "interesting", "plush", "podlike interior"; however, the "updated French classics menu" is typical of the *frères'* cuisine (that is, "not too creative"), and the service is "often negligent."

Café Burq ●🅢 *Wine Bar/Bistro*   - | - | - | M

18ᵉ | 6, rue Burq (Abbesses/Blanche) | 01 42 52 81 27
There's a "bohemian arty feel" at this "rocking" Montmartre wine bistro that's eternally "packed with local hipsters" and "pretty girls" who dig the "delightful" food (the "remarkable honey-roasted Camembert is a must"); with slim pickings in this "extremely touristic neighborhood", it's little surprise this "true find" is "always full."

Café Charbon ● *Classic French*   15 | 16 | 14 | €29

11ᵉ | 109, rue Oberkampf (Parmentier/Rue St-Maur) | 01 43 57 55 13 | fax 01 43 57 57 41
"Up-and-coming models, actors and many would-be writers and artist/philosophers" "linger over an espresso" or a mojito "waiting for the next concert at the [adjacent] Nouveau Casino to begin" in this "dark and dingy" "bohemian" bar on the "lively" Rue Oberkampf; some stay for a "casual" Classic French dinner, which is pretty "average", but "who knows? – the next Audrey Tautou or Vincent Perez could be the waiter who ignores you for 20 minutes, before taking another 15 to bring you your drink."

Café Constant 🅢 *Bistro*   24 | 14 | 19 | €39

7ᵉ | 139, rue St-Dominique (Ecole Militaire) | 01 47 53 73 34 | www.leviolondingres.com
"When you're not up to the big stars", chef-owner Christian Constant's "cozy" (or "tight") "second restaurant" makes a "nice substitute for its posh parent", Le Violon d'Ingres; "no reservations, but it's worth the wait" for "classic (if not classy) bistro food" "prepared with love" at "prices among the most reasonable in the whole 7th"; the "decor's old and tired and that rubs off on the waiters" critics carp; but converts call it "charming", as long as you "get a table on the main floor."

	FOOD	DECOR	SERVICE	COST

Café d'Angel (Le) ⊠ *Bistro*

| - | - | - | M |

17ᵉ | 16, rue Brey (Charles de Gaulle-Etoile/Ternes) | 01 47 54 03 33 | fax 01 47 54 03 33

This divine spot in the 17th is a "perfect Paris bistro" with "excellent" dishes typical of the genre and – as tradition dictates – a daily black-board special, plus "gracious service" and a prix fixe at angelic prices.

⊡ Café de Flore ● ⊠ *Classic French*

| 15 | 20 | 15 | €36 |

6ᵉ | 172, bd St-Germain (St-Germain-des-Prés) | 01 45 48 55 26 | fax 01 45 44 33 39 | www.cafe-de-flore.com

"More than a cafe, this is a historic monument" in Saint-Germain – made "famous" by literary lions – and it's still "equally loved by locals and tourists" (the former "on the terrace, the poets upstairs") who "subscribe to all the expected clichés with gusto"; so while the "simple Classic French food" is "serviceable", the service "diffident" and prices "ridiculously expensive", it remains the "consummately Parisian" place for "watching the world go by" – and "to think that Hemingway once did the same makes it that much sweeter."

Café de la Musique ● *Classic French*

| ▽ 15 | 21 | 17 | €31 |

19ᵉ | Cité de la Musique | 213, av Jean Jaurès (Porte de Pantin) | 01 48 03 15 91 | fax 01 48 03 15 18 | www.cite-musique.fr

While its Classic French menu is "limited", this La Villette cafe plays enough tunes to please customers, who go "to meet people passionate about music" (it's part of a cultural complex), for "brunch outside", a "late-night meal" or just to "collapse with drinks and some hors d'oeuvres after a day at the Cité des Sciences with a child."

Café de la Paix ● *Classic French*

| 19 | 22 | 18 | €61 |

9ᵉ | InterContinental Le Grand Hôtel | 12, bd des Capucines (Auber/Opéra) | 01 40 07 36 36 | fax 01 40 07 36 13 | www.cafedelapaix.fr

Following a "magnificent renovation" a while back, this famous cafe across from the Opéra Garnier remains generally "touristy but reliable"; surveyors clash over the Classic French cuisine, with warriors wailing it's "mediocre and overpriced" and peacemongers positing "it's not what it was when I was younger, but then neither am I"; certainly, the Napoleon III decor retains all its "past glories", as does its "great location" for "watching the passing parade."

Café de la Poste ⊠ *Classic French*

| - | - | - | M |

4ᵉ | 13, rue Castex (Bastille) | 01 42 72 95 35

Eaters with an epistolary bent say this "simple spot" across from an art deco post office "in the Bastille neighborhood" is a fine return address for residents wanting a "quiet getaway", with mosaics, mirrors and "solid traditional French fare."

Café de l'Esplanade (Le) ● ⊠ *Classic/New French*

| 16 | 21 | 15 | €58 |

7ᵉ | 52, rue Fabert (Invalides/La Tour-Maubourg) | 01 47 05 38 80 | fax 01 47 05 23 75

Kitty-cornered to Les Invalides is this "trendy canteen", and "if you look at the menu and think you've seen it before, you're right – it's

another one in the Costes brothers' series", a sampler of "decent" Classic and New French fare; you might also recognize the same "haughty" but "pretty waitresses and crowd wearing black and sporting sunglasses, darling", even when occupying the "ultimate-in-hip" interior.

Café de l'Industrie ◑ *Bistro*   12 | 14 | 11 | €29

11ᵉ | 15-17, rue St-Sabin (Bastille/Bréguet-Sabin) | 01 47 00 13 53 | fax 01 47 00 92 33

"You go more for the atmosphere and to be cool than for the food" at this "buzzy" "super-crowded" "find in the 11th"; still, the bistro fare is "affordable" and "generously served" by staffers that are "polite if often overwhelmed"; many deem the "old-fashioned"-but-"updated" decor "cute."

Café de Mars ◑ *Bistro*   17 | 13 | 16 | €35

7ᵉ | 11, rue Augereau (Ecole Militaire) | 01 47 05 05 91 | fax 01 47 05 05 91 | www.cafe-de-mars.fr

Near the Rue Cler in the 7th, this "typical little French bistro" ("it looks like where they'd shoot a scene establishing this is Paris") has "charming decor" of tiles and mosaics; "the staff dotes on all" the "neighborhood residents" and "unobtrusive tourists" who consume the cuisine with some Eclectic "innovative" touches; "prices are very fair for this level."

Café du Commerce (Le) ◑ *Bistro*   16 | 20 | 15 | €36

15ᵉ | 51, rue du Commerce (Emile Zola) | 01 45 75 03 27 | fax 01 45 75 27 40 | www.lecafeducommerce.com

Ever since it opened in 1921 as an auto workers' canteen, this "bustling" "neighborhood eatery" "well-located near Motte-Picquet" has drawn hordes for its "reasonably priced", "dependable", "basic French food", even if "those in a hurry" wish the staff would step on the gas; but the real attraction in this "multilevel" art deco bistro is the "retractable" skylight that makes it a "destination" "in the summer when it's topless (the roof, not the servers)."

Café du Passage (Le) ◑ *Wine Bar/Bistro*   - | - | - | M

11ᵉ | 12, rue de Charonne (Bastille/Ledru-Rollin) | 01 49 29 97 64

With "an owner who's passionate about wine and whiskey" (including some 80 single-malt scotches), this *bistrot à vins* in the 11th has "a fantastic selection, much of which is served by the glass" and accompanied by "excellent small plates" with an Italian edge; the "old-world" decor makes it "worth a visit."

Café Etienne Marcel ◑ *Eclectic*   ▽ 18 | 21 | 18 | €38

2ᵉ | 34, rue Etienne Marcel (Etienne Marcel) | 01 45 08 01 03 | fax 01 45 08 09 26

"Champagne McDonald's is the best way to describe" this Costes brothers outpost on the northern edge of Les Halles that features much of their "locked-in formula" but is still "just sort of average", from the Eclectic eats to the "slightly kitschy" "*A Clockwork Orange*-style decor" to the "wannabe-hip crowd from the suburbs"; "the

prices are pretty high given the quality of the food and service, but that's typical of fashion restaurants."

Café Faubourg *Classic French*   22 | 20 | 21 | €61

8ᵉ | Sofitel Le Faubourg | 11 bis, rue Boissy-d'Anglas (Concorde/ Madeleine) | 01 44 94 14 24 | fax 01 44 94 14 28 | www.sofitel.com
In the heart of the 8th yet "far from the madding crowd", this "hidden secret" in the Sofitel turns out "surprisingly good food for a hotel" from a Classic French menu that reflects the talents and Southwestern tastes of consulting chef Alain Dutournier (Carré des Feuillants); the "serene view of a courtyard garden" is another reason "everyone smiles" here.

Café Fusion ◐🅭 *Eclectic*   - | - | - | M

13ᵉ | 12, rue de la Butte aux Cailles (Place d'Italie) | 01 45 80 12 02
"A lovely terrace sets the scene for a cafe dinner" at this cheery, modern bistro in charming Butte aux Cailles, where young local residents congregate at stainless-steel tables for fare that, true to the name, fuses French classics with Eclectic offerings; the prices are reasonable in any currency.

Café Guitry 🅭 *Classic French*   - | - | - | M

9ᵉ | Théâtre Edouard VII | 10, pl Edouard VII (Auber/Opéra) | 01 40 07 00 77 | fax 01 47 42 77 68
Situated within the Edouard VII theater, this "quite handsome place" offers soigné, red-and-chestnut-toned comfort and "soft armchairs"; the Classic French cooking's "not bad for cafe fare", and given the location, you can't beat it for a pre- or post-curtain bite when you might "come across actors and directors kissing each other"; P.S. "special mention for the beautiful terrace overlooking the pedestrian square."

Café la Jatte *Eclectic*   14 | 16 | 12 | €44

Neuilly-sur-Seine | 60, bd Vital-Bouhot (Pont-de-Levallois) | 01 47 45 04 20 | fax 01 47 45 19 32 | www.cafelajatte.com
An "enormous" fake skeleton hanging from the ceiling shows the "cavernous" scale of this Ile de la Jatte eatery, a "trendy", "crowded" hangout for Neuilly's smart set who sit indoors or out on a "lovely" terrace; the servers are "not particularly nice or competent" and the Eclectic cooking "is mediocre at best", but these flaws pale compared to the new oyster bar, "lovely" terrace, child-friendly Sunday brunch and "agreeable" setting "away from the tourists."

Café Lenôtre (Le) *New French*   18 | 21 | 16 | €47

8ᵉ | Pavillon Elysée | 10, av des Champs-Elysées (Champs-Elysées-Clémenceau) | 01 42 65 97 71 | fax 01 42 65 76 23 | www.lenotre.fr
With a "charming, simply charming" setting in the Pavillon Elysée, this Italian-accented New French from the Lenôtre caterers is "great on a sunny day" when you can sit on "one of the nicest terraces in Paris"; the "finely displayed foods" are "good", if "limited", and foes find "prices high" for what's essentially "gourmet sandwich fare"; but all ends on a sweet note, since everyone loves the "beautiful pastries."

	FOOD	DECOR	SERVICE	COST

Café Le Petit Pont ◑ *Classic French* | 14 | 14 | 16 | €36
5ᵉ | 1, rue du Petit Pont (St-Michel) | 01 43 54 23 81
"It all feels so Paris" at this "busy cafe": a "killer" Latin Quarter location, "stunning view of Notre Dame" and "good jazz" live nightly; so *c'est dommage* the traditional French fare falls between "bad and mediocre" ("luckily it's not very expensive") and "service is slow"; small wonder "the French seem to avoid" this "touristy" place.

Z Café Les Deux Magots ◑ *Classic French* | 16 | 20 | 16 | €38
6ᵉ | 6, pl St-Germain-des-Prés (St-Germain-des-Prés) | 01 45 48 55 25 | fax 01 45 49 31 29 | www.lesdeuxmagots.fr
"Wear glasses and order in French and you'll feel at home" at this "chapter in Parisian history" that's "a must-do for tourists who have read their Sartre and Beauvoir"; though it's "full of foreigners", the ambiance still "lives up to the hype" and the "window onto the Boulevard Saint-Germain" offers "people-watching supreme"; true, "the viewing beats the chewing", especially given the extraordinary prices for "ordinary" Classic French fare served by "arrogant waiters", so have a drink or at most "a quick bite" and "save dinner for a real restaurant."

Café M 🅢 *New French* | ∇ 19 | 19 | 23 | €48
8ᵉ | Hôtel Hyatt | 24, bd Malesherbes (Madeleine/St-Augustin) | 01 55 27 12 34 | fax 01 55 27 12 35 | www.paris.madeleine.hyatt.com
Guests at this 8th-arrondissement Hyatt hail "the usual professional restaurant" on the premises, this one recently "renovated" in black and gold by architect Pascal Desprez; the "good" New French food is equally "modern" and casually "upscale", while "attentive service" keeps everything moving right along.

Z Café Marly ◑🅢 *Classic/New French* | 16 | 24 | 14 | €44
1ᵉʳ | 93, rue de Rivoli (Palais Royal-Musée du Louvre) | 01 49 26 06 60
When the Louvre has done you in, this on-site Costes eatery is "the finest place to recover from museum fatigue" say fans of the "chic" Empire-style setting and "stellar" views of I.M. Pei's pyramid and the sculpture gallery; the "overpriced" Classic–New French food is "predictable if unspectacular" and the "waiters treat you more like trespassers than customers" – "but who cares?" devotees "would endure any rudeness to sit on this terrace" overlooking the "breathtaking" courtyard.

Café Moderne 🅢 *Bistro* | 21 | 16 | 17 | €41
2ᵉ | 40, rue Notre-Dame-des-Victoires (Bourse) | 01 53 40 84 10 | fax 01 53 40 84 11
"You quickly feel like a regular" at this "endearing" bistro where "a sophisticated, Pan-European clientele", including brokers from the nearby Bourse, comes for "excellent cuisine mixing tradition and innovation", plus a "good choice of wines"; the "tastefully done", "long narrow space" has an ever-changing exhibit of modern paintings and big windows onto a courtyard, creating a "comfortably trendy atmosphere."

	FOOD	DECOR	SERVICE	COST

NEW Café Pleyel 🗷 New French
- | - | - | M

8ᵉ | 252, rue du Faubourg Saint-Honoré (Ternes) | 01 53 75 28 44

Innovative restaurateur Hélène Samuel, who founded the Bon Marché's Delicabar, plays a new tune with this stylish, spacious venue in Paris' renowned concert hall the Salle Pleyel; the eclectic New French menu runs to dishes like split pea soup with sausage, wok-sautéed beef with carrots and cumin and fig tart with almond cream; however, hungry culture vultures can only dine on concert nights (lunch is served every weekday).

Café Ruc ● Bistro
15 | 16 | 14 | €42

1ᵉʳ | 159, rue St-Honoré (Palais Royal-Musée du Louvre) | 01 42 60 97 54 | fax 01 42 61 86 33

"Yet another Costes" address, this bistro in "a critical tourist location" "close to the Louvre" works "for a quick bite with style" – but only if "you're hip and French" opponents opine; otherwise, the "beautiful" but "moody staff" "often seems preoccupied elsewhere", and when they "finally get around to your order, you'll receive" "standard fare" that's "a pretty bad buy for the buck"; but for "excellent views of Paris' human delicacies" amid a "Robert Palmer video" ambiance, it's "unbeatable."

Café Terminus Classic French
- | - | - | M

8ᵉ | Hôtel Concorde St-Lazare | 108, rue St-Lazare (St-Lazare) | 01 40 08 43 30 | fax 01 42 93 01 20 | www.concordestlazare-paris.com

There's "a whiff of old Paris" in this hotel cafe, whose decor represents fashion designer Sonia Rykiel's take on the Belle Epoque (the building dates from the 1880s); the "calm" atmosphere might be a result of its off-the-beaten-track location near Gare Saint-Lazare, while its Classic French cuisine (including "typical shellfish platters") is "refined" if "not outstanding."

Caffé Minotti 🗷🗷 Italian
▽ 22 | 21 | 19 | €66

7ᵉ | 33, rue de Verneuil (Rue du Bac) | 01 42 60 04 04 | fax 01 42 60 04 05 | www.caffeminotti.fr

"As *beau* as it is *bon*" sigh lovers of this "chic" Italian in the ritzy 7th with three small rooms, leather armchairs and "large red" Murano chandeliers hanging from high ceilings; the "terrific food" is as "modern" as the interior – and if the tab is equally eye-popping, at least the servings are "generous"; N.B. a management change post-Survey may outdate the scores.

Caffé Toscano 🗷 Italian
▽ 19 | 17 | 18 | €36

7ᵉ | 34, rue des Sts-Pères (St-Germain-des-Prés) | 01 42 84 28 95 | fax 01 42 84 26 36

It's not easy to find a good, moderately priced meal in the 7th, so this casual Tuscan in the gallery district is a popular spot for antiques dealers and other Left Bankers, with "low-key hospitality" and a wood/terra-cotta interior; the "tasty pasta dishes" are a "welcome Italian diversion from heavy bistro food", since many are made with ingredients like lemon and arugula.

	FOOD	DECOR	SERVICE	COST

Cagouille (La) *Seafood*
25 | 16 | 18 | €55

14ᵉ | 10, pl Constantin Brancusi (Gaîté/Montparnasse-Bienvenüe) |
01 43 22 09 01 | www.la-cagouille.fr

Some come here for "perfectly prepared" fish they claim is "the
freshest you'll get in Paris", others for the "great" cognac collection
comprising "some 200 different varieties"; either way, this meat-free
eatery near Montparnasse is a definite "find" (if "difficult to locate");
what stands out most in the slightly "sterile surroundings" is the "constantly changing" chalkboard menu that "depends on today's market."

Cailloux (Les) 🚫Ⓜ *Italian*
- | - | - | M

13ᵉ | 58, rue des Cinq-Diamants (Corvisart/Place d'Italie) | 01 45 80 15 08
"Worth a trip" "as much for the ambiance as for the pasta" attest
advocates of this "decent" Italian "in the heart of Buttes aux
Cailles"; though humble, the woody decor is "pleasant", and it's "a
good buy" to boot – if "not as economical" since it's been discovered
by a "young, attractive crowd."

Caïus 🚫 *New French*
∇ 19 | 13 | 16 | €50

17ᵉ | 6, rue d'Armaillé (Charles de Gaulle-Etoile) | 01 42 27 19 20 |
fax 01 40 55 00 93

Chef-owner Jean Marc Notelet developed his "original" style at
L'Espérance (in Vézelay) and Boyer (Reims), and his "inspired use of
spices and unusual ingredients" makes his New French in the 17th a
perpetual surprise, especially since the menu changes daily; diners
declare the decor is just "ok", but that's easy to forgive when one
considers the "great-value" menu and "extensive" wine list.

Caméléon (Le) 🚫Ⓜ *Bistro*
20 | 15 | 19 | €49

6ᵉ | 6, rue de Chevreuse (Vavin) | 01 43 27 43 27

This "Montparnasse classic" "changed owners a year or so ago", and,
chameleonlike, "the new management is trying to turn it into a chic
place"; the decor's still "ordinary" and the owner's attitude "a bit too
Rive Droite" for a Left Bank address, "but the bistro food is better",
showing "some creativity" at the hands of young chef David Angelot
(ex the late Jamin), who works *sans* camouflage in an open kitchen.

Camélia (Le) 🚫Ⓜ *New French*
20 | 16 | 20 | €62

Bougival | 7, quai Georges Clémenceau (RER La Défense; Bus Line 258) |
01 39 18 36 06 | fax 01 39 18 00 25 | www.lecamelia.com

The 19th-century *auberge* where Alexandre Dumas (*fils*) met the
woman who inspired *The Lady of the Camellias* is now "an oasis of re-
finement in the culinary desert" of Bougival, where chef-owner
Thierry Conte creates "high-level" New French cuisine in a *sympathique* ambiance that owes much to the "extremely nice" service and
"carefully contemplated" decor in ochre and yellow with columns
and flowered-print banquettes.

Camille ● *Bistro*
16 | 15 | 16 | €38

3ᵉ | 24, rue des Francs-Bourgeois (St-Paul) | 01 42 72 20 50

"Small" yet "charming", this Marais minx is a dependable "neighborhood spot" serving "unpretentious" bistro fare that's "reason-

ably priced", seven days a week (for breakfast too); a "great place for lunch after a visit to the Picasso Museum" or browsing the boutiques, it gets "crowded and noisy", with the sidewalk terrace particularly coveted come summer.

Cantine de Quentin (La) Ⓜ *Wine Bar/Bistro* ‒ ‒ ‒ I

10ᵉ | 52, rue Bichat (Jacques Bonsergent/République) | 01 42 02 40 32 | fax 01 42 02 40 82

With its hand-painted sign on the facade, this "tiny", "lovely" spot is highly recommended for lunch or brunch when cruising the funky Canal Saint-Martin area; a chef who was formerly at Guy Savoy makes "inexpensive" bistro fare, plus a boutique "full of good things" – artisanal foods and modestly priced wines that can be consumed on-site for a small corking fee.

Cap Seguin (Le) 🅂 *Classic French* ‒ ‒ ‒ M

Boulogne-Billancourt | Face au 27, quai le Gallo (Pont-de-Sèvres) | 01 46 05 06 07 | fax 01 46 05 06 88 | www.capseguin.com

Boulogne-area "advertising and media types come in droves" to this barge "facing the Seine", with a riverside terrace and yacht-club ambiance; the "Classic/New French cuisine is agreeable", even if the "service is embarrassingly slow" (though "less pathetic than before"); overall, though, this is "a nice place to be when the sun is shining."

Cap Vernet (Le) 🅂 *New French* 17 16 15 €57

8ᵉ | 82, av Marceau (Charles de Gaulle-Etoile) | 01 47 20 20 40 | fax 01 47 20 95 36

Tucked away at the top of the Champs, this fashionable fish house "has recently renovated décor" that conjures up a chic, sandy-colored beach house; even "in the winter", it's "a wonderful place for oysters" – "but little else" snap those who find the rest of the New French "food disappointing"; still, "it's good for business meals" or at teatime.

Carmine Ⓜ *Italian* ‒ ‒ ‒ M

7ᵉ | 81, ave Bosquet (Ecole Militaire) | 01 47 05 36 15 | fax 01 47 53 88 13

There's a north/south division of opinions on this young Italian in the 7th; partisans proclaim it "a terrific addition to the neighborhood" with a "warm", carmine-colored interior plus "excellent" pastas; but divisionists declare it a "disappointing" experience – "it's near the Eiffel Tower, so what?"

Carpaccio (Le) *Italian* ‒ ‒ ‒ VE

8ᵉ | Hôtel Royal Monceau | 37, av Hoche (Charles de Gaulle-Etoile/Ternes) | 01 42 99 98 90 | fax 01 42 99 89 94 | www.royalmonceau.com

"In a most un-Italian setting" (it's by designer Jacques Garcia), this cosseted Italian in the 8th has been "rejuvenated", which is why the usual clientele – "businessmen at noon" – is evolving in favor of well-dressed shoppers and curious locals; the digs are "luxurious", the "service excellent" and the "food refined", even if some jest "the portions are suited to a slenderizing diet."

	FOOD	DECOR	SERVICE	COST

🅉 Carré des Feuillants 🅢 *Haute Cuisine*   26 | 23 | 25 | €126

1er | 14, rue de Castiglione (Concorde/Tuileries) | 01 42 86 82 82 |
fax 01 42 86 07 71 | www.carredesfeuillants.fr

"One of the great ones", this Haute Cuisine table "adjacent to the
Place Vendôme" "deserves more recognition" than it gets, since "inventive veteran" Alain Dutournier prepares "divine", "classical"
food with Southwestern flavors, plus, in autumn, "possibly the best
game menu in Paris", accompanied by a "wine list that's tops" and
service that's almost "at the level of the food"; while "elegant", "the
decor reminds one of the Ice Queen's palace", but overall, the experience is still "memorable", so "order with abandon if your wallet
can afford it."

Carr's *Irish*   - | - | - | M

1er | 1, rue du Mont-Thabor (Tuileries) | 01 42 60 60 26 | fax 01 42 60 33 32 |
www.carrsparis.com

Though "Irish food is not an obvious choice" in Paris, they give
"great brunch" on weekends at this bit o' "the Emerald Isle" near the
Tuileries; it's "always convivial", with "cordial hosts that look like
they stepped out of Dickens", and has gotten to be quite a singles
venue with the Anglophile-meets-French crowd, even if some of
them "go for the beer" (Guinness, of course) rather than the eats.

Carte Blanche 🅢 *Bistro/New French*   - | - | - | M

9e | 6, rue Lamartine (Cadet) | 01 48 78 12 20 | fax 01 48 78 12 21 |
www.restaurantcarteblanche.com

"Not your father's Paris restaurant", this rustic-looking bistro in the
9th offers "an unusual, witty mix of French ingredients and Asian flavors" on an oft-changing chalkboard menu that ensures you probably won't "eat the same thing twice"; converts call its "creative"
cuisine a "dream", and what's more, there's no rude awakening
when the nicely priced bill arrives.

Cartes Postales (Les) 🅢 *New French*   ▽ 24 | 10 | 16 | €48

1er | 7, rue Gomboust (Opéra/Pyramides) | 01 42 61 02 93 |
fax 01 42 61 02 93

Worth writing home about, this table "the size of a postcard" behind
the Place du Marché Saint-Honoré has long been a "sure bet" for "an
interesting, successful blend of Japanese and French cuisine", prepared by an Asian chef-owner who "was one of the first to start doing
this"; the room is slightly "sterile", but the "reasonable prices" please,
and correspondents concur it's "a fine idea to offer half-portions."

Casa Alcalde *Basque/Spanish*   - | - | - | M

15e | 117, bd de Grenelle (La Motte-Picquet-Grenelle) | 01 47 83 39 71 |
fax 01 45 66 49 01

It's "almost impossible to get a table if you're not a regular – and difficult even if you are" at this "bustling" bastion for Basque bites in
the 15th; although cynics snap this is "Spain for Parisians who've
never crossed the Pyrénées", most maintain it's "worth going to";
P.S. if you can't score a seat in the "cramped" surrounds, get the
paella to go.

	FOOD	DECOR	SERVICE	COST

Casa Bini *Italian* | 21 | 13 | 17 | €47 |

6ᵉ | 36, rue Grégoire de Tours (Odéon) | 01 46 34 05 60 | fax 01 40 46 09 71
"This is the place" for a "real Italian" experience, "from the chef to the staff" say surveyors of this "recently remodeled" address "in the heart of the 6th"; "service and food can be erratic", leading to a "was-it-worth-that-price feeling", but most are delighted with the "delicious" dishes and wines from the northern part of The Boot; P.S. one sometimes "sees French stars dining here."

Casa Olympe (La) 🖂 *Corsica/Provence* | 24 | 15 | 20 | €62 |

9ᵉ | 48, rue St-Georges (St-Georges) | 01 42 85 26 01 |
www.casaolympe.com
Chef-owner Olympe Versini "is a pioneer who has been on the Paris scene for over 30 years", the last 15 running this neighborhood bistro in the 9th, where a "genial crowd" comes for "hearty" Corsican-Provençal food that's "cooked to perfection" and served with "unobtrusive" efficiency; it can be "difficult to make a reservation" even though "they pack you in", but "since the restaurant is teensy, you don't have to look hard to find someone to bring you a check."

Casa Tina ⬤ *Spanish* | – | – | – | M |

16ᵉ | 18, rue Lauriston (Charles de Gaulle-Etoile/Kléber) | 01 40 67 19 24 |
fax 01 41 44 73 63 | www.casa-tina.net
Flamenco music and bullfighting posters leave no doubt that Spanish blood courses through the veins of this "basic", "cozy" eatery close to the Etoile, where a "fun" ambiance goes hand in hand with "decent" tapas, plus more substantial fare such as paella; the nearby annex, Casa Paco, picks up the overflow when this "tiny place" is full.

Caveau du Palais (Le) *Classic French* | 19 | 17 | 17 | €50 |

1ᵉʳ | 17-19, pl Dauphine (Cité/Pont-Neuf) | 01 43 26 04 28 |
fax 01 43 26 81 84
On the "tranquil" place Dauphine, in a "quiet 17th-century courtyard", this "lovely secret spot" is "definitely worth the visit" for its "consistent, delicious food" in the Classic French vein; at lunch the service tends to be "rushed" due to "all the lawyers and judges" from the Palais de Justice nearby, but "on a summer evening, it makes you forget you're in the heart of Paris", especially since your "romantic dinner will not break the bank."

Cave de l'Os à Moëlle Ⓜ *Wine Bar/Bistro* | 22 | 18 | 19 | €34 |

15ᵉ | 181, rue de Lourmel (Lourmel) | 01 45 57 28 28 |
fax 01 45 57 28 00
"Diners eat at communal tables" at this hangout "deep in the 15th", a stone wine cellar that is "informal in the extreme" – you help yourself from "a pot in the back" and the "all-you-can-eat dessert buffet", and "pick your wines (at retail prices) off the wall" (the "genuinely nice staff" opens the bottles); "the self-serve approach can make for commotion at times", but the bistro fare's "simple yet delicious"; so "fill yourself up with joyful satisfaction and learn to love your neighbors."

	FOOD	DECOR	SERVICE	COST

Cave Gourmande (La) - le Restaurant de Mark Singer 🗗 *Bistro*

▽ 25 | 13 | 21 | €49

19ᵉ | 10, rue du Général Brunet (Botzaris/Danube) | 01 40 40 03 30 | fax 01 40 40 03 30

"Maybe it's a bit out of the way for the average tourist", but gourmands gush it's "well worth the Homeric effort to find" this bistro in the far reaches of the 19th, thanks to the "splendid market-driven", "inventive" cuisine concocted "with much thought to taste, texture and presentation" by chef-owner Mark Singer, an "American in Paris"; "efficient service" and an "affordable, sharp wine list" make up for the "modest setting."

Caves Pétrissans 🗗 *Wine Bar/Bistro*

▽ 19 | 15 | 17 | €46

17ᵉ | 30 bis, av Niel (Péreire/Ternes) | 01 42 27 52 03 | fax 01 40 54 87 56

The same family has owned this "classic, timeless bistro" in the 17th "for a very long time" – more than a century, in fact – and "not much of the decor has changed since WWII"; "warmth and welcome" await customers who cram into "tight quarters", then dig into Classic French specialties "like nobody makes anymore"; but the biggest "attraction here is the wine list", sold from the "attached boutique" at retail plus a corkage fee.

Caviar Kaspia ◑🗗 *Russian*

25 | 19 | 22 | €121

8ᵉ | 17, pl de la Madeleine (Madeleine) | 01 42 65 33 32 | fax 01 42 65 66 26 | www.caviarkaspia.com

"If you have a lust for caviar", this "tsarist-decorated" Russian "landmark" is "the perfect place" to satisfy it, preferably at "a table for two in a window overlooking the Place Madeleine"; the "young servers are easy on the eyes" and the "truly wealthy" "customers are a show by themselves"; but the "star" here is the "divine" black gold, backed by the "best blini and smoked fish"– a "light meal", perhaps, but a worthy "sky's-the-limit" "splurge."

Cazaudehore La Forestière 🄼 *Haute Cuisine*

22 | 22 | 20 | €67

Saint-Germain-en-Laye | 1, av Kennedy (RER St-Germain-en-Laye) | 01 30 61 64 64 | fax 01 39 73 73 88 | www.cazaudehore.fr

Attached to a Relais & Chateaux hotel in Saint-Germain-en-Laye, this "venerable house" is an "easy getaway from the city" for Southwestern-influenced, "exquisite" Haute Cuisine "*en terrace*" overseen by "gracious hosts"; the "lovely" setting with a "great view of gardens" is "wonderful on a sunny Sunday for lunch, but late autumn by the fireplace can be even better."

Céladon (Le) *Classic French*

21 | 21 | 22 | €81

2ᵉ | Hôtel Westminster | 15, rue Daunou (Opéra) | 01 47 03 40 42 | fax 01 42 61 33 78 | www.leceladon.com

In the majestic Hôtel Westminster, this "elegant" table is "like dining in the home of a refined friend" – or even your stereotypical "wealthy aunt's parlor", with "luscious" Classic French cuisine and "fancy" service; a few feel it's "a bit too old-fashioned", fretting "substantial price increases aren't reflected in the quality of the cui-

sine", but on weekends it becomes more relaxed, with different decor and a fixed-price menu that may be "the best gourmet deal in Paris"; P.S. "be sure to drop by the Duke's Bar" after dinner.

∇ 144 Petrossian (Le) ⌧ *Seafood* `25` `21` `22` `€84`
7ᵉ | 18, bd de la Tour-Maubourg (Invalides/La Tour-Maubourg) | 01 44 11 32 32 | fax 01 44 11 32 35

Fish egg lovers roe their boats to this caviarteria in the swanky 7th for the "sublime indulgence" of beluga's best; though if black gold is "the highlight" here, the "outstanding" menu also shows "good depth" with products from the depths (the Food score's climbed under chef Rougui Dia); other pluses include the "elegant" decor and "attentive", unobtrusive service, but "if you have to think of price, best not to go" (or else opt for the lunch prix fixe).

Cerisaie (La) ⌧ *Southwest* `21` `11` `18` `€43`
14ᵉ | 70, bd Edgar Quinet (Edgar Quinet/Montparnasse-Bienvenüe) | 01 43 20 98 98 | fax 01 43 20 98 98

A "young chef" and his "charming" wife run this venue that has a "neighborhood feel" despite its location "within sight of the Tour Montparnasse"; the Southwestern-accented "intelligent menu" features "wonderful combinations", so "reservations are a must" for a "jam-packed table" where clients declare their "delight" at such "big flavors" in a "tiny room."

Chai 33 ☻ *Wine Bar/Bistro* `14` `16` `12` `€41`
12ᵉ | 33, Cour St-Emilion (Cour St-Emilion) | 01 53 44 01 01 | fax 01 53 44 01 02 | www.chai33.com

"Walls of windows, large staircases", "unpolished concrete" surfaces and two terraces have turned the "vast open space" of an old Bercy wine warehouse into this "chic", "original" *bistrot à vins*; "spend the night sampling wines from the cellar" of 300 labels, while you nibble on "trendy", albeit "banal" bistro dishes, served by a "*très chic*", if often "busy", staff.

Chalet (Le) *Alpine/Classic French* `-` `-` `-` `M`
Neuilly-sur-Seine | 14, rue du Commandant Pilot (Les Sablons/Porte Maillot) | 01 46 24 03 11 | fax 01 46 37 18 80 | www.lechaletdeneuilly.com

The rustic, mountain-inn decor "transports you to the Alps without being overdone" ("no one's yodeling, luckily") at this Neuilly venue; but if the wooden interior isn't cheesy, the food is - *fondue savoyarde* and other "simple" but "well-prepared", "authentic" Monotagnarde specialties that have habitués hiking in for an "out-of-the-ordinary" experience; N.B. the summer fare is lighter Classic French.

Chalet des Iles (Le) *Classic French* `14` `24` `14` `€57`
16ᵉ | Lac Inférieur du Bois de Boulogne (La Muette/La Pompe) | 01 42 88 04 69 | fax 01 42 88 84 09 | www.chaletdesiles.net

Sunday afternooners feel like "the subject of a Seurat painting" as they "approach by little boat this charming restaurant" on an "enchanting island" in the Bois de Boulogne; "it's a real pity the Classic French cuisine is not at a level this place deserves" - in fact, "it

would be banal" without the "paradisiacal" premises that make it "one of the most romantic in Paris."

Chantairelle ⊠ *Auvergne*

| - | - | - | M |

5ᵉ | 17, rue Laplace (Maubert-Mutualité) | 01 46 33 18 59 | fax 01 46 33 18 59 | www.chantairelle.com

Recorded bird calls, stone walls, a woodsy scent and a forest – or at least a garden – make this "small, friendly" spot "near the Panthéon" like "a trip to the Auvergne", for a discovery of the mountainous region's "fantastic", "hearty" fare ("order the stuffed cabbage") along with "basic and reasonable" wines; surveyors "love the owner", the "cozy terrace", Monsieur Maurice the resident cat and the fact that it's all so comfortably "predictable."

Chardenoux *Bistro*

| ▽ 19 | 15 | 15 | €51 |

11ᵉ | 1, rue Jules Vallès (Charonne/Faidherbe-Chaligny) | 01 43 71 49 52 | fax 01 43 71 80 89

"After a low period it's back at the expected level" laud lovers of this century-old bistro, "one of the best of its type in Paris"; a new chef's menu is a "reference" for "classic offerings", and the building with its original belle epoque interior is a classified historic monument, "worth the trip by métro" to the 11th – and a postcard from the past.

Charlot - Roi des Coquillages ❷ *Brasserie*

| 15 | 13 | 14 | €54 |

9ᵉ | 12, pl de Clichy (Place de Clichy) | 01 53 20 48 00 | fax 01 53 20 48 09 | www.charlot-paris.com

Reflecting the improving demographics of the once "dodgy" Place de Clichy neighborhood, sleek new decor has replaced the kitschy look of this veteran brasserie; menuwise, you can still "always count on the fresh shellfish", and if some find it "hard on the wallet", "order a *plateau* for a group, and it's surprisingly reasonable."

Charpentiers (Aux) ❷ *Bistro*

| 18 | 16 | 19 | €43 |

6ᵉ | 10, rue Mabillon (Mabillon/St-Germain-des-Prés) | 01 43 26 30 05 | fax 01 46 33 07 98

"Linked to the Carpenter's Guild, this solid landmark of French culinary history" – established 1856 – still serves "no-frills bistro" comestibles in a "comfortable", collegial setting ("your new best friend is at the next table"); the "unmovable menu" and "oh-so typical *garçons*" suggest that "it's never changed and, we suspect, never will."

Chartier *Classic French* (aka Bouillon Chartier)

| 13 | 21 | 14 | €24 |

9ᵉ | 7, rue Faubourg Montmartre (Grands Boulevards) | 01 47 70 86 29 | fax 01 48 24 14 68 | www.restaurant-chartier.com

"Tucked away off the Grands Boulevards", "one of the last classic dining halls" of Paris makes you "feel like you're stepping back in time" to an era of "no-frills" Classic French food, "rushed waiters" and communal tables in a "barn"-sized "beautiful building"; the food is "incredibly cheap" – but most jeer you get "the quality you pay for", plus often you "have to wait next to the garbage cans"; but that doesn't stop "both natives and tourists" lining up for the "lively" ambiance.

	FOOD	DECOR	SERVICE	COST

Chateaubriand (Le) 🚫Ⓜ *New French*   22 | 15 | 16 | €48

11ᵉ | 129, av Parmentier (Goncourt/Parmentier) | 01 43 57 45 95
Serving up nothing less than "the future of bistro cuisine", according to its acolytes, this eatery adds to the "buzz of the Oberkampf area" with "surprising and explosive" New French cooking by "young Basque" chef Inaki Aizpitarte; there's "a real bobo atmosphere" in the minimalist interior with its "casual" service, "high" noise level and handwritten blackboard menu, but though this place might be "terribly à la mode", it's also "s-o-o-o good."

Chen Soleil d'Est 🚫 *Chinese*   - | - | - | VE

15ᵉ | 15, rue du Théâtre (Charles Michels) | 01 45 79 34 34 | fax 01 45 79 07 53
"Even if the chef passed away a couple years ago, [it's] "still the best Chinese restaurant in Paris" (certainly, it's one of the most "pricey") declare defiant devotees of this table; in the midst of a somewhat bleak, "out-of-the-way location" in the 15th, it's "a haven" for "divine Peking duck" dinners, "elegantly presented" and made with "French products" – as are the "serious wines."

Cherche Midi (Le) ❶ *Italian*   19 | 15 | 17 | €41

6ᵉ | 22, rue du Cherche-Midi (Sèvres-Babylone/St-Sulpice) | 01 45 48 27 44
"On a lovely quiet street near Saint-Sulpice" in the 6th, this "hole-in-the-wall is an insider's favorite" for "reliably good Italian cuisine" that's often served with "tongue-in-cheek commentary from the waiter"; "ideal for celebrity-spotting", it's usually "crowded and noisy", due to the "elbow-to-elbow seating", so you "better reserve or be a habitué" (who heads straight for the coveted "seats on the sidewalk terrace").

NEW Chéri Bibi ❶ *Bistro*   - | - | - | M

18ᵉ | 15, rue André-del-Sarte (Anvers/Château Rouge) | 01 42 54 88 96
Bobos from the Butte are making tracks for "the new hip spot on the eastern side" of Montmartre, open late and co-owned by Yannig Samot (La Famille, Le Réfectoire), where "1950s flea-market furnishings" set the scene for an "excellent value" meal consisting of "simple", "classic" bistro recipes in "copious" portions and "well-chosen wines"; perhaps "the service is nicer for habitués than for others", but nevertheless this place is "ever full."

Chez André ❶ *Bistro*   20 | 15 | 18 | €51

8ᵉ | 12, rue Marbeuf (Franklin D. Roosevelt) | 01 47 20 59 57 | fax 01 47 20 18 82
"Just a block from the hustle and bustle" of the Champs sits this "epitome of bistros", complete with "oyster shucker outside"; seems as if "nothing here has changed since before World War II", when it opened: neither the "simple and oh-so-good" cuisine nor the "classic environment" nor the "grandmotherly" waitresses, "all dressed in black with white aprons"; however, "if you don't like [sitting] close to strangers, this is not the place for you."

	FOOD	DECOR	SERVICE	COST

Chez Catherine Ⓩ *New French* — 23 | 19 | 22 | €71

8ᵉ | 3, rue Berryer (George V/St-Philippe-du-Roule) | 01 40 76 01 40 |
fax 01 40 76 03 96

While its side-street address in the 8th is "a tad off the beaten track",
it's worth "studying your map" to find this New French, with "pricey"
but "interesting" and "inventive" cuisine offered amid "lovely", gray-
toned decor; the "warm, welcoming service" is led by chef Catherine
Guerraz, who "takes the time to talk to every table and is adorable."

Chez Cécile — - | - | - | M

(La Ferme des Mathurins) Ⓩ *Classic French*

8ᵉ | 17, rue Vignon (Madeleine) | 01 42 66 46 39 | www.chezcecile.com
Owner Cécile de Sintel provides a "terrific evening" at this "excellent-
value" table in the 8th, where "a hardworking chef in a tiny kitchen"
turns out "truly outstanding" Classic French food with "inventive pre-
sentations and flavors", plus "consistently whimsical service"; music
lovers trumpet that the "live jazz on Thursday nights" is "a blast."

Chez Clément ◑ *Classic French* — 15 | 17 | 16 | €35

2ᵉ | 17, bd des Capucines (Opéra) | 01 53 43 52 00 | fax 01 53 43 82 09
4ᵉ | 19, rue Beaumarchais (Bastille) | 01 40 29 17 00 | fax 01 40 29 17 09
4ᵉ | 21, bd Beaumarchais (Bastille/Chemin-Vert) | 01 40 29 17 00 |
fax 01 40 29 17 09
6ᵉ | 9, pl St-André-des-Arts (St-Michel) | 01 56 81 32 00 |
fax 01 56 81 32 09
8ᵉ | 123, av des Champs-Elysées (Charles de Gaulle-Etoile) |
01 40 73 87 00 | fax 01 40 73 87 09
8ᵉ | 19, rue Marbeuf (Franklin D. Roosevelt/George V) | 01 53 23 90 00 |
fax 01 53 23 90 09
14ᵉ | 106, bd du Montparnasse (Vavin) | 01 44 10 54 00 |
fax 01 44 10 54 09
15ᵉ | 407, rue de Vaugirard (Porte de Versailles) | 01 53 68 94 00 |
fax 01 53 68 94 09
17ᵉ | 47, av de Wagram (Charles de Gaulle-Etoile/Ternes) |
01 53 81 97 00 | fax 01 53 81 97 09
17ᵉ | 99, bd Gouvion-St-Cyr (Porte Maillot) | 01 45 72 93 00 |
fax 01 45 72 93 09
Boulogne-Billancourt | 98, av Edouard Vaillant (Marcel Sembat) |
01 41 22 90 00 | fax 01 41 22 90 09
www.chezclement.com
Additional locations throughout Paris

"Everything is average" at this "country-style chain with lots of copper decor" ("kitschy, but not bad") and "standard" Classic French
cuisine; still, it's a "popular spot for tour groups", "cheap reunions"
or "a quick meal before or after a movie."

Chez Denise - — 24 | 18 | 18 | €47

La Tour de Montlhéry ◑Ⓩ *Bistro*

1ᵉʳ | 5, rue des Prouvaires (Châtelet-Les Halles) | 01 42 36 21 82 |
fax 01 45 08 81 99

"Every night's a party" (one that runs all night) at this "wonderful
old-style bistro that has survived for years" in the old Les Halles
("you'll expect Hemingway to be seated next to you any minute");

cuisine "doesn't come more traditionally Parisian" than the "delicious", "hearty portions" of "French rustic food", including "many animal parts that may seem strange to city folk", "served with humor that takes your mind off the noise level" and the fact "you're sitting in your neighbor's lap."

Chez Francis ● Brasserie
17 | 19 | 16 | €58

8e | 7, pl de l'Alma (Alma Marceau) | 01 47 20 86 83 | fax 01 47 20 43 26

"At the very end of the chic Avenue Montaigne", this "stalwart" boasts perhaps "the best view from a restaurant in all of Paris", and throughout the day, shoppers, business-lunchers and theatergoers vie to "grab an outdoor table" with "a straight shot at the Eiffel Tower", or to sit inside for "a taste of the Belle Epoque"; surveyors say the "honest" brasserie cuisine has "improved" since the arrival of a new chef ("have the fish") – but frankly, the fare's "not the point, n'est-ce pas?"

Chez Françoise ● Classic French
17 | 14 | 17 | €55

7e | Aérogare des Invalides (Invalides) | 01 47 05 49 03 | fax 01 45 51 96 20 | www.chezfrancoise.com

Located inside the Invalides aérogare ("don't let this scare you away"), this is a "favorite place for French politicians" from the nearby National Assembly who ignore the "air-terminal ambiance" and concentrate on the "quite acceptable" Classic French cuisine; it's ideal for a business meal, especially as the staff is "efficient and diplomatic."

Chez Fred ⊠ Lyon
- | - | - | M

17e | 190 bis, bd Péreire (Péreire/Porte Maillot) | 01 45 74 20 48

"Staunch Lyonnais cooking" is the specialty of this bouchon (a bistro-style restaurant from the Rhône city), which makes it "a good place to know near Porte Maillot" when you hanker for hearty favorites like côte de boeuf or the inimitable andouillette (tripe sausage); surveyors smile at its slightly "wacky" side, wondering what other venue is "decorated with snapshots of customers and staff, yet offers valet parking"?

Chez Gégène Ⓜ Classic French
- | - | - | M

Joinville-le-Pont | 162 bis, quai de Polangis (RER Joinville-le-Pont) | 01 48 83 29 43 | fax 01 48 83 72 62 | www.chez-gegene.fr

"If you want to have a feel for the '20s around Paris", this century-old guinguette in Joinville-le-Pont, along the Marne River, is "a step back into another epoch, especially on the weekends" when people come to dance; just remember that the "fun" here is all about the fête – waltzers whisper "avoid at all costs" the Classic French food; N.B. closed January–March, open weekends only October–December.

⚡ Chez Georges ⊠ Bistro
24 | 19 | 21 | €60

2e | 1, rue du Mail (Bourse) | 01 42 60 07 11

"A mix of traditional and hip diners" "makes a beeline" to this bistro, a "charming slice of old Paris life" near the Palais-Royal and belonging to "the same family" for several generations; "tradition abounds" here, from the red banquettes to the "motherly waitresses" to the "classic" "comfort" "food of great distinction" – and a higher Food

score; even the "raucous crowd" seated "elbow-to-elbow" is "as French as it gets."

Chez Georges-Porte Maillot ● *Brasserie* ▽ 18 | 16 | 18 | €55

17ᵉ | 273, bd Péreire (Porte Maillot) | 01 45 74 31 00 | fax 01 45 72 18 84 | www.chez-georges.com

Residents of the upscale Porte Maillot area appreciate this "always predictable" institution that's "traditional but not tired", especially after a chef change and recently refreshed decor; "famous for its meats", the kitchen turns out "good solid" brasserie food in "huge portions" and the "solicititous" (though sometimes "spotty") service adds to the "classy ambiance"; as an extra bonus, it's "open Sunday night."

Chez Gérard ⓈI *Auvergne* ▽ 19 | 16 | 18 | €36

Neuilly-sur-Seine | 10, rue Montrosier (Porte Maillot) | 01 46 24 86 37 | fax 01 46 37 21 72

The "menu hasn't changed for 10 years" (even if the chef has) in this "traditional" Neuilly bistro with "refined", "delicious" food from the Auvergne; "but why should it when it is as good" as this shrug surveyors who "feel like they're at home" thanks to the "relaxed atmosphere", "affordable" prices and "service with a smile."

Chez Géraud ⓈI *Classic French* 20 | 15 | 18 | €56

16ᵉ | 31, rue Vital (La Muette) | 01 45 20 33 00

"In a quiet area" of the 16th, this "simple" standby treats even first-timers "like regulars" and is considered by loyal locals to be "one of the best bistros" around, with classic, "old-style bourgeois cooking" using "seasonal or regional delicacies" (including "wow"-worthy game in the fall) and a small but "perfect choice of wines" that spurs oenophiles to cry "break out the Burgundy!"

Chez Grisette ⓈI *Wine Bar/Bistro* - | - | - | M

18ᵉ | 14, rue Houdon (Abbesses/Pigalle) | 01 42 62 04 80 | fax 01 42 62 04 80 | www.chez-grisette.fr

"There's no putting on airs" in this Montmartre wine bistro where the "charming *patronne*", Grisette, creates a "warm and friendly" ambiance and serves "simple but savory" classic cooking (including "excellent blood sausage") accompanied by "great" bottles from "small independent producers", stacked up on the wall as part of the decor; N.B. wine and foie gras available for takeout.

Chez Janou ● *Provence* 23 | 19 | 18 | €36

3ᵉ | 2, rue Roger Verlomme (Bastille/Chemin-Vert) | 01 42 72 28 41 | www.chezjanou.com

"Oh, you just want to hate" this place "next to the Place des Vosges" "for being so cute, trendy and touristy – but it delivers" with "divinely fresh", "sun-drenched" Provençal cuisine, including fish "that tastes like the water is down the hill", at least "80-plus [kinds of] pastis" and a "bottomless" chocolate mousse "like no other"; but "they really pack 'em in tight" at this "boisterous", "buzzing" spot, so "even with a reservation, you'll probably have to wait for your table."

	FOOD	DECOR	SERVICE	COST

Chez Jenny ◗ *Alsace* | 19 | 18 | 19 | €44 |

3ᵉ | 39, bd du Temple (République) | 01 44 54 39 00 | fax 01 44 54 39 09 | www.chezjenny.com

Alsace admirers "always enjoy" this "choucroute paradise" opened in 1932 by a Strasbourg native on the Place de la République (now owned by the Frères Blanc chain); a "traditional brasserie", it's "great" "on a cold night" or late in the evening with a "large group", and though critics call it "more fun than delicious", the "rushed atmosphere", "amiable service" and old-fashioned decor take patrons back to "a bygone time."

Chez Julien *Bistro* | 19 | 22 | 18 | €49 |

4ᵉ | 1, rue du Point-Louis-Philippe (Hôtel-de-Ville/Pont-Marie) | 01 42 78 31 64

The "fabulous" Empire decor has long been the selling point of this "cozy", "romantic" bistro located Seine-side in the Marais, and with its recent takeover by Thierry Costes, the "old-school dining" deserves a second look – though a few deem the cuisine "a bit of a disappointment"; even so, it's "not bad for a quick bite", the "staff's sincere" and in the summer, there's a "lovely outdoor seating area overlooking the Ile Saint-Louis" and the "beautiful old church" Saint-Gervais.

Chez L'Ami Jean ◗ 🗷 Ⓜ *Basque/Bistro* | 24 | 16 | 19 | €49 |

7ᵉ | 27, rue Malar (Invalides/La Tour-Maubourg) | 01 47 05 86 89 | www.amijean.com

Chef Stéphane Jego, "the Basque king of Paris", is basking in compliments nowadays, which explains why his "high-energy" bistro a short walk from Les Invalides is "always packed with fun-loving gourmands" – in fact, the only complaint is it's "too crowded to be comfortable"; but few care since his "fabulous" *nouveau*-Southwestern cuisine, served by a "helpful staff", could be the "best value in town."

Chez la Vieille 🗷 *Bistro* | ▽ 16 | 13 | 15 | €47 |

1ᵉʳ | 1, rue Bailleul (Louvre-Rivoli) | 01 42 60 15 78 | fax 01 42 60 15 78

"Reassuring in an ever-changing world", this "authentic" bistro has long served a hit list of "real" French dishes "from another epoch" in a small, two-story 1950s interior near Les Halles; though some young upstarts find the food "uneven", converts cry the "huge portions" of "fork-licking" fare "delicious" (if "not for the fainthearted").

Chez Léna et Mimile 🗷 Ⓜ *Bistro* | ▽ 15 | 22 | 16 | €42 |

5ᵉ | 32, rue Tournefort (Censier-Daubenton/Place Monge) | 01 47 07 72 47 | fax 01 45 35 41 94

Boasting "one of the nicest terraces around", above a trickling fountain "on a tiny, quiet square off the usually hectic Rue Mouffetard", this traditional '30s bistro is "a treasure" for locals who laud the "well-priced" Classic French menu; but dissidents declare "it's a shame the food is mediocre when the setting is so exceptional."

	FOOD	DECOR	SERVICE	COST

Chez Léon ☒ *Bistro*
| 13 | 11 | 13 | €36 |

17ᵉ | 32, rue Legendre (Villiers) | 01 42 27 06 82 | fax 01 46 22 63 67
This "lively" 1930s bistro in the 17th (not to be confused with the mussels chain with a similar name) "reopened in 2007" under new ownership (the chef and his cousin) with an "engaging staff" and a "lovely redecoration" all adding to the "convivial" ambiance; the "freshness of the cuisine matches the new varnish on the place", while the "refined" traditional dishes (the "meat cooked just so") have a "satisfying" flavor "like you rarely find anymore."

Chez Les Anges ☒ *Brasserie*
| 23 | 19 | 19 | €61 |

7ᵉ | 54, bd de la Tour-Maubourg (La Tour-Maubourg) | 01 47 05 89 86 | www.chezlesanges.com
New owners have returned this 7th-arrondissement address "back to the old" name, yet this time the angels have a "hip", primarily white abode ("sophisticated", if "stark" some say); opinions are more harmonious regarding the "affordable" brasserie fare by new chef Hidenori Kitaguchi (ex Jamin) featuring "creative", "careful" preparations of "traditional" eats, plus an "excellent wine list" with some heaven-sent Burgundies.

Chez Livio *Italian*
| 13 | 11 | 11 | €40 |

Neuilly-sur-Seine | 6, rue de Longchamp (Pont-de-Neuilly) | 01 46 24 81 32 | fax 01 47 38 20 72
A family-run "institution" for 50 years, Neuilly's "popular" trattoria serves up a wide array of Italian eats; detractors dis the "mediocre" "small portions" and "interminable waits", "particularly on the weekends"; but it's "an excellent choice for families with kids", especially "when they open up the roof on a hot summer day."

Chez Ly ◑ *Chinese/Thai*
| - | - | - | M |

17ᵉ | 95, av Niel (Péreire) | 01 40 53 88 38 | fax 01 40 53 88 68
"Yes, Madame Ly exists", and "for those who enjoy Cantonese cooking", her place in the 17th – the family's third in Paris – is "a must" with a "wonderful ambiance", exotic woods and Chinese porcelain, and a "diverse" choice of "tasty" dishes from Hong Kong and Thailand, plus original offerings such as sake-marinated foie gras studded with lotus and rolled in poppy seeds.

Chez Maître Paul *Alsace*
| 21 | 18 | 19 | €48 |

6ᵉ | 12, rue Monsieur-le-Prince (Odéon) | 01 43 54 74 59 | fax 01 43 54 43 74 | www.chezmaitrepaul.fr
"Every foodie loves coming to this bistro" for an insider's take on "utterly delicious", "reliable" regional "cuisine from the Jura" mountains (their signature "chicken in yellow wine with morels is heavenly"); it's served "with a welcoming smile" in a "small, cozy and classy" space near Odéon.

Chez Marcel ☒ *Lyon*
| - | - | - | M |

6ᵉ | 7, rue Stanislas (Notre-Dame-des-Champs) | 01 45 48 29 94
It's "like going to dinner at someone's grandparents'" at this "very small", "quirky", "family-run restaurant" in the 6th, where patrons

find the "historic look" – complete with lace curtains and "faded rose wallpaper" – totally "charming", while the staff is "solicitous" and the "classic" Lyonnais cuisine is both "excellent" and "dependable"; "end your meal with an Armagnac, which [owner] Jean-Bernard Daumail retrieves from a hidden cellar under his bar."

Chez Marianne *Mideastern*
| 18 | 13 | 14 | €23 |

4e | 2, rue des Hospitalières St-Gervais (St-Paul) | 01 42 72 18 86
"Even if you're broke" you can come to this haven in the historical "heart of the Marais" for a "great variety" of "tasty", "solid Middle Eastern" and Eastern European food; but service is "irregular" and "getting a table in the dining room can be a struggle, especially on weekends", as it's "very crowded even by Paris standards"; hence, "if it's nice weather, eating outside is recommended."

Chez Michel ●🗷 *Brittany/New French*
| 24 | 16 | 20 | €46 |

10e | 10, rue de Belzunce (Gare du Nord/Poissonnière) | 01 44 53 06 20 | fax 01 44 53 61 31
With this "tiny shrine" to the food of Brittany "off the beaten path", the "aptly named" chef Thierry Breton has "helped redefine mid-priced Parisian dining"; converts claim his prix fixe menu of "homey but sophisticated" New French cooking is "one of the best bargains" in town, with especially "exceptional" choices "in game season" (though some grouse that "many dishes require a supplement"); "be sure to reserve and reconfirm" before making "the trek" to the 10th, and try not to be "relegated to the basement."

Chez Nénesse 🗷 *Classic French*
| - | - | - | I |

3e | 17, rue de Saintonge (Filles-du-Calvaire/République) | 01 42 78 46 49 | fax 01 42 78 45 51
In the happening northern part of the Marais, this family-run, old-style bistro with a heating stove in the middle of the room is "one of the very few" of its kind left, offering "inexpensive" Classic French food such as *tête de veau* along with "friendly service" in a "homey atmosphere."

Chez Omar ●⇄ *Moroccan*
| 21 | 14 | 17 | €32 |

3e | 47, rue de Bretagne (République/Temple) | 01 42 72 36 26
For "couscous at its most trendy", check out this "casual" "fashion-industry favorite" in the 3rd, where plates are "piled high" with "pleasant" Moroccan morsels, the "jovial" owner makes "you feel like a local on your first" visit and the "waiters never stop joking around"; they "don't take reservations", but "don't be turned off by the line that often extends out the door" – it's "worth the wait."

Chez Papa ● *Southwest*
| 17 | 14 | 15 | €25 |

8e | 29, rue de l'Arcade (Madeleine/St-Lazare) | 01 42 65 43 68
10e | 206, rue la Fayette (Louis Blanc) | 01 42 09 53 87
14e | 6, rue Gassendi (Denfert-Rochereau/Raspail) | 01 43 22 41 19 | fax 01 40 47 55 73
15e | 101, rue de la Croix-Nivert (Commerce/Félix Faure) | 01 48 28 31 88
www.chezpapa.fr
"Cheap and nourishing", this chain is "aimed toward students" and "young, underpaid office workers" with its "huge portions" of "typi-

cally Southwestern fare" ("meaning heavy and full of fat"); "the food is not tops", "the decor's pretty lowbrow" and the servers are geared toward turning over tables, but "if you're hungry, this is the place to go"; P.S. the "salade Boyarde with fried potatoes, Cantal and blue cheese, ham and lettuce is by far the best choice on the menu."

Chez Paul ● *Bistro*

| 21 | 18 | 19 | €39 |

11ᵉ | 13, rue de Charonne (Bastille/Ledru-Rollin) | 01 47 00 34 57 | fax 01 48 07 02 00 | www.chezpaul.com

There's a "good scent of tradition" at this "always-packed" Bastille bistro that's been around since 1945 and still has a "great neighborhood vibe" for "post-Opéra" suppers; "tables are sardined" with eaters enjoying "generous portions" of "Classic French fare done simply and well", plus "plenty of red wines at reasonable prices to help wash it all down"; however, the "meaty" menu and "homemade desserts to die for" are definitely "not for dieters."

Chez Paul ● *Bistro*

| 16 | 12 | 13 | €35 |

13ᵉ | 22, rue de la Butte-aux-Cailles (Corvisart/Place d'Italie) | 01 45 89 22 11 | fax 01 45 80 26 53

"Eat like a Parisian" on grandmotherly dishes ("the baked figs in autumn are the stuff dreams are made of") at this bistro "off the tourist beat" in the 13th; the decor's "not very original" and the service is "up and down", but overall "the energy level is high", fueled by the "affordable prices."

Chez Pauline ⌧ *Bistro*

| 20 | 17 | 21 | €57 |

1ᵉʳ | 5, rue Villedo (Palais Royal-Musée du Louvre/Pyramides) | 01 42 96 20 70 | fax 01 49 27 99 89 | www.chezpauline.com

Near the Palais-Royal, here is "another classic bistro that hasn't lost its skill or charm" with its French "comfort food" ("good game in season"); while it "could use an update, decorwise", the "attentive, though not hovering, service" compensates; it's a bit "expensive" alas.

Chez Prune ● *Eclectic*

| ∇ 18 | 19 | 16 | €26 |

10ᵉ | 36, rue Beaurepaire (Jacques Bonsergent/République) | 01 42 41 30 47

A cool clique frequents this "casual" eatery with a "lovely view of the Canal Saint-Martin", particularly from a "coveted table outside"; "rather rude" waiters serve "pretty good" Eclectic eats, seven days a week from morning till late at night, though many come just for "a drink and to hang with the beautiful crowd."

Chez Ramona Ⓜ *Spanish*

| - | - | - | M |

20ᵉ | 17, rue Ramponneau (Belleville/Couronne) | 01 46 36 83 55

The warm Iberian welcome from chef-owner Ramona and her daughter Cucu, plus their excellent tapas and other Spanish dishes, have trendy young types charging for this affordable bodega in bohemian Belleville; the simple, charming decor recreates an old-fashioned grocery store, and prices are as friendly as the atmosphere.

	FOOD	DECOR	SERVICE	COST

Chez Ramulaud ◐🗷 *Bistro* — 16 | 13 | 17 | €37

11ᵉ | 269, rue du Faubourg St-Antoine (Faidherbe-Chaligny/Nation) |
01 43 72 23 29

A faithful "neighborhood clientele" fills up this "cool" "hangout" not far
from Place de la Nation, where there's a new owner and a chef but the
dishes remain an "original" mix of "exotic" and "classic" bistro cuisine,
studded with "lots of unfamiliar things" that are "worth trying"; the
"wine list is interesting", the staff readily "available" and the cost a
"good value", all reasons why this place "never lets you down."

Chez René 🗷Ⓜ *Lyon* — 21 | 17 | 21 | €47

5ᵉ | 14, bd St-Germain (Maubert-Mutualité) | 01 43 54 30 23

"Think Paris in the '20s and '30s and you'll get the idea" confide clients
of this "old-style, old-world, old-charm" institution in the 5th, where
the waiters wear aprons and "nothing ever changes", even after the re-
tirement of the beloved longtime owner; its regulars, businessmen and
politicians claim the "mainly Lyonnaise cuisine is unequalled" – "this
is the kind of restaurant that gives French food a good name."

Chez Savy 🗷 *Aveyron* — 18 | 15 | 17 | €45

8ᵉ | 23, rue Bayard (Franklin D. Roosevelt) | 01 47 23 46 98

Savvy diners looking for the "most affordable pleasure" near the "chic
boutiques of Avenue Montaigne" head for this "efficient and filling"
bistro where "ancient mirrors" give the setting "timeworn cachet" and
the kitchen turns out "solid" Aveyronnaise cuisine, including "shirred
eggs with Roquefort worth the four hours of walking to burn off."

Chez Vincent ◐🗷 *Italian* — - | - | - | E

19ᵉ | Parc des Buttes Chaumont (Botzaris/Buttes Chaumont) |
01 42 02 22 45 | fax 01 40 18 95 83

Vincent Cozzoli's fans have followed their favorite chef-owner to his
new location in the Parc des Buttes Chaumont for "a fix of good
Italian food" served in "huge portions" that help make up for the fact
it's "not inexpensive"; the "theatrical" personality of the *proprietaro*
makes for interesting – and sometimes even "overwhelming" – service.

Chez Vong ◐🗷 *Chinese* — 21 | 20 | 19 | €54

1ᵉʳ | 10, rue de la Grande Truanderie (Etienne Marcel) | 01 40 26 09 36 |
fax 01 42 33 38 15 | www.chez-vong.com

"Chef Vai Kuan Vong came to Paris over 25 years ago", and what he
cooks is "as close to Haute Chinese cuisine as you can get" converts
claim – though purists pout that the "overpriced", "Frenchified
cooking lacks authenticity"; still, in a shabby part of Les Halles, the
decor of this "upscale" Asian offers a "mysterious atmosphere with
its old stone dining rooms dotted with Buddhas, parasols and bamboo", and the "service is adorable."

Chiberta (Le) 🗷 *New French* — 22 | 21 | 22 | €101

8ᵉ | 3, rue Arsène Houssaye (Charles de Gaulle-Etoile) | 01 53 53 42 00 |
fax 01 45 62 85 08 | www.lechiberta.com

Now "one of Guy Savoy's stable", this venue in the 8th gets mixed
responses: scores side with those who find the "inventive" New

French fare "wonderful", the "modern decor" "elegant" and the "service fine"; but dissenters deem the digs "dark" ("wear a miner's helmet in the restrooms if you want to see") and the "rather simple" cuisine "much too dear for what it is", making this site do-able "only for business lunches."

Chieng Mai ⊠ *Thai*

16	13	13	€32

5ᵉ | 12, rue Frédéric Sauton (Maubert-Mutualité) | 01 43 25 45 45

"Run in an old-fashioned way", this "authentic Thai" in the 5th "near Notre Dame" "is like taking a mini-vacation from Paris"; but while the "multicourse meals are an adventure, it's too bad the rooms are so plain"; luckily service is *un peu* more "pleasant", as are the prices.

Chien qui Fume (Au) ☾ *Brasserie*

18	18	17	€42

1ᵉʳ | 33, rue du Pont-Neuf (Châtelet-Les Halles) | 01 42 36 07 42 | fax 01 42 36 36 85 | www.au-chien-qui-fume.com

At "the edge of the Les Halles garden", this "standard brasserie" with "original" images of "dogs smoking" offers "a good deal for what you get" – namely, Classic French dishes; some growl that it's "living off its history and its name" – in particular, the staff, "although witty, is ineffective" – but you gotta "keep it in perspective: it's about fun, not Haute Cuisine" or service here.

Christine (Le) ☾ *Bistro*

23	20	21	€55

6ᵉ | 1, rue Christine (Odéon/St-Michel) | 01 40 51 71 64 | fax 01 43 26 15 63 | www.restaurantlechristine.com

"Tucked away" on a "charming" street in Saint-Germain, this "welcoming", "romantic" spot with "rustic"-chic decor of stone walls and "quirky art" serves "creative", "well-crafted" bistro cuisine; it fulfills the dream of "what Americans imagine a great French restaurant should be", which explains why it's "often filled" with them, especially in the front room; locals ask for a table in the back, where "French doors open onto a courtyard."

NEW Christophe ⊠ *Bistro*

-	-	-	M

5ᵉ | 8, rue Descartes (Cardinal Lemoine) | 01 43 26 72 49

After training under Eric Briffard at the Plaza-Athénée and Anne-Sophie Pic in Valence, young chef Christophe Philippe goes solo with this tiny, casually upscale bistro in "a really nice section" of the Latin Quarter; the chalkboard menu offers "very good quality for the price", with excellent regional meats, fish from the Poissonerie du Dôme and wines from De Vinis Illustribus, one of the city's finest suppliers, located conveniently a few doors away.

Cibus ⊠ *Italian*

-	-	-	M

1ᵉʳ | 5, rue Molière (Palais Royal-Musée du Louvre/Pyramides) | 01 42 61 50 19

Close to the Palais-Royal, this Italian is a little-known address, and with only 20 seats it's probably better that way; there's no menu – the server tells you what the chef-owner has on offer that day – but regulars know they can count on "perfectly al dente" pastas and

other dishes made with organic ingredients, plus homemade liqueurs and "nice wines by the glass" from Italia.

Cigale Récamier (La) 🗷 *Classic French* | 21 | 18 | 20 | €53 |

7ᵉ | 4, rue Récamier (Sèvres-Babylone) | 01 45 48 86 58
"Lots of neighborhood regulars" gather at this Classic French in a cul-de-sac near the Bon Marché store (it's "lovely dining outside without cars buzzing in your face"); "they really know how to make soufflés", which are "varied and wonderful" – though critics caution "choosing anything else will leave you deflated"; even though "the staff is sometimes overwhelmed", it's "still nice."

🗷 Cinq (Le) *Haute Cuisine* | 28 | 29 | 28 | €178 |

8ᵉ | Four Seasons George V | 31, av George V (Alma Marceau/ George V) | 01 49 52 71 54 | fax 01 49 52 71 81 | www.fourseasons.com/paris
"Come here for the meal of your life" swoon sated surveyors who promise this Haute Cuisine table in the George V, voted Tops in Decor and Service, is "perfect in every way", from the "delectable", oft-"adventurous" menu to the "exquisite" classic decor with "vases of flowers everywhere" to the "surprisingly friendly service", "as personal as it is professional" (even offering "a box of reading glasses" to farsighted diners); yes, this "splendid splurge" "will just about rob you of every last euro", but "the experience is so wonderful, somehow one doesn't mind."

Cinq Mars 🗷 *Bistro* | ▽ 19 | 17 | 19 | €44 |

7ᵉ | 51, rue de Verneuil (Rue du Bac/Solférino) | 01 45 44 69 13
"Chic BCBG locals in tweeds" make this "upbeat" spot "tucked away behind the Musée d'Orsay" their neighborhood canteen, for its retro-"relaxed" interior, "informal but thoughtful" staff and "simple, consistently well-prepared" bistro cuisine, including "great eat-per-your-discretion choices, in particular the chocolate mousse", served family-style.

Citrus Etoile 🗷 *Classic/New French* | 20 | 19 | 18 | €80 |

8ᵉ | 6, rue Arséne Houssaye (Etoile) | 01 42 89 15 51 | fax 01 42 89 28 67 | www.citrusetoile.fr
"Owned by a talented chef" (who spent a decade at L'Orangerie Beverly Hills) and his Californian wife, this "contemporary" table near the Etoile offers "quality" New French cuisine (plus some classics) that's "imaginative" without ever being "fussy", in a "sober, modern", gray-and-orange setting with well-spaced tables; if the "relaxed service" has a slight LA vibe, diners just deem that the "perfect antidote to a hectic day."

Cloche des Halles (La) 🗷🗗 *Wine Bar/Bistro* | - | - | - | M |

1ᵉʳ | 28, rue Coquillière (Les Halles/Louvre-Rivoli) | 01 42 36 93 89
There's "a lot of history" in this "truly Parisian" wine bar named for the bell that signaled the opening and closing of the now-defunct Les Halles market; nostalgic clients can reminisce while munching

"excellent", "fairly priced" "light" fare, like cold meat and cheese platters, washed down with "great Beaujolais"; the cozy ambiance is "especially warm and welcoming when the weather is cold and damp."

Clos des Gourmets (Le) 🗗 M *New French* | 25 | 20 | 21 | €51 |

7ᵉ | 16, av Rapp (Alma Marceau/Ecole Militaire) | 01 45 51 75 61 | fax 01 47 05 74 20 | www.closdesgourmets.com

Converts "cannot recommend this place enough", as it offers a chance to dine on "fine cuisine" "in the shade of the Eiffel Tower for a fraction of the usual upscale prices"; the owner's "inspired" New French cooking appears "wholly understated – and then wow", while the "warm, inviting dining room" is particularly "pleasant", thanks to service so friendly it "ruins Paris' arrogant reputation."

Closerie des Lilas (La) ◑ *Classic French* | 18 | 23 | 19 | €63 |

6ᵉ | 171, bd du Montparnasse (Port Royal/Vavin) | 01 40 51 34 50 | fax 01 43 29 99 94 | www.closeriedeslilas.fr

This Montparnasse "mythical place" "has a great reputation to live up to" and how well it succeeds depends on which part you patronize; "the brasserie is an experience" – "even though Hemingway is long gone, the oysters and drinks are still fine", and in the "charming bar" the piano-playing and people-watching are "divine"; but "the restaurant is formal and stuffy" with merely "reliable" Classic French cuisine that "can get very expensive"; "all in all, this historical landmark is worth a visit", though.

Clos Morillons (Le) 🗗 M *New French* | - | - | - | M |

15ᵉ | 50, rue des Morillons (Porte de Vanves) | 01 48 28 04 37 | fax 01 48 28 70 77

The chef-owner at this longstanding table "in an offbeat location" in the 15th runs a "competent kitchen", and locals say his New French cuisine flavored with exotic spices makes it "a reliable and pleasant place to eat", especially in the evening by candlelight.

Clou (Le) 🗗 *Bistro* | ∇ 19 | 15 | 19 | €40 |

17ᵉ | 132, rue Cardinet (Malesherbes) | 01 42 27 36 78 | fax 01 42 27 89 96 | www.restaurant-leclou.fr

"Helpful service" headed up by chef-owner Christian Leclou (ex Ledoyen and Drouant) makes this Batignolles bistro a bastion for locals, with "consistently excellent" Classic French dishes, a "nice wine list" and daily market-fresh specials; the "low-key, comfortable setting" may be "nothing special", but the "good-value" price for this "quality" certainly is.

Clovis (Le) 🗗 M *New French* | - | - | - | E |

8ᵉ | Sofitel Arc de Triomphe | 14, rue Beaujon (Charles de Gaulle-Etoile) | 01 53 89 50 53 | fax 01 53 89 50 51 | www.sofitel.com

"A couple of steps from the Arc de Triomphe", this New French in the Sofitel provides "refined", "inventive" dishes in a "calm", "agreeable" setting; if critics cavil "it should be better, given the price and reputation" of the chef, who was once Ducasse's second-in-command, expense-account holders hail it as just right "for business lunches."

	FOOD	DECOR	SERVICE	COST

Clown Bar ● 🅑🍴 *Wine Bar/Bistro* | 17 | 17 | 17 | €38 |

11ᵉ | 114, rue Amelot (Filles-du-Calvaire) | 01 43 55 87 35 |
www.clown-bar.fr

Its "clown-laden setting" featuring "colorful" art nouveau
Sarreguemines tiles – a reference to the nearby Cirque d'Hiver –
makes this wine bar a "cute" corner to curl up in; "but fortunately
the food is more serious" – "simple but delicious" bistro fare; even
so, it may not justify going "out of your way" unless you're jammed
into a Volkswagen with a red-nosed crowd.

Coco de Mer ● 🅑 *Seychelles* | - | - | - | M |

5ᵉ | 34, bd St-Marcel (Les Gobelins/St-Marcel) | 01 47 07 06 64

In the 5th, this "second embassy of the Seychelles" serves "very good
cuisine that allows you to travel with your feet in the sand" sprinkled
across the entrance; in particular, the prix fixe offers "excellent fish" at
"reasonable prices"; don't be surprised if "coming out, you'll feel like
taking off for Mahé, La Digue or another of the archipelago's islands."

NEW Cocottes (Les) 🅑 *New French* | ▽ 21 | 18 | 20 | €35 |

7ᵉ | 135, rue St-Dominique (Ecole Militaire/Les Invalides) |
01 45 50 10 31

Christian Constant is at his "simple, affordable best" in this new
"conceptual restaurant" where the "delicious, healthy" New French
dishes are served in "individual casseroles" (made by Staub) at a
"long, communal counter"; even if "service is friendly but slow", this
"gastronomic fast-food" joint (the wine is "poured from cardboard
boxes") is an "amusing" arrival "in the posh 7th."

Coffee Parisien ● 🅑 *American* | 16 | 13 | 13 | €28 |

6ᵉ | 4, rue Princesse (Mabillon) | 01 43 54 18 18
16ᵉ | 7, rue Gustave Courbet (Trocadéro/Victor Hugo) | 01 45 53 17 17
Neuilly-sur-Seine | 46, rue de Sablonville (Les Sablons) | 01 46 37 13 13

"Surprisingly filled with" "trendy Gallic teens", this trio of "crammed"
Yankee-style coffee shops offers a "French take on diner food" ("real
pancakes, eggs Benedict, club sandwiches, hamburgers, etc."); critics claim that though it's among "the best American fare" in town,
it's still "not great", and abhor the "amateurish service"; but "excited expats" aver "if you've the patience to wait a long time" ("particularly on weekends"), you'll feel "just like back home."

Coin des
Gourmets (Au) *Cambodian/Vietnamese* | 22 | 14 | 19 | €35 |

1ᵉʳ | 38, rue du Mont-Thabor (Concorde) | 01 42 60 79 79 🅑
5ᵉ | 5, rue Dante (Cluny La Sorbonne/Maubert-Mutualité) |
01 43 26 12 92

"When you need an Asian food fix" in Paris but don't feel like making
the trip to far-flung *quartiers*, delve into this "delightful" duo that
draws a crowd with "well-executed", "home-cooked" dishes from
Cambodia and Vietnam that are "decent" value, particularly "at
lunch"; the recently renovated branch in the 1st (formerly known as
Indochine) boasts a "more agreeable" setting than the "indifferent"-
looking Latin Quarter address.

	FOOD	DECOR	SERVICE	COST

Comédiens (Les) ◐ ⊠ *Classic French* | - | - | - | M |

9ᵉ | 7, rue Blanche (Trinité) | 01 40 82 95 95 | fax 01 40 82 96 95
Two steps from the Trinité church in the 9th, showbiz denizens
and theatergoers congregate at this Classic French with exposed-
brick walls, a zinc bar and posters galore; amid the boisterous ambiance, it's "fun to watch everything going on in the open kitchen"; the
"superb" service is swift, and the specials on the chalkboard menu
are "always different."

Comptoir (Le) ◐ ⊠ *Eclectic/Moroccan* | 21 | 18 | 19 | €53 |

1ᵉʳ | 37, rue Berger (Les Halles/Louvre-Rivoli) | 01 40 26 26 66 |
fax 01 42 21 44 24 | www.comptoirparis.com
Inveterate travelers congregate in this "relaxed" table with neo-
Moroccan decor in Les Halles, serving real and invented dishes from
around the world, with an emphasis on North Africa ("very good
tagine and mint tea"); roamers report the food's "not exceptional"
but it is "original", plus it's a fine "option at lunch", with "ample
platters" and a terrace where you can "sit outside and people-
watch" the Parisians.

⊠ Comptoir du Relais (Le) *Bistro/Brasserie* | 26 | 14 | 19 | €50 |

6ᵉ | Hôtel Relais Saint-Germain | 9, carrefour de l'Odéon (Odéon) |
01 44 27 07 97 | fax 01 46 33 45 30 | www.hotelrsg.com
It's practically "impossible" "to get into this place" in the 6th – dinner
reservations are "the element unobtainium" "unless you're staying
at the hotel", while lunch means "standing in line" – but determined
foodies overcome the odds for Yves Camdeborde's "brilliant twist
on French bistro fare" with "super brasserie" offerings at noon and a
"no-choices" evening prix fixe, both a "tremendous value"; admirers
admit the space is "small and cramped" ("was that really a table for
four or for one?") and the "efficient" staff is "prissy", but if they
could, they'd "eat every meal there."

Comte de Gascogne (Au) ⊠ *Gascony* | - | - | - | VE |

Boulogne-Billancourt | 89, av Jean-Baptiste Clément
(Pont-de-St-Cloud) | 01 46 03 47 27 | fax 01 46 04 55 70 |
www.aucomtedegascogne.com
Like a tropical greenhouse, with tree branches waving under a lofty
ceiling, this formal restaurant with "magic decor" in the suburb of
Boulogne offers "traditional but savory" Gascon cuisine, starring
various types of foie gras; the "perfect service" starts with chef-
owner Henri Charvet, who was born in Bourgogne, ran Marius et
Janette in Paris and developed a passion for palm trees while at the
restaurant Lafayette in Martinique.

Congrès Maillot (Le) ◐ *Brasserie* | ∇ 18 | 15 | 14 | €54 |

17ᵉ | 80, av de la Grande-Armée (Porte Maillot) | 01 45 74 17 24 |
fax 01 45 72 39 80
Oyster lovers can slurp 'em down until 2 AM, seven days a week,
at this "typical brasserie" near the Palais des Congrès, part of the
Gérard Joulie chain; discordant elements complain the "tables
are cramped, the service rushed" and the traditional fare "too

80   subscribe to ZAGAT.com

expensive" for what it is, but all agree you can't go wrong when you order "a seafood platter paired with a Chablis"; N.B. they serve breakfast too.

Cook Book ⊠ *Eclectic*

| - | - | - | M |

7ᵉ | 9, rue Surcouf (Invalides) | 01 45 51 92 82

Near Les Invalides, this Eclectic with simple but colorful decor (bare wood floors, red and yellow chairs) draws mixed reviews: readers ravenous for "world food" praise the "interesting" eats ranging from Argentine steak to kangaroo to curried fruit, while malcontents mutter about a "mediocre" menu and an "intrusive" staff; still, it can be "nice for lunch if you happen to be in the neighborhood."

Copenhague ⊠ *Danish*

| 18 | 17 | 16 | €75 |

8ᵉ | 142, av des Champs-Elysées (Charles de Gaulle-Etoile/George V) | 01 44 13 86 26 | fax 01 44 13 89 44

Everything's copasetic at this Copenhagen import where little has changed despite a takeover by the Frères Blanc chain; known as an "institution" for "good Nordic" cuisine (and a "nice view of the Champs-Elysées"), clients "are never disappointed by the freshness of the fish", saying the "quality of the food" justifies the "expensive" prices; alas, the "sober" Danish decor lacks "a bit of warmth", while the servers have become downright "cold."

Cordonnerie (La) ⊠ *Classic French*

| - | - | - | M |

1ᵉʳ | 20, rue St-Roch (Pyramides/Tuileries) | 01 42 60 17 42 | www.restaurantlacordonnerie.com

"What a charming place" enthuse patrons of this 17th-century "old house" just off the Rue Saint-Honoré, where the chef-owner, Hugo Wolfer, "inherited his talent and the restaurant from his classically trained father" (who opened it in 1964); he and wife Valérie "provide an intimate", "delightful" experience – diners can "sit right in front of the kitchen" and watch him prepare the "savory" traditional French fare.

Cosi *Sandwiches*

| 19 | 9 | 13 | €14 |

6ᵉ | 54, rue de Seine (Mabillon/Odéon) | 01 46 33 35 36

"You like sandwiches and music?" they come together in this eat-in or take-out "trendy" Saint-Germain shop, a "student hangout gone yuppie" with "delicious combinations of meats, cheese and veggies" on "fresh-from-the-oven breads" as well as "real salads"; a "cool staff and laid-back atmosphere, with Vivaldi playing, complete the experience."

Cosi (Le) ⊠ *Corsica*

| 16 | 15 | 12 | €33 |

5ᵉ | 9, rue Cujas (Cluny La Sorbonne/Luxembourg) | 01 43 29 20 20 | fax 01 43 29 26 40 | www.le-cosi.com

This Latin Quarter purveyor of *stufatu* (macaroni casserole), *brocciu* (sheep's milk cheese) and other specialties of the Maquis has earned a reputation as "one of the best Corsican restaurants in Paris", with a chef who creates "original", "heartwarming" and inexpensive plates using "fresh products" from the island in a "cozy", "stylish" room with jazzy music and book-filled library shelves.

Costes ● *Eclectic*

	FOOD	DECOR	SERVICE	COST
	18	25	15	€72

1ᵉʳ | Hôtel Costes | 239, rue St-Honoré (Concorde/Tuileries) | 01 42 44 50 25

Just being in this "über-hip" eatery in the Hôtel Costes "raises your cool factor by 10", as you join the "jet set", "old men with younger women" and "caricatures of beautiful people" who gather like moths to the flame in a "sexy", "dark brothellike setting" (in the summer, there's "no more glamorous place to have a casual dinner" than the courtyard); insiders report the "expensive" Eclectic food is "reasonably good" while the service is "woefully inefficient" ("failed models do not make as good a staff as failed actors") – but who cares? "the scene is the only thing that matters here."

Cottage Marcadet (Le) 🅱 🅼 *New French*

	FOOD	DECOR	SERVICE	COST
	-	-	-	E

18ᵉ | 151 bis, rue Marcadet (Lamarck-Caulaincourt) | 01 42 57 71 22 | www.cottagemarcadet.com

Behind Montmartre, this most elegant cottage has streamlined Louis XVI decor with white tablecloths and silver candlestick holders on each table, a "pleasant" ambiance "perfect for intimate, romantic dining" and a young chef-owner whose "creative" New French food inspires "overwhelming enthusiasm" among his disciples; the "professional but relaxed" staff remains "attentive", "even if your French is not so great."

Coude Fou (Le) ● *Wine Bar/Bistro*

	FOOD	DECOR	SERVICE	COST
	19	14	19	€34

4ᵉ | 12, rue du Bourg-Tibourg (Hôtel-de-Ville) | 01 42 77 15 16 | fax 01 48 04 08 98 | www.lecoudefou.com

Oenophiles opine this is "the most pleasant wine bar in the neighborhood" behind the Hôtel de Ville; even if the small room offers "not much in terms of decor" (despite native frescoes and tile floors), it's a "good basic place for a nice bite" of "comforting" bistro dishes; "tables are tight, so if you tend to get hot, you won't have a good time", but the staff "is fine with Americans, of which there are multitudes."

Cou de la Girafe (Le) 🅱 *New French*

	FOOD	DECOR	SERVICE	COST
	15	15	15	€44

8ᵉ | 7, rue Paul Baudry (Franklin D. Roosevelt/St-Philippe-du-Roule) | 01 56 88 29 55 | fax 01 42 25 28 82

A "business and shopping crowd" flees the jungle of the Champs at this "trendy" "escape" with an ambiance that's both "convivial" and "intimate", thanks to lounge music and "soft lighting" (not to mention "elbow-to-elbow seating"); the "warm-colored" decor is a good match for the "original, exotic" New French cuisine, and though service can seem "amateurish", prices are relatively "affordable for the area."

Couleurs de Vigne 🅱 *Wine Bar/Bistro*

	FOOD	DECOR	SERVICE	COST
	-	-	-	I

15ᵉ | 2, rue Marmontel (Convention/Vaugirard) | 01 45 33 32 96 | fax 01 45 33 32 96

This "sweet" "intimate *bar à vins* is worth seeking out" in a remote part of the 15th, with "wines that are well chosen" and wrapped up in a "typically French ambiance"; the food is "not bad, but not special – best bet is the quite good charcuterie" – and your accompanying bottle can be "taken home" if you don't finish it at table.

Coupe-Chou (Le) ◑ *Classic French*

	FOOD	DECOR	SERVICE	COST
	23	25	22	€54

5ᵉ | 9-11, rue de Lanneau (Maubert-Mutualité) | 01 46 33 68 69 |
fax 01 46 33 71 96 | www.lecoupechou.com

"Who can resist an open fireplace" sigh lovers of this "rustic" "restaurant in a cozy little alley in the heart of the Latin Quarter", where a "warren" of 17th-century rooms breathes "charm, history and romance" with numerous candles and hearths "ablaze"; unsurprisingly, this is "not the place to come if you're seeking culinary innovation", but classicists concur the ambiance and "excellent, traditional fare" make dining here a "very French experience" – even if it's "frequented by many tourists."

Coupe Gorge (Le) ◑ *Bistro*

	FOOD	DECOR	SERVICE	COST
	-	-	-	M

4ᵉ | 2, rue de la Coutellerie (Hôtel-de-Ville) | 01 48 04 79 24 |
fax 01 49 98 03 57 | www.coupegorge.com

"Good" traditional bistro cuisine that's pleasingly "underpriced" makes it easy to overlook the "mediocre setting" of this century-old standard behind Hôtel de Ville, though the red-banquette-and-wooden-table decor does evolve every couple of months with different art exhibits on the walls.

☑ Coupole (La) ◑ *Brasserie*

	FOOD	DECOR	SERVICE	COST
	19	23	18	€55

14ᵉ | 102, bd du Montparnasse (Vavin) | 01 43 20 14 20 |
fax 01 43 35 46 14 | www.flobrasseries.com/coupoleparis

"The mother of all brasseries" in Montparnasse is an "enduring charmer" with a "huge", "gorgeously appointed art deco" interior and "tremendous ambiance" provided by a "boisterous" crowd and "bustling, efficient waiters with lots of personality"; perhaps this Groupe Flo member is "not quite what it once was" – certainly "the food doesn't live up to the magic of the place", unless you "stick to the seafood platter" – but go anyway, cuz "you haven't been to Paris until you've been here."

NEW Crémerie (La) 🅂 Ⓜ *Wine Bar/Bistro*

	FOOD	DECOR	SERVICE	COST
	-	-	-	M

6ᵉ | 9, rue des Quatre-Vents (Odéon) | 01 43 54 99 30 |
www.lacremerie.fr

A wine-loving architect has taken over this pocket-size wine bar/shop in the 6th, keeping the decorative ceiling and marble counter of the original 1880 dairy; fine palates find it a "place to stop your watch and snack on cold cuts" with prestigious provenances, from a rare Italian Burrata cheese to Spanish Bellota ham, plus "good" natural vintages by the glass.

Crêperie de Josselin (La) ◑ 🅂 Ⓜ ⇄ *Brittany*

	FOOD	DECOR	SERVICE	COST
	22	14	18	€19

14ᵉ | 67, rue du Montparnasse (Edgar Quinet/Montparnasse-Bienvenüe) |
01 43 20 93 50

On a "street filled with 'em in Montparnasse", what's "maybe the most famous crêperie in Paris" wins praise for a pancake filled with "both novel combinations and traditional flavors" that's "so enormous the plate's incapable of containing it"; given the "snug" surrounds, "you'll get to know your neighbors even if you don't want to", but

rest assured, this Breton's "crêpes are worth the crowding" (and "service is fast" too).

NEW Cristal de Sel 🗷 M New French — | — | — | E

15e | 13, rue Mademoiselle (Commerce/Félix Faure) | 01 42 50 35 29 | fax 01 42 50 35 29

It's becoming increasingly difficult to snag a reservation at this recently arrived table near the Place du Commerce, where a "great team" is headed up by chef and co-owner Karil Lopez, who spent five years at Eric Frechon's side at the Bristol; unmissable with his tall white toque in a semi-open kitchen, he turns out sophisticated New French cuisine that contrasts with the chalkboard menus and the gray-and-white interior.

🗷 Cristal Room 🗷 New French — 17 | 28 | 18 | €91

16e | Baccarat | 11, pl des Etats-Unis (Boissière/Iéna) | 01 40 22 11 10 | fax 01 40 22 11 99 | www.baccarat.fr

"In the former palace of the Countess of Noailles" in the 16th (now Baccarat's HQ), the dining room has been turned into a restaurant composed of an "enchanting" "splendid combination" of exposed brick, wood paneling and chandeliers, reflecting Philippe Starck's design and some of the world's finest crystal; but while this glass house is "quite special", critics throw stones at the merely "correct" New French food, the "sometimes haughty service" and a "greedy" policy of "tiny portions and huge tabs."

Crus de Bourgogne (Aux) 🗷 Bistro ▽ 17 | 16 | 15 | €41

2e | 3, rue Bachaumont (Les Halles/Sentier) | 01 42 33 48 24 | fax 01 40 28 66 41

There's "not a trendy item on the old-fashioned menu" of this "charming" century-old bistro with red-checkered tablecloths on an "unexpected side street of le quartier Montorgueil"; detractors mutter the food and service "never fail to disappoint", but it remains a "great place to take out-of-towners for that Frenchy feel."

Cuisine (La) New French ▽ 25 | 21 | 27 | €65

7e | 14, bd de la Tour-Maubourg (Invalides/La Tour-Maubourg) | 01 44 18 36 32 | fax 01 44 18 30 42

A "perfect gem" proclaim pleased patrons of this posh address near Les Invalides, whose "chic", "haute-bourgeois atmosphere" – including a contemporary art deco–style interior, porcelain dishes and well-spaced tables – makes it all the more surprising to find such "solicitous service" ("I'd go back just for the lack of attitude") and prices that range from "low to escalating"; compliments also abound for the New French cooking – "a little slice of culinary magic"; P.S. "they are open on Sunday."

NEW Cuisine (La) 🗷 M Bistro — | — | — | M

11e | 73, rue Amelot (Chemin-Vert) | 01 43 14 27 00

Occupying the long, skinny space once inhabited by Les Jumeaux, this new kitchen on a quiet street in the 11th is attracting the attention of trendy young locals, thanks to a chef-owner from Chez

Paul, colorful modern decor with baroque touches and contemporary bistro fare (rabbit pâté, Creole baba au rhum) on an ever-changing menu.

<table>
<thead>
<tr><th></th><th>FOOD</th><th>DECOR</th><th>SERVICE</th><th>COST</th></tr>
</thead>
<tbody>
</tbody>
</table>

Curieux Spaghetti Bar (Le) ● *Italian*   - | - | - | M

4ᵉ | 14, rue St-Merri (Hôtel-de-Ville/Rambuteau) | 01 42 72 75 97 |
fax 01 40 13 87 58 | www.curieuxspag.com

"Even spaghetti can be fun" discover diners at this "funky and eclectic", "one-of-a-kind" noodle bar behind the Beaubourg that combines "really good pasta" (served with a bib) and disco atmosphere ("don't expect to have too much conversation, as the music is very loud"); nobody comes here in search of *haute gastronomie,* but rather for the "incredible ambiance", right down to the colorful psychedelic decor, long counter, chandeliers and periodically changing wallpaper.

NEW Dali (Le) *Classic French*   - | - | - | E

1ᵉʳ | Hôtel Meurice | 228, rue de Rivoli (Concorde/Tuileries) |
01 44 58 10 44 | www.lemeurice.com

Following Philippe Starck's slick redesign of the Meurice's public spaces, the old winter-garden room has morphed into an Egyptian-inspired palace, complete with a huge painted canvas-tent ceiling and silver winged armchairs; named for one of the hotel's famed guests (and with his surreal details in the furnishings), it showcases house toque Yannick Alléno in a more casual, Classic French mode at – slightly – more relaxed prices than in the main dining room.

Dalloyau *Dessert/Tearoom*   23 | 18 | 18 | €32

4ᵉ | 5, bd Beaumarchais (Bastille) | 01 48 87 89 88 |
fax 01 48 87 73 70
6ᵉ | 2, pl Edmond Rostand (Cluny La Sorbonne/Odéon) | 01 43 29 31 10 |
fax 01 43 26 25 72
8ᵉ | 101, rue du Faubourg St-Honoré (Miromesnil/St-Philippe-du-Roule) |
01 42 99 90 00 | fax 01 45 63 82 92
Boulogne-Billancourt | 67, av J.B. Clément (Boulogne-Jean Jaurès) |
01 46 05 06 78 | fax 01 46 03 90 30
www.dalloyau.fr

"Magnificent éclairs, stupendous tarts and fabulous macaroons" are among the "sweet-tooth satisfiers" offered at these "calm", "high-class" *salons de thé* "all over Paris" – you could "have breakfast at the one on Faubourg Saint-Honoré, then afternoon tea on the terrace across from the Luxembourg Gardens" and finally "before the Opéra Bastille", a light dinner on "something savory to justify a few desserts"; they're also "wonderful" for takeout – in fact, even "flight attendants get their picnics for the plane, and eat better than anyone!"

Dalva *New French*   - | - | - | M

2ᵉ | 48, rue d'Argout (Louvre-Rivoli/Sentier) | 01 42 36 02 11 |
www.dalvarestaurant.fr

There's "stellar karma" in this lovely little New French with a mod but homey interior and a sidewalk terrace on what's perhaps the "hippest street in Paris"; ingredients for the "fresh, inventive fare" come from the nearby Montorgueil market and are whipped into shape by

a chef who earned his chops at L'Arpège and Taillevent, while the entire affordable menu is overseen by Bruno Schaeffer, chef-owner of the late L'Argenteuil.

Dame Tartine *Sandwiches*
| 14 | 15 | 13 | €27 |

4ᵉ | 2, rue Brisemiche (Hôtel-de-Ville) | 01 42 77 32 22 | fax 01 42 77 32 22

"Right next to the Stravinsky Fountain near the Beaubourg", this "unpretentious" *sandwicherie* stands out for tasty *tartines* that, if "not revolutionary", are "always respectable" and quite "affordable"; being able to "eat outdoors makes for good decor."

Da Mimmo ●🗷Ⓜ *Italian*
| - | - | - | M |

10ᵉ | 39, bd de Magenta (Gare de l'Est/Jacques Bonsergent) | 01 42 06 44 47 | fax 01 42 06 31 35

Da pizza enjoys a reputation as "the best" in town at this Neapolitan-style trattoria, a "hangout for the young who's who" of Paris, despite – or due to – a "Scorcese movie" interior that's "so ugly it is funny"; while fans willingly part with their dough for the "expensive" pies, others feel you can get "better food served by nicer people" elsewhere.

Da Rosa *Classic French*
| ▽ 19 | 15 | 15 | €33 |

6ᵉ | 62, rue de Seine (Mabillon/Odéon) | 01 40 51 00 09

"Perfect for watching the shoppers" in Saint-Germain, "this small restaurant" in a "gourmet grocery store" serves up "delicious" Classic French light bites made with "Spanish Bellota ham, cheeses" and other nonpareil products – plus some "wines of the same caliber" – that owner José Da Rosa seeks out and supplies to many chefs around town; some sniff there's "no real cuisine" here, but since they serve continuously from 11 AM to 11 PM, it's "good when everything else is closed."

Daru 🗷 *Russian*
| - | - | - | M |

8ᵉ | 19, rue Daru (Courcelles/Ternes) | 01 42 27 23 60 | www.daru.fr

"Real Russians who attend the Orthodox church down the block" faithfully frequent this "idiosyncratic" but "charming" 8th-arrondissement institution created in 1918 by an officer of the Czar; supporters swear it has "some of the best" Soviet fare – from smoked salmon to beef stroganoff – and the service is "simple but warm", while prices exhibit a policy of "containment" that's rare; P.S. the "iced vodka in all varieties is a must."

Dauphin (Le) 🗷 *Southwest*
| 20 | 17 | 18 | €50 |

1ᵉʳ | 167, rue St-Honoré (Palais Royal-Musée du Louvre) | 01 42 60 40 11 | fax 01 42 60 01 18

Just "40 paces from the Louvre", this princeling provides "ample servings of all the favorite" Southwestern staples in a setting that's "classic bistro: mosaic floor, zinc-topped bar" and "windows that open onto the street"; sliding scores suggest it's "lost some charm", cuisine-and servicewise, but "in a heavy tourist area generally known for rip 'n' heat food", "satisfied regulars" say this spot is still *sympathique.*"

	FOOD	DECOR	SERVICE	COST

Davé *Chinese/Vietnamese*

18 **14** **19** **€54**

1ᵉʳ | 12, rue de Richelieu (Palais Royal-Musée du Louvre) | 01 42 61 49 48

"An institution for fashion-world [types] when they're in Paris" ("Marc Jacobs has parties here"), this "cool", compact Chinese-Vietnamese in the 1st "boasts images of the celebrities who've dined" and been doted on by the namesake owner, who is something of "a legend" himself; lesser mortals call the place "overrated, overpriced, just plain over" – but they're overridden by devotees who declare "eccentric service is what makes this place charming."

D'Chez Eux ⊠ *Bistro/Southwest*

25 **19** **25** **€68**

7ᵉ | 2, av Lowendal (Ecole Militaire) | 01 47 05 52 55 | fax 01 45 55 60 74 | www.chezeux.com

"Come hungry" to this "old-school neighborhood bistro" "two steps from Les Invalides", where "sturdy", "stunning" Southwestern "comfort" food is served in "copious" portions ("huge baskets of charcuterie", an "all-you-can-eat dessert trolley") "perfect for American appetites"; the "convivial" setting owes much to "happy" waiters in "long white *tabliers*" making clients feel as "relaxed" as if they "were in the owner's home" or, as the French say, *chez eux.*

Delicabar ⊠ *New French*

13 **14** **12** **€30**

7ᵉ | Bon Marché | 26-38, rue de Sèvres (Sèvres-Babylone) | 01 42 22 10 12 | fax 01 42 22 08 60 | www.delicabar.fr

"Stylish" shoppers of the Bon Marché "refuel" at the department store's "chic snack bar" whose "modern design" mixes a white background with "multicolored banquettes" and barstools; it's "convenient" for a "quick but civilized lunch", especially on the terrace, though some find the New French food "extremely expensive" given the delicate portions.

Délices d'Aphrodite (Les) *Greek*

▽ **18** **15** **17** **€38**

5ᵉ | 4, rue de Candolle (Censier-Daubenton) | 01 43 31 40 39 | fax 01 43 36 13 08 | www.mavrommatis.fr

A "simpler, no-fuss version of its big brother, Mavrommatis", also in the 5th, this Grecian goddess attracts a good many followers, so "the staff sometimes is overwhelmed" – especially on summer evenings when the "agreeable" sidewalk seats fill up quickly.

Dell Orto ● ⊠ Ⓜ *Italian*

- **-** **-** **E**

9ᵉ | 45, rue St-Georges (St-Georges) | 01 48 78 40 30

Its name is Italian for 'from the garden', but there's nothing garden-variety about this 9th-arrondissement address that *amici* applaud as "one of the city's tops" for "a multitude of inventive fresh pasta" and other Tuscan dishes; "a warm neighborhood welcome" comes from the owner, a French filmmaker.

Dessirier ● *Seafood*

20 **16** **19** **€75**

17ᵉ | 9, pl du Maréchal Juin (Péreire) | 01 42 27 82 14 | fax 01 47 66 82 07 | www.michelrostang.com

Near the Place Péreire, this "well-mannered" Michel Rostang-run "grand fish specialist" serves "delicious seafood", which makes it a

bull's-eye for business dining – though even the executive clientele goes ballistic over the "breathtaking prices"; malcontents are mollified, however, by the "pleasant service" and an "excellent wine list."

Deux Abeilles (Les) 🅱 Dessert/Tearoom ▽ 21 | 17 | 16 | €41

7ᵉ | 189, rue de l'Université (Alma Marceau) | 01 45 55 64 04 | fax 01 45 55 64 04

"Ladies who lunch" buzz into this "cozy", "welcoming" spot run by a "welcoming mother and daughter" behind the Musée Branly with a "quiet", "English tearoom" ambiance that's particularly inviting "on a rainy day", plus "delicious" salads and "homemade pastries" including a "lemon meringue pie to die for"; when the weather's fine, "bring grand-mère" for a view of the Eiffel Tower from sidewalk tables.

Deux Canards (Aux) 🅱 Classic French 18 | 17 | 17 | €46

10ᵉ | 8, rue du Faubourg Poissonnière (Bonne Nouvelle) | 01 47 70 03 23 | fax 01 47 70 18 85 | www.lesdeuxcanards.com

Fans say you'd have to be a quack not to love this rather offbeat Classic French in the 10th, where "chatty" owner Gérard Faesch "makes you feel like part of his family"; "his narration of the chalkboard menu is priceless" too, and "obviously the duck is a must"; some find the decor, adorned with "jars of oranges in various states of fermentation", "a little overwrought" but most say it's "warm" and "rustic" – and "nicely nonsmoking."

2 Pieces Cuisine 🅱 Bistro - | - | - | M

18ᵉ | 65, rue du Ruisseau (Jules Joffrin) | 01 42 23 31 23 | www.2pieces-cuisine.com

A "nice neighborhood place – no more, no less" declare the few that have found this casual bistro tucked away in a gentrifying corner of Montmartre; within its warm-toned premises, it feeds the starving artists of today with a good-value Classic French prix fixe that changes every two months.

Devèz (Le) ◗ Steak ▽ 16 | 10 | 12 | €47

8ᵉ | 5, pl de l'Alma (Alma Marceau) | 01 53 67 97 53 | fax 01 47 23 09 48 | www.devezparis.com

"Before going to see a show", beef eaters come to sink their teeth into "superb steaks", meaty tapas or a "delicious mac'Aubrac" burger – all made from one of the finest races of French cattle, and washed down with a full-bodied red from "a serious wine list"; the ambiance is cozy in the winter, while in summer clients stake out a place on the "large outdoor terrace on Place de l'Alma."

Diamantaires (Les) 🅱 Armenian/Greek - | - | - | M

9ᵉ | 60, rue La Fayette (Cadet/Le Peletier) | 01 47 70 78 14 | fax 01 44 83 02 73 | www.lesdiamantaires.com

Founded in 1929 and aptly located in the 9th, the neighborhood long known as New Athens, this "old Greco-Armenian address" still serves the same standards: meze, souvlaki, kebabs and grilled lamb, while live musicians give wannabe Zorbas the chance to dance the sirtaki Thursday–Sunday nights.

Diapason (Le) 🅵 *Southwest*   - | - | - | E

18ᵉ | Terrass Hôtel | 12-14, rue Joseph de Maistre (Abbesses/
Place de Clichy) | 01 44 92 34 00 | fax 01 42 52 29 11 |
www.terrass-hotel.com

It's all about eating alfresco at this Montmartre hotel venue that
boasts "one of the best views in Paris" from its seventh-floor terrace
(open May through September); it actually serves Southwestern
fare year-round, in a neutral-toned Asian interior, but most feel the
"food and service seem automatically better" "on summer evenings,
when there is no more romantic" place in town.

Diep 🌑🅵 *Asian*   21 | 17 | 18 | €59

8ᵉ | 55, rue Pierre Charron (Franklin D. Roosevelt) | 01 45 63 52 76 |
fax 01 42 56 46 56 | www.diep.fr

"Good but expensive" – the latter "due to the location" in a pricey
part of the 8th – is the majority read on this "jet-setty" Asian; "it's
not a place to recommend for a romantic dinner", given the gallop-
ing service of "waiters who are in a hurry for you to leave, bringing
the check before you ask" and the "ok, not extraordinary" Oriental
decor; on the other hand, the victuals are "among the best Chinese-
Thai-Vietnamese in Paris" and – for those who care about such
things – it's "an indispensable [site] for seeing and being seen."

Divellec (Le) 🅵 *Seafood*   24 | 20 | 21 | €132

7ᵉ | 107, rue de l'Université (Invalides) | 01 45 51 91 96 |
fax 01 45 51 31 75 | www.ledivellec.com

"Conservative but sound" sums up this "traditional French seafooder" on the Esplanade des Invalides that nets "local bigwigs"
with "excellent" fish (including the "legendary pressed lobster") and
"attentive but unintrusive service"; while the recently redone decor's now "handsome", some still sniff over the "stiff atmosphere" –
folks "speaking softly as if in church" – and the "sky-high prices" are
"not for everyday"; "but from time to time, it's worth it" to splurge.

🅭 1728 🅵 *New French*   19 | 27 | 17 | €73

8ᵉ | 8, rue d'Anjou (Concorde/Madeleine) | 01 40 17 04 77 |
fax 01 42 65 53 87 | www.restaurant-1728.com

Boasting "gorgeous", "regal" décor, paintings (for sale) on the walls,
and "private salons for intimate dinners", "the setting alone is worth
the trip" to this 18th-century manse just off the Faubourg Saint-
Honoré, Lafayette's final home; while it "doesn't live up to the setting", the New French fare with a soupçon of "Sino sophistication" is
"unusual" and at times "delightful"; and if that's not your cup of tea,
it's also open afternoons for a "perfect" pot of chamomile and "great
pastries" by dessert deity Pierre Hermé.

Dix Vins (Le) 🅵 *Wine Bar/Bistro*   - | - | - | M

15ᵉ | 57, rue Falguière (Pasteur) | 01 43 20 91 77

This "nice neighborhood place" in the 15th has gained a following
with fresh, inexpensive bistro food, including game in season, and
an ever-changing *carte des vins*; the small, informal space with oil
lamps on the tables works equally well "for a tête-à-tête or a group."

	FOOD	DECOR	SERVICE	COST

Djakarta Bali 🏧Ⓜ️ *Indonesian*

	20	18	18	€41

1er | 9, rue Vauvilliers (Châtelet-Les Halles/Louvre-Rivoli) |
01 45 08 83 11 | fax 01 45 08 17 81 | www.djakarta-bali.com

A "serene ambiance" reigns at this Indonesian table next to Les
Halles run by a brother/sister team, offering "refined", "authentic"
cooking filled with "exotic flavors" from the archipelago; "stress-
free" service and traditional decor almost make patrons "believe
they are over there" – especially on Friday nights, when dancers
from Bali take to the floor.

Domaine de Lintillac 🏧 *Southwest*

	▽ 18	13	18	€28

2e | 10, rue St-Augustin (Quatre Septembre) | 01 40 20 96 27 |
www.lintillac-paris.com
7e | 20, rue Rousselet (Duroc) | 01 45 66 88 23 |
www.restaurantdomainedelintillac.com Ⓜ️
9e | 54, rue Blanche (Blanche/Trinité) | 01 48 74 84 36 |
www.lintillac-paris.com ◗

"Lovers of duck in all its varieties" migrate to this trio of tables where
the "tasty Southwestern" cuisine is "cheap and plentiful", from the
foie gras to the "must-have" confit de canard that come straight
from the Périgord "producer to the consumer"; it's rustic, "casual"
and "fast", so it's easy to fill up "and waddle home."

Dôme (Le) ◗ *Seafood*

	22	23	21	€70

14e | 108, bd du Montparnasse (Vavin) | 01 43 35 25 81 |
fax 01 42 79 01 19

This "lovely, luxurious" seafooder with "a rich literary" heritage has
a "traditional atmosphere with overstuffed booths and large floral
arrangements filling nooks and crannies"; "you can spend an afternoon just sampling the oyster selection" and "the best bouillabaisse" ("we so obviously enjoyed it, they offered us seconds");
"service is precise", if "in a hurry", and while the "expensive" prices
make some mourn its bohemian brasserie past, for most it's "worth
a visit to Montparnasse."

Dôme du Marais (Le) 🏧Ⓜ️ *New French*

	22	22	20	€47

4e | 53 bis, rue des Francs-Bourgeois (Hôtel-de-Ville/Rambuteau) |
01 42 74 54 17 | fax 01 42 77 78 17

True to its name, this "spacious" place in the Marais boasts courtyard dining under "a magnificent dome" in a "beautifully restored
space that was once Paris' official pawn shop"; but while this
"unique" address is "historical", the "tasty, imaginative" cuisine is
New French, with a "good-value" quotient that extends to the kiddie
menu, priced according to each child's age.

🆉 Dominique Bouchet 🏧 *Haute Cuisine*

	27	21	24	€86

8e | 11, rue Treilhard (Miromesnil) | 01 45 61 09 46 | fax 01 42 89 11 14 |
www.dominique-bouchet.com

Although it's "hidden" in the upper 8th, those who find this Haute
Cuisine haven declare it "delivers 100% on the promise of greatness
reflected in Bouchet's résumé", which includes Les Ambassadeurs;
a "joy of a man", the chef-owner makes "creative preparations" of

French classics while steering clear of trendy "foams and froths"; converts also compliment the "modern but warm interior" and "polite, attentive service from English-speaking waiters"; so, travelers, take note: "this is the food that you went to Paris for."

Don Juans (Les) Ⓢ *Mediterranean/New French* | - | - | - | M |

3e | 19, rue de Picardie (Filles-du-Calvaire/Temple) | 01 42 71 31 71
This *roué* in the northern Marais wins the hearts of local hipsters with Mediterranean-influenced New French cuisine that's "carefully prepared", yet "never overly sophisticated"; the service is "congenial", the setting features contemporary furniture in a two-story space of exposed beams and concrete, and the reasonable price is a definite virtue.

Dos de la Baleine (Le) ⓈⓂ *Bistro* | ▽ 20 | 18 | 20 | €45 |

4e | 40, rue des Blancs-Manteaux (Hôtel-de-Ville/Rambuteau) | 01 42 72 38 98 | fax 01 43 45 43 34 | www.ledosdelabaleine.com
The "sweet" staff "tries hard to make an enjoyable evening" for the diverse clientele that's largely, though not exclusively, gay at this "modest" bistro that's long been "one of the stars of the Marais"; served within cozy, old stone walls, the "good food", including "crowd-pleasing fish and duck specialties", is priced to constitute "one of the great bargains of the 4th."

Drouant ● *Classic French* | 22 | 21 | 20 | €82 |

2e | 16-18, pl Gaillon (Opéra/Quatre-Septembre) | 01 42 65 15 16 | fax 01 49 24 02 15 | www.drouant.com
The "revelation of the year" roar reviewers about chef-owner Antoine Westermann's "superb reinvention" of this "historical" table near the Opéra Garnier; architect Pascal Desprez's "magnificent" update of the original décor is the backdrop for "stunning" "small bites" of Classic French cuisine (starters, sides and "desserts come in groups of four") that "allow elegant tastings of a variety of dishes without culinary overload"; only a heretical handful hiss that the results are "disappointing", given the "high prices."

Duc (Le) ⓈⓂ *Seafood* | 23 | 15 | 20 | €81 |

14e | 243, bd Raspail (Raspail) | 01 43 20 96 30 | fax 01 43 20 46 73
Ah, but life is good when you're seated in front of "a buttery *sole meunière* served in a room resembling a ship of the French line" – as you are at this "sedate" but "sublime" seafooder in Montparnasse; after nigh on 40 years, perhaps the "tired" hull needs overhauling, but "watching waiters fillet the fish is great fun", so plenty are pleased to put into port at "one of the top" *poisson* palaces in Paris.

Duc de Richelieu (Le) ●Ⓢ *Lyon* | - | - | - | M |

12e | 5, rue Parrot (Gare de Lyon) | 01 43 43 05 64 | fax 01 40 19 08 70
"Cooking from the heart" is what draws people to this Lyonnais-like bistro near, naturally, the Gare de Lyon; "even if the decor is

unremarkable", this place pleases with "chatty, ultraefficient" service and "fabulous wine choices" to back up the "terrific value" of a menu.

Durand Dupont Drugstore ● *Eclectic* | - | - | - | M |
Neuilly-sur-Seine | 14, pl du Marché (Les Sablons) | 01 41 92 93 00 | fax 01 46 37 56 79

It may be "trendy, but don't expect more" of this Eclectic brasserie frequently "frequented by families in Neuilly" (especially for brunch on the "agreeable terrace"); the "disappointingly inconsistent menu and service make every visit hit-or-miss", and given that risk-reward ratio, it's "too expensive."

Ebauchoir (L') Ⓢ Ⓜ *Bistro* | - | - | - | M |
12ᵉ | 43-45, rue de Citeaux (Faidherbe-Chaligny) | 01 43 42 49 31 | www.lebauchoir.com

With its "old-style" decor in red and yellow (it's even been "used as a movie set on occasion"), this "typical neighborhood place" quickly fills up with a young, cool crowd of regulars from the funky area between Bastille and Nation; the inventive bistro cooking "never disappoints" ("the rice pudding alone is worth the trip to Paris"), and it's "good value for the price" – especially the "wine *au compteur*", where you only pay for what you drink.

Ebouillanté (L') Ⓜ *Classic French/Tearoom* | - | - | - | I |
4ᵉ | rue des Barres (St-Paul) | 01 42 71 09 69 | www.restaurant-ebouillante.com

On a quiet, cobblestone pedestrian lane with steps leading from the Pont Marie into the Marais, this small *salon de thé* enjoys an exceptional location for its light meals such as stuffed pastry *briques* (Tunisian crêpes) and salads; the terrace is irresistible when the weather's fine – if only you can find a free table.

Ecaille de la Fontaine (L') Ⓢ *Shellfish* | - | - | - | M |
2ᵉ | 15, rue Gaillon (Opéra) | 01 47 42 02 99 | fax 01 47 42 82 84 | www.la-fontaine-gaillon.com

Don't be surprised if you bump into Gérard Depardieu here, since he owns this "intimate seafooder that shares a kitchen with a more expensive place across the street" (La Fontaine Gaillon); located in a "lovely neighborhood" near the Opéra Garnier, it's a "great pick before a show" with a choice selection of French shellfish, plus "nice outdoor seating" in the summer – and if you don't see the celebrity patron, you can always admire the photos of his life that line the walls.

Ecailler du Bistrot (L') Ⓢ Ⓜ *Seafood* | ∇ 19 | 15 | 19 | €49 |
11ᵉ | 20-22, rue Paul Bert (Faidherbe-Chaligny) | 01 43 72 76 77 | fax 01 43 72 24 66

Birthed by the "mother house next door", the Bistrot Paul Bert, this spawn specializes in "seafood, seafood, seafood" that utilizes the "freshest" shellfish around, including "little guys you've never seen before"; though "sometimes the oyster opener is a little clumsy", it's "worth the trip" to the 11th because it's a terrific catch "for the buck."

	FOOD	DECOR	SERVICE	COST

NEW **Eclaireur (L')** ⌧ *New French* | - | - | - | VE

8ᵉ | 10, rue Boissy d'Anglas (Concorde) | 01 53 43 09 99 |
fax 01 53 43 03 71 | www.leclaireur.com

An avant-garde, eternally chic chain of boutiques branches out into
food with a fashionable new lounge/eatery attached to the address
in the 8th; the decor, conceived with Barnaba Fornasetti (son of
Piero, whose 1950s dishes are sold in the store), is a fabulous mix of
his father's baroque and surrealism, the bar concocts creative cocktails and the chef prepares New French food served by an unexpect-
edly friendly staff against a soundscape of cool tunes.

Ecluse (L') ◑ *Wine Bar/Bistro* | 16 | 13 | 18 | €35

1ᵉʳ | 34, pl du Marché St-Honoré (Pyramides/Tuileries) | 01 42 96 10 18 |
fax 01 42 96 10 17
6ᵉ | 15, quai des Grands-Augustins (St-Michel) | 01 46 33 58 74 |
fax 01 44 07 18 76
8ᵉ | 15, pl de la Madeleine (Madeleine) | 01 42 65 34 69 |
fax 01 44 71 01 26
8ᵉ | 64, rue François 1er (George V) | 01 47 20 77 09 | fax 01 40 70 03 33
17ᵉ | 1, rue d'Armaillé (Charles de Gaulle-Etoile) | 01 47 63 88 29 |
fax 01 44 40 41 91
www.leclusebaravin.com

"A chain but a good one" oenophiles opine about these rustic wine
bars around town, offering an especially "great selection of Bordeaux
by the glass"; clearly the Classic French "food is secondary", "but you
do have to eat something with the wine", and since "the staff knows"
its stuff, a "reasonably priced", "pleasant experience is guaranteed."

Editeurs (Les) ◑ *Brasserie* | 14 | 20 | 15 | €38

6ᵉ | 4, Carrefour de l'Odéon (Odéon) | 01 43 26 67 76 | fax 01 46 34 58 30 |
www.lesediteurs.fr

Rapidly becoming the "cornerstone of the square" around the Odéon,
this "sophisticated rendezvous" is renowned for its "congenial" "library decor", with "comfortable chairs and shelves filled with books
you can take down and actually read"; it's the "great setting that
makes it a busy place all day – you don't come here for the food" ("solid
but overpriced" brasserie eats) or the somewhat "slow service"; indeed, the bookish believe it's "best just for drinks and snacks."

El Mansour ⌧ *Moroccan* | 17 | 17 | 17 | €52

8ᵉ | 7, rue de La Trémoille (Alma Marceau) | 01 47 23 88 18 |
fax 01 40 70 13 53

"Morocco is close enough to touch" at this "refined" table in the 8th;
the menu is "an invitation to travel" with "slightly industrial" but
"good couscous and tagine", and the exotic decor "fits perfectly
with the meal"; "though not friendly at first, the service warms up as
the night progresses."

El Palenque ⌧Ⓜ⇄ *Argentinean* | 19 | 10 | 12 | €34

5ᵉ | 5, rue de la Montagne Ste-Geneviève (Maubert-Mutualité) |
01 43 54 08 99

"Heaven for homesick Argentines", this pint-sized patch of the pam-
pas in the Latin Quarter is a *bueno, bueno* address for "delicious

meat", along with "typical dishes, including dulce de leche and wonderful wines"; "a student-y atmosphere" and "friendly service from the Latin American waiters" ensure it's "excellent value for the money."

Elysées (Les) ☒ *Haute Cuisine*

23	24	25	€126

8ᵉ | Hôtel Vernet | 25, rue Vernet (Charles de Gaulle-Etoile/George V) | 01 44 31 98 98 | fax 01 44 31 85 69 | www.hotelvernet.com

This perpetual sleeper in the Hôtel Vernet holds a place on many foodies' lists as the "great Eric Briffard" lives up to his "Joël Robuchon training" with "delightful" Haute Cuisine; the "magnificent room" features a "beautiful stained-glass ceiling" and a "not-snobby", "unusually friendly atmosphere"; what's more, it's "not as expensive as many other grand palaces (and the chef is actually in the kitchen!)."

Elysées Hong Kong *Chinese*

-	-	-	M

16ᵉ | 80, rue Michel-Ange (Exelmans) | 01 46 51 60 99 | fax 01 46 51 60 99

Chinese food is not the City of Light's specialty, yet for some 30 years this recently remodeled space in the silk-stocking 16th has pulled in a soigné crowd of regulars, including French showbiz types, with "consistently excellent" classics; the authentic-minded attack the food as "Westernized", but most find it suits them to a tea, especially since prices are moderate.

Emporio Armani Caffè ☒ *Italian*

19	19	16	€57

6ᵉ | 149, bd St-Germain (St-Germain-des-Prés) | 01 45 48 62 15 | fax 01 45 48 53 17

"As you would expect", "a fab fashion attitude – dramatic decor, beautiful people galore and a staff straight off a catwalk" – dominates this "sooo chic" cafe "on the second floor of the Emporio Armani"; but "surprisingly, there's actually decent food to go with the design", a "light" but "true taste of Northern Italy", "nicely presented"; yes, those pretty servers can be "haughty", and many moan the "model-sized portions for exorbitant prices" appeal to "Armani, not the appetite"; most, though, are "impressed."

Enoteca (L') ● *Italian*

20	16	17	€44

4ᵉ | 25, rue Charles V (St-Paul/Sully Morland) | 01 42 78 91 44 | fax 01 44 59 31 72 | www.enoteca.fr

"In pasta e vino veritas" declare devotees of this "intimate" Italian vino bar in a centuries-old Marais house; massive beams overhead create a "romantic" but "low-key" setting in which to sample possibly the "best list of wines from The Boot" (with the "good by-the-glass selection changing weekly") and "unfussy", "well-cooked" *cucina*; surveyors also salute "the staff that knows its stuff", even though some warn they grow "distant if you refuse their expensive suggestions."

Entoto ☒Ⓜ *Ethiopian*

-	-	-	I

13ᵉ | 143-145, rue L.M. Nordmann (Glacière) | 01 45 87 08 51

"If you've never eaten Ethiopian food, you are in for a treat" confide clients of this "simple" though "friendly" venue in the 13th, where "flavorful" dishes with "interesting seasonings" include *wot*, a

platter of meat and vegetables eaten by hand with injera bread; but this East African offers more than just a cultural adventure – "it's a bargain" too.

Entracte (L') (Chez Sonia et Carlos) Ⓜ Bistro

FOOD	DECOR	SERVICE	COST
-	-	-	E

18ᵉ | 44, rue d'Orsel (Abbesses/Anvers) | 01 46 06 93 41

"A favorite with the locals" and "colorful" types from the "theater across the street", this traditional "treasure" in the 18th also attracts trekkers "on the way up the hill to Sacré Coeur", who are drawn by the "beautiful flowers that brighten the decor", the "wonderful atmosphere" and the "warm welcome" of the owner, whose functions also include greeter, bartender and chef; his "exquisitely prepared" bistro food is "served with justifiable pride."

Entredgeu (L') Ⓢ Ⓜ Bistro

FOOD	DECOR	SERVICE	COST
17	9	13	€42

17ᵉ | 83, rue Laugier (Porte de Champerret) | 01 40 54 97 24 | fax 01 40 54 96 62

"Jammed and jamming", this "quirky bistro at the top end of the 17th" belongs to "a former sous-chef of Yves Camdeborde's", who prepares an "imaginative" menu that "changes with the market" while his wife oversees the room; alas, while "affordable", it's "awfully average" antagonists argue, while sensitive souls shrink from the "surly service"; at least "they've installed air-conditioning."

Enzo Ⓢ Italian

FOOD	DECOR	SERVICE	COST
-	-	-	M

14ᵉ | 72, rue Daguerre (Denfert-Rochereau/Gaîté) | 01 43 21 66 66 | www.pizzaenzo.fr

Eponymous chef-owner Enzo Camerino earns kudos for what many consider the "best pizza in town", thin-crusted and always freshly made, plus pastas and "good vegetarian options" at this tiny trattoria in the 14th; but it's all just pie in the sky for those who show up too late to claim one of the 30 "less than comfortable", but highly coveted, seats.

Epicure 108 Ⓢ Alsace/Asian

FOOD	DECOR	SERVICE	COST
-	-	-	M

17ᵉ | 108, rue Cardinet (Malesherbes) | 01 47 63 50 91

"Unjustly overlooked due to the lack of tourist traffic in the area", this intriguing and thoroughly original table in the 17th offers an "Alsatian menu from an Asian chef-owner"; happily, his efforts such as fish choucroute and green tea crème brûlée avoid "crazy fusion", showing instead the delicious results of a "respectful interaction between two traditions."

Epi d'Or (L') Ⓢ Bistro

FOOD	DECOR	SERVICE	COST
16	15	17	€41

1ᵉʳ | 25, rue Jean-Jacques Rousseau (Louvre-Rivoli) | 01 42 36 38 12 | fax 01 42 36 46 25

It's "small and not fancy", "but everyone here is serious about the food" at this "authentic" bistro near the Bourse, with a "moody old interior" that dates back to 1935 and a "warm welcome" for all; malcontents mutter "there was a time when it was better" (and indeed, the Food score's slipped), but since this old-fashioned type of

"good-value" place is "getting harder and harder to find", disciples deem it "worth the detour."

☑ Epi Dupin (L') Ⓢ *Bistro*

24	14	19	€51

6ᵉ | 11, rue Dupin (Sèvres-Babylone) | 01 42 22 64 56 | fax 01 42 22 30 42 | www.epidupin.com

There's "good reason" this "bubbly" bistro near the Bon Marché is "always packed" exclaim "gobsmacked" gastronomes who guarantee the "inspired", "innovative" prix fixe is such "great value" it's practically "a giveaway" – overriding serenity-seekers shuddering it's "not worth the cattle-car experience" ("cramped tables" and a "rushed", albeit "nice" staff); P.S. you "must book" one of the two nightly seatings, remembering that the tourist-heavy early one feels like "eating in the States."

NEW Epigramme (L') ⓈⓂ *Bistro*

-	-	-	M

6ᵉ | 9, rue de l'Eperon (Odéon/St-Michel) | 01 44 41 00 09

It can be surprisingly tough to find good ol' French food in Saint-Germain, site of so many Italian eateries, which explains why early scouts have been writing epigrams about this tiny new bistro; exposed-stone walls create a warm country-house type atmosphere in which to enjoy the good-value chalkboard menu that runs to dishes like cauliflower soup, grilled veal breast with pumpkin purée and Campari-flavored orange and grapefruit gelée.

Erawan Ⓢ *Thai*

17	10	12	€41

15ᵉ | 76, rue de la Fédération (La Motte-Picquet-Grenelle) | 01 47 83 55 67 | fax 01 47 34 85 98

Bangkok buffs affirm that this intimate spot near Ecole Militaire offers "authentic" Thai food, "not the watered-down French version" – indeed, this is "one of the few places where you can ask for *prig nam pla* (a condiment with chiles in fermented fish sauce) and actually get it"; the personnel is "affable", and despite "uninteresting decor", it still manages to conjure a "lovely atmosphere."

Escale du Liban (L') ● *Lebanese*

-	-	-	I

4ᵉ | 1, rue Ferdinand Duval (St-Paul) | 01 42 74 55 70 | fax 01 42 74 55 27

This Lebanese port of call in a 17th-century building in the Marais has been taken over by a new chef-owner, but nothing has changed, from the busy take-out counter to the tables on two floors above, where patrons sit and graze on meze and sticky-sweet pastries.

Escargot Montorgueil (L') *Bistro*

21	22	21	€62

1ᵉʳ | 38, rue Montorgueil (Les Halles) | 01 42 36 83 51 | fax 01 42 36 35 05 | www.escargot-montorgueil.com

The golden snail over the door of this "unique old" "ornate" bistro is an unmistakable sign that this is "a must-stop if you love escargot", served in sauces as disparate as "traditional, curry and Roquefort", or "crêpes suzette made tableside" (another star of a menu "that couldn't be more Classic" French); located near Les Halles since 1832, this place still has decor "straight out of the 19th century", although "it's easy to overspend" given the 21st-century prices.

	FOOD	DECOR	SERVICE	COST

☑ Espadon (L') *Classic French*
`26` `27` `28` `€149`

1ᵉʳ | Hôtel Ritz | 15, pl Vendôme (Concorde/Opéra) | 01 43 16 30 80 |
fax 01 43 16 33 75 | www.ritzparis.com

It's "like being invited to dinner by Louis XVI" at this "over-the-top"
table in the Hôtel Ritz with "sublime" formal surroundings, a "beautiful summer patio" and "royal treatment" from "surprisingly
friendly" servers; most marvel at chef Michel Roth's "lovely", "perfectly executed" Classic French cuisine – even if a few subjects sigh
it doesn't merit "prices that register on the ridiculous scale."

Espadon Bleu (L') *Seafood*
`21` `18` `20` `€60`

6ᵉ | 25, rue des Grands-Augustins (Odéon/St-Michel) | 01 46 33 00 85 |
fax 01 43 54 54 48 | www.jacques-cagna.com

Chef-restaurateur Jacques Cagna's eateries "at the least are always
really good", and that's the case with his cheerful, colorful seafooder in the 6th – a real catch for its "extremely fresh *fruits de mer*"
and "very friendly service"; "the setting is perhaps too nautical"
(even the chalkboard menu is shaped like a fish), but that doesn't
deter the "noisy young crowd" fueling the "thriving bar scene."

Etoile (L') ◐ ☑ *Classic French*
▽ `24` `25` `23` `€59`

16ᵉ | 12, rue de Presbourg (Charles de Gaulle-Etoile) | 01 45 00 78 70 |
fax 01 45 00 78 71 | www.letoileparis.com

Though it's almost a decade old, the stars still come out to this
nightclub/restaurant with a "dramatic" view of the Arc de Triomphe
right outside the window; while it's a "great scene", the "excellent"
Classic French food is more than just an afterthought; swinging surveyors also rave about the "discotheque down below", equally "expensive", but highly "hip."

Etoile Marocaine (L') *Moroccan*
`-` `-` `-` `M`

8ᵉ | 56, rue Galilée (George V) | 01 47 20 44 43 | fax 01 47 23 53 75 |
www.etoilemarocaine.com

"It's not fancy and the service can be slow", but this place serves
some of "the most delicious and authentic Moroccan food in town";
intricately painted and glazed "tiled walls and small fountains" create "nice ambiance", and prices are "reasonable" for the pricey 8th.

Eugène ☑ *Eclectic*
`-` `-` `-` `M`

8ᵉ | 166, bd Haussmann (St-Philippe-du-Roule) | 01 42 89 00 13 |
fax 01 42 89 01 14

Just steps from the charming Musée Jacquemart-André lies this
"decent neighborhood bistro with Eclectic furnishings and menu";
the former features warm orange-and-brown furnishings with a big
picture window (designed by Gustave Eiffel) and long pewter bar,
while the latter features market-fresh fish and lamb; a 22.5€ prix
fixe makes it a particularly "nice place to have lunch."

Fables de La Fontaine (Les) *Seafood*
`24` `16` `21` `€54`

7ᵉ | 131, rue St-Dominique (Ecole Militaire) | 01 44 18 37 55

Chef Christian Constant nets a lot of praise for his "wonderful fish
restaurant" "overlooking a cute traffic-free" square in the 7th, where

the catch of the day on the "small chalkboard menu" is "fresh, simple and outstanding"; the service is "prompt and friendly" and prices are "reasonable" for such "transcendent seafood", so "the only thing it needs is more tables."

Fakhr el Dine ● *Lebanese*

▽ 24 | 20 | 18 | €49

16ᵉ | 30, rue de Longchamp (Trocadéro) | 01 47 27 90 00 | fax 01 53 70 01 81 | www.fakhreldine.com

"Less showy than others on the Right Bank", this elegant Lebanese offers "a range of interesting tagines" and other "excellent, abundant dishes"; the shawarma-warm milieu is "pleasant to linger in", but also good "for a quick lunch."

Famille (La) 🗷Ⓜ *New French*

19 | 15 | 17 | €49

18ᵉ | 41, rue des Trois-Frères (Abbesses/Anvers) | 01 42 52 11 12 | fax 01 42 52 11 12

This "convivial", loftlike space on a tiny cobbled street in Montmartre pulls a hip, younger crowd with an inventive New French menu that changes every 15 days; if fans find the food "delicious", foes feel it's "expensive for such small portions" – but then, "you always have to be patient with your family", *n'est-ce pas*?

Fellini *Italian*

21 | 14 | 17 | €51

1ᵉʳ | 47, rue de l'Arbre-Sec (Louvre-Rivoli) | 01 42 60 90 66
15ᵉ | 58, rue de la Croix-Nivert (Commerce/Emile Zola) | 01 45 77 40 77 | fax 01 45 77 22 54 🗷

Spearheaded by "good-humored", "personable service", a "warmly welcoming atmosphere" pervades this pair of pasta purveyors in the 1st (with "mellow stone walls" and a Sardinian slant) and 15th (with Neopolitan cuisine); patrons also are "pleased" by the "appetizing *plats*" and the "well-selected list of wines"; some say it seems "a little expensive" for spaghetti, but most shrug "that's the price you pay" for "a trip to Italy in the course of an evening."

Ferme (La) *Sandwiches*

- | - | - | I

1ᵉʳ | 55-57, rue St-Roch (Opéra/Pyramides) | 01 40 20 12 12 | fax 01 40 20 06 06

Now nearly a decade old, this rustic, wood-paneled *sandwicherie* was one of the first in the 1st to challenge the traditional city-center steak-frites lunch with predominantly organic, "good and healthy food, reasonably priced whether it's a salad, a yogurt or a cookie"; though it's self-service, the "help is nice", and while "handy for lunch on the run", it's also a "good place for breakfast."

Ferme St-Simon (La) 🗷 *Classic French*

23 | 22 | 23 | €62

7ᵉ | 6, rue de St-Simon (Rue du Bac/Solférino) | 01 45 48 35 74 | fax 01 40 49 07 31 | www.fermestsimon.com

The "charming", "cozy" decor of exposed beams and etched glass "makes for a pretty fancy" farm at this "old-world hangout"; it's a great "place to see how French politicians dine" – the Assemblée Nationale's nearby – as you enjoy the "luscious" "Classic French dishes served by classy pros"; and if whippersnappers whine it's "older-style dining", "lots of regulars" revel in the level of "luxury

and calm that hasn't faltered over the last 20 years" – even with a "new owner and chef since June 2007."

Fermette Marbeuf 1900   18 | 24 | 18 | €56
(La) ●⊠ *Classic French*
8ᵉ | 5, rue Marbeuf (Alma Marceau/Franklin D. Roosevelt) | 01 53 23 08 00 | fax 01 53 23 08 09 | www.fermettemarbeuf.com

"A jewel of art nouveau" declare decorators who "love the stained-glass ceiling" and "walls of mirrors and gold" at this Classic French just off the Champs-Elysées in the 8th; such "a shame", then, that the "food is good, but nothing special" and the servers swing from "disinterested" to "friendly"; of course, one option is to "ogle the place and leave."

Ferrandaise (La) ⊠ *Bistro*   21 | 16 | 21 | €50
6ᵉ | 8, rue de Vaugirard (Odéon/Cluny/Luxembourg RER) | 01 43 26 36 36 | www.laferrandaise.com

Just across from the Luxembourg Gardens, this "charming neighborhood bistro serves delicious hearty dishes, including Ferrandaise beef from the Auvergne"; some cavil there's "not much in the way of ambiance" – the decor's mostly "pictures of lovely cows lining the rustic walls" – but the "service is friendly and unhurried" and the prix fixe "a great buy."

Findi ● *Italian*   16 | 16 | 16 | €55
8ᵉ | 24, av George V (Alma Marceau/George V) | 01 47 20 14 78 | fax 01 47 20 10 08 | www.findi.net

"You'd think you were in a smart home" – provided home was an "à la mode" "Italian palazzo" – at this "upscale date place"; the food is almost as "smart", especially the "good, fresh homemade pastas", and "the waiters really try to please"; costs seem "reasonable, given the prestigious location" on the swank Avenue George V.

NEW Fines Gueules   - | - | - | M
(Les) ● *Wine Bar/Bistro*
1ᵉʳ | 43, rue Croix-des-Petits-Champs (Bourse/ Palais Royal-Musée du Louvre) | 01 42 61 35 41

Those intrepid few who have discovered this new "hip wine bar" just off the Place des Victoires in the 1st praise its "good selection" of vinos and its daily changing bistro menu that includes the best ingredients, including meat from star butcher Hugo Desnoyer; the stylish interior includes exposed-stone walls and a waxed cement floor.

Fins Gourmets (Aux) ⊠Ⓜ⇥ *Southwest*   19 | 16 | 16 | €53
7ᵉ | 213, bd St-Germain (Rue du Bac) | 01 42 22 06 57

Breathe "the atmosphere of eternal Paris" at "one of the last of the old bistros" in Saint-Germain, where "pleasant personnel" serve "carefully prepared" Southwestern specialties in a "typical, traditional" room; true, the setting seems "tired" at times, but "you eat well and you don't pay too much", so if it "hasn't changed" since 1959, many "hope it never does."

	FOOD	DECOR	SERVICE	COST

Finzi *Italian*

∇ 13 | 8 | 15 | €46

8ᵉ | 182, bd Haussmann (St-Philippe-du-Roule) | 01 45 62 88 68 | fax 01 45 61 41 05

"Always lively", this long-running "neighborhoodlike" Italian serves "refined cuisine" suited to this business-y part of the 8th; even so, a fallen Food score suggests many now find it pasta prime, saying "everything's going downhill here except the prices."

First (Le) *New French*

18 | 21 | 17 | €72

1ᵉʳ | Westin Hotel | 234, rue de Rivoli (Concorde) | 01 44 77 10 40 | fax 01 44 77 14 70 | www.lefirstrestaurant.com

With its low-lit, supper-club/"boudoir atmosphere", designer Jacques Garcia's decor for the Westin's New French is just the ticket "if you like cozy places where purple is the dominant color"; "but the food and service have a lot of catching up to do": the staff can be "a little bit stuffy" and the menu, while "sophisticated", is "not good value for money."

☒ Fish La Boissonnerie Ⓜ *Provence*

22 | 15 | 19 | €40

6ᵉ | 69, rue de Seine (Odéon) | 01 43 54 34 69

"In overpriced, touristy Saint-Germain", this "hectic but friendly" old *poissonerie* serves "remarkably good" food – dishes prepared with "a taste of Southern France", with "fish the obvious specialty", plus "exceptional wines supplied by co-owner Juan Sanchez, who has a shop around the corner"; at times service seems "overburdened and untrained", and as a virtual "home for the American expat", the room rings with "noisy", English-speaking voices

Flandrin (Le) ➊ *Brasserie*

15 | 14 | 14 | €62

16ᵉ | 80, av Henri Martin (Rue de la Pompe) | 01 45 04 34 69 | fax 01 45 04 67 41

"A golden girl/boy staple", "this old train station–turned-brasserie" is "the place to be seen in the posh" 16th, particularly the "sunny patio"; but "unless you want to show off your Ferrari" (the car-watching is as big as the people-watching here), many moan it's "not worth going", since it's "expensive for no real reason" – certainly not the "mediocre dishes" or the servers "only interested in the regulars."

Flora Danica *Classic French/Danish*

19 | 18 | 16 | €58

8ᵉ | 142, av des Champs-Elysées (Charles de Gaulle-Etoile/George V) | 01 44 13 86 26 | fax 01 44 13 89 44 | www.restaurantfloradanica.com

Amid "a neighborhood filled with tourist traps", this "ultimate Nordic experience in the heart of the Champs" is "the place to go if you want to eat salmon" or herring (plus some Classic French favorites); there's a "beautiful courtyard for summer dining", which many prefer to the "noisy", Danish "modern" dining room; prices are "reasonable" compared to Copenhague, its "expensive upstairs brother."

Flore en l'Ile (Le) ➊ *Classic French*

18 | 19 | 18 | €30

4ᵉ | 42, quai d'Orléans (Cité/Pont-Marie) | 01 43 29 88 27 | fax 01 43 29 73 54

Boasting a "strategic location on the tip of the Ile Saint-Louis", this busy "neighborhood place" has "great views" of Notre Dame to en-

	FOOD	DECOR	SERVICE	COST

hance its "consistent and appealing" Classic French meals, including "brunch, lunch, tea" and "late-night Berthillion" ice cream; if several find it "overpriced", most say "it's worth whatever they charge" for that "movie-set" setting, despite "impersonal" service.

Florimond (Le) ⚠ *Classic French* | 24 | 19 | 26 | €50 |

7ᵉ | 19, av de la Motte-Picquet (Ecole Militaire/La Tour-Maubourg) | 01 45 55 40 38 | fax 01 45 55 40 38

"What a find!" crows the crowd over this "delightful" Classic French where a staff that's "so kind and helpful" and "effortlessly attentive" delivers "delicious" dishes ("the incredible stuffed cabbage" is a real *chou*-in), supervised by the "warm, friendly owner"; the "small store-front space" may not be much, but who cares when the tab is "reasonable", given the "pricey neighborhood" near Les Invalides.

Fogón ●Ⓜ *Spanish* | 21 | 15 | 18 | €53 |

6ᵉ | 45, quai des Grands-Augustins (Odéon/St-Michel) | 01 43 54 31 33 | fax 01 43 54 07 00

"It's pricey for paella, but this is Paris' only Spanish restaurant worthy of the name" aver amigos of this Seine-side site in Saint-Germain ("dynamite location"); whether devouring "interesting, unique tapas" or items on the "super-inventive tasting menu", the "crowd is young and fun", which – along with "kind and *muy* professional" staffers – creates a "good atmosphere" amid the "original modern decor."

⚠ Fontaine de Mars (La) *Southwest* | 21 | 19 | 21 | €50 |

7ᵉ | 129, rue St-Dominique (Ecole Militaire) | 01 47 05 46 44 | fax 01 47 05 11 13

"The remodel in 2007 made room for more tables", and though cynics carp "they've doubled the room's size and lost half of its charm", most still "love this place" in "the shadow of the Eiffel Tower" because it's exactly what a "typical bistro should be": "charming owners" and staff, "huge checked" linens, moleskin banquettes and traditional, "memorable" Southwestern cuisine; even if it's getting "a little on the pricey side", it "never fails to make you happy"; P.S. weather permitting, "opt for a table outside near the fountain."

Fontaine Gaillon (La) ●⚠ *Classic French* | 22 | 22 | 20 | €75 |

2ᵉ | 1, pl Gaillon (Opéra/Quatre-Septembre) | 01 42 65 87 04 | fax 01 47 42 82 84 | www.la-fontaine-gaillon.com

Best-known for playing Cyrano, actor Gérard "Depardieu demonstrates his panache", providing "a visual and culinary delight" with this celebrity-studded Classic French in the 2nd; the "food can be delicious" – especially the "fresh fish" – and the "surroundings are beautifully appointed", particularly if you sit outside "next to the [namesake] fountain"; while "the staff appears a bit haughty at first, that goes away", making this "pleasant" place "worth the price."

Fontaines (Les) *Bistro* | 17 | 11 | 15 | €37 |

5ᵉ | 9, rue Soufflot (Cluny La Sorbonne/Luxembourg) | 01 43 26 42 80 | fax 01 43 54 44 57

"A lively choice by the Panthéon" ("the sidewalk tables offer great views"), "this bistro has all the typical" dishes in such "huge por-

tions" that one "serving is enough for a family"; the "decor's pretty pitiful", and the "staff is available, without much else", but overall, the place is "tasty, unpretentious" and relatively "cheap."

Fontanarosa *Italian*   - | - | - | E

15ᵉ | 28, bd Garibaldi (Cambronne/Ségur) | 01 45 66 97 84 |
fax 01 47 83 96 30 | www.fontanarosa-ristorante.eu

"Fantastic Sardinian food", "convivial service" (perhaps including a chat with English-speaking owner Flavio Mascia) and "an impressive wine list, including a fair bit of juice from Sardinia, keep 'em coming back" to this Italian with an "enjoyable patio" in the 15th; sole regret: it "has become really expensive."

Foujita *Japanese*   - | - | - | M

1ᵉʳ | 41, rue St-Roch (Pyramides) | 01 42 61 42 93 🗷
1ᵉʳ | 7, rue 29 Juillet (Tuileries) | 01 49 26 07 70 | fax 01 49 26 07 60
There are almost "no amenities" at this sushi-purveying pair in the 1st; but if you need a fix of "stark, fresh" fish, at "great quality for the price", they're "the best."

Fouquet's (Le) ●🗷 *Classic French*   18 | 21 | 17 | €67

8ᵉ | 99, av des Champs-Elysées (George V) | 01 47 23 60 50 |
fax 01 40 69 60 35 | www.lucienbarriere.com

"It's all about the view and the history" at this "Parisian landmark" on the Champs-Elysées, with its "tourist magnet" of a terrace without and a "charming boudoir atmosphere" (all "old-line red velvet") within; be prepared to spend *beaucoup d'* euros for what most call "distinctly average" Classic French fare, and be aware that "ego has crept into" the staff attitude; still, you too can "feel like someone famous here" – and that makes it "worth sampling, at least once."

Fous d'en Face (Les) ● *Bistro*   - | - | - | M

4ᵉ | 3, rue du Bourg-Tibourg (Hôtel-de-Ville) | 01 48 87 03 75 |
fax 01 42 78 38 03
Overlooking a pretty square near the Hôtel de Ville ("good for people-watching"), this traditional bistro offers "nicely prepared" "solid country French" food, including a "great" pot-au-feu; owner Philippe Llorca is a "gregarious guy who wants you to have a nice experience."

Frégate (La) 🗷 *Seafood*   ▽ 24 | 17 | 21 | €38

12ᵉ | 30, av Ledru Rollin (Gare de Lyon/Quai de la Rapée) | 01 43 43 90 32 |
fax 01 43 43 90 32
Located "right on the *quai*" in the 12th (its name means 'frigate'), this "elegant" seafooder is "an enchanted island" that's featured "fabulous food, full of intense flavors" in "a nice, quiet" setting for the last 30-odd years; "the clientele tends to be businesspeople and/or the middle-aged" who savor "service so attentive, you feel like a private guest."

Fumoir (Le) ● *Eclectic*   17 | 21 | 18 | €43

1ᵉʳ | 6, rue de l'Amiral de Coligny (Louvre-Rivoli) | 01 42 92 00 24 |
fax 01 42 92 05 05 | www.lefumoir.com
Since its main drawback – having to "endure the smoke" – is now history, there's nothing to impede one's enjoyment of this "ineffably

cool", "*très* NYC" "meet-for-a-drink spot" "facing the Louvre"; it's "always packed" with a "seriously hip" crowd soaking up "the warm ambiance of the library room", the "nice strong cocktails" and the "reliable" Eclectic fare (though, truthfully, "you'll be so busy checking out the people checking you out that you won't notice what you're eating").

Gallopin ● 🖟 🖾 *Brasserie* | 16 | 20 | 17 | €47 |

2ᵉ | 40, rue Notre-Dame-des-Victoires (Bourse/Grands Boulevards) | 01 42 36 45 38 | fax 01 42 36 10 32 | www.brasseriegallopin.com

"Big, busy and [blessed] with belle epoque decor" sums up this "classic brasserie" with an "inviting bar" behind the Bourse in the 2nd; "it's a pity that the cuisine isn't up to" the environs, and that the gallopin' waiters, "garbed in long aprons", tend to be "impersonal"; still, this veteran works as "a really reliable standby."

Gamin de Paris (Au) ● 🖾 *Southwest* | 21 | 18 | 16 | €34 |

4ᵉ | 51, rue Vieille-du-Temple (Hôtel-de-Ville/St-Paul) | 01 42 78 97 24

This "hidden gem in the Marais" sparkles with "lots of candles", a wood-burning fireplace and twinkling lights in the abundant foliage of the dining room; proffered by "relaxed servers", the "affordable" Southwestern menu features "delectable duck dishes", "old-style steak" and a "gooey to-die-for chocolate cake" that many melt for.

🆕 Garance *Bistro/New French* | – | – | – | M |

10ᵉ | 96, quai de Jemmapes (Jacques Bonsergent/République) | 01 42 02 87 95

Overlooking the Canal Saint-Martin in the ever-trendier 10th, this relaxed bistro has quickly become a favorite with hip, young locals for its modestly priced offbeat menu – think sea-bream tartare with Thai pesto, sesame-seed-covered tuna steak and spice-bread tiramisu with pears; a friendly atmosphere prevails in the dining room where dark furniture stands out against the exposed-stone walls.

Gare (La) ● *Classic French* | 14 | 21 | 15 | €46 |

16ᵉ | 19, Chaussée de la Muette (La Muette) | 01 42 15 15 31 | fax 01 42 15 15 23 | www.restaurantlagare.com

If you're one of the 16th's "golden youth" (entry "forbidden to those over 18" some jest) you go to this "chic" Classic French "for the setting" – "a great renovation of an old railway station", recently refreshed to include plasma TVs and mirrors – and "for the really pleasant terrace"; unchanged, though, are criticisms of the cooking – which ranges from "culinary disaster" to "very ordinary" – and the staff, which is a bit too "casual" for comfort.

Garnier ● *Brasserie* | 22 | 18 | 18 | €82 |

8ᵉ | 111, rue St-Lazare (St-Lazare) | 01 43 87 50 40 | fax 01 40 08 06 93

Things go swimmingly at this brasserie just across the street from the Gare Saint-Lazare, "an area with few good restaurants"; not only does it serve some of the "best seafood in Paris" – "there's shellfish, and then there's Garnier's shellfish" – it also offers a setting that somewhat "surrealistically" blends aquariums with Lalique lamps

and mirrors; however, dissidents deride the "disorganized" staff (confirmed by a Service score drop).

Gauloise (La) 🗷 *Bistro* ▽ 15 | 16 | 13 | €40

15ᵉ | 59, av de la Motte-Picquet (La Motte-Picquet-Grenelle) | 01 47 34 11 64 | fax 01 40 61 09 70

Those in search of some "reasonably priced class" find this traditional bistro in the 15th fills the bill with "jovial atmosphere" and "quite adequate cooking"; however, the circa-1900 "decor's aging" a bit, and the "service is "accommodating – for locals."

Gavroche (Le) ●🗷 *Bistro* 17 | 14 | 16 | €48

2ᵉ | 19, rue St-Marc (Bourse/Richelieu-Drouot) | 01 42 96 89 70

"Carnivores rejoice" to taste "*côte de boeuf* at its best" at this traditional bistro in the 2nd that's "worth a trip to see what Paris was really like before World War II"; despite the "atmosphere of camaraderie", however, some sigh it costs "such a lot of euros", given the "gritty" digs, "slow service" and general sense – supported by sliding scores – that it's "gone downhill of late."

Gaya 🗷 *Seafood* 23 | 16 | 19 | €79

7ᵉ | 44, rue du Bac (Rue du Bac) | 01 45 44 73 73 | fax 01 45 44 73 73 | www.pierre-gagnaire.com

"Even more chic" since baroque toque Pierre Gagnaire acquired it, this vintage Left Bank fish house is now a cutting-edge catch-of-the-day place; his "alchemic concoctions" (tandoori-style monkfish, red pepper iced parfait) are served in a Corian table and stainless-steel setting that strikes some as "almost as cold as the room that the fish is kept in"; "it was always excellent and pricey – since the takeover, it's excellent, pricey – and hard to get a reservation."

Gazzetta (La) 🗷Ⓜ *Mediterranean/New French* – | – | – | M

12ᵉ | 29, rue de Cotte (Ledru-Rollin) | 01 43 47 47 05 | fax 01 43 47 47 17 | www.lagazzetta.fr

The few who've recently discovered this relatively young venue in the 12th salute it as "the surprise of the year"; Swedish chef Petter Nilsson's (ex Troisgros, in the Rhône Valley) New French–Med menu changes daily, but runs to "excellent" unusual dishes, like lamb with pickled lemons and honey, or banana terrine; equally "remarkable" is the decor – featuring a crazy quilt tiled floor and framed antique posters – and the "impeccable welcome."

Ⓩ Georges ● *Eclectic* 18 | 25 | 15 | €62

4ᵉ | Centre Georges Pompidou | 19, rue Beaubourg (Hôtel-de-Ville/ Rambuteau) | 01 44 78 47 99 | fax 01 44 78 48 93

"God, what a scene" it is, as "beautiful people" (they "turn away the unfashionable") mix it up with "visiting housewives from Dallas" amid the "smashing" "space-age decor" of this "glamorous" Costes brothers venue on the roof of the Pompidou Center – "one of the most gorgeous views in Paris"; also offering an eyeful are the "snooty", "modellike waitresses in micro-minis" "carrying big heavy trays that weigh more than they do"; the Eclectic fare "is too

expensive for the quality", but who cares – "even a McDonald's up here would warrant a visit."

Georgette 🅂🅼 *Bistro* ▽ 22 | 13 | 21 | €40

9ᵉ | 29, rue Saint-Georges (Notre-Dame-de-Lorette) | 01 42 80 39 13

"Exactly the kind of place that makes eating out in Paris so charming" confide converts to this contemporary bistro in the 9th; the owner "is both delightful and delighted to explain" the New French menu of "simple" foods that "mix well with the homestyle service and dinerlike decor"; admittedly, the latter's "a bit '60s, with brightly colored Formica tables", but overall, this is "an entire pleasure."

🆉 Gérard Besson 🅂 *Classic French* 25 | 21 | 24 | €121

1ᵉʳ | 5, rue du Coq-Héron (Louvre-Rivoli/Palais Royal-Musée du Louvre) | 01 42 33 14 74 | fax 01 42 33 85 71 | www.gerardbesson.com

"Small, intimate and semi-formal", "much frequented" by foreigners, this carved-wood-and-velvet veteran in the 1st pleases with "retro" "food to be relished", especially by "those who like game in season", and with service that's "polite" "without being condescending"; "perhaps it's hurt a bit by not adhering to fashionisms, but if you want great Classic French fare, this is one of the best."

Gitane (La) 🅂 *Classic French* - | - | - | M

15ᵉ | 53 bis, av de la Motte-Picquet (La Motte-Picquet-Grenelle) | 01 47 34 62 92 | fax 01 40 65 94 01 | www.la-gitane.com

"This modest place is perfect for a dinner with friends after a day's hard labor" say habitués happy to set up camp with this gypsy (*gitane*) in the 15th; the "food's mainly traditional" French, served by an "easygoing staff" to a "varied clientele" that includes everyone from old ladies with their dogs to dating couples.

Giulio Rebellato *Italian* ▽ 20 | 14 | 20 | €59

16ᵉ | 136, rue de la Pompe (Victor Hugo) | 01 47 27 50 26

"In a *quartier* that's frequented by the chic clique" of the 16th, this "small", "low-key" Italian offers Venetian victuals that are "very good" but "very dear" as well; a "nice welcome" accompanies the "well-prepared" fare, though a few fear it's somewhat Frenchified.

Gli Angeli ●🅂 *Italian* 18 | 14 | 15 | €40

3ᵉ | 5, rue St-Gilles (Chemin-Vert/St-Paul) | 01 42 71 05 80

When the "Italians who live in Paris eat there", you know you have "a great place for pasta", and that's why "a reservation is a must" at this trattoria near the Place des Vosges; though "service can be a bit rude", the "authentic" "affordable" eats are absolutely angelic.

Gorille Blanc (Le) 🅂 *Bistro* ▽ 21 | 14 | 20 | €41

7ᵉ | 11 bis, rue Chomel (Sèvres-Babylone/St-Sulpice) | 01 45 49 04 54 | fax 01 45 49 04 54

"Just steps away from the bustle of the Bon Marché" store, this "cozy little box" of a bistro pulls a stylish crowd with "delightful" cuisine that swings from "creative" to "classic"; whether French or foreign, "guests are well served", and the pretty room is a perfect place to "relax after a long day of shopping in Saint-Germain."

	FOOD	DECOR	SERVICE	COST

Goumard ☒ Seafood
24 | 22 | 23 | €94

1ᵉʳ | 9, rue Duphot (Madeleine) | 01 42 60 36 07 | fax 01 42 60 04 54 | www.goumard.fr

At this "magic address" near the Madeleine, "terrific seafood" – from "flavorful, succulent oysters" to "excellent sea bass" – reels in compliments from surveyors, who also salute service that's "polite without being snooty" and the "maple-paneled dining room" with Lalique inserts that "makes you feel like you're on a '"30s oceanliner like La Normandie" (don't miss the "belle epoque toilets" either); "prices are nose-bleed", so unless "a rich uncle wants to treat you to dinner", check out the (relatively) "bargain lunch."

Gourmand (Au) ☒ Classic/New French
20 | 17 | 19 | €47

1ᵉʳ | 17, rue Molière (Palais Royal-Musée du Louvre/Pyramides) | 01 42 96 22 19 | fax 01 42 96 05 72 | www.augourmand.fr

"Moving from the 6th" to the 1st has caused a "great rebirth of this fine place"; the French "food is creative, yet nods to the past", with a produce-only prix fixe that's "ideal for vegetarians"; the "warm colors" of the trompe l'oeil theatrical decor and equally "warm, well-paced service" make reviewers vow "I will return."

Gourmets des Ternes (Les) ☒ Bistro
∇ 19 | 14 | 15 | €45

8ᵉ | 87, bd de Courcelles (Ternes) | 01 42 27 43 04

"Politically incorrect and unabashedly so", this "down-and-dirty meat-and-potatoes" bistro near the Place des Ternes is "cramped and loud – but hey, it's been like that for decades" shrug supporters who still line up for the "steak lover's dream" of a menu; a score rise confirms the service "standard is way up" ("the snootiness is just shtick"); even so, several say "you can do better elsewhere."

Graindorge Belgian/Northern France
22 | 18 | 19 | €55

17ᵉ | 15, rue de l'Arc-de-Triomphe (Charles de Gaulle-Etoile) | 01 47 54 00 28

"Notoriously great for beers", this north star near the Etoile also offers "fine Belgian and Northern French food", "original", "meticulously prepared" and presented by "immaculate servers" in "homey" digs.

Grand Café (Le) ● Brasserie
13 | 15 | 12 | €45

9ᵉ | 4, bd des Capucines (Opéra) | 01 43 12 19 00 | fax 01 43 12 19 09 | www.legrandcafe.com

"Right near the opera house" in the 9th, this "huge, classic" brasserie is "definitely a tourist-type place", with "very pretty" belle epoque decor and prices "too high for what they serve" ("le grand mediocre"); the service is rather variable ("professional when it's by one of the 'old guys', amateurish when not"), but at least they sling the "fresh shellfish" and other staples into the wee hours.

Grand Colbert (Le) ●☒ Brasserie
19 | 24 | 20 | €54

2ᵉ | 2, rue Vivienne (Bourse/Palais Royal-Musée du Louvre) | 01 42 86 87 88 | fax 01 42 86 82 65 | www.legrandcolbert.com

As a sample of the "glorious Belle Epoque", "the decor remains the draw" of this "boisterous" brasserie tucked away in the Passage

Vivienne – that, "and nostalgia for the scene from a Diane Keaton/Jack Nicholson movie shot here"; cynics sniff *Something's Got to Give* with the bland food" and attitude ("they're a little high on themselves after the film"), but fans find the "old standbys competently executed" and the staff "as warm and inviting as ever"; P.S. tip: "go late to avoid too many Americans."

Grande Armée (La) ● *Classic French*

15	15	15	€46

16ᵉ | 3, av de la Grande-Armée (Charles de Gaulle-Etoile) | 01 45 00 24 77 | fax 01 45 00 95 50

"Simple but chic" – think striped canvas walls in military-tent mode – this Classic French is "pleasant" "if you like Napoleonic memorabilia" and want to be part of a well-heeled younger crowd around the Arc de Triomphe; though foes assault it on gastronomic grounds ("nothing good, nothing bad"), fans battle back, citing the "varied menu"; at least the service sparks a ceasefire, since everyone likes the "efficient waiters."

Grand Louvre (Le) *Classic French*

18	18	15	€41

1ᵉʳ | Musée du Louvre | below the Pyramid (Palais Royal-Musée du Louvre) | 01 40 20 53 41 | fax 01 42 86 04 63

"A huge flower arrangement greets you at the entrance" to this Classic French with "a wonderful location on the courtyard of the Louvre" ("under the I.M. Pei glass pyramid") and "sleek and sophisticated" decor by Jean-Michel Wilmotte; ok, "so it's not great cuisine", but it's "not bad for a museum restaurant", either, "with varied choices"; besides, it's "a boon for tired feet" and is "perfect for a quick bite" "while the gargoyles stare down at you"; N.B. dinner Wednesday and Friday only.

NEW Grand Pan (Le) 🅢 *Bistro*

-	-	-	M

15ᵉ | 20, rue Rosenwald (Convention/Plaisance) | 01 42 50 02 50

In a quiet corner of the 15th, young chef-owner Benoît Gauthier's new, "excellent bistro" is a great destination for anyone who wants to sample Gallic grill skills, since the short and simple chalkboard menu offers up various *viandes* (pork, beef, etc.), served with homemade frites and a green salad; the small space gets noisy with a diverse crowd that appreciates the huge, shareable portions and good wines by the carafe.

☑ Grand Véfour (Le) 🅢 *Haute Cuisine*

28	29	28	€157

1ᵉʳ | Palais Royal | 17, rue de Beaujolais (Palais Royal-Musée du Louvre) | 01 42 96 56 27 | fax 01 42 86 80 71 | www.grand-vefour.com

Chef Guy Martin's "exquisite" Haute Cuisine offers "a glorious feast for the senses in the midst of old-world luxury" at this "mythic address" in the 1st; "dripping with atmosphere", the "exceptional setting", a gilded box of a room with a painted ceiling and brass plaques engraved with the names of its celebrated clientele (Colette, Maria Callas), is animated by a staff that's "professional, courteous and welcoming"; true, this "royal treatment needs a royal treasury" when the bill comes – but "it meets each and every expectation."

Grand Venise (Le) 🅐🅜 *Italian*

∇ 25 | 20 | 23 | €88

15ᵉ | 171, rue de la Convention (Convention) | 01 45 32 49 71 | fax 01 45 32 07 49

Tucked way in the 15th, "one of the very best Italian restaurants in Paris" offers up a "warm welcome", "spectacular flower arrangements" and leisurely served *cucina* with "superb flavors from a loving mama"; however, you may want to "fast for a week before" going, since portions are "gigantic" and it's "expensive."

Grange Batelière (La) 🅐 *Classic French*

- | - | - | E

9ᵉ | 16, rue de la Grange Batelière (Richelieu-Drouot) | 01 47 70 85 15 | fax 01 47 70 85 15

Though little-known, this "pleasant" traditional bistro in the 9th charms with its Second Empire decor; owned by comedienne Mimie Mathy and her chef-husband Gérard Benoist, it gets animated with auctioneers from Drouot nearby, as well as fans of Mimie's; happily, the elegant Classic French cuisine compensates for the crowds, if not the sturdy prices; N.B. open for dinner two Wednesdays a month only.

Grille (La) 🅐 *Bistro*

17 | 14 | 15 | €40

10ᵉ | 80, rue du Faubourg Poissonnière (Poissonnière) | 01 47 70 89 73

"The grilled turbot for two is so fresh it jumps off your plate", and it's made the reputation of this "small, authentic" "old-fashioned neighborhood bistro" in the 10th; co-owner "Madame Geneviève's hospitality is worth the trip", which also offers a chance to eyeball the "eccentric" decor of lace, dolls and gewgaws that decorate the room.

Grille St-Germain (La) ● *Bistro*

∇ 17 | 17 | 17 | €44

6ᵉ | 14, rue Mabillon (Mabillon) | 01 43 54 16 87 | fax 01 43 54 52 88

With "Bordeaux-colored velvet curtains at the door and beautiful [black-and-white] celebrity photos on the wall", "a pleasant atmosphere" prevails at this "comfy neighborhood joint" in Saint-Germain; the "solid bistro food" makes most happy, since "the kitchen works with good quality produce", and if "service can be a little slow", few mind when "it's such a good buy for the money."

Guinguette de Neuilly (La) *Classic French*

- | - | - | M

Neuilly-sur-Seine | 12, bd Georges Seurat (Pont-de-Levallois) | 01 46 24 25 04 | fax 01 47 38 20 49 | www.laguinguette.net

This "old-fashioned *guinguette*" on the Ile de la Jatte is a "pleasant" place to paddle down memory lane, since it serves up the same relaxed, blowsy atmosphere that made these waterside cafes/dance halls so popular with Parisians a century ago; "you could say it's living off its reputation and Seine-side setting", but many find the Classic French fare "reliable" and even "agreeable in summer"; the servers, however, seem ready for "a career change."

Guirlande de Julie (La) *Classic French*

15 | 16 | 15 | €46

3ᵉ | 25, pl des Vosges (Bastille/St-Paul) | 01 48 87 94 07 | fax 01 48 87 01 22 | www.latourdargent.com

Armed with "an elegant location under the arches of the Place des Vosges", this Classic French comes trailing "garlands of taste, sophis-

tication and cachet" (it's owned by La Tour d'Argent's Terrail family); if the fare is "just so-so", at least the "sympathetic" servers create a "convivial" atmosphere in the rosy-toned dining room – as does the good wine list, composed by the sommelier from the mother ship.

☑ Guy Savoy,

28	25	27	€179

Restaurant 🅱 Ⓜ *Haute Cuisine*

17ᵉ | 18, rue Troyon (Etoile) | 01 43 80 40 61 | fax 01 46 22 43 09 | www.guysavoy.com

Clearly, his "ventures in Las Vegas haven't distracted" chef-owner Guy Savoy – his "modern", "elegantly understated" Rue Troyon flagship remains "consistently superior in every way"; the "innovative" cooking "brings Haute Cuisine as close to art as it can come", the "formal but friendly" service hits a "high watermark" ("the staff all but spoon-fed us") "and – unusual for a big-name chef – M. Savoy often is actually at the restaurant"; yes, they charge "ridiculous prices", but since "you can't take it with you, leave some of it here."

Hangar (Le) ◗ 🅱 Ⓜ⇄ *Classic French*

18	12	15	€46

3ᵉ | 12, impasse Berthaud (Rambuteau) | 01 42 74 55 44

There's "hardly any decor" at this "pleasantly casual" "little bistro" around the corner from the Pompidou, but "the atmosphere's cozy" and the Classic French food "delicious" (especially "the magnificent seared foie gras"), if "not always original"; "they don't take credit cards – pretty annoying", but it keeps the prices "reasonable."

☑ Hélène

25	22	22	€122

Darroze 🅱 Ⓜ *New French/Southwest*

6ᵉ | 4, rue d'Assas (Rennes/Sèvres-Babylone) | 01 42 22 00 11 | fax 01 42 22 25 40 | www.helenedarroze.com

"La belle Hélène" is one of "the best female chefs in France", and her "innovative" New French–Southwestern creations, served in a "striking" room with parquet floors and plum accents in the 6th, are "exquisite"; but even *amis* admit they're "priced way above what they should be", especially given that they only arrive "after an interminable wait" despite the "cordial" staff; one tip: "eat in the ground-floor tapas bar – it's the same cooking, small-plates–style, at lower prices"; P.S. "the Armagnacs are worth the splurge."

Hier & Aujourd'hui 🅱 *New French*

-	-	-	M

17ᵉ | 145, rue de Saussure (Perreire) | 01 42 27 35 55 | fax 01 47 64 30 85 | resto.hieraujourdhui.free.fr

"Good food, friendly people" and an "excellent value/quality ratio" make it "worth going" to this gray-toned bistro, "a bit lost at the top of the 17th"; the few who've found it deem it "a welcome addition" to their culinary list, since the daily changing New French fare comes courtesy of a chef who cooked with Guy Savoy; warm service from wife/co-owner/fellow Savoy alum Karin is part of the bargain too.

Higuma *Japanese*

15	5	11	€19

1ᵉʳ | 163, rue St-Honoré (Palais Royal-Musée du Louvre) | 01 58 62 49 22 | fax 01 58 62 49 27

(continued)

(continued)

Higuma

1ᵉʳ | 32 bis, rue Ste-Anne (Pyramides) | 01 47 03 38 59 ⊠

Providing a "perfect" gyoza/noodle fix, these Asian "canteens" offer "huge, delicious" plates of "authentic" fare (as borne out by "their popularity with the Paris Japanese community"); neither looks great (though the newer one "near the Palais-Royal has nicer decor than its Rue Sainte-Anne cousin"), but at least you're "served immediately."

Hippopotamus ● *Steak*   11 | 11 | 12 | €28

1ᵉʳ | 29, rue Berger (Les Halles) | 01 45 08 00 29
2ᵉ | 1, bd des Capucines (Opéra) | 01 47 42 75 70 | fax 01 42 65 23 08
4ᵉ | 1, bd Beaumarchais (Bastille) | 01 44 61 90 40 | fax 01 44 61 90 46
5ᵉ | 9, rue Lagrange (Maubert-Mutualité) | 01 43 54 13 99
6ᵉ | 119, bd du Montparnasse (Vavin) | 01 43 20 37 04 | fax 01 43 22 68 95
8ᵉ | 20, rue Quentin-Bauchart (George V) | 01 47 20 30 14 | fax 01 47 20 95 31
10ᵉ | 8, bd St-Denis (Strasbourg-St-Denis) | 01 53 38 80 28 | fax 01 53 38 80 26
NEW **12ᵉ** | 145 bis, av Daumesnil (Daumesnil) | 01 53 02 40 40
14ᵉ | 68, bd du Montparnasse (Montparnasse-Bienvenüe) | 01 43 20 37 04 | fax 01 43 21 46 10
14ᵉ | 80, av du Général Leclerc (Alésia) | 01 53 90 31 20 | fax 01 53 90 31 24
15ᵉ | 12, av du Maine (Duroc/Montparnasse-Bienvenüe) | 01 42 22 36 75
www.hippopotamus.fr
Additional locations throughout Paris

"Curiously, the quality and the service vary from one restaurant to another" at this "factory chain" – sort of a "TGI Fridays of France" – "catering to conventioneers, students and tourists" with steak "filets and frites"; but overall, the bar's pretty low ("who says you can't get a bad meal in Paris?") – even though parents proclaim "if you're traveling with kids, the place will save your sanity."

Ⓩ Hiramatsu ⊠ *Haute Cuisine/New French*   26 | 25 | 26 | €122

16ᵉ | 52, rue de Longchamp (Boissière/Trocadéro) | 01 56 81 08 80 | fax 01 56 81 08 81 | www.hiramatsu.co.jp

The "meticulous attention to detail, immaculate presentation, and delicate sauces and flavors" offer a "spectacular experience" at this Haute Cuisine destination owned by chef Hiroyuki Hirmatsu in the 16th; though it's "becoming more Frenchified", the "inventive" fare still offers "an uncanny union of Gallic complexity and Japanese elegance", while waiters who are "responsive, helpful and elegant without being stuffy" warm the slightly "cold", if "refined", dining room; most are "just waiting to go back", even though it's "sooo expensive."

Hôtel Amour ● *New French*   ▽ 8 | 18 | 9 | €46

9ᵉ | Hôtel Amour | 8, rue Navarin (St-Georges) | 01 48 78 31 80 | fax 01 48 74 14 09 | www.hotelamour.com

Co-owned by a sprig of the Costes brothers tree, this eclectically decorated restaurant/lounge in the "very hip" Hôtel Amour has "good music" and a "nice" garden patio; but there's not much *amour* for the New French fare ("nothing great on your plate") or the "dis-

appointing service", both of which, says one reviewer, "reminds me of my college days (the prices less so)."

Huîtrerie Régis ●Ⓜ Shellfish ▽ 22 | 14 | 19 | €43

6ᵉ | 3, rue de Montfaucon (Mabillon) | 01 44 41 10 07

"World-class oysters", along with a "wonderful owner", make this Saint-German raw bar a pearl of a place for bivalve lovers; "it's a little cramped for space", but "everyone eating here knows exactly what they're here for and they're rarely disappointed"; P.S. "go early or be willing to wait."

Huîtrier (L') Ⓜ Seafood 20 | 12 | 15 | €47

17ᵉ | 16, rue Saussier-Leroy (Ternes) | 01 40 54 83 44 | fax 01 40 54 83 86

The crustaceans may "cost their weight in gold" and some find the vintage '70s decor "dubious", but this maritime-themed seafooder in the 17th "offers a great selection" of shellfish, plus a few cooked dishes ("great deep-fried calamari"); "everything's so amazingly fresh", and the "really nice" crew assures smooth sailing too.

I Golosi Ⓩ Italian 17 | 11 | 17 | €48

9ᵉ | 6, rue de la Grange-Batelière (Grands Boulevards/Richelieu-Drouot) | 01 48 24 18 63 | www.igolosi.com

Though the Food score's dipped recently, this "convivial" spot with a "convenient location" in the 9th remains a "preferred place" for its "original dishes from different Italian regions" on a "menu that changes constantly"; "the tabs can get a little hefty" and the "decor's a bit basic", but for most "this is a secret address to guard jealously."

Il Barone ●Ⓩ Italian ▽ 21 | 11 | 18 | €38

14ᵉ | 5, rue Léopold Robert (Raspail/Vavin) | 01 43 20 87 14 | fax 01 43 20 87 14

"Finding a good Italian restaurant in Paris can be difficult", but this "real trattoria" in Montparnasse offers a "charming experience", starring "truly homemade pasta", robustly flavored and served by a staff that's as "friendly as an Italian crew usually is"; "don't sweat the lack of decor", but do "try to avoid the hallwaylike front room" (strictly for tourists).

Il Cortile Ⓩ Italian 23 | 20 | 20 | €76

1ᵉʳ | Hôtel Castille Paris | 37, rue Cambon (Concorde/Madeleine) | 01 44 58 45 67 | fax 01 44 58 44 00

Chef Vittorio Beltramelli, a lieutenant of renowned Milanese toque Gualtiero Marchesi, mans this hotel dining room in the 1st, and fans applaud his "well-proportioned, delectable" dishes, an "inventive" version of Lombardian cuisine; in summer, "try for the outside courtyard and view the lovely fountain" – it'll distract from the "spotty service", which swings from "sublime" to "exasperatingly slow."

Ile (L') ● Classic/New French 18 | 21 | 15 | €51

Issy-les-Moulineaux | Parc de l'Ile St-Germain | 170, quai de Stalingrad (RER Issy-Val de Seine) | 01 41 09 99 99 | www.restaurant-lile.com

Prices are "high, but justified" by the "leafy", "exceptionally agreeable" waterside setting on the Ile Saint-Germain that's won this

"stylish site" a loyal following, despite the "undistinguished", if "decent" Classic–New French cuisine; one tip is to "go early – afterwards, it's a factory" with correspondingly "industrialized service."

Il Etait une Oie dans le Sud-Ouest 🗷Ⓜ Southwest

			M
-	-	-	

17ᵉ | 8, rue Gustave Flaubert (Courcelles/Ternes) | 01 43 80 18 30 | fax 01 43 80 99 50

"Foie gras heaven" awaits at this plum-toned Southwestern French in the 17th, where delights like duck, puréed potatoes and the aforementioned liver may amount to "heart attack on a stick, but worth the near-death experience"; you'd have to be quackers to pass this place up, especially given the reasonable prices.

Ilot Vache (L') ◑ Classic French

18	18	16	€48

4ᵉ | 35, rue St-Louis-en-l'Ile (Pont-Marie) | 01 46 33 55 16

"With a kitschy cow theme, this little spot on the Ile Saint-Louis" is "recommended" for Classic French cuisine ("the chocolate mousse is moo-licious"); some malcontents mutter that, "under new management", the food's fallen to "mediocre" levels, but most feel it remains "ideal for tourists wishing to discover traditional *gastronomie française*" (and indeed, "there will be Americans at every meal").

Il Viccolo 🗷 Italian

			E
-	-	-	

6ᵉ | 34, rue Mazarine (Odéon) | 01 43 25 01 11

A chic crowd of pasta lovers, including the occasional well-known face, camps out at this "genuinely Italian" spot in Saint-Germain; the "food is good, if not high-end", the "service almost shockingly friendly" and, with a glassed-in sidewalk space, it "feels cozy, despite its modern-leaning decor"; however, "prices are a bit high" for what's essentially a "neighborhood place."

🆕 Il Vino ◑ Classic French/Mediterranean

			VE
-	-	-	

7ᵉ | 13, bd de la Tour-Maubourg (Invalides/La Tour-Maubourg) | 01 44 11 72 00 | www.ilvinobyenricobernardo.com

An award-winning former sommelier at Le Cinq, Italian-born Enrico Bernardo has opened this unique new eatery near Les Invalides that exalts the art of wine pairings; once guests have chosen their preferred pour, he and chef David Barilone decide which dishes from the Classic French–Med best accompany it (tasting menus are the way to go, both for variety and affordability); already a crowd of politicians, editors and oenophiles is packing the sleek dining room with cobalt-blue carpet and modern art on the walls, in search of the benefits of Bacchus.

Inagiku 🗷 Japanese

18	14	12	€45

5ᵉ | 14, rue de Pontoise (Maubert-Mutualité) | 01 43 54 70 07 | fax 01 40 51 74 44

"Chefs who cook meat, fish and vegetables on a teppanyaki table" "before your eyes" is the "original" – for Paris, anyway – concept of this Latin Quarter Japanese; however, surveyors split over the service ("polite, but they don't talk much") and decor ("very Zen"),

adding that, aside from "the Benihana-style show", it's "expensive for what you get."

Indiana Café ◐ *Tex-Mex* | 7 | 8 | 8 | €26 |

3ᵉ | 1, pl de la République (République) | 01 48 87 82 35 | fax 01 48 87 82 35

6ᵉ | 130, bd St-Germain (Odéon) | 01 46 34 66 31 | fax 01 46 34 66 31

8ᵉ | 235-237, rue du Faubourg St-Honoré (Ternes) | 01 44 09 80 00 | fax 01 44 09 80 00

9ᵉ | 79, bd de Clichy (Place de Clichy) | 01 48 74 42 61 | fax 01 48 74 42 61

NEW 10ᵉ | 42 bis, bd de Bonne Nouvelle (Bonne Nouvelle) | 01 45 23 01 77 | fax 01 45 23 00 04

11ᵉ | 14, pl de la Bastille (Bastille) | 01 44 75 79 80 | fax 01 44 75 79 80

14ᵉ | 1, av du Général Leclerc (Denfert-Rochereau) | 01 40 47 60 41 | fax 01 40 47 57 65

14ᵉ | 72, bd du Montparnasse (Montparnasse-Bienvenüe) | 01 43 35 36 28 | fax 01 43 35 07 25

14ᵉ | 77, av du Maine (Gaîté) | 01 43 22 50 46 | fax 01 40 47 09 22 www.indiana-cafe.fr

"So touristy you'd think you actually were in Indiana", this "noisy" "mass-market version of a French idea of a Western-themed restaurant" serves a "tired attempt at Tex-Mex" food (if the "forgetful waitresses" remember how, that is); it'll do "when you're craving a greasy burger and beer" perhaps – "the happy-hour prices are a good deal" – otherwise, leave it "for your concierge's kids."

Indra ⊠ *Indian* | - | - | - | M |

8ᵉ | 10, rue du Commandant Rivière (St-Philippe-du-Roule) | 01 43 59 46 40 | fax 01 42 25 70 32 | www.restaurant-indra.com

One of the oldest subcontinental eateries in Paris (established 1976) occupies a primo spot just off the Champs; it serves all the classics – tandoori meats, naan, kulfi – in a traditional, warm-hued setting; but heat-seekers say "the spices they use don't seem as interesting", advising "if it's good Indian food you're after, take the Chunnel train to London."

Isami ⊠Ⓜ *Japanese* | 25 | 14 | 16 | €62 |

4ᵉ | 4, quai d'Orléans (Pont-Marie) | 01 40 46 06 97

"The best sushi in Paris" is the draw at this small (some say "cramped"), "simple" Japanese "with a nice Seine view" of the Ile Saint-Louis; if a few things seem fishy – the "haughty service" and "extremely expensive" tabs – the "good selection of cold sakes" erases any unease; but "come only if you're a serious sushi aficionado, because there's almost nothing else on the menu."

Issé ⊠ *Japanese* | ▽ 23 | 16 | 22 | €42 |

1ᵉʳ | 45, rue de Richelieu (Palais Royal-Musée du Louvre/Pyramides) | 01 42 96 26 60

From "old favorites" ("possibly the best tempura ever") to "inventive ice creams", the small-plates menu offers "a delectable journey

through Japanese cuisine" at this "unusual" Asian in the 1st; "the minimalist Zen decor may leave something to be desired for some, but others will like its clean lines."

☑ Jacques Cagna ⓩ *Haute Cuisine*

FOOD	DECOR	SERVICE	COST
26	23	25	€107

6ᵉ | 14, rue des Grands-Augustins (Odéon/St-Michel) | 01 43 26 49 39 | fax 01 43 54 54 48 | www.jacques-cagna.com

"Civilized, old-world charm and delicious", classic "Haute Cuisine par excellence" – no wonder "it's like stepping back in time" to visit this "elegant" Saint-Germain stalwart adorned with 17th-century artwork and jacket-clad customers; yes, it's "a bit too expensive", the staff's "a tad snooty" and sentimentalists sob "it's not what it was", but chef-owner Cagna and his sister "put you at ease", visiting each table, and overall, "if you want to pamper yourself, this is the place."

Jardin des Cygnes *Classic French*

FOOD	DECOR	SERVICE	COST
22	23	21	€81

8ᵉ | Hôtel Prince de Galles | 33, av George V (George V) | 01 53 23 78 50 | www.luxurycollection.com

"A classic in a tranquil setting" – a courtyard overlooking a "delightful garden" in the 8th – this hotel restaurant is "perfect for that romantic date"; while "the food simply doesn't match" the ambiance, it's still "very good traditional French cuisine" and supplied by a "gracious staff"; prices are somewhat "pretentious", however.

Jardinier (Le) ⓩ *Bistro*

FOOD	DECOR	SERVICE	COST
-	-	-	M

9ᵉ | 5, rue Richer (Bonne Nouvelle) | 01 48 24 79 79 | fax 01 47 70 95 79

With pretty Napoleon III decor that includes cast-iron columns, an elaborate chandelier and lavish moldings, this relaxed bistro not far from the Folies Bergère is "a fun place" where young chef-owner Stéphane Furnaz serves up "well-priced creative cuisine" with lots of lovely legumes; Furnaz's friendly wife runs the dining room.

Jardins de Bagatelle (Les) *Classic French*

FOOD	DECOR	SERVICE	COST
17	18	15	€56

16ᵉ | Parc de Bagatelle | Route de Sèvres (Pont-de-Neuilly) | 01 40 67 98 29 | fax 01 40 67 93 04

"Wander the rose gardens and then have a leisurely lunch [or dinner] under the trees" – "in spring and summer, this is one of the most romantic places in Paris" say believers in this Bois de Boulogne site; given the "wonderful venue", it's understandable the Classic French "food and service are disappointing" in comparison, but you'll hear few complaints from the cosmopolitan "clientele craving greenery"; better "bring your bank book", though.

Jarrasse, l'Ecailler de Paris *Seafood*

FOOD	DECOR	SERVICE	COST
-	-	-	E

Neuilly-sur-Seine | 4, av de Madrid (Pont-de-Neuilly) | 01 46 24 07 56 | fax 01 40 88 35 60 | www.michelrostang.com

Since chef-restaurateur Michel Rostang took it under his wing two years ago, this Neuilly veteran has become an "excellent suburban seafooder", with "nice service" and offbeat decor (Japanese-style cloth lanterns and velvet banquettes) that's "fair enough"; it's "a little expensive" – but then, so is Neuilly.

	FOOD	DECOR	SERVICE	COST

Jean 🅢 New French
19 | 16 | 19 | €56

9ᵉ | 8, rue St-Lazare (Notre-Dame-de-Lorette) | 01 48 78 62 73 |
fax 01 48 78 66 04 | www.restaurantjean.fr

Surveyors split when they come to this "ambitious" New French in the
"not-too-glamorous 9th" ("pay attention so you can find your way
back to the métro"); if dissenters are "disappointed that two Taillevent
alumni couldn't come up with better food", friends find it "truly
fine", and the "prices modest", given the "memorable" experience.

Jean-Paul Hévin 🅢 Dessert/Tearoom
24 | 15 | 16 | €26

1ᵉʳ | 231, rue St-Honoré (Madeleine/Tuileries) | 01 55 35 35 96 |
fax 01 55 35 35 97 | www.jphevin.com

Upstairs from "*chocolatier extraordinaire*" Jean-Paul Hévin's shop in
the 1st is this "lovely tearoom", aka "hot chocolate heaven"; it's
"enough to make you rethink any diet", since "you'll want to have all
of the desserts", maybe preceded by a "quick [bite of] traditional
French fare"; there's some grousing about "inconsistent service" and
"faded decor", but for most this is "perfect for a pick-me-up after a
morning of shopping" – and, of course, "a must for any chocoholic."

Je Thé . . . Me 🅢 Ⓜ Classic French
- | - | - | M

15ᵉ | 4, rue d'Alleray (Convention/Vaugirard) | 01 48 42 48 30 |
fax 01 48 42 70 66 | www.jetheme.net

"Probably one of the quaintest restaurants in Paris", this "cozy" (ok,
maybe "a little cramped") venue attracts 15th-arrondissement locals
with its landmarked locale in a "quirky" old grocery store full of mirrors, earthenware jugs and bric-a-brac; the "charming" chef-owner
provides "true Classic French fare" that's "well up to standard – but
it's the overall ambiance that's so good" here.

J'Go ● Southwest
▽ 14 | 14 | 13 | €43

NEW 6ᵉ | 3, rue Clément (Mabillon) | 01 43 26 19 02
9ᵉ | 4, rue Drouot (Richelieu-Drouot) | 01 40 22 09 09 |
fax 01 40 22 07 15 🅢
www.lejgo.com

"The atmosphere is all rugby and *corrida* (bull fights)", the twin pas-
sions of the French Southwest, at this Toulouse-based "temple to lamb
and pork" in the 9th (with a newborn calf in the 6th); even if the service
can be "middling", "it's perfect for business at noon, and buddies at
night", especially as it's pretty reasonably priced – "but be careful, because the native Southwestern products" can cause the bill to charge.

Joe Allen ● American
13 | 13 | 16 | €40

1ᵉʳ | 30, rue Pierre Lescot (Etienne Marcel) | 01 42 36 70 13 |
fax 01 42 36 90 80 | www.joeallenparis.com

With "a somber red-brick interior lined with classic [star's] Hollywood
photos", it "feels like NYC's theater district" at this "casual" Les
Halles veteran, a virtual "American pied-à-terre in Paris" in terms of
clientele and cuisine; it's "best to stick with the basic burgers" and
brunches, ignoring the servers who often seem to be "having a bad
day"; critics claim the whole place "needs to be refreshed, but why
change a formula that's worked for so long?"

	FOOD	DECOR	SERVICE	COST

Joséphine "Chez Dumonet" 🅈 *Bistro* — 23 | 16 | 19 | €63

6ᵉ | 117, rue du Cherche-Midi (Duroc/Falguière) | 01 45 48 52 40 |
fax 01 42 84 06 83

"Like walking into a period-set piece" – full of beveled glass dividers
and brass gas jets that are "truly old Paris" – this veteran in the 6th
offers "great preparations of bistro classics", from "excellent confit de
canard to Grand Marnier soufflé", with the welcome innovation of
"huge" half portions for many dishes; supporters don't even mind that
"prices have skyrocketed", because there's "not many of these left."

🆉 Jules Verne (Le) *Classic French* — - | 26 | 24 | €117

7ᵉ | Tour Eiffel | Champ-de-Mars, 2nd level (Bir-Hakeim) | 01 45 55 61 44 |
fax 01 47 05 29 41 | www.toureiffel.fr

Globe-trotting gastronaut "Alain Ducasse had taken over, but hadn't
yet put his stamp on the place" when our Survey closed, but early re-
ports on Paris' favorite room-with-a-view – reached by private ele-
vator to the Eiffel Tower's second level – indicate that designer
Patrick Jouin has given the perched space a "futuristic, yet swank",
low-lit look of caramel, camel and black, while chef Pascal Féraud
helms a modernized Classic French menu, served by a staff that's
"attentive", "without being condescending (even when my husband
mistook the sommelier for the waiter)"; yet, some suspect all will
"still be overshadowed by that view" – it's "like floating on a cloud,
watching the city unfold in front of you."

Juvéniles 🅈 *Wine Bar/Bistro* — 16 | 13 | 19 | €35

1ᵉʳ | 47, rue de Richelieu (Bourse/Palais Royal-Musée du Louvre) |
01 42 97 46 49 | fax 01 42 60 31 52

"The food is fine, and the wine's divine" at this "scruffy but atmospheric" *bar à vins* in the 1st, where there are just enough
Eclectic eats to provide ballast for the "beautiful selection of bottles
from all over the world"; all unfolds under the "watchful eye of the
owner", a "quick-quipping" Scot, who supplies samples for all
you "sherry aficionados."

Kai 🅜 *Japanese* — - | - | - | E

1ᵉʳ | 18, rue du Louvre (Louvre-Rivoli) | 01 40 15 01 99

"Expensive and classy, this Japanese place" not far from the
Louvre remains rather confidential, but those in-the-know say it offers "great food": "from the presentation to the textures, every dish
is a little surprise, and the Pierre Hermé desserts are to die for";
the "accommodating service" caters to the "fashion crowd" within
the "small space."

Kaïten ◑🅈 *Japanese* — - | - | - | E

8ᵉ | 63, rue Pierre Charron (Franklin D. Roosevelt) | 01 43 59 78 78 |
fax 01 43 59 71 51

Some of "the best sushi we've had in Paris" is on hand at this counter-
top just off the Champs-Elysées; true, prices veer toward the "expensive", but it's "useful for noonday" lunch, the "staff is quick and
efficient", and there's "the all-important conveyor belt to keep
the kids amused."

Kambodgia ⊠ SE Asian

16ᵉ | 15, rue de Bassano (Charles de Gaulle-Etoile/George V) | 01 47 23 31 80 | fax 01 47 20 41 22 | www.kambodgia.com

"Reminiscent of an opium den" in its vaguely louche, "dark" decor, this "beautiful" basement in the 16th offers a chance to sample some of "Southeast Asia's best" cuisines, mainly Cambodian and Vietnamese; some find the prices for the "highbrow" cooking higher than usual, but most just enjoy the "romantic venue."

NEW Karl et Erich ⊠ New French

17ᵉ | 20, rue de Tocqueville (Villiers) | 01 42 27 03 71 | fax 01 42 27 03 71

The twin brothers – one in the kitchen, the other in the dining room – who ran the late Les Jumeaux have crossed town to the 17th and set up shop in a sleek, very contemporary loftlike space; not many surveyors have made the move with them, but the few who have laud the "inventive" New French fare.

Khun Akorn Ⓜ Thai

11ᵉ | 8, av de Taillebourg (Nation) | 01 43 56 20 03 | fax 01 40 09 18 44

"On the edge of the 11th, Bangkok opens its arms to you" at this "authentic" Thai with "pretty", "exotic decor" (regulars "try for the rooftop terrace in summer"); but even those who deem the cuisine "delicious" for its "truly spicy" flavors castigate the servers, who seem so "indifferent" "that we laughed out loud in disbelief."

Kifune ⊠ Japanese

17ᵉ | 44, rue St-Ferdinand (Porte Maillot) | 01 45 72 11 19

"Tops in tuna", this Japanese in the 17th remains the hidden favorite of fin fans in search of authenticity and "exquisite raw fish"; service can be a bit brusque, and it's not cheap, but you put up with these shortcomings when you've got "one of the capital's best sushi bars."

Kim Anh Ⓜ Vietnamese

15ᵉ | 51, av Emile Zola (Charles Michels) | 01 45 79 40 96 | fax 01 40 59 49 78

Its "menu doesn't change", but since the "nice owners" serve "some of the best Vietnamese cuisine in the city, year in and year out", positives "have no problem" with the "refined food" at this 15th-arrondissement "Zen setting for a romantic date"; "however, it is more expensive than expected."

Kinugawa ⊠ Japanese

1ᵉʳ | 9, rue du Mont-Thabor (Tuileries) | 01 42 60 65 07 | fax 01 42 60 57 36
8ᵉ | 4, rue St-Philippe-du-Roule (St-Philippe-du-Roule) | 01 45 63 08 07

NEW Hanawa ⊠ Japanese

8ᵉ | 26, rue Bayard (Franklin D. Roosevelt) | 01 56 62 70 70 | fax 01 56 62 70 71
www.kinugawa-hanawa.com

A sizable Asian clientele persuades many surveyors that this trio of sushi slingers, which also delivers delicate dishes from Kyoto and Tokyo, is "almost as good as what you'll find in Japan" – and certainly among "the best in Paris"; both the "sublime" sashimi and the

"excellent" cooked fare are "charmingly served"; "but the prices cut like a samurai's sword", and "the Armani/Zen minimalism" of the decor seems "somewhat corporate in feel"; N.B. new sibling Hanawa serves more fusion-y fare – e.g. both Toraya and Jean-Paul Hévin pastries in its tea salon.

Kiosque (Le) 🈂Ⓜ *Classic French*   15 | 12 | 14 | €37

16ᵉ | 1, pl de Mexico (Trocadéro) | 01 47 27 96 98 | fax 01 45 53 89 79
Despite an original "journalism theme" – they "offer a daily newspaper with your meal, and the menu simulates a paper as well" – cynics suggest this site is old news, since the Classic French menu seems "mundane" (even though it's "constantly evolving" with different regional dishes each week), and "the sexy servers don't know how to explain the *plats*"; still, "it's always packed in the evening", perhaps because it's "one of the only places in the 16th [that serves] as late as 11 PM."

Kong ◗ *Eclectic*   14 | 25 | 14 | €55

1ᵉʳ | Pont Neuf Bldg. | 1, rue du Pont-Neuf (Pont-Neuf) | 01 40 39 09 00 | fax 01 40 39 09 10 | www.kong.fr
"The ambiance may be fantastic" and the "Philippe Starck decor second to none" at this double-decker, "glass-domed, trendy restaurant in the sky" in the 1st, but while it's "an excellent, see-and-be-seen place", the Eclectic Franco-Japanese menu is "only passable" and the staff has "an attitude problem", so "go for the drinks" (like Carrie did in *Sex and the City*), enjoy "the spectacular rooftop view" and move on.

Lac-Hong 🈂 *Vietnamese*   ▽ 20 | 11 | 16 | €51

16ᵉ | 67, rue Lauriston (Boissière/Victor Hugo) | 01 47 55 87 17
Even if the setting is "modest", the "food is wonderful" at this "not-cheap" Vietnamese in the 16th; service varies from "attentive and professional" to "brusque and disinterested", so you go for the "sublime" cooking instead.

❷ Ladurée *Classic French/Tearoom*   23 | 24 | 17 | €35

6ᵉ | 21, rue Bonaparte (St-Sulpice) | 01 44 07 64 87 | fax 01 44 07 64 93
8ᵉ | 16, rue Royale (Concorde/Madeleine) | 01 42 60 21 79 |
fax 01 49 27 01 95
8ᵉ | 75, av des Champs-Elysées (George V) | 01 40 75 08 75 |
fax 01 40 75 06 75 ◗
9ᵉ | Printemps | 52, bd Haussmann (Havre-Caumartin) | 01 42 82 40 10 |
fax 01 42 82 62 00 🈂
www.laduree.fr
Dating back to 1862, these "tearooms *extraordinaire*" are "a Paris institution for good reason" – namely, the "best macaroons in the world", plus other "orgasmic sweets", "heavenly hot chocolate" and light eats like a "sophisticated club sandwich"; "refined but not snooty" sums up their atmosphere, especially "at the original Rue Royale location (a great Proustian *patisserie*)"; so, the only sour note is the somewhat "brisk" staff, but as the "chic Parisiennes" say, "when you go to Ladurée, it feels like everything will be all right."

| | FOOD | DECOR | SERVICE | COST |

Languedoc (Le) *Southwest*
| | - | - | - | M |

5e | 64, bd de Port-Royal (Les Gobelins/Glacieres) | 01 47 07 24 47

Apparently "unchanged for 30 years", this "mom-and-pop operation" in the 5th still delights with "dependable" dishes of "authentic Southwestern food", particularly from the namesake region; while the digs are "small enough to have the owner's dog under your legs", the "portions are generous" and the "staff good-humored"; best of all, it's as "reasonable" as it is "reliable."

Lao Siam ● *Thai*
| | 15 | 9 | 11 | €26 |

19e | 49, rue de Belleville (Belleville/Pyrénées) | 01 40 40 09 68 | fax 01 42 03 14 26

"For nearly 30 years", this "amusing" Asian has lured believers up to Belleville for "a large choice" of Thai and Laotian dishes; true, the "kitschy" decor "needs some serious refreshing" and the service can be "mediocre, because it's always so crowded"; even so, almost everyone agrees it offers a "great bang for the buck."

Lao Tseu *Chinese*
| | - | - | - | M |

7e | 209, bd St-Germain (Rue du Bac) | 01 45 48 30 06 | fax 01 40 59 91 21

When craving "a taste of authentic Chinese in Paris", regulars – including writer-philosopher Bernard-Henri Lévy – make tracks to this tri-level veteran; along with the "thoughtfully prepared" fare, an "atmosphere of neighborhood friendliness" prevails; best of all, it's "reasonably priced, considering the location" in swanky Saint-Germain.

☒ Lapérouse ☒ *Haute Cuisine*
| | 21 | 27 | 24 | €108 |

6e | 51, quai des Grands-Augustins (Pont-Neuf/St-Michel) | 01 43 26 90 14 | fax 01 43 26 99 39 | www.restaurantlaperouse.com

"Wonderfully romantic", this Seine-side "Paris landmark" is "a beautiful throwback" to the 18th century, with plush "old-world" decor ("check out the upstairs assignation rooms", private dining salons where the scratches on the mirrors were reportedly made by ladies verifying the veracity of offered gems); the "traditional" Haute Cuisine "has its ups and downs" but is "fine" overall, and – as befits the *amour*-oriented ambiance – the "service is attentive, but not intrusive"; P.S. "the prix fixe lunch is an elegant bargain."

☒ Lasserre ☒ *Haute Cuisine*
| | 27 | 28 | 28 | €153 |

8e | 17, av Franklin D. Roosevelt (Franklin D. Roosevelt) | 01 43 59 02 13 | fax 01 45 63 72 23 | www.restaurant-lasserre.com

Experience "elegance personified" at this "old-world" "orchid-filled" establishment in an 8th-arrondissement mansion; combining "great classics with innovations", chef Jean-Louis Nomicos' "brilliant" Haute Cuisine bags bushels of compliments, as does the "flawless" staff, but the real raves are for the "fabulously '60s" technical touches, "from the James Bond entrance by the mini-lift" to the "unique open roof" (it's the "best topless place in town!"); "it all adds up to one magical evening for which you'll pay – but without the sense of being robbed."

	FOOD	DECOR	SERVICE	COST

⚡ Laurent ⊠ *Haute Cuisine*   24 | 26 | 23 | €139

8ᵉ | 41, av Gabriel (Champs-Elysées-Clémenceau) | 01 42 25 00 39 |
fax 01 45 62 45 21 | www.le-laurent.com

"If you're looking for a romantic garden in the middle of Paris, this is
it" crow converts of this "elegant" pavilion on the edge of the
Champs-Elysées; while the "traditional" Haute Cuisine and service
"shine", several say they're "not as good as the prices would indicate"; still, this is "where the movers and shakers have lunch" ("better lunch than dinner") – because "it's tough to beat dining on the
patio on a beautiful spring" day.

Lavinia ⊠ *Classic French*   17 | 17 | 18 | €39

1ᵉʳ | 3-5, bd de la Madeleine (Madeleine) | 01 42 97 20 20 |
fax 01 42 97 54 50 | www.lavinia.fr

"Just steps from the Madeleine", "plunge into a universe of wine" at
this "impressive" store – 6,500 labels, baby – where you can eat
"surrounded by gleaming bottles" amid an "atmosphere of wine
geeks and social butterflies"; while "good", the Classic French fare
is "a little pricey for what it is, considering the wait time before getting served", but "who cares about the food or service – what you
care about here is the vino"; best of all, "any bottle in the shop is
available in the restaurant at the retail price"; P.S. "lunch only"
(sandwiches until 8 PM).

Legrand Filles et Fils ⊠ *Wine Bar/Bistro*   - | - | - | M

2ᵉ | Galerie Vivienne | 1, rue de la Banque (Bourse/Palais Royal-
Musée du Louvre) | 01 42 60 07 12 | fax 01 42 61 25 51 |
www.caves-legrand.com

"Don't tell everyone – this is still a reasonably well-kept secret"
plead patrons of this *bar à vins*, "a great little place for a quick snack
and a glass of one of the truly outstanding wines served by the
legendary shop" Caves Legrand; "sitting at this casual spot, you
know you are in Paris" – "atmospheric Old Paris" to be exact – since
it's located "in one of the city's most beautiful" arcades, the glass-
roofed Galerie Vivienne.

Lei *Italian*   ▽ 21 | 24 | 18 | €49

7ᵉ | 17, av de la Motte-Picquet (Ecole Militaire/La Tour-Maubourg) |
01 47 05 07 37

"A hit with the fashion crowd in the 7th", this "modern Italian" with
sleek, stone-paneled decor "has made a lot of progress" since it
opened five years ago; some aspects can be "a bit expensive", but
"stick to the tagliata and you'll never go wrong."

Léon de Bruxelles ● *Belgian*   16 | 10 | 14 | €29

1ᵉʳ | 120, rue Rambuteau (Les Halles) | 01 42 36 18 50 | fax 01 42 36 27 50
4ᵉ | 3, bd Beaumarchais (Bastille) | 01 42 71 75 55 | fax 01 42 71 75 56
6ᵉ | 131, bd St-Germain (Mabillon/Odéon) | 01 43 26 45 95 |
fax 01 43 26 47 02
8ᵉ | 63, av des Champs-Elysées (Franklin D. Roosevelt/George V) |
01 42 25 96 16 | fax 01 42 25 95 42
9ᵉ | 8, pl de Clichy (Place de Clichy) | 01 48 74 00 43

(continued)

Léon de Bruxelles

11ᵉ | 8, pl de la République (République) | 01 43 38 28 69 |
fax 01 43 38 33 41
14ᵉ | 82 bis, bd du Montparnasse (Edgar Quinet/Montparnasse-
Bienvenüe) | 01 43 21 66 62 | fax 01 43 21 66 76
17ᵉ | 95, bd Gouvion-St-Cyr (Porte Maillot) | 01 55 37 95 30 |
fax 01 55 37 95 35
www.leon-de-bruxelles.fr

"All mussels, all the time" is the mantra at this "bright, bustling"
bevy of Belgians that bring out bucketfuls of bivalves, "lots of beer"
and "all-you-can-eat frites"; "the service is indifferent and the decor
far from inspiring" (unless you like that "plastic-y" "family restaurant look"), but "for what it is, a cheap chain with a theme, it's not
bad at all."

Lescure ☒ *Bistro*   17 | 12 | 16 | €37

1ᵉʳ | 7, rue de Mondovi (Concorde) | 01 42 60 18 91
Unless "you're shy, it's impossible not to enjoy yourself with a variety
of strangers, both local and tourist, when you're packed in family-
style" at this 1st-arrondissement "hole-in-the-wall" with rustic decor
(is that "garlic and onions hanging from the ceiling"?); it's been
serving the same "tried-and-trusted French bistro fare" since 1919
at a "remarkable value"; yes, it's "too small, too loud and the food's
average – but it's absolutely charming" anyway.

Libre Sens ◐☒Ⓜ *Classic French*   - | - | - | E

8ᵉ | 33, rue Marbeuf (Franklin D. Roosevelt) | 01 53 96 00 72 |
fax 01 53 96 00 84
Perhaps the "trendy decor", including an Op Art '70s cognac bar and
a room with a white bed for supine supping, is more of a hit than the
Classic French fare at this "happening place" just off the Champs;
still, fans praise the "compose-your-own salad" menu "and good
service", and while some say it's "just for lunch", it gets "quite busy
late in the evening" too.

Lina's *Sandwiches*   16 | 10 | 12 | €16

2ᵉ | 50, rue Etienne Marcel (Bourse/Etienne Marcel) | 01 42 21 16 14 |
fax 01 42 33 78 03 ☒
7ᵉ | 22, rue des Sts-Pères (St-Germain-des-Prés) | 01 40 20 42 78 |
fax 01 40 20 42 79 ☒
8ᵉ | 61, rue Charon (Franklin D. Roosevelt/George V) | 01 42 25 34 24 |
fax 01 42 25 34 25 ☒
8ᵉ | 8, rue Marbeuf (Alma Marceau) | 01 46 23 04 63 |
fax 01 47 23 93 09 ☒
9ᵉ | 30, bd des Italiens (Opéra/Richelieu-Drouot) | 01 42 46 02 06 |
fax 01 42 46 02 40 ☒
12ᵉ | 102, rue de Bercy (Bercy) | 01 43 40 42 42 | fax 01 43 40 65 11 ☒
16ᵉ | 116, av Kléber (Trocadéro) | 01 47 27 28 28 |
fax 01 47 27 60 26
17ᵉ | 23, av de Wagram (Charles de Gaulle-Etoile/Ternes) | 01 45 74 76 76 |
fax 01 45 74 76 77 ☒

(continued)

(continued)

Lina's
Neuilly-sur-Seine | 156, av Charles de Gaulle (Pont-de-Neuilly) | 01 47 45 60 60 | fax 01 47 45 34 68 🆔
www.linascafe.fr

"While shopping and schlepping", this string of "American-style sandwich/salad shops" makes a "good pit stop", offering "simple, dependable" "fast food with a human face"; but cynics say it's "not super-exciting" and warn "watch out – all of the extras add up", so that a seemingly "affordable" meal can turn "surprisingly expensive."

Liza *Lebanese*   24 | 24 | 20 | €45
2ᵉ | 14, rue de la Banque (Bourse) | 01 55 35 00 66 | fax 01 40 15 04 60 |
www.restaurant-liza.com

"What a nice surprise", "a place that looks, tastes and sounds like modern Lebanon" enthuse the many fans of "charming" Liza Soughayar's "amazing restaurant" on a "quiet street" in the 2nd; not only is the "decor stunning", but the food is "interesting and original" – think "Lebanese nouvelle cuisine"; the service is "good" too, and aside from the "expensive wines", the prices are reasonable.

Loir dans la Théière (Le) *Dessert/Tearoom*   16 | 15 | 13 | €24
4ᵉ | 3, rue des Rosiers (St-Paul) | 01 42 72 90 61

"Ideal for brunch and snacks" ("huge lemon tart!"), this tearoom "in the middle of the Marais" is "warm and cozy", with a bobo atmosphere – "like the edgy arty neighborhoods in New York" – and "nice, if inefficient" service; given all this, plus the "affordable" tabs, you'll have to "get past the crowds to bag a table."

Lô Sushi ● *Japanese*   15 | 13 | 12 | €40
8ᵉ | 8, rue de Berri (Franklin D. Roosevelt/George V) | 01 45 62 01 00 |
fax 01 45 62 01 10 | www.losushi.com

Fans of "sushi on the fly" can "watch the chefs preparing dishes and sending them down the conveyor belt along the edge of the counter-top seating" at this "temple of techno-Zen" in the 8th, which boasts "TVs to keep you entertained"; while "inventive", the rolls are only "remotely Japanese", and "expensive", given they're "not the best"; still, they're "quite popular, especially with the lunch crowd."

Louchebem (Le) ●🆔 *Steak*   15 | 12 | 12 | €37
1ᵉʳ | 31, rue Berger (Châtelet-Les Halles) | 01 42 33 12 99 |
fax 01 40 28 45 50 | www.le-louchebem.fr

With "a pretty view of the church of Saint-Eustache" (focus on that, because "the interior is design-challenged"), this "butcher's shop-turned-restaurant" "is a place to go for grills and [old] Les Halles ambiance"; "fine dining it ain't, but if you're not too proud to queue for a table, there's nothing pretentious about the excellent-value steaks."

Louis Vin (Le) ⌀ *Wine Bar/Bistro*   19 | 16 | 17 | €47
5ᵉ | 9, rue de la Montagne Ste-Geneviève (Maubert-Mutualité) |
01 43 29 12 12 | fax 01 43 29 12 20 | www.fifi.fr

Reviewers raise a toast to this "reliable *bistrot à vins*, with an ever-changing menu" of "traditional French" fare and – *bien sûr* – a

The values with the ▽ symbol for La Lozère.

	FOOD	DECOR	SERVICE	COST

"good selections of wines"; "service can be uneven", but "the owner likes chatting with his patrons, which is always pleasant"; P.S. "FYI: cash only."

Lozère (La) 🅢🅜 Auvergne   ▽ 18 | 11 | 19 | €27

6e | 4, rue Hautefeuille (St-Michel) | 01 43 54 26 64 | fax 01 43 54 55 66 | www.lozere-a-paris.com

"Simple", "delicious cuisine from a lesser-known region" – Lozère in the south – delights reviewers who are into "robust" eats and "rustic" scenes; "now that everyone knows about it", its "narrow" quarters get "crowded" ("reservations are a must") but it's "in a convenient location" in the 6th, and "what's more, it's not expensive"; P.S. "the Thursday night special is a great treat" – a creamy, cheesy mashed potato dish, *aligot*.

Luna (La) 🅢 Seafood   17 | 13 | 13 | €56

8e | 69, rue du Rocher (Europe/Villiers) | 01 42 93 77 61 | fax 01 40 08 02 44

Surveyors split over this veteran seafooder, tucked away in a small street behind the Gare Saint-Lazare: though stalwarts insist it "deserves its reputation as one of the best fish places in Paris", a Food score slide supports a sense of "drop in quality" – or perhaps the place just seems "overpriced" given that "the physical characteristics are pretty ordinary" and the "service leaves something to be desired"; still, few deny the dishes are "delicate and original", with "wonderfully fresh" fish.

NEW Lup (Le) ◐🅢 Eclectic   - | - | - | E

6e | 2-4, rue Sabot (St-Germain-des-Prés) | 01 45 48 86 47 | www.lelup.com

Tucked away in a tiny street, this after-hours novice renews the famous nightlife vibe of Saint-Germain, with late hours, nightly entertainment, exotic cocktails and an Eclectic, offbeat snacking menu that runs from risotto with shrimp to crab and mango salad, served up in a mirrored, bordello-red setting.

☑ Lyonnais (Aux) 🅢🅜 Lyon   21 | 19 | 19 | €57

2e | 32, rue St-Marc (Bourse/Richelieu-Drouot) | 01 42 96 65 04 | fax 01 42 97 42 95 | www.alain-ducasse.com

Sure, the "Alain Ducasse name brings in the crowds" to this veteran in the 2nd – but they stay for the "subtle twists on classic Lyonnais cooking", like "a delicious pig's foot and foie gras starter", and the "wonderful atmosphere" of the tiled 1900-vintage dining room; cynics say "it's become a victim of its own success" (other bistros "are half the price and better foodwise"), but positives proclaim "it's a perfect Lyon *bouchon*" – "cramped" conditions, "surly servers" and all.

Ma Bourgogne ◐⊠ Burgundy   18 | 18 | 16 | €40

4e | 19, pl des Vosges (Bastille/St-Paul) | 01 42 78 44 64 | fax 01 42 78 19 37

"Even by Paris standards, the setting under the arches of the Place des Vosges is unique", which is why this "bistro is a must" "on beautiful days"; be advised, though, that the "service is brusque" and the

"simply good, not exceptional" Burgundian–Classic French "food is heavy in the warmer months" (the key time to go); so some say it's "best for a coffee and croissant" before "the crowds make it crazy."

Macéo 🛇 *Classic/New French*
23 | 21 | 21 | €64

1er | 15, rue des Petits-Champs (Bourse/Palais Royal-Musée du Louvre) | 01 42 97 53 85 | fax 01 47 03 36 93 | www.maceorestaurant.com

"Run by Mark Williamson of Willi's Wine Bar", this more formal eatery behind the Palais-Royal offers an "agreeable", "interesting" combination of Classic and New French flavors, plus a "good vegetarian menu for those looking" and, of course, a "handpicked wine list that can't be beat"; "happy, helpful waiters" wander the wood-paneled, "bright, spacious" setting, with "tables set apart enough for real conversation."

Magnolias (Les) 🛇 Ⓜ *New French*
▽ 25 | 21 | 21 | €72

Perreux-sur-Marne | 48, av de Bry (RER Nogent-le-Perreux, Ligne E) | 01 48 72 47 43 | fax 01 48 72 22 28 | www.lesmagnolias.com

The "astonishing creativity" of chef-owner Jean Chauvel makes it "well worth the cab ride" to suburban Perreux-sur-Marne and his "magical" New French, a parquet-floored dining room with "pretty decorations" and well-spaced tables; occasionally the food gets "a bit too out there (we couldn't even figure out how to consume one amuse-bouche)" – but most salute this "superb address", with "rather reasonable prices for such" "brilliantly presented" eats.

Maharajah (Le) ● *Indian*
▽ 17 | 12 | 18 | €29

5e | 72, bd St-Germain (Maubert-Mutualité/St-Michel) | 01 43 54 26 07 | fax 01 40 46 08 18 | www.maharajah.fr

"One of the first Indian restaurants in Paris", this Latin Quarter stalwart curries mixed sentiments from surveyors; some find their northern regional fare "delicious", while skeptics say sari, it's just "ordinary"; but there's no denying "it's one of the best, value-for-money–wise."

Main d'Or (La) ● *Corsica*
- | - | - | M

11e | 133, rue du Faubourg St-Antoine (Ledru-Rollin) | 01 44 68 04 68 | fax 01 44 68 04 68

"A pleasant surprise in an out-of-the-way spot" sums up this "spicily marvelous", "genuine Corsican" near the Bastille; the personnel's "very solicititous" too, so that even if this millstone-and-wrought-iron dining room is a little spartan, a meal here is a guaranteed good time, especially given the "fair prices."

Maison Blanche *New French*
20 | 24 | 18 | €102

8e | 15, av Montaigne (Alma Marceau) | 01 47 23 55 99 | fax 01 47 20 09 56 | www.maison-blanche.fr

Though its "cutting-edge" menu was designed by "two brothers with excellent culinary" credentials (the Pourcel twins of Montpellier's acclaimed Le Jardin des Sens), it's the "wonderful location" atop Avenue Montaigne, with "fantastic" Eiffel Tower views, that makes this "white-on-white" New French "an amazing place to [see and] be seen" for fashionistas and "terminally trendy" types; *hélas*, a

sense of "style over substance" applies to everything else, from the "variable" food to the "uninvolved" servers.

Maison Courtine (La) 🗷 *Southwest*

FOOD	DECOR	SERVICE	COST
▽ 24	16	21	€57

14ᵉ | 157, av du Maine (Mouton-Duvernet) | 01 45 43 08 04 | fax 01 45 45 91 35

There's no ducking the fact that the Southwestern French food – including "a *magret de canard* for an army" – can be "really excellent" at this "modern" Montparnasse mainstay; "gracious service", a "pleasant setting" and relatively "reasonable prices" (given the quality) add up to "a winner."

Maison de l'Amérique Latine 🗷 *Classic French*

FOOD	DECOR	SERVICE	COST
▽ 18	28	18	€75

7ᵉ | 217, bd St-Germain (Solférino) | 01 49 54 75 10 | fax 01 40 49 03 94 | www.mal217.org

With "a great garden in a great location", this "lively" Classic French in a 7th-arrondissement mansion is a fine choice when a breath of fresh air is essential; the cuisine's "good, if not exciting" and the interior "lacks personality", so "go mostly for the setting and sit" outdoors; N.B. dinner May–September only.

Maison du Caviar (La) ◗ *Russian*

FOOD	DECOR	SERVICE	COST
▽ 22	14	19	€109

8ᵉ | 21, rue Quentin-Bauchart (George V) | 01 47 23 53 43 | fax 01 47 20 87 26 | www.caviar-volga.com

"Good caviar and even better vodka" make an unbeatable combination at this luxurious Russian in the silk-stocking 8th arrondissement; it's a "bustling scene with global socialites" dining on "decadent meals" that include Soviet specialties and an "excellent crab salad"; perhaps the vaguely art deco decor could use "rethinking", but ambiance enough is provided by all the beautiful "people putting on a show"; as to price – well, that depends "on how much caviar you consume."

Maison du Jardin (La) 🗷 *Bistro*

FOOD	DECOR	SERVICE	COST
24	19	23	€43

6ᵉ | 27, rue de Vaugirard (Rennes/St-Placide) | 01 45 48 22 31 | fax 01 45 48 22 31

This "true gem" "near the Luxembourg Gardens" is a "favorite little" bistro for "remarkable" New French food served by "dedicated", "personable" people in a "cozy" dining room; the fact that it offers "excellent value for money" also makes it "one to recommend", even if many beg to "keep it secret."

Maison Prunier 🗷 *Seafood*

FOOD	DECOR	SERVICE	COST
21	20	19	€77

16ᵉ | 16, av Victor Hugo (Charles de Gaulle-Etoile) | 01 44 17 35 85 | fax 01 44 17 90 10 | www.prunier.com

"Landmarked for its decor" – "gorgeous art deco rooms" below and a "lavish" Russian salon above – this long-running seafooder in the 16th is "still a treasure" for its "classic" but "irreproachable" *fruits de mer,* smoked salmon and caviar and service that's "professional", if *un peu* "pompous"; and while many mutter it's "too expensive" given the increasingly limited offerings, it's still "cheaper than a round trip to the seaside."

Mandalay (Le) 🖄 Ⓜ *Eclectic*

FOOD	DECOR	SERVICE	COST
-	-	-	M

Levallois-Perret | 35, rue Carnot (Anatole France/Louise Michel) | 01 47 57 68 69 | fax 01 40 89 05 76

Chef-owner Guy Guenego's Eclectic "exotic cuisine, full of flavors and fragrances" from around the world, makes this modest place worth the trek to quiet suburban Levallois-Perret; the tables are a tad "tight" in the colorful dining room with African-Asian "ethnic decor", but the "welcome is warm" and the prices are reasonable.

Mansouria 🖄 *Moroccan*

FOOD	DECOR	SERVICE	COST
22	18	20	€42

11ᵉ | 11, rue Faidherbe (Faidherbe-Chaligny) | 01 43 71 00 16 | fax 01 40 24 21 97

One of "the top Moroccans in Paris – and it shows" say surveyors of this "wonderful" eatery with a "well-priced, lengthy menu" and "fun waiters"; "in between the food and decor, it transports you straight to North Africa" – doubtless a better place to be than its "lost location" near the Bastille.

Marée (La) 🖄 *Seafood*

FOOD	DECOR	SERVICE	COST
23	19	21	€110

8ᵉ | 1, rue Daru (Courcelles/Ternes) | 01 43 80 20 00 | fax 01 48 88 04 04 | www.lamaree.fr

For more than 40 years this "haute" seafooder in the 8th has hooked politicians and other big *poissons* with "fish of the highest quality", prepared in both classic and "inventive" ways, "and incredible desserts"; "classically decorated" with painted hunting scenes, it still boasts "professional service", but a few feel that "since it was sold to a chain last year", "it's no longer the world-class experience it used to be."

🆕 Marée Denfert (La) *Seafood*

FOOD	DECOR	SERVICE	COST
-	-	-	E

14ᵉ | 83, av Denfert-Rochereau (Denfert-Rochereau) | 01 43 54 99 86

Marée Passy (La) *Seafood*

16ᵉ | 71, av Paul Doumer (La Muette /Trocadéro) | 01 45 04 12 81 | www.lamareepassy.com

Fearless fish lovers wade deep into the 14th or 16th for a first-rate feed at these trendy, "pricey but excellent" seafooders: decked out with bright-red furnishings and nautical artifacts, they're landing an arty crowd with its catch-of-the-day menu, friendly staff and seven-days-a-week service; "don't miss the baba au rhum dessert."

Marée de Versailles (La) 🖄 Ⓜ *Seafood*

FOOD	DECOR	SERVICE	COST
19	18	18	€44

Versailles | 22, rue au Pain (RER Versailles-Rive Droite) | 01 30 21 73 73 | fax 01 39 49 98 29 | www.restaurantlamaree.com

It's always high tide at this seafooder in Versailles, which keeps its many fans aboard its yachtlike, wood-paneled dining room with the "very freshest", luxe fish (lobster, etc.) prepared according to "creative recipes"; a "warm welcome" and "lovely" terrace also make this a great place to drop anchor, and if it's not cheap, at least "you get your money's worth."

Mariage Frères *Dessert/Tearoom*

FOOD	DECOR	SERVICE	COST
21	22	20	€31

4ᵉ | 30, rue du Bourg-Tibourg (Hôtel-de-Ville) | 01 42 72 28 11 | fax 01 42 74 51 68

(continued)

Mariage Frères

6ᵉ | 13, rue des Grands-Augustins (St-Michel) | 01 40 51 82 50 |
fax 01 44 07 07 52

8ᵉ | 260, rue du Faubourg St-Honoré (Ternes) | 01 46 22 18 54 |
fax 01 42 67 18 54

www.mariagefreres.com

A "temple of tea" with three "shrines" in the city, this "divine time warp" has a "colonial ambiance" "straight out of the movie *Indochine*" – right down to the "solicitous" waiters "in spotless white jackets"; even the "couture prices" don't deter the lines at the door for "refined" lunches and brunch, "heavenly" cakes and an "extraordinary selection" of brews "from the far reaches of the world" with "heady aromas" and "names that make you dream."

Marius ⊠ *Seafood*

18 | 13 | 17 | €57

16ᵉ | 82, bd Murat (Porte de St-Cloud) | 01 46 51 67 80 | fax 01 40 71 83 75
Its "regular" clientele of "locals" from the 16th ensures this "classic" seafooder is "always almost full"; for nigh on 18 years it's reeled 'em in with "delicious" shellfish of "exceptional freshness" and a whale of a bouillabaisse; customers also commend the "affordable" prices and "agreeable terrace in summer."

Marius et Janette ◐ *Seafood*

25 | 18 | 20 | €96

8ᵉ | 4, av George V (Alma Marceau) | 01 47 23 84 36 | fax 01 47 23 07 19
It may be "way too expensive" ("bring your banker – you'll need him"), and the "extreme nautical decor" is a bit much, but "the fish is superbly prepared" at this old-timer, "one of the better seafood houses" in Paris; if the clientele's "slightly snobbish" (reflecting the stylish address in the 8th), the service is "surprisingly warm"; however, it does get "crowded and noisy", so try to snag a terrace table in summer, with its enviable "view of the Eiffel Tower" across the Seine.

Market ◐ *Eclectic*

22 | 23 | 19 | €74

8ᵉ | 15, av Matignon (Champs-Elysées-Clémenceau) | 01 56 43 40 90 |
fax 01 43 59 10 87 | www.jean-georges.com

"Hip and happening", chef-restaurateur Jean-Georges Vongerichten's Paris outpost has "cool, modern" "Manhattan-like" decor (a bit "me-too minimalist" some snipe) and an equally "chic" "Asian-inspired" Eclectic menu; if "not his best", it's still "high-quality", and highly "popular with the young and trendy, and businesspeople" "who don't want to get fat"; it's "not cheap, but you can't expect a bargain, considering the location" "just off the Champs"; P.S. while "often reported as cold", the service "flows with grace" – and upward, as a higher score attests.

Marlotte (La) ⊠ *Classic French*

16 | 12 | 15 | €44

6ᵉ | 55, rue du Cherche-Midi (Sèvres-Babylone/St-Placide) |
01 45 48 86 79 | fax 01 45 44 34 80 | www.lamarlotte.com

Ratings may not fully reflect that a new team from La Bastide Odéon has taken over this long-running "neighborhood place" not far from the Bon Marché; the newly freshened digs host basically the same

"unoriginal" but "fine traditional French food" ("don't miss the lentil salad") brought by "slow" but "sociable" servers; prices continue to be "affordable."

Martel (Le) ◐🗷 *Classic French/Moroccan* | - | - | - | M |
10ᵉ | 3, rue Martel (Château d'Eau) | 01 47 70 67 56

"Hang with the fashionistas" at the "hippest couscous joint in the city", where owner Mehdi Gana, ex-waiter at Chez Omar, has created a hideaway "for non-dieting Parisians with a sense of style" in the shabby-chic 10th; the menu includes Moroccan mainstays, Classic French fare and "a dessert tray that'll kill you", while the "cool" ambiance includes 1900-era bistro decor, soft lighting "and Coleman Hawkins music"; if few know this place, that suits fans just fine – "it's too good to be publicized."

Marty *Brasserie* | 16 | 17 | 15 | €53 |
5ᵉ | 20, av des Gobelins (Les Gobelins) | 01 43 31 39 51 | fax 01 43 37 63 70 | www.marty-restaurant.com

"Finally, a brasserie that's a little different" say patrons of this "jovial" family business, opened in the 5th in 1913 and now run by the founders' granddaughter; she's created a "chic" art deco setting where reproductions of paintings by Picasso and Erté hang on the walls, while her chef creates "flavorful" dishes to accompany the enticing seafood; however, hostiles hiss at the "highish prices" for "smallish portions."

Mascotte (La) ◐ *Auvergne* | - | - | - | M |
18ᵉ | 52, rue des Abbesses (Abbesses/Blanche) | 01 46 06 28 15 | fax 01 42 23 93 83 | www.la-mascotte-montmartre.com

Surveyors seeking a "typical Montmartre place" ("back when Montmartre was the place to be") find it at this "old institution", a family-owned brasserie where locals dig into "superlative oysters" and "fine" Auvergnat fare "with appropriate accompanying alcohols"; "ambiance is guaranteed on Sundays", when "an amazing cast of characters, from little old ladies to local drag queens", congregates.

Mathusalem (Le) 🗷 *Bistro* | - | - | - | M |
16ᵉ | 5 bis, bd Exelmans (Exelmans) | 01 42 88 10 73 | fax 01 42 88 42 43 | www.restaurant-mathusalem.com

Habitués raise a glass to this "unpretentious" neighborhood bistro named for a six-liter champagne bottle; a "good pick in the depths of the 16th", at lunch it's "packed with media people" from nearby France Télévision, who call it "one of the best buys in the area" for "typical" "filling" Classic French fare and ever-"smiley service."

Matsuri *Japanese* | 14 | 13 | 13 | €38 |
1ᵉʳ | 36, rue de Richelieu (Pyramides) | 01 42 61 05 73 | fax 01 42 96 60 64 🗷
16ᵉ | 2-4, rue de Passy (Passy) | 01 42 24 96 85 | fax 01 42 24 14 54
La Défense | Tour Coeur Défense | 70, Esplanade Charles de Gaulle (La Défense) | 01 49 01 27 09
www.matsuri.fr

"Instant sushi gratification" is on offer 365 days a year at this "convivial" chain where the Japanese specialties constantly circle "on a

conveyor belt"; it's "practical at lunch", given the guarantee of "extremely fast service from the parading plates"; but skeptics sneer at the "worn-out gimmick", saying the morsels taste "machine-made."

Maupertu (Le) 🗷 *Classic French* 21 | 19 | 25 | €46

7ᵉ | 94, bd de la Tour-Maubourg (Ecole Militaire/
La Tour-Maubourg) | 01 45 51 37 96 | fax 01 53 59 94 83 |
www.restaurant-maupertu-paris.com

"With its fantastic view of Les Invalides", it's no wonder tourists and locals alike love this "wonderful neighborhood place"; "to add to the lovely atmosphere", there's an "extremely warm welcome from the gracious, bilingual owner" and staff, who serve "expertly prepared" Classic French fare "at a reasonable price."

Mauzac (Le) *Wine Bar/Bistro* - | - | - | M

5ᵉ | 7, rue de l'Abbé de l'Epée (Luxembourg) | 01 46 33 75 22 |
fax 01 46 33 25 46 | www.lemauzac.com

Since the "welcome is warm" and "the wine selection robust", don't let "the awful '70s decor" put you off this "pleasant neighborhood hangout" "on an arbored street" in the Latin Quarter; in between sips, you can "stuff yourself with an assortment of pâté" and other bistro bites; the "small sidewalk terrace is a real plus in nice weather."

Mavrommatis 🗷 M *Greek* 19 | 14 | 16 | €48

5ᵉ | 42, rue Daubenton (Censier-Daubenton) | 01 43 31 17 17 |
fax 01 43 36 13 08 | www.mavrommatis.fr

Devotees would sail the wine-dark sea to eat at this "classy" Hellenic haven, the "best in Paris" for its "traditional Greek food with Cypriot influences" "updated to the 21st century"; the fare's "beautifully presented" in a space that "feels like an old Athenian home" in the Latin Quarter; and although the tab strikes some as "above average", most feel it's "justified."

Maxan (Le) 🗷 *New French* - | - | - | E

8ᵉ | 37, rue de Miromesnil (Miromesnil) | 01 42 65 78 60 |
fax 01 49 24 96 17 | www.rest-maxan.com

Young chef Laurent Zajac, who sharpened his skills in several Haute Cuisine havens, goes it alone at this small insider's address "in a ritzy neighborhood" near the Faubourg Saint-Honoré; the funky-"chic" decor – felt strips hanging from the ceiling, plaster dots on the walls – acts as backdrop to the "surprisingly good", inventive New French fare that is "expensive, but a treat" to a clientele ranging from cabinet ministers to fashion designers.

Maxim's 🗷 M *Classic French* 18 | 25 | 20 | €106

8ᵉ | 3, rue Royale (Concorde/Madeleine) | 01 42 65 27 94 |
fax 01 42 65 30 26 | www.maxims-de-paris.com

Restaurantwise, this Rue Royale venue may be the most "famous French spot" in the world, site of key scenes in *Gigi* and countless other films, plays and books set in belle epoque Paris; *hélas,* "fantasy decor" can't compensate for Classic French "dishes that lack magic", leading most to moan "the only thing maxim here these

days are the prices" ("I never knew that a $150 green salad existed on God's green earth until I ate here"); at least the "waiters look spiffy" – as will you: "men are required to wear jacket and tie."

NEW M Comme Martine 🖪Ⓜ *Bistro*   - | - | - | M

17ᵉ | 33, rue Cardinet (Courcelles/Wagram) | 01 43 80 63 60 | fax 01 43 80 63 60

Veteran restaurateur M-for-Martine Engelhardt's young, 34-seat bistro is already "a hit" with those "looking for a good quality/price ratio" place in the 17th; juxtaposing traditional chandeliers with contemporary furniture, the plum-and-ivory decor is "modern, without being flashy", while the "truly excellent food" takes a light, slightly Italian tinge (the signature artichoke salad, tiramisu).

Meating Ⓜ *Steak*   ∇ 17 | 11 | 14 | €62

17ᵉ | 122, av de Villiers (Péreire) | 01 43 80 10 10 | fax 01 43 80 31 42

If "you're hunkering for a big piece of meat [broiled] to perfection", this Franco-American steakhouse in the 17th is a good steer; however, the traditional Gallic side of the menu is "mediocre", and some "arrogant" servers are admonished "don't forget – the client is king."

Méditerranée (La) *Seafood*   21 | 21 | 19 | €59

6ᵉ | 2, pl de l'Odéon (Odéon) | 01 43 26 02 30 | fax 01 43 26 18 44 | www.la-mediterranee.com

"The charming decor with Cocteau drawings" is a big draw at this "bustling" sixtysomething Classic French "located on a lively intersection" in the 6th; while the old-time "dash is gone", it "still serves good seafood" (don't miss the "real bouillabaisse"), and if the service can be "sullen" sometimes, the "sunny, bright" setting will leave you "very relaxed" – at least, until you get the check.

Mesturet (Le) 🖪 *Southwest*   - | - | - | M

2ᵉ | 77, rue de Richelieu (Bourse) | 01 42 97 40 68 | fax 01 42 97 40 68 | www.lemesturet.com

"A zoo at lunch", this "casual restaurant" with a "great owner" (Alain Fontaine, founder of Baracane) near the old Bourse is "delightful at night" for "foot-weary tourists" in search of "a nice dinner" of Southwestern "food that combines finesse with bistro cooking" for "not a lot of euros."

🛛 Meurice (Le) 🖪 *Haute Cuisine*   27 | 28 | 27 | €153

1ᵉʳ | Hôtel Meurice | 228, rue de Rivoli (Concorde/Tuileries) | 01 44 58 10 55 | fax 01 44 58 10 76 | www.meuricehotel.com

"One of the great French chefs in one of Paris' prettiest dining rooms" sums up "the Haute Cuisine experience" at the Hôtel Meurice; loaded with luxe items like truffles and caviar, "culinary wizard" Yannick Alléno's "food is just exquisite", and "the cuisine's matched" by the "balletlike service" "gliding" within the "grand, gorgeous" and "gilded" space recently redone with Philippe Starck's silver chairs and abstract glass sculpture; "yes, it's expensive" – but "the experience is magnificent."

	FOOD	DECOR	SERVICE	COST

Z Michel Rostang Ⓩ *Classic French* — 27 | 24 | 27 | €150

17ᵉ | 20, rue Rennequin (Péreire/Ternes) | 01 47 63 40 77 |
fax 01 47 63 82 75 | www.michelrostang.com

"Where charm and sophistication intersect", you find chef-owner
Michel Rostang's "chic" table in the 17th, whose "every detail is perfect", from the "superb" cuisine ("rich, rich" "but delicious none the
same") to the "charming maitre d'" and "flawless staff" to the
"wood-paneled beauty" of the decor; yes, it's "a bit too pricey" – but
after 30 years, this is "still among the best of the Classic French" establishments; P.S. "in season, ask to be truffled for the entire meal."

NEW Mini Palais *New French* — - | - | - | E

8ᵉ | av Winston Churchill (Champs-Elysées-Clémenceau) |
01 42 56 42 42 | www.minipalais.com

Its earth tones infused with red accents, this young New French
at the Grand Palais is a striking space with a long cement bar,
Baccarat lighting and "a grandiose terrace"; already a hip crowd is
flocking "for a meal under the columns", savoring chef Gilles
Choukroun's (Angl'Opéra) offbeat dishes like foie gras crème
brûlée and banana gazpacho, brought by "spectacular – as in
spectacularly disorganized" service.

Mirama *Chinese* — 20 | 6 | 12 | €28

5ᵉ | 17, rue St-Jacques (Maubert-Mutualité/St-Michel) | 01 43 54 71 77 |
fax 01 43 25 37 63

"If you really crave Chinese while in Paris", this Latin Quarter "dive"
with smoked ducks hanging in the front window is perfect for "authentic Cantonese" cooking, including "wonderful shrimp dumpling
soup" and "killer roast pork"; there's "not much decor" or service,
but since the "food's always good" and the prices low, the academic
and arty regulars don't much mind.

Moissonnier Ⓩ Ⓜ *Lyon* — 19 | 13 | 19 | €49

5ᵉ | 28, rue des Fossés St-Bernard (Cardinal Lemoine/Jussieu) |
01 43 29 87 65 | fax 01 43 29 87 65

This "longstanding" Latin Quarter Lyonnais is so "reliable", "there's
doubt you'd find any better in Lyon" itself – or so believe boosters of
this bistro and its "efficient but discreet servers"; the "unpretentious" "decor doesn't detract" from the "impeccably prepared traditional cuisine", some of whose specialties (such as tripe) are
admittedly "an acquired taste – but worth acquiring."

Monsieur Lapin Ⓜ *Classic French* — 18 | 16 | 17 | €46

14ᵉ | 11, rue Raymond Losserand (Gaîté/Pernety) | 01 43 20 21 39 |
fax 01 43 21 84 86

"Less rabbit-fixated since the change in ownership", this "charming"
little Classic French in the 14th still has "bunny love on full dis-
play, from the seven-course, rabbit-only chef's menu to the absolutely delightful wall dioramas that depict French life with the
bunnies standing in for their human counterparts"; "deft service"
and "great bang for the buck" prices make this an address worth
high-tailing it to.

Montalembert (Le) *New French*

	FOOD	DECOR	SERVICE	COST
	19	21	18	€61

7ᵉ | Hôtel Montalembert | 3, rue de Montalembert (Rue du Bac) | 01 45 49 68 03 | fax 01 45 49 69 49 | www.montalembert.com

The "trendy interior" of this "small" "slick-looking" eatery in the 7th "attracts businessmen and –women for the ideal power breakfast" or lunch of "modern" French fare; although it offers "better-than-average hotel dining", this "calm" spot is "expensive for what it is", especially given the "nice" but "relaxed service (you have to wait to be noticed)."

Mont Liban (Le) *Lebanese*

	FOOD	DECOR	SERVICE	COST
	-	-	-	M

17ᵉ | 42, bd des Batignolles (Rome) | 01 45 22 35 01 | fax 01 43 87 04 59

Meze maniacs find "delicious" morsels "at bargain prices" in this casual, modern Lebanese on a busy boulevard near the Place de Clichy; a "nice kofta kebab or chiche taouk sandwich" can be washed down with a shot of anise-flavored arak; N.B. takeout also available.

Montparnasse 25 (Le) ☒ *New French*

	FOOD	DECOR	SERVICE	COST
	16	14	15	€60

14ᵉ | Le Méridien Montparnasse | 19, rue du Commandant René Mouchotte (Montparnasse-Bienvenüe) | 01 44 36 44 25 | fax 01 44 36 49 03 | www.m25.fr

Maybe because it's tucked away upstairs at the Méridien Montparnasse hotel, this "intimate" black-and-silver dining room "remains too little-known"; among the knowledgeable, however, it's "celebrated for its cheese selection and art deco–style ambiance" and chef Christian Moine's "classy" New French cuisine; since this venue is most popular for business dining, service is "polite" and prices are "slightly high."

☒ Mon Vieil Ami Ⓜ *Bistro*

	FOOD	DECOR	SERVICE	COST
	24	20	21	€55

4ᵉ | 69, rue St-Louis-en-l'Ile (Pont-Marie) | 01 40 46 01 35 | fax 01 40 46 01 36 | www.mon-vieil-ami.com

Tucked away on the "charming Ile Saint-Louis", chef-owner Antoine Westermann's "wonderful bistro" serves "innovative" "modern Alsatian food" ("this chef truly knows how to make vegetables sing") and French country classics in an "intimate" – ok, "cramped" – dining room with black, half-timbered walls; it's "always packed, often with Americans", and some find it "overhyped", but given the "accommodating staff", it's a "good gathering place for a group" of *amis*, either *vieils* or new; P.S. "beware – they have two seatings, and if you choose the first one, you'll be rushed through dinner."

NEW Mood (Le) ◑ *Asian Fusion*

	FOOD	DECOR	SERVICE	COST
	-	-	-	M

8ᵉ | 114, av de Champs-Elysées (George V) | 01 42 89 98 89 | www.groupe-bertrand.com

Right on the Champs, this split-level space with low-lit, red-hued decor by fashionable Parisian decorator Didier Gomez is "good for a quick business lunch", while "the bar's big selection of cocktails" gets a "trendy" crowd in the mood at night; the Franco-Asian "fusion food" is "nothing special", but a decent deal given this expensive area.

	FOOD	DECOR	SERVICE	COST

Mori Venice Bar ●☒ *Italian*   17 | 16 | 16 | €69

2ᵉ | 2, rue du Quatre Septembre (Bourse) | 01 44 55 51 55 |
fax 01 44 55 00 77 | www.mori-venicebar.com
Near the old Bourse, "this flashy Italian" grabs a "glamorous" crowd
with its "original", rather baroque decor; while many find the Venetian
fare "a nice surprise", the mori-ose mutter you should walk pasta
this "overrated" place; perhaps you need to be one of the "famous
faces" – "you're treated better if the maitre d' knows you."

Moulin à Vent (Au) ☒Ⓜ *Bistro*   19 | 13 | 17 | €45

5ᵉ | 20, rue des Fossés St-Bernard (Cardinal Lemoine/Jussieu) |
01 43 54 99 37 | fax 01 40 46 92 23 | www.au-moulinavent.com
This "longtime favorite" in the Latin Quarter pulls "a great mix of locals and tourists" who love the "traditional" ambiance and bistro
cuisine, with carnivores clamoring for the "Châteaubriand and
crispy potatoes (yes, cooked in duck fat!)"; given the "crowded"
conditions, the "service is not quite as attentive" as it used to be, but
at least "you get to know your neighbors."

Moulin de la Galette (Le) *Classic French*   15 | 15 | 14 | €45

18ᵉ | 83, rue Lepic (Abbesses/Lamarck-Caulaincourt) | 01 46 06 84 77 |
fax 01 46 06 84 78
Immortalized in Renoir's paintings, this famous former dance hall in
an old Montmartre windmill is now the "original" setting for a "dy-
namic team" – Antoine Heerah and Jerome Bodereau, formerly of Le
Chamarré; they're trying hard to dispel the place's "touristy" reputation via "delicious" Classic French fare with a Mauritian touch
(e.g. suckling pig with dark muscavado sugar); however, many lament that "light" portions make the prices seem "onerous."

Mousson (La) ☒ *Cambodian*   - | - | - | M

1ᵉʳ | 9, rue Therese (Pyramides) | 01 42 60 59 46
Connoisseurs of Khmer cuisine head to this "delightful Cambodian"
near the Palais-Royal for classic dishes from the Mekong Delta, including "divine loc lac beef"; true, the room's "too tiny", but prices
are just right.

Murano (Le) ● *New French*   16 | 21 | 15 | €62

3ᵉ | Murano Urban Resort | 13, bd du Temple (Filles-du-Calvaire/
République) | 01 42 71 20 00 | fax 01 42 71 21 01 |
www.muranoresort.com
"Hip" habitués and hotel guests frequent this "fabulous" watering hole
in the northern Marais, where the mega-white, "magnificent contemporary" decor is accented with "spectacular" colored lighting; tren-
doids tuck into "inventive" New French food that's "minimalist" in style
(and content), then head to the bar for "very good cocktails" and
164 brands of vodka; P.S. "the inner courtyard is lovely in summer."

Murat (Le) ● *Classic French*   ▽ 13 | 17 | 12 | €50

16ᵉ | 1, bd Murat (Porte d'Auteuil) | 01 46 51 33 17 | fax 01 46 51 88 54
In a setting rich with red velvet, Paris Hilton wannabes, Maserati
drivers and "advertising/media types at play" "vie for the attention

of the beautiful staff" at this "trendy" Classic French near the Porte d'Auteuil; but "there's no chance of that, so just sit back and soak up the atmosphere."

Muscade ☒ *Eclectic/Tearoom*

FOOD	DECOR	SERVICE	COST
-	-	-	M

1ᵉʳ | 36, rue Montpensier (Palais Royal-Musée du Louvre/Pyramides) | 01 42 97 51 36 | fax 01 42 97 51 36

"Sitting surrounded by the Palais-Royal makes for a perfect lunch" or "afternoon tea pick-me-up" at this "nice little spot" that offers "huge salads" and other Eclectic fare; dinner is also served – in summer, tables overlooking the historical gardens are prime real estate – but do reserve in winter, to ensure they'll be open.

Muses (Les) ☒ *Haute Cuisine*

FOOD	DECOR	SERVICE	COST
19	13	17	€80

9ᵉ | Hôtel Scribe | 1, rue Scribe (Opéra) | 01 44 71 24 26 | fax 01 44 71 24 64 | www.sofitel.com

"Although it's down below, the Haute Cuisine is quite a-muse-ing" pun pleased patrons about the Hôtel Scribe's subterranean table (the "basement ceiling is too low"); yes, it's "rather expensive", but given chef Franck Charpentier's "spectacular dishes" and the "personal" service, you'll "feel pampered and not pimped."

Musichall ●☒ *New French*

FOOD	DECOR	SERVICE	COST
15	19	12	€62

8ᵉ | 63, av Franklin D. Roosevelt (St-Philippe-du-Roule) | 01 45 61 03 63 | fax 01 45 61 03 88 | www.music-hallparis.com

It's a never-ending spectacle at this "lively" club/eatery off the Champs that keeps jumping until 4 AM on weekends; the decor is "as kitsch as it could be", with "all-white" walls bathed by "continually changing" colored lights and "tight tables" so low they're "practically on the floor"; cynics sneer "the action's all on the walls, not on the plates", but defenders declare the New French cuisine is "better than you would expect" for such a "trendy" spot, with special mention for the "remarkable" desserts.

Natacha ●☒ *Classic French*

FOOD	DECOR	SERVICE	COST
-	-	-	M

14ᵉ | 17 bis, rue Campagne-Première (Raspail) | 01 43 20 79 27 | fax 01 43 22 00 90

"New chef-owners are just settling in" to this veteran Montparnasse bistro, leaving unchanged the warm-toned, "artistic setting" with contemporary paintings, and ensuring the Classic French cuisine is "still good"; though "few of the [old] movie-star-and-celebrity clientele are now seen", it remains a "premier street restaurant", so "don't accept a table in the cellar – the action (if any) is on the first floor."

Nemrod (Le) ●☒ *Auvergne*

FOOD	DECOR	SERVICE	COST
16	12	16	€32

6ᵉ | 51, rue du Cherche-Midi (Sèvres-Babylone/St-Placide) | 01 45 48 17 05 | fax 01 45 48 17 83

Shoppers "take a break from the Bon Marché" and other boutiques for the "hustle and bustle" of this "hopping" Auvergnat cafe, serving "hearty portions" of "authentic cooking", plus "huge salads"; it's "old-fashioned fun" with "good terrace seating" and "people-watching", despite the "pure craziness" of lunch hour.

	FOOD	DECOR	SERVICE	COST

New Jawad ● *Indian/Pakistani* — ▽ 18 | 15 | 18 | €38

7ᵉ | 12, av Rapp (Alma Marceau) | 01 47 05 91 37 | fax 01 45 50 31 27
When struck by sudden Sunday night subcontinental cravings, residents of the posh 7th head to this "spacious" Indo-Pakistani that, while "not extraordinary", is a "good standby when you don't want to leave the neighborhood for 'ethnic' food"; "helpful staffers" "will serve it spicy when asked."

New Nioullaville ● *Chinese* — ▽ 16 | 11 | 12 | €28

11ᵉ | 32-34, rue de l'Orillon (Belleville) | 01 40 21 96 18 | fax 01 41 58 55 14
"Without a doubt one of the most authentic Chinese in Paris" (though it also offers "Pan-Asian cooking from five different kitchens"), this busy Belleville site seems "just like Hong Kong" with a "gigantic menu" and "waitresses coming through with steam carts" full of "delicious dim sum" delicacies; the "impersonal" decor doesn't amount to much, but then neither does the bill.

Noces de Jeannette (Les) *Bistro* — - | - | - | M

2ᵉ | 14, rue Favart (Richelieu-Drouot) | 01 42 96 36 89 | fax 01 47 03 97 31 | www.lesnocesdejeannette.com
With its central location off the Grands Boulevards and five salons decorated in a range of styles, this "tourist-group destination" for traditional bistro fare is often "crowded" with foreigners, who find the food "uneven" (some suspect the caliber "depends on the price of your tour"); "the staff allows plenty of time for people-watching."

Nos Ancêtres les Gaulois, A ● *Classic French* — 13 | 20 | 15 | €40

4ᵉ | 39, rue St-Louis-en-l'Ile (Pont-Marie) | 01 46 33 66 07 | fax 01 43 25 28 64 | www.nosancetreslesgaulois.com
Ok, so this Ancient Gaul-themed restaurant on the Ile Saint-Louis "won't check your gourmet-meal box" – it's "very touristy", with "below-average" Classic French food and service that runs to "wandering warriors banging their staffs on your table"; even so, in between the strolling minstrels, the singing and the "all-you-can-eat crudités and charcuterie and red wine", it manages to be "as much fun as you can have in Paris with your clothes on."

No Stress Café ● *Eclectic* — - | - | - | M

9ᵉ | 2, pl Gustave Toudouze (St-Georges) | 01 48 78 00 27 | fax 01 42 81 36 03
"In a quiet part of the 9th", touchy-feely types come to this "popular" place for its "cool laid-back atmosphere", Med-inspired setting and hands-on service, including the option of a "massage before, during or after your meal"; while the oft-changing Eclectic menu is mostly "mediocre", there's a "great terrace" for hanging loose on the square Gustave Toudouze; N.B. it's no stress – and no reservations either.

Noura *Lebanese* — 19 | 14 | 16 | €40

2ᵉ | 29, bd des Italiens (Chaussée d'Antin/Opéra) | 01 53 43 00 53 | fax 01 53 43 83 53 ●

(continued)

(continued)

Noura

6e | 121, bd du Montparnasse (Vavin) | 01 43 20 19 19 |
fax 01 43 20 05 40 ☕

16e | 21, av Marceau (Alma Marceau/George V) | 01 47 20 33 33 |
fax 01 47 20 60 31 ☕🅂

16e | 27, av Marceau (Alma Marceau/George V) | 01 47 03 02 20 |
fax 01 47 23 99 80

www.noura.fr

There's almost always a Noura nearby when a hankering for hummus hits; true, "the decor is plain" and the staff "could try harder", but it's "a safe choice for Lebanese fare" – hence, this "high-quality chain" is "constantly crowded"; P.S. "for more chic quarters and refined service, choose the Pavilion" at 21 Avenue Marceau.

Nouveau Village Tao-Tao ☕ *Chinese/Thai* ▽ 18 | 16 | 16 | €30

13e | 159, bd Vincent Auriol (Nationale) | 01 45 86 40 08 |
fax 01 45 86 46 21

Though this Asian in the 13th is "big" enough to feed a village, its popularity means reservations are required if you want to taste traditional dishes from China and Thailand; the experience can be akin to eating at a "large factory" foes find; yet advocates argue it's "always a sure value" for the "real" thing, including an "especially good" Peking duck.

NEW Nouvelle Athenes (La) 🅂 *New French* – | – | – | M

9e | 6, pl Pigalle (Pigalle) | 01 49 70 03 99

The glory days of Pigalle's frisky nightlife are long gone, but the *quartier* still can be a destination for inventive New French fare, such as that offered by an ex-sous-chef of L'Atelier de Joël Robuchon at this new venue, named for a historic Impressionists hangout; a dramatic circular staircase leads to the contemporary digs upstairs, while downstairs, the bar swings with live jazz Tuesdays and on weekends.

Obélisque (L') *Classic French* 23 | 21 | 22 | €77

8e | Hôtel de Crillon | 10, pl de la Concorde (Concorde) | 01 44 71 15 15 |
fax 01 44 71 15 02 | www.crillon.com

"In the Crillon's second restaurant", diners can enjoy "delicious" Classic French cuisine amid plush "red velvet, mirrored" decor; "lacking an identity", it reminds some of an "upscale hotel coffee shop", but it offers what's "truly an affordable lunch for such a prestigious place."

Oeillade (L') 🅂 *Bistro* ▽ 14 | 11 | 13 | €47

7e | 10, rue de St-Simon (Rue du Bac/Solférino) | 01 42 22 01 60

"Tucked away" in the posh 7th, this bistro for the bourgeoisie serves up a "true Gallic meal" from a "limited menu" that is "good if uninspired" fans find; but the less-forgiving declare it downright "lackluster", adding that this restaurant's decor "needs a redo" too.

Oenothèque (L') 🅂 *Wine Bar/Bistro* – | – | – | M

9e | 20, rue St-Lazare (Notre-Dame-de-Lorette) | 01 48 78 08 76 |
fax 01 40 16 10 27

Diners looking to drink in a "good wine education" raise a glass to this welcoming, red-hued *cave* "with a lovely owner" near the Gare

Saint-Lazare; it offers a "great cellar" of "well-priced" bottles to accompany a daily changing chalkboard of Classic French dishes and game in season.

Olivades (Les) ☒ Provence
(aka Bruno Deligne-Les Olivades)

FOOD	DECOR	SERVICE	COST
17	14	16	€47

7ᵉ | 41, av de Ségur (Ségur/St-François-Xavier) | 01 47 83 70 09 | fax 01 42 73 04 75 | www.deligne-lesolivades.fr.tc

You can almost "hear the grasshoppers singing" at this "charming, easy bistro" in the 7th, where the Provençal-accented menu runs to "well-presented and conceived dishes", which "often include olives"; though "plain", the dining room also has a southern French allure, and if a sagging Food score suggests it's "less special" than before, you still get "good prices for the quality of the food."

☑ Ombres (Les) New French

FOOD	DECOR	SERVICE	COST
18	27	15	€79

7ᵉ | Musée du Quai Branly | 27, quai Branly, Portail Debilly (Alma Marceau) | 01 47 53 68 00 | fax 01 47 53 68 18 | www.elior.com

This "spectacular", all-glass Jean Nouvel–designed dining room in the Musée du Quai Branly "defies the stereotype that great views and fine food are rarely found together": while the star here is clearly the "to-die-for" panorama of Paris, the New French fare is "interesting and tasty, if not outstanding"; yes, the "staff manages to be rushed and slow at the same time", and it's "too expensive", but it's still worth dining in this "enormous, dramatic stage" of a space; besides, "what's not to like with the Eiffel Tower as your dining companion?"

Opportun (L') ●☒ Lyon

FOOD	DECOR	SERVICE	COST
15	11	17	€47

14ᵉ | 64, bd Edgar Quinet (Edgar Quinet) | 01 43 20 26 89 | fax 01 43 21 61 88

"Surrounded by locals", a meal at this "convivial" bistro near Montparnasse is "like eating at home" "as much for the personality of the owner" as for the "typical Lyonnais bistro cuisine", featuring "perfectly cooked sweetbreads"; but malcontents moan the meaty menu's "lacking in imagination" and dismiss the "imitation retro decor."

Orangerie (L') ● Classic French

FOOD	DECOR	SERVICE	COST
22	22	20	€88

4ᵉ | 28, rue St-Louis-en-l'Ile (Pont-Marie) | 01 46 33 93 98 | fax 01 43 29 25 52

For many, this "intimate", long-running establishment remains "the epitome of romance in the heart of the Ile Saint-Louis", with "elegant" decor and an "enjoyable", if "limited" Classic French menu; but since the loss of legendary owner Jean-Claude Brialy, foes find "the warmth is lacking" ("I feel like I've crashed a private party"), making the experience seem "too expensive" "for what you get."

Orénoc (L') ☒ Asian/Classic French

FOOD	DECOR	SERVICE	COST
▽ 17	18	16	€72

17ᵉ | Le Méridien Etoile | 81, bd Gouvion-St-Cyr (Porte Maillot) | 01 40 68 30 40 | fax 01 40 68 30 81 | www.lemeridien-etoile.com

After a stint in New York, chef Claude Colliot (ex Bamboche) has settled in at the sprawling, colonial-themed dining room "in the bee-

hive of the Méridien Etoile" (a "good address for a business lunch"); often Asian-inspired, his Classic French cooking remains "original", but, as with many a corporate hotel, it's "expensive for the quality."

Orient-Extrême ●🈂 *Japanese* | 18 | 17 | 17 | €47

6ᵉ | 4, rue Bernard-Palissy (St-Germain-des-Prés) | 01 45 48 92 27 | fax 01 45 48 20 94

Sashimi-philes would swim miles to get to this "fashionable" Saint-Germain site serving with a "wider selection than the run-of-the-mill" Japanese joints; "among the best in Paris", it's also "the place to go if you want celebrity with your sushi" – so while the "service is spotty" (unless "you're known"), it's rarely a raw deal.

🆉 Os à Moëlle (L') ●🈂🅜 *Classic French* | 25 | 16 | 20 | €44

15ᵉ | 3, rue Vasco de Gama (Lourmel) | 01 45 57 27 27 | fax 01 45 57 28 00

Despite its huge popularity, chef-owner and "Crillon alumnus" Thierry Faucher's "tiny bistro" with "decor of beams and mirrors" in the 15th "still retains its simple charm", wowing the crowds with a "divine", "delicious" prix fixe of "market-based" Classic French dishes (e.g. "lovely cold pea soup, skate in brown butter and floating island just like *grand-mère* used to make"); it can be "crowded and noisy", but the staff is "friendly" as it offers up "an incredible meal for the price."

Ostéria (L') 🈂 *Italian* | 22 | 14 | 17 | €54

4ᵉ | 10, rue de Sévigné (St-Paul) | 01 42 71 37 08 | fax 01 48 06 27 71

"Though it changed hands" two years ago, this literally "hidden jewel" – "no sign or street number to identify it" – still serves some of "the most authentic Italian food" in town ("they cook risotto as it should be cooked") in "extremely small" Marais quarters; on the downside, "if you're not a VIP, you get the feeling you're bothering the bosses", and "prices are now too high" ("sign of the times in Paris").

Osteria Ascolani ●⇌ *Italian* | - | - | - | M

18ᵉ | 98, rue des Martyrs (Abbesses/Pigalle) | 01 42 62 43 94 | www.osteria-ascolani.com

Led by a "female chef-owner who's serious about food", a "friendly staff" serves "homemade, uncomplicated Italian" *cucina,* mostly from mountainous Abruzzo, on the Parisian hill of Montmartre at this "perfect neighborhood place"; the "casually elegant" dishes "change every day", and a hip young clientele appreciates the *dolce* prices and la dolce vita hours, daily until 2 AM.

Oudino (L') 🈂 *Bistro* | - | - | - | M

7ᵉ | 17, rue Oudinot (Duroc) | 01 45 66 05 09 | fax 01 45 66 53 35 | www.oudino.com

Since it has "a charming staff and an inventive menu", this "intimate bistro tucked away in a quiet backstreet" in the 7th is well worth seeking out for a tasty meal; the '30s-style dining room makes a "nice spot for a casual evening."

	FOOD	DECOR	SERVICE	COST

Oulette (L') Ⓢ Southwest   19 | 14 | 17 | €68

12ᵉ | 15, pl Lachambeaudie (Cour St-Emilion/Dugommier) | 01 40 02 02 12 | fax 01 40 02 04 77 | www.l-oulette.com

"If you can't make it to Southwest France", this site in the 12th is "well worth the métro ride" for cuisine that includes both classic, like a "duck confit to die for", and "innovative" dishes (maybe a bit "too modern for me"); even so, sliding scores support the sense it's "not quite what it once was, especially the service" and the "austere decor."

Oum el Banine Ⓢ Moroccan   - | - | - | E

16ᵉ | 16 bis, rue Dufrenoy (Porte Dauphine/Rue de la Pompe) | 01 45 04 91 22 | fax 01 45 03 46 26 | www.oumelbanine.com

"Watch your waistline" at this "wonderful neighborhood Moroccan" in the 16th, where the "authentic" tagines and couscous cause "gourmets to cross town for the pure delight"; despite the "rather gloomy" digs, "meticulous" service is guaranteed because the "*patronne* keeps an eye" on everything.

Ourcine (L') ⓈⓂ Classic/New French   24 | 14 | 21 | €43

13ᵉ | 92, rue Broca (Glacière/Les Gobelins) | 01 47 07 13 65 | fax 01 47 07 18 48

"The sign above the door says it all: 'a cook's cuisine, a winemaker's wines'" at this "cozy, new-style bistro" in the13th, where "really talented" chef-owner Sylvain Danière (ex La Régalade) serves "classic, with a hint of contemporary", French food "at prices that couldn't be gentler" – "30€ buys a three-course menu without a single been-there, done-that option"; the "staff works really hard to complete the experience", but surveyors "hesitate to say" any more: "there are few tables and I want to get one."

Ozu Japanese   ▽ 23 | 24 | 17 | €69

16ᵉ | 2, av des Nations-Unies (Trocadéro) | 01 40 69 23 90 | fax 01 40 69 23 96 | www.ozu-paris.com

Perhaps "the samurai decor looks a little Las Vegas", and it's definitely "weird to watch your dinner swimming" around the huge aquarium – but that doesn't stop supporters from taking the plunge at this glass-walled Japanese in the 16th; "sensational sushi" shares the menu with "wonderful fusion dishes"; just be prepared to reel in a big-fin bill.

Palanquin (Le) Ⓢ Vietnamese   18 | 13 | 16 | €39

6ᵉ | 12, rue Princesse (Mabillon/St-Germain-des-Prés) | 01 43 29 77 66 | www.lepalanquin.com

Those looking for "a break from standard French" cooking can savor a soupçon of Saigon in Saint-Germain at this Vietnamese, which features "authentic, fresh" favorites like pho soup, *Banh cuon* (steamed ravioli) and ginger duck; the "cozy setting" displays the exposed beams and stones of its 18th-century building.

Pamphlet (Le) Basque/Southwest   23 | 19 | 23 | €50

3ᵉ | 38, rue Debelleyme (Filles-du-Calvaire) | 01 42 72 39 24

"Excellent, "exquisitely prepared" Southwestern French and Basque-inspired dishes make this "cozy", "casual neighborhood place" in

the Marais "well worth a visit", especially since the prices are so "reasonable"; the new decor of "taupe stone walls and red accents" gets a thumbs up too, but the real praise (and higher score) goes to "the staff – sweet, funny and kinder than kind."

Paolo Petrini ⬧ *Italian* | - | - | - | E |

17ᵉ | 6, rue du Débarcadère (Argentine/Porte Maillot) | 01 45 74 25 95 | fax 01 45 74 12 95 | www.paolo-petrini.fr

"*Bravissimo!*" bellow fervent fans of this "excellent Italian" near Porte Maillot, where chef-owner Paolo Petrini's "refined" cooking is inspired "by his memories of teenage experiences in Tuscany and Venezia"; the dining room may be "modest" but the decor is "elegant", and the business types who fill the room at noon and well-heeled locals who come for dinner appreciate the "warm and enchanting" service.

Papilles (Les) ⬧⬧ *Classic French* | 23 | 15 | 20 | €43 |

5ᵉ | 30, rue Gay-Lussac (RER Luxembourg) | 01 43 25 20 79 | fax 01 43 25 24 35

Patrons' *papilles* (taste buds) are tantalized at this "adorable little address, something between a gourmet grocery and gastronomic port of call" near the Panthéon, where "superb wines" "shown, store-style, on the walls" complement a "one-choice menu" of "consistently flavorful" Classic French food; it's "bright and lively" (some say "noisy"), so "go with a group, but not on a first date" – especially since "you'll need a nap after" all that well-priced vino.

Paradis du Fruit (Le) ⬧ *Eclectic* | 14 | 11 | 12 | €23 |

1ᵉʳ | 4, rue St-Honoré (Les Halles) | 01 40 39 93 99
2ᵉ | 23, bd des Italiens (Opéra) | 01 44 94 08 48
5ᵉ | 1, rue des Tournelles (Bastille) | 01 40 27 94 79
6ᵉ | 29, quai des Grands-Augustins (St-Michel) | 01 43 54 51 42
8ᵉ | 35, rue Marbeuf (Alma Marceau) | 01 45 62 47 22
8ᵉ | 47, av George V (George V) | 01 47 20 74 00
11ᵉ | 12, pl de la Bastille (Bastille) | 01 43 07 82 25
14ᵉ | 21, bd Edgar Quinet (Edgar Quinet) | 01 40 47 53 44
17ᵉ | 32, av de Wagram (Ternes) | 01 44 09 02 02
Neuilly-sur-Seine | 205, av Charles de Gaulle (Pont-de-Neuilly) | 01 46 24 66 15
www.leparadisdufruit.fr
Additional locations throughout Paris

Students sick of spaghetti swarm to this Eclectic chain for a "natural, fresh" fix from the "fruit-based menu", including "copious" salads and "delicious", "healthy" smoothies served amid "kitschy" "coconut tree–style" decor; "it's a nice place to refuel", but certainly "not refined", and the "young" servers are often "overwhelmed" by the crowds; in short, while cheaper than spring break in the Caribbean, it's "a bit expensive for the quality."

Paradis Thai ⬧ *Thai*   ▽ | 15 | 20 | 17 | €28 |

13ᵉ | 132, rue de Tolbiac (Tolbiac) | 01 45 83 22 26 | fax 01 45 83 22 26 | www.paradisthai.com

The "original" "templelike decor within a huge warren of rooms with tropical fish" swimming under a glass floor impresses patrons

more than the "decent" Thai dishes at this stylish Southeast Asian in the 13th; still, the service is soigné, the "menu enormous" and the prices *petits*.

	FOOD	DECOR	SERVICE	COST

Parc aux Cerfs (Le) *Bistro*

∇ 21	18	23	€47

6ᵉ | 50, rue Vavin (Notre-Dame-des-Champs/Vavin) | 01 43 54 87 83 | fax 01 43 26 42 86

Vintage '30s decor channels a Montparnasse frame of mind at this former artists' atelier-turned-bistro with "thoughtfully prepared dishes" both traditional and contemporary (special kudos to "their unique two-cabbage salad"); the "servers go to any lengths to look after you", and in summer, the small terrace out back is ideal for dining alfresco.

Paris (Le) 🅩 *Haute Cuisine*

20	17	18	€83

6ᵉ | Hôtel Lutétia | 45, bd Raspail (Sèvres-Babylone) | 01 49 54 46 90 | fax 01 49 54 46 00 | www.lutetia-paris.com

A "small jewel in the Hôtel Lutétia" in the 6th, this Haute Cuisine table with "classy" if slightly "dated" art deco–style decor by Sonia Rykiel offers "refined" fare "in the grand style"; service is "alert and efficient" if "a little distant", and "prices are high, but justified."

Paris Seize (Le) 🅩 *Italian*

18	11	16	€40

16ᵉ | 18, rue des Belles-Feuilles (Trocadéro) | 01 47 04 56 33

"Noisy, animated" and "always packed with locals" from the upper-crust 16th, this "neighborhood" Italian doles out "generous servings" of "homemade pasta" at "reasonable" prices; but while some cherish the "young atmosphere", others are irate that it's "invaded by trendy rich kids."

Pasco 🅜 *Mediteranean/Southwest*

22	21	21	€45

7ᵉ | 74, bd de la Tour-Maubourg (La Tour-Maubourg) | 01 44 18 33 26 | fax 01 44 18 34 06 | www.restaurantpasco.com

"With a cozy setting across from Les Invalides", this "fairly priced" eatery (run by a pair of pals named Pascal) caters to "a mix of Americans and locals" within its "light, modern" confines; there's a Southwestern-"Mediterranean tilt to the menu" – many recommend the risotto with Serrano ham and Parmesan cheese – and while it may "need more staff to handle the crowds", it's "excellent for a Sunday dinner when many places are closed."

Passage des Carmagnoles (Le) ◐🅩 *Wine Bar/Bistro*

-	-	-	M

11ᵉ | 18, Passage de la Bonne Graine (Ledru-Rollin) | 01 47 00 73 30 | fax 01 47 00 65 68

"The attraction of this charming place is actually the host, Antoine Toubia", whose popular wine bar in a passage near Bastille proposes a "superb selection" of bottles and a "well-prepared" menu of meaty Classic French dishes such as andouillette or steak tartare with mint; food for thought as well as stomach is provided by well-lubricated philosophical debates held on the first Thursday of every month.

Ⓩ **Passiflore** ⓧ *Asian/Classic French* | 26 | 20 | 21 | €79 |

16ᵉ | 33, rue de Longchamp (Boissière/Trocadéro) | 01 47 04 96 81 | fax 01 47 04 32 27 | www.restaurantpassiflore.com

"East meets West on the Right Bank" – specifically, the 16th – where chef-owner Roland Durand's "über-creative" "Asian-inspired" Classic French fare (lobster ravioli in a mulligatawny sauce, for example) is "prepared with a lot of finesse"; if the "ambiance can be a bit on the business side" at lunch, the evening atmosphere is "elegant and refined", yet "without stiffness", thanks largely to the "personal" service; yes, it's "pricey all around", but after seven years, this trendsetter "reveals new surprises every trip."

Passy Mandarin *Asian* | 20 | 17 | 21 | €49 |

16ᵉ | 6, rue Bois-le-Vent (La Muette) | 01 42 88 12 18 | fax 01 45 24 58 54

Passy Mandarin Opéra ⓦ *Asian*

2ᵉ | 6, rue d'Antin (Opéra) | 01 42 61 25 52 | fax 01 42 60 33 92

Reportedly, "this is where Joël Robuchon comes for Peking duck – enough said" proclaim converts who crowd this Asian with two addresses, one out in the 16th with "wonderful" authentic Chinese digs, and the other "close to the Opéra Garnier" whose "decor takes you back to the '70s"; at both, though, you'll enjoy "one authentic flavor after another", served by a staff that's "quick", despite "occasional problems understanding your requests."

Paul Chêne ⓦⓧ *Classic French* | 20 | 17 | 20 | €59 |

16ᵉ | 123, rue Lauriston (Trocadéro/Victor Hugo) | 01 47 27 63 17 | fax 01 47 27 53 18 | www.paulchene.com

"One of the 16th's treasures", this "standby" may be "stuck in a time warp" but that's what its regulars have come to expect: "French comfort food at its best" in a "relaxed", "intimate dining room" where "old-line elegance and service" are assured; it's "not inexpensive", but it's "perfect for a discreet affair or a romantic first date."

Ⓩ **Pavillon de la Grande Cascade** *Haute Cuisine* | 25 | 29 | 26 | €137 |

16ᵉ | Bois de Boulogne | Allée de Longchamp (Porte Maillot) | 01 45 27 33 51 | fax 01 42 88 99 06 | www.lagrandecascade.fr

"Feel like royalty for an evening" or afternoon when you visit this Second Empire pavilion; it's always had an "ultraromantic setting" in the Bois de Boulogne ("spectacular" in summer, while in winter "the glass walls bring the outside in"), but after the advent of "creative" chef Frédéric Robert, the Haute Cuisine has "definitely improved to excellent", and so has the staff – "unobtrusive, but always anticipating one's needs"; some swoon at the "hysterical, are-you-kidding-me prices", but overall, this "over-the-top" experience is "a step back in time that's worth the trip."

Ⓩ **Pavillon Ledoyen** ⓧ *Haute Cuisine* | 26 | 26 | 26 | €170 |

8ᵉ | 8, av Dutuit (Champs-Elysées-Clémenceau/Concorde) | 01 53 05 10 01 | www.ledoyen.com

For a "truly elegant" Haute Cuisine experience, head for this "magical" pavilion with "palatial" Napoleon III–style decor by star de-

signer Jacques Grange and a "beautiful setting" under the chestnut trees at the lower end of the Champs; chef Christian Le Squer's efforts, especially with seafood, are "subtle, brilliant" and brought to table "by an army of highly trained footmen" ("attentive", though some seem to "lack the joy of waitering"); "from the portable champagne bar to the choice of sugars with coffee, this is sybaritic dining – and priced accordingly."

Pavillon Montsouris *Classic French*   ∇ 17 | 23 | 16 | €60

14ᵉ | 20, rue Gazan (Porte d'Orléans) | 01 43 13 29 00 | fax 01 43 12 29 02 | www.pavillon-montsouris.fr

With an "enchanting", glass-roofed dining room and "exceptional terrace", it's "like eating in the middle of the park" at this Classic French that in fact overlooks the Parc Montsouris; the "refined dishes", well-"spaced" tables and "discreet, attentive" waiters make this perpetual garden party "perfect" for "grand occasions"; it's technically "expensive, but good value for the money."

Père Claude (Le) ⊠ *Classic French*   ∇ 17 | 13 | 15 | €51

15ᵉ | 51, av de la Motte-Picquet (La Motte-Picquet-Grenelle) | 01 47 34 03 05 | fax 01 40 56 97 84

At this "institution for those meat-craving moments", this "casual, friendly" rotisserie is where "regulars from the neighborhood" around the Ecole Militaire come to chow on "serious" Classic French grilled goodies; first-timers are struck by the "bustling" "'60s-chic" ambiance – "I felt like I was in a movie by Roger Vadim" (who peddled flesh of a different sort).

Pères et Filles *Bistro*   ∇ 16 | 15 | 17 | €36

6ᵉ | 81, rue de Seine (Mabillon/Odéon) | 01 43 25 00 28

A "young crowd" appreciates this "convenient" Saint-Germain address that's replete with all the classic bistro trimmings (zinc bar included); still, several scoff that, when it comes to the Classic French fare, "the food is better at home"; as for the welcome, it's less preferable to be a *père* than a *fille* – you can count on "better service if you are skinny, pretty and 25."

Perraudin (Le) *Bistro*   ∇ 13 | 13 | 15 | €37

5ᵉ | 157, rue St-Jacques (Cluny La Sorbonne/Luxembourg) | 01 46 33 15 75 | fax 01 46 33 52 75 | www.restaurant-perraudin.com

Straight "out of the movies, with checkered tablecloths and aged decor", this "classic", "noisy" bistro "near the Sorbonne" is "popular among students" and "many Americans" looking for "a breath of old Paris"; "after more than 100 years, it's still reliable" for "Classic French dishes in a convivial atmosphere"; "arrive early or be sure to reserve" or you'll have to "hang out at the bar, brushing up on your savoir-faire."

Perron (Le) ⊠ *Italian*   18 | 16 | 17 | €52

7ᵉ | 6, rue Perronet (St-Germain-des-Prés) | 01 45 44 71 51 | fax 01 45 44 71 51

On a Saint-Germain side street, this "cozy", clubby and slightly "cave"-like Italian "always fills up" with editors, antiques dealers

and other "colorful locals" consuming "good, standard fare" within the "exposed beams and stone walls"; "service is passable, if not exactly on top of things", but "everyone is having a great time" nonetheless.

Pershing, Restaurant ● *Eclectic/New French* | 17 | 23 | 14 | €72 |

8ᵉ | Hôtel Pershing Hall | 49, rue Pierre Charron (George V) | 01 58 36 58 36 | fax 01 58 36 58 01 | www.pershinghall.com

"Tremendous decor", with an "amazing [inside] garden wall", makes this hotel eatery in the 8th "rather 'in'"; but critics would "rather stay out" – while the Eclectic–New French "food is improving", it's still "a rip-off", and if the "pretty waitresses make you forget the uninteresting dishes and overpriced wines", they "must be grabbed to speed along the meal"; so unless you like "paying for the scene", maybe "it's most enjoyable just for drinks"; P.S. "don't touch anything in the garden, or you'll get yelled at."

Petit Bofinger *Brasserie* | 18 | 18 | 18 | €36 |

4ᵉ | 6, rue de la Bastille (Bastille) | 01 42 72 05 23 | fax 01 42 72 04 94 ● 🗷
17ᵉ | 10, pl du Maréchal Juin (Péreire) | 01 56 79 56 20 | fax 01 56 79 56 21 ●
La Défense | 1, pl du Dôme (La Grande Arche) | 01 46 92 46 46 | fax 01 46 92 46 47 🗷
Vincennes | 2, av de Paris (Château de Vincennes) | 01 43 28 25 76 | fax 01 49 57 02 79

These "offshoots" of the original, historic Bofinger are "typical brasseries" serving up "classic" "if unsurprising" fare – including oysters that are "some of the freshest in town" – "without chichi"; operated by Groupe Flo, there's no surprise it has "a bit of a chain restaurant" feeling; the Bastille branch is voted "the best" with "food nearly as good as its mother's across the street", "but cheaper."

Petit Châtelet (Le) *Classic French* | - | - | - | M |

5ᵉ | 39, rue de la Bûcherie (St-Michel) | 01 46 33 53 40

"Wedged amongst a bevy of cafes capitalizing on their proximity to Notre Dame", this "cute spot" is a "haven of good Classic French cuisine" "in the midst of a touristy area"; "the food is pleasantly straightforward", the service is so "welcoming" it's "endearing" and if you "eat outside" facing the cathedral "you won't soon forget the view."

Petit Colombier (Le) 🗷 *Classic French* | 18 | 16 | 18 | €59 |

17ᵉ | 42, rue des Acacias (Argentine/Charles de Gaulle-Etoile) | 01 43 80 28 54 | fax 01 44 40 04 29

The name of the game is game ("the selection is fresh and unique") at this "cozy" "welcoming" auberge with "an old-style country decor" near the Etoile; "solid French classics" round out the rest of the menu, aided by "amiable service", and many find the prices "reasonable" "for a romantic evening out."

Petite Chaise (A la) *Classic French* | 19 | 18 | 20 | €43 |

7ᵉ | 36, rue de Grenelle (Rue du Bac) | 01 42 22 13 35 | fax 01 42 22 33 84 | www.alapetitechaise.fr

This "1600s Classic French" in the 7th claims to be the "oldest restaurant in Paris", which makes it a big draw for foreigners and an

"eccentric university clientele" seduced by the "charming", "retro" ambiance and a "good-value", "old-fashioned" menu of "dependable comfort food" "served with attention"; "try to sit downstairs" since the "top floor is frequently filled with American tour groups."

Petite Cour (La) *New French* 21 | 22 | 21 | €52

6e | 8, rue Mabillon (Mabillon/St-Germain-des-Prés) | 01 43 26 52 26 | fax 01 44 07 11 53 | www.la-petitecour.com

In the past the cuisine's "been up and down", but a rising Food score suggests the kitchen's found its footing at this "charming" New French "on a quiet side street [near] Saint-Sulpice Cathedral"; even if it hadn't, the "lovely", "vine-cloaked" "sunken garden patio" would "compensate for all sins", aided by the "surprisingly sophisticated" service; be warned though, "it's on every concierge's list of places to go" – hence, "lots of Americans."

Petite Sirène de Copenhague (La) 🖼 Ⓜ *Danish* - | - | - | M

9e | 47, rue Notre-Dame-de-Lorette (St-Georges) | 01 45 26 66 66

Aptly situated in the northern 9th, this bit of "Copenhagen in Paris" is "worth the detour" for fare "with a Scandinavian flair" courtesy of its "charming" Danish chef-owner; his siren song is "remarkable fish", along with "warm" service in a "sober" yet "light-filled" setting.

NEW Petites Sorcières de Ghislaine Arabian (Les) *Northern French* - | - | - | M

14e | 12, rue Liancourt (Denfert-Rochereau) | 01 43 21 95 68

After a few years off-stage, chef-owner Ghislaine Arabian is back with a cozy little shopfront in the 14th; known for her Northern French and Flemish fare, she feeds the masses with dishes like breaded shrimp croquettes and cod in beer sauce; already the cramped, red-and-beige dining room is getting packed with guests who go for the good-value lunch menu (prices head north at dinner).

Petite Tour (La) 🖼 *Classic French* - | - | - | M

16e | 11, rue de la Tour (Passy) | 01 45 20 09 31 | fax 01 45 20 09 31

"Worth trying if you're in the neighborhood" say surveyors of this "good local" that's been serving Classic French fare to the Passy bourgeoisie for over 20 years; while new owners have spruced up the decor (which "needed some life"), longtimers lament that the menu now "appears to be too ambitious for the chef."

Petit Lutétia (Le) *Brasserie* 19 | 20 | 20 | €47

6e | 107, rue de Sèvres (Vaneau) | 01 45 48 33 53 | fax 01 45 48 74 59

"Belle epoque atmosphere and vest-wearing waiters" continue to charm at this "perfect neighborhood brasserie" in a silk-stocking section of the 6th; the "short but ever-changing menu" runs to "yummy mussels", "fresh oysters", "homemade terrines" and "quite good *fruits de mer*", brought by one of the "happiest staffs in Paris"; in short, a good time is had by all, "365 days a year."

| | FOOD | DECOR | SERVICE | COST |

Petit Marché (Le) ● *New French* | 22 | 17 | 19 | €39 |

3e | 9, rue de Béarn (Bastille/Chemin-Vert) | 01 42 72 06 67 |
fax 01 42 76 00 03

Near the Place des Vosges, this "neighborhood joint" is "jumping with a younger crowd" that comes for "fantastic" New French cuisine with "an Asian twist" at "reasonable" prices; with an open kitchen that keeps humming till midnight and "frenetic but effective" service, it's "perfect for a late-night bite on a hot summer night", especially if you can snag a table on the tiny terrace.

Petit Marguery (Le) 🗷 Ⓜ *Bistro* | 21 | 17 | 19 | €48 |

13e | 9, bd de Port-Royal (Les Gobelins) | 01 43 31 58 59 |
fax 01 43 36 73 34 | www.petitmarguery.fr

This "eternal" bistro has got game, and "outstanding game" at that, along with "good old-fashioned French cuisine that practically doesn't exist anymore" (e.g. a Grand Marnier soufflé that's "out of this world"); boasting "crisp service", a "fine wine list" and "impeccably traditional ambiance", the place in the 13th is "not elegant, not fancy" but quite simply "the real thing."

Petit Niçois (Le) *Provence* | 16 | 12 | 18 | €42 |

7e | 10, rue Amélie (La Tour-Maubourg) | 01 45 51 83 65 |
fax 01 47 05 77 46 | www.lepetitnicois.com

The "best bouillabaisse in Paris" is the bait at this Provençal venue, a "typical neighborhood place" in the 7th; if the rest of the menu is "a disappointment", at least "you can get by paying less here for an honest meal than almost anywhere else in the area", and the "owner's extremely personable (his dog running around is a true Parisian experience)."

Petit Pascal (Le) 🗷 *Bistro* | - | - | - | M |

13e | 33, rue Pascal (Les Gobelins) | 01 45 35 33 87 | fax 01 45 35 33 87

Petit but busy, this bistro is always packed with picky penny-pinchers who appreciate the excellent quality and generous portions of the Classic French cooking; quick service and a warm atmosphere explain why it grabs the Gobelins neighborhood set.

Petit Pergolèse (Le) 🗷 *Bistro* | 23 | 16 | 19 | €62 |

16e | 38, rue Pergolèse (Argentine/Porte Maillot) | 01 45 00 23 66 |
fax 01 45 00 44 03

Resembling a "neighborhood club that welcomes everyone into the family" – thanks largely to owner Albert Corre, who "greets and moves around, watching everything" – this "sophisticated yet cozy" bistro in the 16th supplies "varied", "creative" New French cuisine and "warm service"; "it's tight and noisy, but that's what makes it so much fun."

Petit Pontoise (Le) *Bistro* | 22 | 16 | 21 | €44 |

5e | 9, rue de Pontoise (Maubert-Mutualité) | 01 43 29 25 20 |
fax 01 43 25 09 43

"Wow" exclaim enthusiasts of this "wonderful, unspoiled Parisian bistro" in the Latin Quarter serving up "classic homestyle comfort food" "at great prices"; a "deserved favorite with Americans" along

with professors and students from the Sorbonne, this "small venue with big flavors" is "noisy" and "always full", which can "overburden" the "pleasant staff."

Petit Poucet (Le) *New French* — | — | — | M

Levallois-Perret | 4, rd-pt Claude Monet (Pont-de-Levallois) | 01 47 38 61 85 | fax 01 47 38 20 49 | www.le-petitpoucet.net

"See and be seen" "on the banks of the Seine" at this "trendy", spacious Ile de la Jatte New French that caters to "bourgeois families in the evening and advertising types at noon"; wet blankets bark the eats are rather "industrial" but all concur that the "agreeable terrace" is "unbeatable in summer."

Petit Prince de Paris (Le) ◐ 🖾 Ⓜ *Bistro* — | — | — | M

5ᵉ | 12, rue de Lanneau (Maubert-Mutualité) | 01 43 54 77 26

"You'll feel like you're on another planet" at this "terrific" table "in an old townhouse by the Sorbonne", "tightly packed" with a "mixed gay-straight crowd", a "funky", "vibrant atmosphere" and the "sassiest" waiters in town; open late, it's perfect either "for couples *en tête-à-tête* or a group of friends", and the bistro menu, "an amazing deal", is as "adventuresome" as the Little Prince himself.

Petit Rétro (Le) 🖾 *Bistro* 16 | 16 | 16 | €38

16ᵉ | 5, rue Mesnil (Victor Hugo) | 01 44 05 06 05 | fax 01 47 55 00 48 | www.petitretro.fr

Like the name suggests, this "little" venue is "highly appreciated for its super-retro character", created out of "charming" belle epoque tiles and the "perfume of good traditional French dishes"; jaded natives may sneer it's "nothing special", but "if you want a typical bistro", this is "one of the best secrets of the 16th."

Petit Riche (Au) ◐ 🖾 *Bistro* 18 | 19 | 16 | €49

9ᵉ | 25, rue le Peletier (Le Peletier/Richelieu-Drouot) | 01 47 70 68 68 | fax 01 48 24 10 79 | www.aupetitriche.com

Traditional French bistros are going, going, "mostly gone", but steps from the Drouot auction house in the 9th is this "survivor from the 19th century" serving "*très riche*" "old-fashioned classics" that inspire a mixed lot of views, from "so-so" to "excellent"; but in any case, "you go here for the ambiance", to sit on red velvet banquettes amid the "authentic" 1880s decor – ideal for a business lunch, entertaining out-of-town guests or "after the theater."

Petit St. Benoît (Le) 🖾 ⇗ *Classic French* 16 | 14 | 16 | €32

6ᵉ | 4, rue St-Benoît (St-Germain-des-Prés) | 01 42 60 27 92 | www.petit-st-benoit.fr

"Shoehorn yourself into a table, steel yourself for curt service" and tuck in for a "noisy dinner with the locals" at this Saint-Germain "canteen" that's "been here forever" (or at least 1901); you'll find the same "good old family cooking *à la française* (not that we always liked what *maman* served)", the same setting, which "hasn't been redecorated since about 1929", and almost the same prices, making this one of "the cheapest eats in Paris."

	FOOD	DECOR	SERVICE	COST

Petit Victor Hugo (Le) ●🅱 *Classic French* | ▽ 19 | 16 | 15 | €52

16ᵉ | 143, av Victor Hugo (Rue de la Pompe/Victor Hugo) |
01 45 53 02 68 | fax 01 44 05 13 46 | www.petitvictorhugo.com
Following "a change in ownership", some say this Classic French in
the 16th "isn't what it used to be", but fans insist it remains a pleasant "neighborhood place" with "good food from a varied menu" and
"great people-watching" amid "plenty of green foliage."

Petit Zinc (Le) ● *Brasserie* | 18 | 22 | 18 | €56

6ᵉ | 11, rue St-Benoît (Mabillon/St-Germain-des-Prés) | 01 42 86 61 00 |
fax 01 42 86 61 09 | www.petitzinc.com
"Named for its zinc bar that's been around forever", this "art nouveau-
style gem" in Saint-Germain serves brasserie fare ("seafood is the
specialty") that's "surprisingly good for such a touristy" area; but
nostalgists mutter it was "more fun before it became part of a big
French chain", finding the "decor more interesting than the formulaic
food" and service that swings from "absent-minded" to "attentive."

Pétrelle (Le) 🅱🅼 *New French* | - | - | - | E

9ᵉ | 34, rue Pétrelle (Anvers) | 01 42 82 11 02 | fax 01 40 23 05 69
"The best restaurant with its own cat in Paris" is tucked away on a
cobbled side street in the increasingly bobo 9th; the "eclectic decor"
of flea-market finds creates a "delightful ambiance" that often attracts a boldface name or two (Christian Lacroix, Madonna); the
"seasonal menu" of New French dishes is "worth every centime",
however, "one waiter really is no longer enough for the whole place."

Pétrus *Brasserie* | ▽ 21 | 18 | 19 | €74

17ᵉ | 12, pl du Maréchal Juin (Péreire) | 01 43 80 15 95 | fax 01 47 66 49 86
Previously a plush seafood house, this business dining favorite in the
17th has been transformed into "an excellent brasserie serving well-
prepared food, notably fish"; pastel- and taupe-toned, "discreetly
modern decor" and a "friendly staff" make it a good catch, even if it's
"a bit expensive – but you leave with a good memory."

Pharamond 🅱🅼 *Classic French* | 19 | 20 | 20 | €72

1ᵉʳ | 24, rue de la Grande Truanderie (Etienne Marcel/Les Halles) |
01 40 28 45 18 | fax 01 40 28 45 87 | www.pharamond.fr
Nobody's talking tripe when they say this "noisy, crowded, simple
place" near Les Halles is "as much a taste of Old France as you can find
today" – and by old, we mean dating back to 1832, when it began serving tripe *à la mode de Caen*; still on the menu, it will "melt in your
mouth", along with the other classics proffered by "friendly" servers;
though "recently renovated" after a management change, its "genuine" belle epoque decor remains intact, leading some to quip "new
owner, new chef, same old furniture" (seriously, "it's a lovely place").

Pichet de Paris (Le) 🅱 *Seafood* | 16 | 11 | 14 | €59

8ᵉ | 68, rue Pierre Charron (Franklin D. Roosevelt) | 01 43 59 50 34 |
fax 01 42 89 68 91
"If you're a tourist, it's a find; if you're a local, you're unhappy all the
tourists have found it" say surveyors about this "unpretentious ad-

	FOOD	DECOR	SERVICE	COST

dress" approximately "50 meters from the Champs-Elysées"; the seafood remains as "solid as it's been for 30 years", even if "prices are a little excessive" given the "unoriginal" decor and service that varies, "depending on the client and the mood" of the staffer.

Pied de Chameau (Au)/ Al Nour ◑🅩 *Moroccan*

-	-	-	M

3ᵉ | 173, rue St. Martin (Châtelet-Les Halles/Rambuteau) | 01 42 78 35 00 | fax 01 42 78 00 50 | www.alnour.fr

Those "longing for a vacation in the Maghreb" get their fix at this Moroccan with a "trendy reputation" in the 3rd; the "low-lit", "exotic" decor "makes this a perfect romantic evening in Casablanca", but if you're on a first date, "beware: the belly dancer makes you dance!"

Pied de Cochon (Au) ◑ *Brasserie*

18	19	17	€49

1ᵉʳ | 6, rue Coquillière (Châtelet-Les Halles) | 01 40 13 77 00 | fax 01 40 13 77 09 | www.pieddecochon.com

"Call me Miss Piggy" squeal supporters of this "lively" "remnant of the old Les Halles", who pork out on "abundant" portions of traditional brasserie fare, including "the pig's feet that give the restaurant its name"; "open nonstop", it can feel rather "factory"-like, but for foreign visitors, its "archetypal Parisian waiters" and "kitschy" (even "gaudy") decor make it "a must, at least – but probably only – once."

Pierre au Palais Royal ◑🅩 *Classic French*

17	15	15	€54

1ᵉʳ | 10, rue Richelieu (Palais Royal-Musée du Louvre) | 01 42 96 09 17 | fax 01 42 96 26 40

Scores may not fully reflect the advent of "new owner Eric Sertour and his chef Pascal Bataillé" to this "delightful little" site "near the Palais-Royal", but those who know say they're "making marvels" with the L'Arome alum's Classic French fare, both earthy and elevated, and "handsome new" monochromatic decor; while the hoi polloi might hesitate at the prices, there are "menus of thirtysomething euros, even in the evening", and a post-theater prix fixe too.

🆉 Pierre Gagnaire 🅩 *Haute Cuisine*

28	25	27	€194

8ᵉ | Hôtel Balzac | 6, rue Balzac (Charles de Gaulle-Etoile/George V) | 01 58 36 12 50 | fax 01 58 36 12 51 | www.pierre-gagnaire.com

"Let your senses explore uncharted territory" during a "breathtaking meal" at this "brilliant", completely "unforgettable" Haute Cuisine haven in the 8th, serving what many describe as "the most innovative food" in Paris ("Pierre Gagnaire is to gastronomy what Picasso was to contemporary art"); yes, the master's "science experiment"-like creations, while "out of this world", are "too out there" for some; but the "exceptional service" in the discreet dove-gray and blonde wood dining room makes you "feel like royalty", and to the vast majority, it's "worth every euro (damn dollar!)."

Pinxo *New French*

21	18	19	€64

1ᵉʳ | Renaissance Paris Vendôme | 9, rue d'Alger (Tuileries) | 01 40 20 72 00 | fax 01 40 20 72 02

Owned by "star-studded chef" Alain Dutournier, this "stylish spot" in the 1st "combines aspects of a traditional tapas bar with

those of a contemporary French restaurant" where "two or three people can share dishes" of "exotic Basque-influenced cuisine" that are "not copious, but flavorful"; perhaps the best seats in the "sleek minimalist room" are "at the bar with a view of the open kitchen", but the "noise level is low" throughout, providing a "Zen-chic" experience.

Pitchi Poï *Jewish/Polish*

| | | | M |

4e | 7, rue Caron (St-Paul) | 01 42 77 46 15 | fax 01 42 77 75 49 | www.pitchipoi.com

"Discover Jewish cuisine" with a Polish twist at this "small, lively" eatery, known for its "scrumptious" blini washed down with a large selection of vodkas and its highly "hyped", all-you-can-eat Sunday brunch buffet; even devotees declare "the decor is pretty basic" but "the courtyard is nice" with its coveted location "on a tranquil square in the Marais."

Pizzeria d'Auteuil *Italian*

| | | | M |

16e | 81, rue la Fontaine (Michel-Ange-Auteuil) | 01 42 88 00 86

"Overflowing with regulars" from the ritzy 16th, "this pizzeria is in fact a real Italian restaurant" – and a "good" one too; "but it's best not to go hungry" since you'll probably have to wait for service that "runs the gamut from passable to scandalous"; since "it's always full", though, clearly the "cool crowd" doesn't care that "the welcome is not their strong suit" and the decor's "uninteresting"; P.S. "you can also order pizzas to go."

Pizzetta (La) 🗷 *Italian*

| | | | M |

9e | 22, av Trudaine (Anvers/Pigalle) | 01 48 78 14 08 | fax 01 48 78 14 08 | www.lapizzetta.fr

"Hip and hip-to-hip", Sardinian chef Ricardo Podda's "simple place" packs 'em in with "great pizzas" and other Italian eats "on the lovely Avenue Trudaine"; "efficient" servers skillfully negotiate the Napoleon III–meets-Milanese modern decor.

Ploum 🗷🅼 *Japanese/New French*

| | | | M |

10e | 20, rue Alibert (Goncourt) | 01 42 00 11 90 | www.ploum.fr

"Yet another example of how the French make delightful dining seem effortless", this futuristic fusion venue "with huge windows and raw interiors" – like "a UFO that landed in the middle of nowhere" "near the Canal Saint-Martin" – serves sushi and "simple dishes" that, though "traditional French-sounding", are "innovative and exciting"; service is "friendly", and prices reasonable.

Point Bar 🗷🅼 *New French*

| 22 | 17 | 17 | €40 |

1er | 40, pl du Marché St-Honoré (Pyramides) | 01 42 61 76 28 | fax 01 42 96 46 90

Run by Alice Bardet, the daughter of a renowned chef in Tours, this "pleasant place" is "probably the best on the Marché Saint-Honoré" for its "light yet delicious" New French made with "super-fresh ingredients"; enthusiasts also emphasize its "above-average service and affordable" prices.

	FOOD	DECOR	SERVICE	COST

Polichinelle Cafe *Bistro*

-	-	-	M

11e | 64-66, rue de Charonne (Charonne) | 01 58 30 63 52

Yes, it looks "like a '30s soup kitchen with absolutely no updating since", but that's part of "the charm of this place", yet another of the eateries turning the 11th into neo-bistro central; regulars rave about the relaxed atmosphere and modest prices for modern dishes cooked with a lot of loving care; there's live entertainment every Sunday in the ever-bustling bar.

Polidor ● *Bistro*

17	16	15	€30

6e | 41, rue Monsieur-le-Prince (Luxembourg/Odéon) | 01 43 26 95 34 | fax 01 43 26 22 79

"Steeped in history", this "old bistro" (est. 1845) near the Luxembourg Gardens is where students, starving artists and tourists "looking for the 'authentic' Paris" "sit elbow-to-elbow" at "long communal tables" to eat "decent, inexpensive" ("if uninspired") "comfort meals" in an "unpretentious" room adorned by a cubbyholed napkin holder where the likes of Baudelaire and Hemingway once kept their linen; old-timers opine it "hasn't changed in 40 years" – "even the waitresses seem the same" with their "genuine rude service."

Pomponette (A la) ●⊠ *Bistro*

▽ 17	15	14	€46

18e | 42, rue Lepic (Abbesses/Blanche) | 01 46 06 08 36 | fax 01 42 52 95 44 | www.alapomponette.fr

"A real institution, managed by the fourth generation" of the clan that opened it in 1909, this bistro serves "good, if not light" comfort food amid "very Montmartre decor" – "the walls are adorned by works of local painters who were short of cash (and sometimes of talent)"; the "honest neighborhood ambiance" is accented by monthly concerts ("you may wait awhile for your check since your waiter may be busy dancing").

Pomze ⊠ *New French*

18	17	19	€50

8e | 109, bd Haussmann (Miromesnil/St-Augustin) | 01 42 65 65 83 | fax 01 42 65 30 03 | www.pomze.com

"Admirers of William Tell" and apple addicts are thrilled to the core by this "wonderfully inventive" "concept" eatery in the 8th, where the New French menu "is built around *la pomme* in all its forms", adding "subtle flavors" to dishes from starters to dessert; augmenting them is an impressive selection of – what else? – "the best ciders" from around France; N.B. there's also a ground-floor gourmet shop.

Port Alma ⊠Ⓜ *Seafood*

▽ 17	13	18	€68

16e | 10, av de New York (Alma Marceau) | 01 47 23 75 11 | fax 01 47 20 42 92

Some surveyors say it's smooth sailing at this "solid" seafooder on the Seine in the 16th, but other reviewers report stormy weather – "you never know if you'll eat well here from one day to the next", while the "high prices" are all too constant; the maritime-themed "dining room could use some updating" too; P.S. there's a "good view of the Eiffel Tower – from two tables."

Potager du Roy (Le) 🅢🅜 *Classic French* | 19 | 17 | 16 | €53 |

Versailles | 1, rue du Maréchal-Joffre (RER Versailles-Rive Gauche) | 01 39 50 35 34 | fax 01 30 21 69 30

Visitors to Versailles hail this "lovely retreat" near the palace, where the chef makes "exceptional" Traditional French "cuisine with a touch of originality", giving "a place of honor to vegetables" (the name refers to the royal garden); the decor is equally "classic" – though perhaps the tables are "a little too close together" – and while it's "a little dear", you won't need a king's ransom to pay the bill.

Pouilly Reuilly 🅢 *Bistro* | - | - | - | M |

Le Pré-St-Gervais | 68, rue André Joineau (Hoche) | 01 48 45 14 59 | fax 01 48 45 93 93

It's just east of the city in Le Pré-Saint-Gervais, but suburban surveyors say this "old favorite" can be "out of this world" for "heavy", "typical bistro food" (think organ meats, blood sausage and giant éclairs); as they walk through to the post-war dining room, customers get a close-up look at the kitchen – but be advised that it stops taking orders after 9:45 PM.

Poule au Pot (La) ◗🅢🅜 *Bistro* | 23 | 19 | 23 | €46 |

1er | 9, rue Vauvilliers (Châtelet-Les Halles/Louvre-Rivoli) | 01 42 36 32 96 | fax 01 40 91 90 64 | www.lapouleaupot.fr

There's "a chicken in every pot" – or nearly – at this "classic spot" in Les Halles, a "local place" where peckish diners can count on "large portions" of the "signature dish", as well as onion soup, bone marrow, profiteroles and other bistro faves; the service is "very amiable", right up until closing time at 5 AM.

🆉 Pré Catelan (Le) 🅢🅜 *Haute Cuisine* | 27 | 28 | 26 | €159 |

16e | Bois de Boulogne, Route de Suresnes (Pont-de-Neuilly/Porte Maillot) | 01 44 14 41 14 | fax 01 45 24 43 25 | www.precatelanparis.com

"Haute Cuisine of the highest order", "impeccable service" and, of course, that "beautiful location" in the Bois de Boulogne – small wonder that a "phenomenal dining experience" awaits at this "elegant, enduring" classic; though recently redone in contemporary tones of beige, bronze and gray, the decor retains its "magical" imperial aura; even advocates allow the "prices are budget-busting", but "cost be damned" – "lunch in the garden on a summer afternoon is pure bliss."

Pré Salé (Le) 🅢 *Northern France* | - | - | - | M |

1er | 9, rue d'Argenteuil (Palais Royal-Musée du Louvre/Pyramides) | 01 42 60 56 22

Run by a "young couple that deserves our support", this cozy spot in the 1st provides a nod to Normandy, both in the photos adorning its sunny beige and bordeaux decor and in its creative cuisine; the name refers to the region's famed salt marshland–raised lamb, which is, not surprisingly, the specialty here; bankers and business types are pre-sold at lunch, but at quieter nights it becomes the happy secret of knowing locals.

	FOOD	DECOR	SERVICE	COST

Press Café ☒ *Bistro*   - | - | - | I

2ᵉ | 89, rue Montmartre (Sentier) | 01 40 26 07 30 |
www.presscafe.net

A stone's throw from the offices of Agence France-Presse (hence, its
name), this "nice neighborhood bistro" in the 2nd arrondissement delights journalists and other hard-pressed locals with its
"exceptional service and food"; the latter consists of simple
cuisine – foie gras, hand-cut beef tartare, chocolate mousse – at
prices so low they're newsworthy.

Pré Verre (Le) ☒ Ⓜ *New French*   22 | 13 | 16 | €38

5ᵉ | 8, rue Thénard (Maubert-Mutualité) | 01 43 54 59 47 |
www.lepreverre.com

Diners "who like to be surprised" "wait in line" for a table at this
"young, animated" Latin Quarter New French, which "has achieved
cult culinary status by reinventing classics" with a "fusion of spices"
that "get you traveling without moving" – and all for an "unbeatable
price" too; but no matter how "crowded" and "noisy" the "narrow"
main room gets, claustrophobic clients should "avoid at all costs"
the "low-ceilinged basement."

Procope (Le) ⬤ *Classic French*   16 | 22 | 16 | €55

6ᵉ | 13, rue de l'Ancienne Comédie (Odéon) | 01 40 46 79 00 |
fax 01 40 46 79 09 | www.procope.com

"You have to eat in this 17th-century establishment once, just to
check it off your list" – for this Classic French in Saint-Germain is
practically "a museum" with its "portrait-laden walls, apartment-
sized rooms" and antiques (you "like the idea of dining next to
Voltaire's desk"?); once patronized by "luminaries of literature, the
arts" and politics, it's "now frequented largely by tourists" – "the
servers are clearly fed up with them" – and critics call the cuisine
"great for history buffs, but not for gourmets."

NEW P'tit Casier (Le) ☒ *Seafood*   - | - | - | M

15ᵉ | 49, rue Olivier De Serres (Convention) | 01 56 08 36 22

This bona fide minnow of a place in the 15th has become an insider's
address among fish lovers thanks to the minimalist but inventive
cooking of chef/co-owner Iza Guyot, a Franco-Moroccan who combines her bloodlines with dishes like cod tagine and oyster tartare
with lime and onions.

P'tit Troquet (Le) ☒ *Bistro*   22 | 17 | 23 | €40

7ᵉ | 28, rue de l'Exposition (Ecole Militaire) | 01 47 05 80 39 |
fax 01 47 05 80 39

Now, "this is the bistro atmosphere you crave when you arrive in
Paris" declare devotees of this "wife-, husband- and daughter-run
little restaurant" "in an unassuming alleyway near the Eiffel Tower";
the service is "very nice" and the food "simply delightful"; true, the
decor of flea-market finds is a tad "tired", but "with traditional food
at reasonable prices becoming increasingly rare" these days, small
wonder the place been "discovered by tourists (so go late and eat
with the French)."

	FOOD	DECOR	SERVICE	COST

Publicis Drugstore ● *Brasserie* — 11 | 11 | 10 | €35

8ᵉ | 133, av des Champs-Elysées (Charles de Gaulle-Etoile/George V) |
01 44 43 77 64 | fax 01 44 43 79 02 | www.publicisdrugstore.com

Boasting an "idyllic location on the Champs" within the glass-
fronted Publicis entertainment/shopping complex, this "hip, modern"
French take on an American coffee shop serves an eclectic brasserie
menu throughout the day; "the decor is a little too bat cave-ish", and
the food "banal, but the Parisians love it, so you have to try it."

Pure Café ● *Eclectic* — - | - | - | M

11ᵉ | 14, rue Jean Macé (Faidherbe-Chaligny) | 01 43 71 47 22 |
fax 01 43 71 47 22

There are no guarantees you'll spot actress Julie Delpy, but still this
"classic cafe", featured in the film *Before Sunset,* makes a "lovely, casual date" (or reunion) place, thanks to its "fresh, delicious" Eclectic
fare, "inexpensive drinks" from a horseshoe-shaped bar and "relaxed
setting", courtesy of its "off-the-beaten-track location" in the 11th.

Pur'Grill *New French* — 19 | 18 | 18 | €83

2ᵉ | Park Hyatt Paris-Vendôme | 5, rue de la Paix (Opéra) | 01 58 71 12 34 |
fax 01 58 71 10 32 | www.paris.vendome.hyatt.com

With "impressive circular design" (by American-in-Paris Ed Tuttle,
who's done several Aman resorts), the Park Hyatt's "stylish" dinner-
only eatery offers a "view of the artists of the kitchen" as they grill
"tasty meats" and other New French fare; but some purists pout the
decor's "impersonal" and the "prices are bit steep for the offerings."

Quai (Le) *New French* — - | - | - | M

7ᵉ | Quai Anatole France - Port de Solférino (Solférino) | 01 44 18 04 39 |
fax 01 44 18 09 52 | www.restaurantlequai.com

"Nothing better than being on a barge on a beautiful day" say sea-
faring surveyors of this houseboat moored at the foot of the Musée
d'Orsay; "charming servers" offer "enjoyable" New French lunches,
in a glass-enclosed room or outside on the Seine-side terrace where
the splendid view lets "you wave to the *bateaux-mouches* passing by."

Quai Ouest ● *Eclectic* — 13 | 14 | 11 | €47

Saint-Cloud | 1200, quai Marcel Dassault (Pont-de-St-Cloud) |
01 46 02 35 54 | fax 01 46 02 33 02

If everyone likes the "nice view" of the Seine from this "huge hangar-
like" ship in suburban Saint-Cloud, opinions are mixed when it
comes to the Eclectic menu; if amiable mateys maintain it's "better
than what you usually find at other barge restaurants", cynical sail-
ors snap the kitchen "could do better", and so could the "slow" staff;
but then, "you come here not for the food, but for the setting" and to
"see and be seen" by the TV-industry and trendy types.

404 (Le) ● *Moroccan* — 22 | 25 | 20 | €43

3ᵉ | 69, rue des Gravilliers (Arts et Métiers) | 01 42 74 57 81 |
fax 01 42 74 03 41

It's like a "berber's tent deep in the medina" at this "lively" Moroccan
near Arts et Métiers, with an "exotic", "sumptuous" decor like "the

inside of a genie bottle", "frenzied music" and a "sexy, moody, party atmosphere"; just "prepare to be sardined" into the "cool crowd" that packs the place seven days a week for "tasty, reasonably priced" couscous and tagines, and avoid the first seating if you don't want to be "rushed out" before your mint tea arrives.

Quincy (Le) 🖪🎏 *Bistro* - | - | - | M

12ᵉ | 28, av Ledru-Rollin (Gare de Lyon/Quai de la Rapée) | 01 46 28 46 76 | fax 01 46 28 46 76 | www.lequincy.fr

"It doesn't get any more local than this" cry converts to this "cozy", "very Parisian" veteran bistro near the Gare de Lyon, which delights with traditional French dishes like "great snails and frogs' legs", and chef-owner Michel Bosshard, who "comes to the table and helps you decide what to order"; fans fear that after 38 years, he "will need to retire soon, so rush to try it before it's too late."

Quinzième (Le) 🖪 *New French* - | - | - | E

15ᵉ | 14, rue Cauchy (Javel) | 01 45 54 43 43 | www.restaurantlequinzieme.com

"In a quiet corner of the 15th, near the Parc André Citroën" lies "the restaurant everyone's talking about" these days – "TV chef Cyril Lignac's" first physical kitchen; fans find the New French fare quite "pleasing to the palate", while opponents argue it's "overpriced, overrated and overexposed in the media" – but none of that stops media mavens from flocking to the "lovely" contemporary digs.

🆕 Racines (Les) 🖪 *Wine Bar/Bistro* - | - | - | M

2ᵉ | 8, passage des Panoramas (Grands Boulevards) | 01 40 13 06 41 | www.morethanorganic.com

The romantic Passage des Panoramas, an ancient arcade in the 2nd, is the location of one of the hottest new *bistrot à vins* in Paris; a mélange of vinophiles, boutique-owners and fashion types mix it up over pours – many of them organic – and plates of cheese and charcuterie plus a few hot Classic French dishes and pastas, made with quality produce (meat comes from star butcher Hugo Desnoyer and vegetables from chef Alain Passard's farm).

Radis Roses Restaurant 🖪Ⓜ *New French* - | - | - | M

9ᵉ | 68, rue Rodier (Anvers) | 01 48 78 03 20

This tiny, modern venue in the ever-trendier 9th is a friendly, "casual" spot, whose New French menu features "updated specialties from – of all places – the Drôme, [a region] not normally known for its cuisine"; there's a New York feeling to the hip room and "pleasant service", but since it only "seats 23, reservations are essential."

Ragueneau (Le) *Classic French/Tearoom* - | - | - | I

1ᵉʳ | 202, rue St-Honoré (Palais Royal-Musée du Louvre) | 01 42 60 29 20 | fax 01 42 60 29 70 | www.ragueneau.fr

"A few meters from the Louvre and La Comédie Française", this theatrical-looking venue named for the poetry-loving pastry chef in *Cyrano de Bergerac* is ideal for a cuppa in the main floor tea salon, but it also serves "pretty good" Classic French food in the

upstairs dining room; "it may not be gastronomy, but it's good value" for the money.

Ravi ●☒ *Indian*  ▽ 21 | 20 | 19 | €48

7ᵉ | 50, rue de Verneuil (Rue du Bac) | 01 42 61 17 28 | fax 01 42 61 12 18

"Definitely known only to the locals", "this tiny – we mean tiny – treasure in Saint-Germain" offers "dark ambiance" and "detailed decor" of carved wooden screens and artwork to back up its "delicious" Indian cuisine; while "adorable", the staff sometimes seems "on vacation"; nevertheless, subcontinental supporters swear "if you want a romantic dinner, there's nowhere better."

Rech (Le) ☒Ⓜ *Seafood* - | - | - | E

17ᵉ | 62, av des Ternes (Charles de Gaulle-Etoile/Ternes) | 01 45 72 29 47 | fax 01 45 72 41 60 | www.rech.fr

It was "recently taken over by Alain Ducasse", and fish fans are flipping over the "great rebirth of this great old place" just off the Place des Ternes; gently "upgraded", it "keeps the best of the old", from the "fabulous" seafood to the softly lit 1920s blond-wood interior on the second floor; the first is a more casual cafe, with "nice *coquillages.*"

Réconfort (Le) *New French* - | - | - | M

3ᵉ | 37, rue de Poitou (St-Sébastien Froissart) | 01 49 96 09 60 | fax 01 49 96 09 62

"Few restaurants so surely justify their name" – 'comfort' – as this "apartmentlike" eatery in the northern Marais; "hidden inside of an old novel", the menu offers "simple modern French food without too many frills"; a "lively crowd" sometimes makes it "noisy", but "subtle lighting" makes it "a place to stare into your date's eyes and chat late into the evening."

Refectoire (Le) *Bistro* - | - | - | M

11ᵉ | 80, bd Richard Lenoir (Richard Lenoir/St-Ambroise) | 01 48 06 74 85 | www.lerefectoire.com

A "kitschy atmosphere" – the "chairs, tables and so on are quite close to that of French public school" cafeterias (*refectoires*) – makes this 11th-arrondissement bistro a "cool, undiscovered place"; the "creative kitchen's" offerings are "accompanied by a lively staff", and all told, even grown-ups find it "thoroughly enjoyable", especially if they "try the restrooms", a true sound-and-light show.

Ⓩ Régalade (La) ☒ *Basque/Bistro* 25 | 17 | 20 | €51

14ᵉ | 49, av Jean Moulin (Alésia) | 01 45 45 68 58 | fax 01 45 40 96 74

Nostalgists naturally say it "isn't what it used to be", but scores support the sentiment that this "consummate bistro" is now "even better than under its legendary previous chef-owner" Yves Camdeborde; chef Bruno Doucet's "country French" cuisine with "a Basque influence" is "hearty and generous" – "where else will a waiter put down a two-ft.-long terrine and bucket of cornichons just for starters?" – and the staff has actually gotten "friendly"; sure it's "noisy" and prices have drifted up, but it's "still a winner" and "well worth the trip to the southern confines of the 14th."

	FOOD	DECOR	SERVICE	COST

☑ Relais d'Auteuil
"Patrick Pignol" 🖼 Ⓜ *Haute Cuisine*   27 | 20 | 26 | €137

16ᵉ | 31, bd Murat (Michel-Ange-Molitor/Porte d'Auteuil) | 01 46 51 09 54 | fax 01 40 71 05 03

"If you're adventuresome", join the "well-to-do neighborhood clientele" that congregates at this Haute Cuisine table out toward the Porte d'Auteuil; while "outrageously expensive", it's "one of the best in Paris" for the eponymous chef-owner's traditional French food and "outstanding wine", plus the "warm welcome of Madame Pignol", within the wood-paneled, slightly "dim" setting; a "really lovely" experience, all 'round.

☑ Relais de l'Entrecôte (Le) ☾ *Steak*   22 | 14 | 18 | €39

6ᵉ | 20, rue St-Benoît (St-Germain-des-Prés) | 01 45 49 16 00 | fax 01 45 49 29 75
8ᵉ | 15, rue Marbeuf (Franklin D. Roosevelt) | 01 49 52 07 17 | fax 01 47 23 34 98
www.relais-entrecote.com

They're "one-trick ponies, but it's a great trick" maintain meateaters of these two "cafeterialike" carnivores' caves in the 6th and 8th, where the "only item on the menu is steak" "with plate-licking secret sauce", salad and "frites that just keep coming", plus a "side of grumpy waitresses"; skeptics sneer it's "France's answer to Outback Steakhouse", complete "with lines snaking outside the door daily", but it's ideal "for people who can't make up their minds what to order."

Relais de Venise (Le) ☾ *Steak*   24 | 16 | 19 | €37

17ᵉ | 271, bd Péreire (Porte Maillot) | 01 45 74 27 97

"No surprises" await at this steakhouse at Porte Maillot, an "address handed down from generation to generation", where "the wait for a table is interminable" and then the "friendly but abrupt" waitresses are almost too "quick"; the fixed menu stars an "eternal entrecôte" with "mysterious sauce" that has "spies the world over trying to find out the recipe", along with "terrific frites" ("whatever you do, don't ask for ketchup!"); P.S. the "bargain price" includes "second helpings."

Relais du Parc (Le) 🖼 Ⓜ *Classic/New French*   19 | 18 | 16 | €73

16ᵉ | Hôtel Le Parc | 55-57, av Raymond Poncaré (Trocadéro/Victor Hugo) | 01 44 05 66 10 | fax 01 44 05 66 39 | www.leparcparishotel.com

"Robuchon meets Ducasse meets current chef" at this "expensive" hotel venue near Trocadéro, where both master toques consecutively worked (the "varied" Classic–New French menu offers the signature dishes of each); with its white clapboard walls, and seasonally changing colors, the decor channels a New England frame of mind, but the crowd is definitely *très Parisien,* particularly on the "beautiful outdoor patio."

Relais Louis XIII 🖼 Ⓜ *Haute Cuisine*   25 | 24 | 25 | €104

6ᵉ | 8, rue des Grands-Augustins (Odéon/St-Michel) | 01 43 26 75 96 | fax 01 44 07 07 80 | www.relaislouis13.com

"Feel like Louis himself and dine like a king" at this "wonderful, atavistic" table in Saint-Germain, with a "romantic châteaulike set-

ting", "outstanding Haute Cuisine" and "wine list that doesn't disappoint", proffered by an "impeccable" staff; sure, it seems "stuffy" and "unadventurous" to modernists (and "expensive" to everybody), but "staunch fans" feel it's just the "sort of place Americans dream about – and too rarely experience – in Paris."

Relais Plaza (Le) ◐ *Brasserie/Eclectic* | 23 | 22 | 22 | €76 |

8ᵉ | Plaza-Athénée | 25, av Montaigne (Alma Marceau/ Franklin D. Roosevelt) | 01 53 67 64 00 | fax 01 53 67 66 66 | www.plaza-athenee-paris.com

"Celebrities and a chic clientele" add a "touch of glamour" to this "sophisticated, intimate" art deco "brasserie deluxe"; "the more casual dining experience of the Plaza-Athénée", it's run by the same chefs behind the main restaurant, and their "seductive" Eclectic fare inspires clients to confide "you feel like you're cheating – Alain Ducasse–inspired dishes at a fraction of the price."

Rendez-vous des Chauffeurs (Au) 🗷🅼 *Bistro* | - | - | - | I |

18ᵉ | 11, rue des Portes-Blanches (Marcadet-Poissonniers) | 01 42 64 04 17

Nothing apparently changes (not even the menu) at this century-old "bistro with a real sense of neighborhood" – specifically, an untouristy part of the 18th; a "convivial" "hole-in-the-wall", it has "no decor" to speak of – just copious portions of "simply wonderful food" (including hand-cut fries that some call "the best in the world") at "very gentle prices."

Renoma Café Gallery ◐ *Italian* | - | - | - | E |

8ᵉ | 32, av George V (George V) | 01 47 20 46 19 | fax 01 40 70 90 71 | www.renoma-cafe.com

With a "resolutely modern setting" that mixes antique furniture with contemporary photos, this art gallery–like Italian makes a good canvas for a meal; "served by a friendly staff", the "food's quite nice, but needs to be more creative"; though hardly cheap, it clocks in as "one of the bargains" of the expensive 8th.

Repaire de Cartouche (Le) 🗷🅼 *Bistro* | 16 | 12 | 12 | €41 |

11ᵉ | 8, bd Filles du Calvaire (St-Sébastien Froissart) | 01 47 00 25 86 | fax 01 43 38 85 91

A "nice local feel, with few tourists" pervades this "relaxed" venue in the 11th, a site for family groups who are fans of the "rich", traditional bistro cooking; but the decor's "banal" and the service "glacial" ("maybe I came at a bad time?"), leaving some to suggest it's "not worth the 40-odd euros."

Restaurant (Le) 🗷🅼 *Classic French* | ▽ 26 | 27 | 26 | €76 |

6ᵉ | L'Hôtel | 13, rue des Beaux-Arts (St-Germain-des-Prés) | 01 44 41 99 01 | fax 01 43 25 64 81 | www.l-hotel.com

Philippe Belissent, "a chef from Ledoyen", assumed command of the venue a while back, and "what a great surprise!" – it now offers "a dreamy dinner in the dreamy decor" of the "luxuriant" Left Bank hotel "where Oscar Wilde spent his last days"; "if only he could have lived to enjoy the" "creative", "light Classic French cuisine" ("foams

and emulsions abound but not to excess"), served amid the "lushly" louche look of a low-lit space with leopard print accents, small tables and cushy chairs that "will make anyone look divine"; "servers are at the ready, but never pretentious", so if you don't mind hefty prices, hie thee to this "hedonistic experience."

Restaurant de la Tour ☒ *Classic French* ▽ 21 | 21 | 23 | €54

15ᵉ | 6, rue Desaix (Dupleix/La Motte-Picquet-Grenelle) | 01 43 06 04 24 | fax 01 44 49 05 66

"A charming place, with owners who seem genuinely pleased to welcome customers", this "colorful" site dishes up highly "delicious" Classic French fare, including "foie gras, langoustines, boned pigeon, wild boar stew and crêpes suzette"; dominated by a "business crowd at lunch", it's "very close to the Eiffel Tower, so expect Americans and Brits" as well, all attracted by the "prettily priced" prix fixes.

Restaurant du Marché ☒Ⓜ *Bistro* – | – | – | M

15ᵉ | 59, rue de Dantzig (Porte de Versailles) | 01 48 28 31 55 | fax 01 48 28 18 31

Celebrating its 40th year, this longstanding, low-key bistro in the 15th draws locals with oft-changing, "good, unpretentious country cuisine" and vaguely rustic, classic decor of red banquettes, pewter bar and the archetypical blackboard; Saturday morning cooking classes are led by chef-owner Francis Lévêque.

Restaurant du Musée d'Orsay Ⓜ *Classic French* 17 | 23 | 17 | €35

7ᵉ | Musée d'Orsay | 1, rue de la Légion d'Honneur (Solférino) | 01 45 49 47 03 | fax 01 42 22 34 12 | www.museedorsay.fr

When Manet and Monet start to merge in your mind, the Musée d'Orsay's eatery offers a "regal" "respite from museum overload" with a "stunning" river view and belle epoque decor of "painted ceilings, crystal chandeliers and mirrored walls" that is "just as interesting" as the institution itself; the Classic French fare is a bit "institutional" too, but even if "the food's better on an airplane, you couldn't ask for a prettier place to sit after a day of Impressionist art."

Restaurant du Palais Royal ☒ *Classic French* 19 | 20 | 19 | €63

1ᵉʳ | 110, Galerie de Valois (Bourse/Palais Royal-Musée du Louvre) | 01 40 20 00 27 | fax 01 40 20 00 82 | www.restaurantdupalaisroyal.com

"What better decor than the leaf-dappled shade of the Jardins du Palais-Royal?" sigh surveyors seduced by the "magnificent terrace" of this Classic French overlooking one of the city's prettiest gardens; some find it might be a little "too expensive" for food that's just "above average", but all reviewers agree that it is absolutely "idyllic on a beautiful summer evening."

Restaurant GR5 ☒ *Alpine* ▽ 24 | 17 | 22 | €33

16ᵉ | 19, rue Gustave Courbet (Rue de la Pompe) | 01 47 27 09 84
17ᵉ | 14, rue Saussier-Leroy (Ternes) | 01 47 66 15 11

"In case of an irresistible desire for fondue or raclette, make a beeline" to the nearest of these two Savoyard tables in the 16th

and 17th, a "great value" for stick-to-your-ribs, melted-cheese meals; named for an alpine footpath, either is "a good address when the cold weather hits" with a "convivial ambiance that feels like home" (assuming you live in a "noisy, tight" place with "typical Chamonix atmosphere" – red-checkered tablecloths and old-fashioned skis).

Restaurant Manufacture 🅢 *Bistro*

∇ 21 | 18 | 19 | €40

Issy-les-Moulineaux | 30, rue Ernest Renar (Corentin-Celton/ Porte de Versailles) | 01 40 93 08 98 | fax 01 40 93 57 22 | www.restaurantmanufacture.com

A "canteen for the TV-industry types working nearby", this "cool" loft space in Issy-les-Moulineaux has a "superb" setting (and camera-worthy terrace) dating from its former life as a tobacco factory; the "original" bistro food is "a clever mix of traditional products and modern flavors"; all told, it manufactures "one of the best price/ value ratios in the suburbs."

Restaurant Paul 🅜 *Bistro*

 20 | 17 | 18 | €36

1er | 15, pl Dauphine (Pont-Neuf) | 01 43 54 21 48 | fax 01 56 24 94 09

"Pretend you are in 1940s Paris" at this "quiet oasis" "on a lovely square on the Ile de la Cité", a "landmark setting" where former neighbors Yves Montand and Simone Signoret used to dine on Classic French fare; it's still served today, from "sublime breakfasts" to dinners in the traditional, mirrored bistro setting or under the stars – "an outdoor table and almost anything grilled will never disappoint" you here.

Resto (Le) 🅢 *Classic French*

- | - | - | E

8e | 10, rue de Castellane (Madeleine) | 01 40 07 99 99 | fax 01 40 07 99 49

Those seeking a stopover while shopping around the Madeleine might well find it in this "nice" intimate enclave, which juxtaposes "expensive" Classic French cuisine with retro-chic decor of aluminum foil wallpaper and '50s-style tables and chairs; the market-fresh menu changes weekly and the staff is friendly, but definitely reserve at lunchtime, since it's on a key corner in the 8th.

Reuan Thai *Thai*

 - | - | - | I

11e | 36, rue de l'Orillon (Belleville) | 01 43 55 15 82

It's a short trip from Belleville to Bangkok, thanks to this "tasty" Thai table, a "great find" for "flavorful" fare, including curries and coconut ice cream, served by a "busy" but "friendly" staff; low prices seal the deal.

Réveil du 10e (Le) 🅢 *Bistro*

 - | - | - | M

10e | 33, rue du Château d'Eau (Château d'Eau/Jacques Bonsergent) | 01 42 41 77 59

Head for the increasingly trendy 10th to try this retro-looking site (a 1960s vintage cafe); it's a "wonderful neighborhood bistro" that charms with hearty eats and, despite its small size, a "terrific wine selection", including *beaucoup de* Beaujolais by the glass.

	FOOD	DECOR	SERVICE	COST

Riad (Le) 🚫 *Moroccan* | - | - | - | M |

Neuilly-sur-Seine | 42, av Charles de Gaulle (Les Sablons/Porte Maillot) |
01 46 24 42 61 | fax 01 46 40 19 91

Composed of silk-covered banquettes and marble columns, this upscale Moroccan provides "exotic atmosphere" to the ultra-
bourgeois neighborhood of Neuilly; locals laud its "genuine North
African flavors", along with the "solicitous service" of its "friendly
staff"; there's "a good choice of interesting Moroccan wines" as well.

Ribouldingue 🚫Ⓜ *Classic French* | 18 | 15 | 14 | €40 |

5ᵉ | 10, rue St-Julien-le-Pauvre (St-Michel) | 01 46 33 98 80 |
fax 01 46 54 09 34

A few "just don't get it", but most find "fascinating" "the exquisite
way the chef prepares organs" at this offal-oriented Classic French
("I'm pretty sure I ate cow's udders and liked them"); if the decor's
"a bit rummage"-sale-like, it's because it's left over from the previous tenant; besides, what they saved on redesign is reflected in the
bill: "it's rare to find these prices" in the touristy Latin Quarter.

River Café *Classic/New French* | 14 | 15 | 11 | €48 |

Issy-les-Moulineaux | 146, quai de Stalingrad (RER Issy-Val de Seine) |
01 40 93 50 20 | fax 01 41 46 19 45 | www.lerivercafe.net

"Rare-for-Paris waterfront dining" is the daily special on this "nice
houseboat" "permanently moored" in Issy-les-Moulineaux with
"mini-terraces on each side"; but seafarers snap the combo of
Classic and New French cooking is "not inspirational" and "you have to
have time to spare" because the deck hands are in no hurry to serve.

Robe et le Palais (La) 🚫 *Wine Bar/Bistro* | 19 | 14 | 17 | €38 |

1ᵉʳ | 13, rue des Lavandières-Ste-Opportune (Châtelet-Les Halles) |
01 45 08 07 41 | fax 01 45 08 07 41

Boasting an appropriate "ambiance of cases of grand crus" (literally), this *bistrot à vins* is a "favorite" in the 1st, since its status as a
"great place to discover new wines" is supplemented by the "simple
but good" fare; the staff, however, leaves "a hot-and-cold impres-
sion": "service is slow, but the waiters are friendly."

Robert et Louise Ⓜ *Bistro* | 21 | 14 | 16 | €39 |

3ᵉ | 64, rue Vieille-du-Temple (Rambuteau) | 01 42 78 55 89

"Guests from all over the world sit together at long tables" at "this
palace of meat" in the Marais – a 50-year-old, "extremely popular"
place for its "great steaks" cooked over an open fire "right in
front of you", along with other traditional bistro dishes; the setting
amounts to a "hole-in-the-wall, with a kitchen the size of a closet",
but the welcome is "warm"; just avoid the bathroom which is, to put
it politely, rather "rustic."

Roi du Pot-au-Feu (Le) 🚫 *Bistro* | - | - | - | M |

9ᵉ | 34, rue Vignon (Havre-Caumartin/Madeleine) |
01 47 42 37 10

"Real pot-au-feu" fans make pilgrimage to this "cramped" bistro for
princely portions of the "hearty" "traditional dish" and other "beefy"

"French staples"; while its 1930s setting almost "seems too kitschy", it's a "must-do" "for a meal to put you to sleep or to last you all day" shopping nearby on the Grands Boulevards.

Romantica (La) ☒ *Italian* ▽ 23 | 20 | 19 | €59

Clichy | 73, bd Jean Jaurès (Mairie-de-Clichy) | 01 47 37 29 71 | fax 01 47 37 76 32 | www.claudiopuglia.com

Latin food lovers say this idyllic Italian in the Clichy suburbs "lives up to its name", with a flower-filled courtyard, "very friendly" service and "excellent" pasta; "don't miss the house specialty", tagliolini flambéed tableside in a Parmesan wheel, but "be warned" that this filling dish might leave you "too sleepy to be romantic afterwards."

Rose Bakery Ⓜ *British/French* 17 | 12 | 13 | €27

9ᵉ | 46, rue des Martyrs (Notre-Dame-de-Lorette) | 01 42 82 12 80

A "media favorite" that "emphasizes market freshness", this Anglo-French tearoom/bakery/takeaway on the hippest street in the 9th offers "original", often organic fare from morning until early evening (it's especially "great for brunch"); but the rose is not without its thorns: if "long on food, it's short on ambiance", and "much too small for its enthusiastic clientele (you can spend a lot of time waiting)."

Rose de France *Bistro* - | - | - | M

1ᵉʳ | 24, pl Dauphine (Pont Neuf/Cité) | 01 43 54 10 12 | www.larosedefrance.com

Located on a calm, tree-lined square on the Ile de la Cité, this "small" but "warm and welcoming" bistro beckons with "a choice of French classics with new wave flair"; the "co-owner will advise on the wines" – some from his own vineyard – and the experience is especially "charming" if you snag a sidewalk seat, "sheltered from the city noise."

Rosimar ☒ *Spanish* - | - | - | M

16ᵉ | 26, rue Poussin (Michel-Ange-Auteuil/Porte d'Auteuil) | 01 45 27 74 91 | fax 01 45 20 75 05

"Almost everyone's a regular, yet newcomers are well treated" at this "neighborhood place" "in the heart of the 16th" arrondissement; "authentic Catalan cuisine", "world-class paella" (order it when you book) and a "heartwarming welcome" make up for the "mirrored" but "gloomy decor."

Rôtisserie d'en Face (La) ☒ *Bistro* 21 | 18 | 20 | €51

6ᵉ | 2, rue Christine (Odéon/St-Michel) | 01 43 26 40 98 | fax 01 43 54 22 71 | www.jacques-cagna.com

Diners whose appetites are richer than their wallets make a habit of Jacques Cagna's "casual", "always buzzing" bistro in Saint-Germain supplying "simple, excellently prepared food for a fraction of the price" of the chef-owner's Haute Cuisine table nearby; but if the menu is full of "solid" Gallic "staples" (notably "rotisserie chicken to beat the band"), the clientele is too close to home – seems like "every person in the restaurant is American!"

	FOOD	DECOR	SERVICE	COST

Rôtisserie du Beaujolais (La) *Bistro*   23 | 18 | 21 | €47
5e | 19, quai de la Tournelle (Jussieu/Pont-Marie) | 01 43 54 17 47 | fax 01 56 24 43 71 | www.tourdargent.com
Overlooking the Seine, this "bustling" bistro might be "next to La Tour d'Argent", but it's "completely different" from its grandiose parent; it's "one heck of a lot more reasonable", with "down-home" Beaujolais fare, including "perfectly cooked meat" from a rotisserie overlooking the room, and a "cramped but charming" atmosphere made even more "homey" by the "owners' cat, named Beaujolais, often sleeping next to the bar" ("admire the feline and you'll get a better table").

Rotonde (La) ● *Brasserie*   15 | 14 | 14 | €49
6e | 105, bd du Montparnasse (Vavin) | 01 43 26 48 26 | fax 01 46 34 52 40 | www.rotondemontparnasse.com
In Montparnasse, a "neighborhood populated by famous cafes from a bygone era", this "elegant old-time brasserie" is a "favorite" for its "ruby-red decor" and "padded little nooks"; while critics carp the cuisine's "correct" but "not exceptional", at least the "genuinely surly but efficient waiters" add to the authentic atmosphere of yore.

Rouge St-Honoré *Eclectic*   ∇ 13 | 14 | 14 | €34
1er | 34, pl du Marché St-Honoré (Pyramides/Tuileries) | 01 42 61 16 09 | fax 01 42 61 17 01
Although they've diversified somewhat, the menu's still "based on the tomato and its derivatives" at this "cute" Eclectic with grocery-store-like decor; "perfectly adequate for somewhere cheap and cheerful, it's nothing to get excited about" – though the location overlooking the Place du Marché Saint-Honoré is "pleasant for sitting outside on a warm evening."

Rouge Vif (Le) ⊠ *Southwest*   15 | 13 | 16 | €42
7e | 48, rue de Verneuil (Musée d'Orsay/Solférino) | 01 42 86 81 87
"Just up the street from the Musée d'Orsay", this "real down-home" bistro in the 7th offers "a huge chalkboard" menu of Southwestern dishes for "reasonable prices"; "the owner and his wife are full of bright smiles, but they need to up the ambiance level" – and maybe modernize the "heavy, traditional" cuisine as well.

Royal Madeleine *Classic French*   19 | 16 | 17 | €55
8e | 12, rue du Chevalier St-Georges (Madeleine) | 01 42 60 14 36 | fax 01 42 61 02 16 | www.royalmadeleine.com
On a side street "near the Madeleine", this "charming bistro" boasts a "typically Parisian", old-fashioned dining room "with garnet velvet banquettes, period engravings", copper pans and a vintage zinc bar; an "amiable" staff serves "refreshingly down to earth" Classic French dishes, and if it's "a little expensive", that's not surprising given the "good-quality" fare, "warm" decor and "froufrou neighborhood."

Rubis (Le) ⊠ *Wine Bar/Bistro*   15 | 10 | 15 | €27
1er | 10, rue du Marché St-Honoré (Tuileries) | 01 42 61 03 34
Here's one ruby (*rubis*) that's a real "gem" declare devotees who haunt this "essential" wine bar steps from the Place du Marché

Saint-Honoré; it "hasn't changed in 25 years", but still overflows with "atmosphere, true French personality", a "sublime value-for-money lunch" of classic Gallic fare (or just charcuterie and cheese plates at night) and an inexpensive selection of Beaujolais that's drunk liberally around "barrels on the sidewalk when it's nice out."

Rucola (La) 🅢 Italian

-	-	-	M

17e | 198, bd Malesherbes (Wagram) | 01 44 40 04 50 | fax 01 47 63 13 20

"In a neighborhood filled with mediocre Italian food", the "elegant" offerings of this table ("no pizzas!") attract lots of locals; but the candlelit dining room, decorated with wines in open bins, "welcomes even tourists as prodigal sons and daughters" to this section of the 17th.

Rue Balzac 🌒🅢 New French

17	17	16	€65

8e | 3-5, rue Balzac (George V) | 01 53 89 90 91 | fax 01 53 89 90 94

"Johnny's restaurant" remains a "place to be seen" in the 8th, thanks to France's eternal rocker, co-owner Johnny Hallyday ("you come across him here sometimes"); a "hip crowd" circulates amid the "funky" red-and-blue decor and "original" New French food, and if critics carp the portions, available in both full and half sizes, are "meager for the cost", at least that's "good for your diet."

Rughetta (La) 🌒🅢 Italian

-	-	-	M

18e | 41, rue Lepic (Abbesses/Blanche) | 01 42 23 41 70

"Always packed with the young crowd and celebrities" from the neighborhood, this "lively" Montmartre trattoria serves "very good" pizza and pasta that are redolent of Rome; so what if "the personnel is not always nice" and the decor is minimal – "the terrace is really cool in the summer."

Sale e Pepe 🌒🅢Ⓜ Italian

-	-	-	M

18e | 30, rue Ramey (Château Rouge/Jules Joffrin) | 01 46 06 08 01 | fax 01 42 62 45 49

"You'll feel at home as heaping portions of pasta are served onto your plate from a steaming sauté pan" at this "affordable" "cozy" Sicilian in the 18th, where "a bubbly Italian duo greets you" then treats you to "delicious thin-crust pizzas as well as pastas" made with "fresh ingredients"; "but don't expect a menu, as the chef typically brings out whatever he's compelled to prepare."

Salon d'Hélène 🅢Ⓜ Southwest

19	18	17	€70

6e | 4, rue d'Assas (Sèvres-Babylone) | 01 42 22 00 11 | fax 01 42 22 25 40

"More casual than her fine-dining restaurant" on the floor above, Hélène Darroze's tapas bar-like canteen in the 6th is "popular with the young slick crowd" that covets her "dreamy" "small-portioned" Southwest French–inspired plates, including "the best foie gras on earth"; "the food's quite good, but it's not worth the ticket with the non-decor and frosty service" snarl cynics (though others find the staff "affable" enough); P.S. sybarites suggest "if your wallet and schedule allow, indulge in the lunchtime tasting menu" – 10 courses for 88€.

		FOOD	DECOR	SERVICE	COST

NEW Salon du Panthéon ☒ *Bistro*
| | | - | - | - | M |

5ᵉ | Cinéma du Panthéon | 13, rue Victor Cousin (RER Luxembourg/
Cluny-La Sorbonne) | 01 56 24 88 80 | www.cinemadupantheon.fr
Located on the top floor of the Cinéma du Panthéon, this smart '60s-
style café was decorated by screen goddess Catherine Deneuve
(with an antiques dealer's help); ever since its autumn 2007 premiere,
it's been pulling a hip crowd that loves to lounge on the generously
spaced sofas, lingering over a drink or a light meal of bistro bites.

Samiin *Korean*
| | | - | - | - | M |

7ᵉ | 74, av de Breteuil (Sèvres-Leçourbe) | 01 47 34 58 96 |
www.samiin.com
"Delicious Korean cuisine in a lovely setting" is the lure at this original little place near the Ecole Militaire; "the female servers are
charming and helpful", and prices are "so reasonable for the quality
and creativity" of the homestyle fare.

San *Italian*
| | | - | - | - | M |

3ᵉ | 27, bd du Temple (République) | 01 44 61 73 45 | fax 01 44 61 73 45 |
www.sanristorante.com
In place of the usual clichéd decor (murals of Vesuvius, a visible
wood-burning oven), this hip pie palace near the Place de la
République pulls in trendsters with a loftlike scene of designer table-
ware, red chairs and movies projected on the white walls; pizzas
with imaginative toppings and sassy service give the place a lot of
buzz, and those seeking a pizza the action appreciate that you don't
knead too much dough to eat well.

Sardegna a Tavola ☒ *Italian*
| | | ▽ 21 | 12 | 12 | €55 |

12ᵉ | 1, rue de Cotte (Ledru-Rollin) | 01 44 75 03 28 | fax 01 44 75 03 02
It's not rare to be surrounded by Italian families enjoying this crowded,
"superb" Sardinian out in the 12th; regulars ignore the "brusque"
service and concentrate on the "finesse" of the "creative preparations" and regional wines, saying "enormous portions" ("sharing's
encouraged") make the "inflated prices" a little easier to swallow.

Sarladais (Le) ☒ *Southwest*
| | | - | - | - | E |

8ᵉ | 2, rue de Vienne (St-Augustin) | 01 45 22 23 62 | fax 01 45 22 23 62 |
www.lesarladais.com
Patrons who venture into this venue "off the beaten path" near the
Gare Saint-Lazare are "amazed" to dig into a "tremendous cassoulet" and other seafood-oriented, "consistent" classics from the
Southwest; the staff "serves with easy assurance", and the "warmly
decorated" digs make it "dependable" for a business lunch or "quiet
meal with a friend."

Saudade ☒ *Portugese*
| | | - | - | - | M |

1ᵉʳ | 34, rue des Bourdonnais (Châtelet-Les Halles) | 01 42 36 03 65 |
fax 01 42 36 30 71 | www.restaurantsaudade.com
Perfect for "anyone who loves cod in all its preparations", this long-
running Lusitanian near Châtelet is considered by many to be the
best outpost of Portugal in Paris; perhaps the azulejo-tiled dining

room is "ready for an update", but you still get "guaranteed atmosphere", especially when the live music plays on fado night.

NEW Saut du Loup (Le) ● *New French*   14 | 17 | 15 | €51

1er | Musée des Arts Décoratifs | 107, rue de Rivoli (Palais Royal-Musée du Louvre/Tuileries) | 01 42 25 49 55 | www.lesautduloup.com

Tucked away inside the newly renovated Musée des Arts Décoratifs, this "fashionable" New French offers "gorgeous views" over the Louvre courtyard; while the menu is "good", it "doesn't have many surprises", so enjoy the "nifty" setting instead – a "chic" black-and-white dining room decked out with designer furniture – or, "if the weather's nice, opt for the terrace" with that "Parisian dreamscape" of the I.M. Pei pyramid, the Jardins du Carrousel and the Tuileries.

Sauvignon (Au) *Sandwiches/Wine Bar*   14 | 13 | 13 | €35

7e | 80, rue des Sts-Pères (Sèvres-Babylone) | 01 45 48 49 02 | fax 01 45 49 41 00

"A chic crowd" that spends more shopping than eating "grabs a quick lunch" or après-store munchie at this "delightful" *bar à vins* with "lovely *tartines*" (open-face sandwiches) "and a wonderful selection of wines by the glass"; "such a deal you will not find elsewhere" rave bargain-hunters, "especially considering the neighborhood" (the tony 7th).

Saveurs de Claude (Aux) 🅢 *Classic/New French*   - | - | - | M

6e | 12, rue Stanislas (Notre-Dame-des-Champs/Vavin) | 01 45 44 41 74 | fax 01 45 44 41 95 | www.auxsaveursclaude.com

"Charming" chef-owner Claude Lamain honed his skills working with Guy Savoy before opening this "small" "neighborhood find" in Montparnasse with an "excellently prepared and beautifully presented" Classic and New French menu; the relaxed ambiance owes much to the "warm" "unrushed service" and "well-spaced tables" in an intimate room with low lighting and a stripped-down art deco design.

Saveurs de Flora (Les) 🅢 *New French*   21 | 21 | 20 | €66

8e | 36, av George V (George V) | 01 40 70 10 49 | fax 01 47 20 52 87 | www.lessaveursdeflora.com

Chef-owner Flora Mikula's hideaway just off the Champs-Elysées "feels almost like somebody's private dining room" with "a cozy atmosphere" created by wallpaper, mirrors and candlelight; her "personal", "inventive-but-not-over-the top" New French fare is served by a "warm", if often "overwhelmed" staff; though it's not cheap, most find it "reasonably priced", given the expensive neighborhood.

Saveurs du Marché (Aux) 🅢 *Bistro*   - | - | - | M

Neuilly-sur-Seine | 4, rue de l'Eglise (Pont-de-Neuilly) | 01 47 45 72 11 | fax 01 46 37 72 13

This "good little" place in posh suburban Neuilly boasts fresh, often organic products from the nearby local *marché* (market) and "pleasing" Classic French dishes by chef-owner David Cheleman, who cut his teeth working with Jean-Pierre Vigato (Apicius); be aware, the black-and-beige bistro is "unfortunately not open during the weekend."

	FOOD	DECOR	SERVICE	COST

Sawadee ⓈThai
| | - | - | - | M |

15ᵉ | 53, av Emile Zola (Charles Michels) | 01 45 77 68 90
Its friendly "multilingual staff" makes this "excellent Thai" in a "somewhat concrete corner" of the 15th a "place one returns to with pleasure", even if "the menu hasn't changed in years"; the pretty dining room with golden Buddhas offers a bit of Bangkok to boot.

Scheffer (Le) Ⓢ Bistro
| | 18 | 13 | 19 | €36 |

16ᵉ | 22, rue Scheffer (Trocadéro) | 01 47 27 81 11
"The old owner is gone, taking some of his posters with him, but they've done a great job of maintaining the old atmosphere, good food and low prices" at this "terrific bistro near Trocadéro"; a "simple place", it's often "noisy" and "jam-packed", but it proves that getting "value for money" "is not impossible" in the "snooty 16th."

Scoop Eclectic
| | ▽ 17 | 12 | 12 | €28 |

1ᵉʳ | 154, rue St-Honoré (Louvre-Rivoli/Palais Royal-Musée du Louvre) | 01 42 60 31 84 | fax 01 42 36 01 81 | www.scoopcafe.com
Here's a scoop: when shopping on the Rue Saint-Honoré, refresh yourself with the Eclectic offerings of this "charming ice cream place", which also serves "ample salads" and "absolutely fabulous burgers"; aiming for "an American-style ambiance", the "narrow" red-and-white space "doesn't have enough style" some scold, but "you get your money's worth."

Sébillon ● Brasserie
| | 15 | 14 | 14 | €52 |

Neuilly-sur-Seine | 20, av Charles de Gaulle (Les Sablons/Porte Maillot) | 01 46 24 71 31 | fax 01 46 24 43 50 | www.rest-gj.com
A "Parisian-style brasserie in Neuilly", this "noisy" veteran has been "serving traditional French meals" since World War I; however, old-timers advise "go for one reason only: the famous, eat-as-much-as-you-can lamb" carved tableside, as the "rest of the menu is mediocre", and both the decor and "the service were a lot better 30 years ago" (and on our previous Survey).

16 Haussmann (Le) Ⓢ New French
| | 18 | 18 | 17 | €70 |

9ᵉ | Hôtel Ambassador | 16, bd Haussmann (Chaussée d'Antin/Richelieu-Drouot) | 01 44 83 40 58 | fax 01 44 83 40 57 | www.hotelambassador-paris.com
Philippe Starck's "splendid", nouveau-"baroque" decor is a fitting backdrop for the "innovative" New French cooking at this "luxury hotel restaurant" steps from the Opéra Garnier; clients get "cozy" in the "comfortable chairs" and "well-spaced tables", unperturbed at the slightly "absent-minded service" and "high-end" prices (though some say it all "would be better if the exchange rate were better" too).

ⓏSenderens Brasserie/New French
| | 26 | 22 | 23 | €115 |

8ᵉ | 9, pl de la Madeleine (Madeleine) | 01 42 65 22 90 | fax 01 42 65 06 23 | www.senderens.fr
"Isn't it refreshing when a 70-year-old chef breaks all conventions and reinvents what a restaurant should be?"; that's what happened

when chef-owner Alain Senderens transformed "the venerable Lucas Carton" in the 8th into a "more casual" *brasserie de luxe,* with "creative" New French cuisine and "modernized" design (think a tented ceiling, Corian-topped tables and metallic leather chairs); many "miss Carton's decor and superior service", especially since "the price tag is [still] not insignificant", but almost all agree the "food's fabulous", and find "the new formula a winner."

Sens ●🅩 *Mediterranean*   — | — | — | E

8ᵉ | 23, rue de Ponthieu (Franklin D. Roosevelt) | 01 42 25 95 00 | fax 01 42 25 95 02 | www.sens-paris.com

The Pourcel twins, chef-owners behind Montpellier's famed Jardin des Sens, take on the affluent Golden Triangle with this slick see-and-be-seen venue; the futuristic gray decor, topped by a glass-roofed bar, creates a chic background to the designer thread-garbed clientele consuming "good" seafood-oriented Med specialties, brought by befittingly blasé staffers.

Sensing (Le) 🅩 *New French*   24 | 21 | 21 | €71

6ᵉ | 19, rue Brea (Vavin) | 01 43 27 08 80 | fax 01 43 26 99 27 | www.restaurant-sensing.com

"Be sure to ask for the rear dining room" (it's where the fashionable folks flock) at this "affordable high-end restaurant" owned by chef-restaurateur "Guy Martin from Grand Véfour"; most find the New French fare "a gastronomic delight, so gorgeous we actually took photos", and the "staff is astonishingly friendly"; we're sensing some dissent over the tobacco-brown and limestone decor – "sophisticated" vs. "kinda cold" – but overall, this "trendy anti-bistro" is "a grand addition" to Montparnasse.

7ème Sud ● *Mediterranean/Moroccan*   15 | 15 | 14 | €33

7ᵉ | 159, rue de Grenelle (La Tour-Maubourg) | 01 44 18 30 30 | fax 01 44 18 07 42 🅩
16ᵉ | 56, rue de Boulainvilliers (La Muette) | 01 45 20 18 32

"Very BCBG" (French for 'preppy'), this pair, each an "understated" "cross between a cafe and a restaurant" in the 7th and 16th arrondissements, is "always a good time" if you're "loud, hip and young"; big at brunch, the "sunny" Med-Moroccan menu is "on the high side of average" and the "service is nice – even toward Americans who don't speak French well"; no wonder many "wish they could be a regular" here.

Sept Quinze
(Le) 🅩 *Californian/Mediterranean*   ▽ 21 | 14 | 18 | €45

15ᵉ | 29, av Lowendal (Cambronne/Ségur) | 01 43 06 23 06

"Reservations are a must since the locals dine frequently" at this "bustling, lively restaurant on the border between the 7th and the 15th" arrondissements (hence the name); an "enthusiastic staff serves Mediterranean-French fusion cuisine" with some "creative" Californian quirks (one of the owners "spent many successful years in San Francisco"); since it "sometimes can get noisy", "choose the terrace" if weather permits.

	FOOD	DECOR	SERVICE	COST

Severo (Le) 🍷 *Steak*

20 | 12 | 16 | €46

14ᵉ | 8, rue des Plantes (Mouton-Duvernet) | 01 45 40 40 91

"Meat eaters and wine drinkers unite" at this small site in the 14th, where the owner, "formerly a butcher", emphasizes beef (in fact that's all he serves) and ages it too, serving it with some of "the best varietals in France"; the atmosphere is "typical Parisian" bistro, from the blackboards on the walls to the "service that lacks friendliness."

Sinago (Le) 🍷 *Cambodian*

- | - | - | I

9ᵉ | 17, rue de Maubeuge (Cadet/Notre-Dame-de-Lorette) | 01 48 78 11 14

Converts to Cambodian cuisine caution you "must reserve" ahead for this "friendly neighborhood favorite" in the 9th; it's a Phnom-enal address for "excellent", "fresh" Khmer dishes, even if the narrow room with slightly incongruous decor of wood paneling and rigging from an old Breton boat is "mediocre."

6 New York 🍷 *New French*

17 | 17 | 18 | €55

16ᵉ | 6, av de New York (Alma Marceau) | 01 40 70 03 30 | fax 01 40 70 04 77

As "modern" as Manhattan (with "wonderful views of the Eiffel Tower" across the Seine to prove where you really are), this "aptly named", "chic" table in the 16th boasts "contemporary", "sober" surrounds and a "good-looking" staff to back up the "innovative" French cuisine; though a Food score drop confirms culinary "standards have slipped recently", it still draws an "upper-crust clientele" that doesn't mind the "stiff prices."

Sizin ●🍷 *Turkish*

- | - | - | M

9ᵉ | 47, rue St-Georges (St-Georges) | 01 44 63 02 28 | www.sizin-restaurant.com

"Not your corner kebab joint" bellow Byzantine experts of this "superb value-for-money" "family restaurant" in the 9th, decorated with old postcards of Istanbul; a "warm, welcoming staff serves fine Turkish cuisine" and wines as "authentic" as they are unusual.

Soleil (Le) Ⓜ *Bistro*

- | - | - | M

Saint-Ouen | 109, av Michelet (Porte de Clignancourt) | 01 40 10 08 08 | fax 01 40 10 16 85

Since "there are not many good dining choices" "near the Clignancourt flea market", this bistro becomes a "don't-miss" for hungry antique-hunters; fortunately, the traditional French fare is "wonderful", with "outrageous Breton butter" to smear on the bread; only the "offhand" service mars the experience.

Soleil (Le) 🍷 *Mediterranean*

∇ 19 | 19 | 22 | €49

7ᵉ | 153, rue de Grenelle (La Tour-Maubourg) | 01 45 51 54 12

The only thing missing from this "small", "sweet Mediterranean bistro" "on the great Rue de Grenelle" is the sea itself, but the food and Antibes-style decor of white wrought-iron chairs, pink cushions and sun-adorned tiles put you in a Provençal state of mind; sister to Le Soleil in Saint-Ouen, it also offers "terrific" service.

	FOOD	DECOR	SERVICE	COST

Sora Lena 🗷 *Italian/Mediterranean*

	-	-	-	E

17ᵉ | 18, rue Bayen (Ternes) | 01 45 74 73 73 |
fax 01 45 74 73 52

Near the Place des Ternes, this "trendy nouvelle Italian-Med" has "a lot of atmosphere" that attracts well-heeled locals who laud the "originality (like the beef carpaccio with shellfish)" of the southern regional dishes and the "professional, discreet service"; though it's named for the owners' grandmother, the "refined setting" and "professional, discreet service" translate to a tab more typical of louche lounge than home cooking.

Sormani 🗷 *Italian*

	23	16	20	€76

17ᵉ | 4, rue du Général Lanrezac (Charles de Gaulle-Etoile) |
01 43 80 13 91 | fax 01 40 55 07 37

"Everyone raves" that this "institution" near the Etoile is one of "the best Italians in Paris"; with "divine" dishes often "bathed in truffles", it's "as close to Italy as you are going to get without going there" (but don't expect an economic advantage, since the "prices are astounding"); the Venetian-style, "lively red decor partially offsets" the "oppressive" air generated by the number of "business and older patrons."

Sot l'y Laisse (Le) 🗷Ⓜ *Bistro*

	-	-	-	M

11ᵉ | 70, rue Alexandre Dumas (Alexandre Dumas) | 01 40 09 79 20 |
fax 01 40 09 79 20

Named for a particularly choice piece of poultry, this yellow-toned, "lovely discovery in a lost corner of Paris" south of Père Lachaise is a "charming bistro", with fare that combines "finesse and simplicity" and a "superb wine list"; all's served with "remarkable gentility" in "truly warm" digs.

🗷 Soufflé (Le) 🗷 *Classic French*

	22	17	22	€50

1ᵉʳ | 36, rue du Mont-Thabor (Concorde) | 01 42 60 27 19 |
fax 01 42 60 54 98

"Beloved by natives and tourists alike", this 1st-arrondissement "institution" is known, like the name says, for "soufflés in more possibilities than you thought were possible" – "you can even get a three-course menu" of the puffers – "baked with loving hands" and "served with panache" amid an atmosphere of "old-school charm"; the savvy "steer clear of the rest of the Classic French menu", and eventually the egg-white "novelty wears off" – but when the need strikes, this is a "sure cure for your soufflé jones."

Soupière (La) 🗷 *Classic French*

	-	-	-	E

17ᵉ | 154, av de Wagram (Wagram) | 01 46 22 80 10 |
fax 01 46 22 27 09

This "little storefront at the top of the Avenue de Wagram" is an underground favorite for fungiophiles who crown it "the king of mushrooms", given "the creative chef's incomparable talent for preparing" them on the "exceptional" Classic French menu; a "familial ambiance" prevails, despite the "no-frills" decor, thanks to the "helpful, friendly *patron* and *patronne*."

	FOOD	DECOR	SERVICE	COST

Spoon, Food & Wine ⊠ *Eclectic/New French*   22 | 20 | 22 | €74

8ᵉ | Hôtel Marignan | 14, rue de Marignan (Franklin D. Roosevelt) | 01 40 76 34 44 | fax 01 40 76 34 37 | www.spoon.tm.fr

"An adventure in world-influenced cuisine" "à la Alain Ducasse" lures a "young" international crowd to this hotel venue with a purple-hued, "clean, modern setting" just off the Champs; "you are in control" as you "mix and match" the Eclectic–New French "dishes paired in and across columns" on the menu, aided by "very friendly servers"; if a few find it "disappointing" – "small tastes, fairly large prices" – most say "just splurge and do it."

Spring ⊠Ⓜ *Bistro*   23 | 15 | 20 | €48

9ᵉ | 28, rue de la Tour d'Auvergne (Anvers) | 01 45 96 05 72

"Astonishing food" from American chef-owner Daniel Rose ("the nicest guy") has made this 16-seat storefront in the 9th one of the toughest reservations in town; "a dinner-party atmosphere" prevails as the young toque, who worked with Paul Bocuse and Yannick Alléno at Le Meurice, often "serves wine and clears plates" as well as cooks his "single set menu" of "fresh, well-executed" contemporary bistro fare; "where else will you find such passion?"

Square (Le) ⊠ *Classic French*   - | - | - | M

7ᵉ | 31, rue St-Dominique (Invalides/Solférino) | 01 45 51 09 03 | fax 01 45 50 48 70

This "chic", "lively" "hot spot" covers all the right angles with a "noisy", "friendly vibe" provided by a "young crowd" and "charming servers"; while the Classic French food is "perfectly fine", folks come "more for fun than cuisine"; still, the "great prix fixes" offer a "bang for your buck" that's "nice in a neighborhood" (the 7th) where "reasonable" is rare.

Square (Le) ⊠Ⓜ *Classic/New French*   - | - | - | M

18ᵉ | 227 bis, rue Marcadet (Guy Moquet) | 01 53 11 08 41 | www.le-square.fr

A hipster crowd makes a straight line for this casual, "excellent" address in the faraway 18th, where huge blackboards present the day's offerings, an inventive mix of Classic and New French cuisine; "a fine time" can be had wherever one perches: the bar area with banquettes, the dining room with wooden bistro tables overlooking a patio garden or the garden itself, with vine-covered walls.

Square Trousseau (Le) ●⊠Ⓜ *Bistro*   ∇ 19 | 19 | 17 | €43

12ᵉ | 1, rue Antoine Vollon (Bastille/Ledru-Rollin) | 01 43 43 06 00 | fax 01 43 43 00 66

"Off the beaten track", this "friendly bistro" "just across from the charming Square Trousseau" in the 12th is a "nice neighborhood place", with "charming", "old-fashioned classic" decor (banquettes, zinc bar, etc.), a kitchen that "brings a new twist to the standards (our favorite: the veal shank with honey)" and "swift, sharp staffers"; a "lively crowd" heads for the "patio seating in the warmer weather."

Stella (Le) ● *Brasserie*

FOOD	DECOR	SERVICE	COST
20	16	18	€49

16ᵉ | 133, av Victor Hugo (Rue de la Pompe/Victor Hugo) | 01 56 90 56 00 | fax 01 56 90 56 01

What may be "the chicest brasserie in Paris" – "it's located in the wealthy 16th" – swings with smart-looking "neighborhood foodies" dining on "an ever-fresh supply of seafood", "fabulous steak tartare" and other "clichés of French cooking" (seriously, "the cuisine has recently improved"); the staff, which "comes and goes with incredible speed", has a "fun, slap-on-the-bottom, malicious air"; "low-key and easy", it's especially "worth it on those evenings when everything else is closed" (it serves until 1 AM).

☑ Stella Maris ⑤ *Classic French*

FOOD	DECOR	SERVICE	COST
26	17	21	€95

8ᵉ | 4, rue Arsène Houssaye (Charles de Gaulle-Etoile) | 01 42 89 16 22 | fax 01 42 89 16 01

A "hidden jewel off the Champs-Elysées" enthuse admirers of this "inventive" establishment owned by Tateru Yoshino, a "Japanese chef who breathes elegant Asian undertones into Classic French fare" – just try the cabbage pâté or Indian-spiced lobster to experience his "exquisite" creativity; admittedly, "prices have gone up", many find the "minimalist decor more suited to business than romance" and the service, though "warm", often "drags as the evening wears on"; but these things only slightly mar a mostly "magical" time.

Stéphane Gaborieau-Le Pergolèse ⑤ *Haute Cuisine*

FOOD	DECOR	SERVICE	COST
-	-	-	VE

16ᵉ | 40, rue Pergolèse (Argentine) | 01 45 00 21 40 | fax 01 45 00 81 31 | www.lepergolese.com

After working in luxury hotels in Lyon and the south of France, chef-owner Stéphane Gaborieau now runs this plush old-timer in the 16th, and is "slowly introducing his own flavors" into the classic Haute Cuisine menu; the wood-paneled dining room with oil paintings on the walls and crisp linen tablecloths is "intimate and quiet", even "romantic"; expect suave service and steep prices.

Stéphane Martin ⑤Ⓜ *Classic French*

FOOD	DECOR	SERVICE	COST
-	-	-	M

15ᵉ | 67, rue des Entrepreneurs (Charles Michels/Commerce) | 01 45 79 03 31 | fax 01 45 79 44 69

"With chef-owner Stéphane Martin doing fantastic things in the kitchen, and his wife Marie-Lucille charming guests in the dining room", this Classic French is "a great non-touristy place" tucked away in the "unassuming" 15th; both the decor and service have a "warm feel", and even if the latter's a little "rushed on weekends", the place remains "a find!"

Strapontins (Les) *Classic French*

FOOD	DECOR	SERVICE	COST
-	-	-	M

10ᵉ | 16, av Richerand (Bonsergent/République) | 01 42 41 94 79 | fax 01 42 41 74 49

A "lively young crowd" battles for a "table in the sun" on the "calm, pretty little terrace" of this casual Classic French "just off the Canal" Saint-Martin and "overlooking the 16th-century walls of the Hôpital Saint-Louis"; the "owners try hard to please and usually succeed."

	FOOD	DECOR	SERVICE	COST

Stresa (Le) 🏠 *Italian*

	22	16	19	€87

8ᵉ | 7, rue Chambiges (Alma Marceau) | 01 47 23 51 62

The "stars" come out to this "wonderful" Italian in the 8th, where it's "tough to get a table" unless "you know someone" (or, better yet, *are* someone); the refined cuisine is "highly recommended for cognoscenti", though prices are so high the figures "while in euros, seem to be in lira", and some say simply "do not go" unless you get off on "clients who spend their time looking at each other in an aquarium of mirrors."

Studio (The) ● *Tex-Mex*

	-	-	-	M

4ᵉ | 41, rue du Temple (Hôtel-de-Ville/Rambuteau) | 01 42 74 10 38 | fax 01 42 41 50 34 | www.the-studio.fr

"If you're in the mood for Mexican in a funky setting" – a 17th-century courtyard, shared with a dance studio – then head to this Tex-Mex in the Marais; "coming from a Texan" surveyor, "this place may have the best in Paris" – or at least, "the closest to the real thing."

Suave 🏠 *Vietnamese*

	-	-	-	I

13ᵉ | 20, rue de la Providence (Corvisart/Tolbiac) | 01 45 89 99 27 | fax 01 45 81 34 60

Reservations are imperative at this "small" but "cute" site near Butte aux Cailles, often "crowded" with admirers of its "ample portions of Vietnamese food – less spicy than [in the U.S.], but very good nevertheless"; "kind service" and a suave use of "fresh" ingredients make it stand out in a neighborhood filled with Asian eateries.

Sud (Le) 🏠 *Mediterranean/Provence*

	▽ 16	18	16	€52

17ᵉ | 91, bd Gouvion-St-Cyr (Porte Maillot) | 01 45 74 02 77 | fax 01 45 74 35 36 | www.lesud.fr

"Ah, the sound of crickets in the middle of a Paris winter" sigh surveyors who "feel like they're on vacation" at this Provençal oasis "next to the traffic jams of Porte Maillot"; "exotic Med cuisine and a mix of colors in the plate" reflect the "southern ambiance" of the "under-the-olive-trees" decor; recently acquired by the Frères Blanc group, it seems "less good" to some, and the bill is "a little pricey"; nevertheless, the place can get as "crowded" as Aix in August.

Suffren (Le) ● *Brasserie*

	14	12	13	€43

15ᵉ | 84, av de Suffren (La Motte-Picquet-Grenelle) | 01 45 66 97 86 | fax 01 47 34 68 82

This family-owned, "bustling brasserie" in the 15th has long been a "popular", "neighborhood standard"; "regulars who stick to the classics and don't [challenge] the kitchen's creativity" report it "delivers what it promises: well-executed versions of basic French fare"; prices are higher and the staff's gotten "a little slower", but "great people-watching" from a large sun-filled terrace passes the time.

🆕 SYDR (Syderie de l'Etoile) 🏠 Ⓜ *Southwest*

	-	-	-	M

8ᵉ | 6, rue de Tilsitt (Charles de Gaulle-Etoile) | 01 45 7241 32

Taking his inspiration from Basque tapas bars, chef-owner Alain Dutournier (Carré des Feuillants) has brought an idiosyncratic slice

of the Southwest to Paris with this huge, all-white canteen near the Arc de Triomphe; popular with rugby fans (former star Philippe Sella is a co-owner), it serves up hearty eats and regional wines in gregarious surrounds that include a communal table for 22 people.

Table d'Anvers (La) *Classic French* — 17 | 16 | 15 | €55

9ᵉ | 2, pl d'Anvers (Anvers) | 01 48 78 35 21 | fax 01 45 26 66 67 | www.latabledanvers.com

"Discreet and low-key" ("the signature orchid on the table says it all"), this Classic French on the edge of Montmartre appeals to tourists and locals alike with its "copious meals" and weekday jazz concerts; however, cynics say it's "expensive for the type of food" – "basic, if well prepared."

Table de Babette (La) ⓩ *Creole* — - | - | - | E

16ᵉ | 32, rue de Longchamp (Boissière/Trocadéro) | 01 45 53 00 07 | fax 01 45 53 00 15

TV chef Babette de Rozières unveils the upper-crust side of French Caribbean cooking – usually found in more casual places – in her colonial Louisiana–like dining room in the 16th; within its formal, hushed confines, the kitchen does urbane takes on such Creole classics as blood sausages and gumbo; still, old-world types find "the prices high" for what they deem "regional cuisine."

ⓩ Table de Joël Robuchon (La) *Haute Cuisine* — 26 | 21 | 25 | €119

16ᵉ | 16, av Bugeaud (Victor Hugo) | 01 56 28 16 16 | fax 01 56 28 16 78 | www.joel-robuchon.com

"Haute Cuisine presented by a master" sums up owner Joël Robuchon's "elegant" eatery in the 16th, which offers his "trademark" "food that tastes likes real food" (regulars recommend "ordering from the small-plates side of the menu" or "trying the tasting menu – a nonstop delight"); most like the "modern, without-excess" decor, even if the "ambiance is rather businesslike", and the "professional, yet unfussy service"; in short, "it's what a great restaurant should be: sophisticated, friendly and always on" – literally: it's "open every day and all year (even in August!)"

Table d'Hédiard (La) ⓩ *New French* — 22 | 17 | 21 | €50

8ᵉ | 21, pl de la Madeleine (Madeleine) | 01 43 12 88 99 | fax 01 43 12 88 98 | www.hediard.fr

"Pick up groceries and get a quick bite to eat" at this New French "perched above a wonderful gourmet shop" in the 8th; all through the day, there's "light, fresh food and divine desserts" (though "it can be difficult to swallow the prices"); the "staff's attitude" ranges from "affected" to "attentive", but overall, it's a "wonderful place for resting those weary, overworked tourist feet."

Table du Baltimore (La) ⓩ *Haute Cuisine* — - | - | - | VE

16ᵉ | Sofitel Demeure Hôtel Baltimore | 88 bis, av Kléber (Boissière) | 01 44 34 54 34 | fax 01 44 34 54 44 | www.sofitel.com

"Always reliable" for a "business lunch or dinner", this "luxurious hotel restaurant" near Trocadéro provides a "comfortable" setting

(including "great air-conditioning, a rare thing in Paris"), "attentive service" and a "nice wine list"; but there are tempered tributes for the Haute Cuisine: "good, even very good, but not extraordinary."

Table du Lancaster (La) *Haute Cuisine* | 23 | 23 | 23 | €109 |

8ᵉ | Hôtel Lancaster | 7, rue de Berri (Franklin D. Roosevelt/ George V) | 01 40 76 40 18 | fax 01 40 76 40 00 | www.hotel-lancaster.fr

While fans of Rhône Valley chef Michel Troisgros' Hôtel Lancaster outpost judge his Asian-influenced Haute Cuisine "exciting" and "exotic", doubters dish their "disappointment" over the "too-predictable" offerings; but if the "food's slipped a little, the garden is still beautiful", as is the "civilized" interior and "quiet location away from the madness of the nearby Champs."

Table Lauriston (La) 🅱 *Classic French* | 20 | 16 | 19 | €50 |

16ᵉ | 129, rue Lauriston (Trocadéro) | 01 47 27 00 07

Not far from Trocadéro, this Classic French finds fans aplenty for its "excellent, unpretentious" cooking by chef–owner Serge Barbey (who worked under Bernard Loiseau and Guy Savoy) and its staffers, supervised by his wife, who "really listen to the customer" in a "convivial", silver-accented dining room; given this, and the swank 16th address, it's "a good buy."

🆉 Taillevent 🅱 *Haute Cuisine* | 28 | 28 | 28 | €164 |

8ᵉ | 15, rue Lamennais (Charles de Gaulle-Etoile/George V) | 01 44 95 15 01 | fax 01 42 25 95 18 | www.taillevent.com

"You're at home the minute you enter" this "elegant", "spectacular modern art"–adorned townhouse in the 8th, which – though mourning the loss of legendary owner Jean-Claude Vrinat – shines on as Paris' No. 1 for Food and Popularity; guests would "gladly borrow from the kids' college fund" to sample "service that's not just an art form, but a religion" as it delivers chef Alain Solivérès' "classic", sometimes "inventive", but always "decadent and luscious" Haute Cuisine, backed by "a prodigious wine list"; in short, "why wait for heaven, when you can go to Taillevent?"

Taïra 🅱 *Japanese/New French* | - | - | - | E |

17ᵉ | 10, rue des Acacias (Argentine) | 01 47 66 74 14 | fax 01 47 66 74 14

Fin fans find "first-rate fish" – and forgive the "sad-looking room" – at this "discreet, exceptional address" "a stone's throw from the Arc de Triomphe"; Nippon native Taïra Kurihara's "unique" menu, a "Japanese adaptation of French cuisine", is so "superb" and "well priced" "it's a scandal this phenomenally talented chef is ignored by the media" (except for us, of course).

Tan Dinh 🅱🕏 *Vietnamese* | 23 | 14 | 21 | €71 |

7ᵉ | 60, rue de Verneuil (Rue du Bac/Solférino) | 01 45 44 04 84 | fax 01 45 44 36 93

A "fashionable", "dedicated clientele" adds to the cachet of this "sedate Vietnamese charmer" in the 7th, where the cuisine is "delicate", the "service refined" and an "amazing wine list (particularly the

Burgundies) keeps customers coming back"; malcontents mumble that it's "overrated" and the "portions are small" for the price – which, by the way, requires a pocketful of cash, because "they don't accept credit cards."

Tang ⊠ Chinese | 17 | 15 | 16 | €58 |

16ᵉ | 125, rue de la Tour (Rue de la Pompe) | 01 45 04 35 35 | fax 01 45 04 58 19

This chichi Chinese in the 16th enjoys a high-ranking reputation, and while many feel it's merited, thanks to the "solicitous" owner and "memorable" food from a "diversified menu", scores side with the sizable number of dissidents who declare it "too expensive" for dishes that are merely "good."

Tante Louise ⊠ Burgundy/Classic French | 22 | 18 | 20 | €70 |

8ᵉ | 41, rue Boissy-d'Anglas (Concorde/Madeleine) | 01 42 65 06 85 | fax 01 42 65 28 19 | www.bernard-loiseau.com

"Near the Madeleine", this "luxury bistro" specializing in "traditional Burgundian"-accented French cuisine "cooked to perfection" remains a "good bet for a business lunch or a date" and a "favorite standby" with "the American Embassy crowd nearby"; its "cozy" setting with wood paneling and big armchairs is ideal on "a coolish winter evening", even if the staff seems "attentive and perfunctory at the same time."

Tante Marguerite ⊠ Classic French | ▽ 22 | 19 | 22 | €69 |

7ᵉ | 5, rue de Bourgogne (Assemblée Nationale/Invalides) | 01 45 51 79 42 | fax 01 47 53 79 56 | www.bernard-loiseau.com

"Located on a divine little square behind the Assemblée Nationale", this "beautiful neighborhood" bistro does a "good job" with "nice traditional French cuisine" brought to table by "well-trained" "servers who float through the dining room"; popular with politicians at noon, it pulls in residents of the swanky 7th in the evening with its "quiet, special" ambiance.

Tastevin Ⓜ Classic French | ▽ 24 | 20 | 24 | €69 |

Maisons-Laffitte | 9, av Eglé (RER Maisons-Laffitte) | 01 39 62 11 67 | fax 01 39 62 73 09

It may be "hard to get to without a car" but that doesn't stop clients who "come back religiously over the decades" to this family-run "historic restaurant" serving "well-prepared" Classic French cuisine in a century-old house and "beautiful" gardens in Maisons-Laffitte; admirers appreciate the "quiet" setting ("don't go if you're younger than 35") and "special personal service" in this "old-world" "treasure."

Taverna de Gli Amici ●⊠ Italian | - | - | - | M |

7ᵉ | 16, rue du Bac (Rue du Bac) | 01 42 60 37 74 | fax 01 42 60 37 74

"A wonderful owner" and "quality food at reasonable prices" – plus some "good bottles" of vino – make it easy for this Italian near the Musée d'Orsay to live up to its name, 'the tavern of friends'; the woodsy decor, while "warm", is a little rustic for some.

	FOOD	DECOR	SERVICE	COST

Taverne de Maître Kanter ● *Brasserie*
▽ 16 | 18 | 15 | €35

1ᵉʳ | 16, rue Coquillière (Châtelet-Les Halles/Louvre-Rivoli) |
01 42 36 74 24 | fax 01 42 21 42 31 | www.tmk-leshalles.com

"Typical Alsatian fare in typical Alsatian surroundings" sums up this
two-story Les Halles brasserie abounding in "fresh sauerkraut" and
"trays of shellfish"; it's pretty "basic, but a better standby than one
might expect" – especially since "it's never closed."

Taverne du Sergent Recruteur (La) ● *Classic French*
16 | 16 | 17 | €37

4ᵉ | 41, rue St-Louis-en-l'Ile (Pont-Marie) | 01 43 54 75 42 |
fax 01 44 07 02 58 | www.lesergentrecruteur.com

There are "more tourists jammed in [here] than in Notre Dame" at
this Ile Saint-Louis veteran that "attempts to re-create Middle Ages
communal dining" with "ye olde" decor of beamed stone walls, farm
tools and long wood tables; "excellent baskets of charcuterie, [cru-
dités] and cheese are provided when you sit down", but otherwise
the Classic French fare's fairly "marginal" and some feel it's "from a
former era and should be left there"; still, with "the right group and
sufficient wine, it can be fun."

Taverne Henri IV (La) ⊠ *Wine Bar/Bistro*
16 | 16 | 18 | €40

1ᵉʳ | 13, pl du Pont-Neuf (Pont-Neuf) | 01 43 54 27 90 |
fax 01 43 54 27 90

"Curators and carpenters sit side by side for a glass" at this "working
man's wine bar" on the tip of Ile de la Cité, a "historical institution"
and "an old favorite" of many (including writer Georges Simenon);
to accompany the "nice selection of wines at good prices", present-
day patrons tuck into "homey platters of country pâtés, cheeses"
and charcuterie, noting the "owners have spruced up the tired old
decor" (it's still "nothing spectacular", though).

Temps au Temps (Le) ⊠Ⓜ *Bistro*
25 | 16 | 25 | €38

11ᵉ | 13, rue Paul Bert (Faidherbe-Chaligny) | 01 43 79 63 40 |
fax 01 43 79 63 40 | www.tempsautemps.com

After four years, this "teeny" bistro in the 11th "remains a breath of
fresh air", thanks to chef-owner Sylvain Cendra's "fabulous food at
a price you won't believe" – "a three-course meal for 30€"; reserve
at least four days in advance, since the room with a big enameled
clock face is usually "jam-packed with a total of 26 guests and one
hard-working waitress" – in fact, some surveyors were "hesitant to
share [their opinions], because I may not get in next time!"

Temps des Cerises (Le) ●⊠ *Bistro*
- | - | - | M

13ᵉ | 18, rue de la Butte-aux-Cailles (Place d'Italie) | 01 45 89 69 48 |
fax 01 45 88 18 53

Egalitarians eat up this "lively legacy of the Paris Commune days", a
Butte aux Cailles bistro "run as a cooperative" where "all the staffers,
from chef to dishwasher, are owners" and patrons sit together at
"large tables"; it's "genuine, gruff and earthy" – "please put in modern toilets!" – but the "generous portions" of "hearty traditional
French fare" are cheap enough for the masses.

	FOOD	DECOR	SERVICE	COST

Terminus Nord ❶ *Brasserie*

17 | 19 | 17 | €45

10ᵉ | 23, rue de Dunkerque (Gare du Nord) | 01 42 85 05 15 |
fax 01 40 16 13 98 | www.terminusnord.com

"Exuding the bustle and expectation of its namesake across the
road", the Gare du Nord, this "classic" brasserie with its "fin de siècle
decor" is "the perfect spot for Eurostar travelers" to "go back in
time"; while the food quality can be "random", passengers profess
that the "platters of briny seafood are always a safe bet" and the
"rushed", white-aproned waiters are "fun to watch."

Terrasse Mirabeau (La) 🗷 *Bistro*

- | - | - | M

16ᵉ | 5, pl de Barcelone (Javel/Mirabeau) | 01 42 24 41 51 |
fax 01 42 24 43 48 | www.terrasse-mirabeau.com

What "a revelation" rave epicureans who "dream of going all the
time" to this "upscale bistro – or is it a reasonably priced creative
restaurant?" – in the 16th; the kitchen's "superb creativity", including "excellent terrines", matches the sleek, mirrored maroon-and-
chocolate-colored decor with "real paintings on the tabletops" and
big bay windows overlooking a "beautiful terrace."

Terres de Truffes 🗷 *Classic French*

▽ 19 | 14 | 17 | €81

8ᵉ | 21, rue Vignon (Madeleine) | 01 53 43 80 44 | fax 01 42 66 18 20 |
www.terresdetruffes.com

Funghi-philes pant that "no place is better at delivering superb truffle
dishes, from starter to dessert", than this recently enlarged "connoisseurs' mecca" near the Madeleine; however, dissidents declare it
has to dig deeper: "since a management change, the former generosity
is gone, the recipes have changed and the prices have gone up."

Terroir (Le) 🗷 *Bistro*

- | - | - | E

13ᵉ | 11, bd Arago (Les Gobelins) | 01 47 07 36 99

"A perennial favorite" of "local people" and tourists on the trail of a
"real French restaurant", this bistro in the 13th serves "no trendy
nonsense, just top-rate traditional cooking" in "high-priced" but "incredible portions" ("try the terrine de maison and see if you can
even eat anything else"); "hearty regional wines", plus a "warm welcome", round out the "marvelous" experience.

Tête Ailleurs (La) 🗷 *Mediterranean*

- | - | - | M

4ᵉ | 20, rue Beautreillis (St-Paul/Sully Morland) | 01 42 72 47 80 |
fax 01 42 74 66 85

Southern warmth is served at this "casual", "charming" Marais table
with "delicious Med food" (including a "heavenly lamb") and an
"eager-to-please staff" (it's "one of the friendliest places in town");
the "bright, arty decor" combines rich orange shades with exposed-
stone walls and natural light from a glass rooftop.

Thierry Burlot 🗷 *New French*
(aka Le Quinze)

- | - | - | M

15ᵉ | 8, rue Nicolas Charlet (Pasteur) | 01 42 19 08 59

Namesake owner Burlot has an enthusiastic following, both at the
Cristal Room where he is head chef, and here in the 15th at his own

New French table, a "great find" for "gourmet, creative food" "at un-expectedly reasonable prices"; regulars "love the contemporary decor" and the "precise flavors" of his "inventive" menu, confiding that "the caramel ice cream is a life-altering experience."

Thiou *Thai* — 21 | 21 | 20 | €61
7ᵉ | 49, quai d'Orsay (Invalides) | 01 40 62 96 50 | fax 01 40 62 97 30 🗷
8ᵉ | 12, av George V (Alma Marceau) | 01 47 20 89 56 | fax 01 47 20 76 16
Petit Thiou 🗷 *Thai*
7ᵉ | 3, rue Surcouf (Invalides) | 01 40 62 96 70
"When the mood moves you for a chic Asian dinner, come" to these venerable venues, which offer "the best Thai in Paris – and know it, judging by the prices" some quip; the "food is like the decor – smooth" and the scene "social-trendy"; some surveyors prefer Petit Thiou, as it's "less noisy" (and less expensive).

Thoumieux *Bistro/Southwest* — 19 | 19 | 20 | €45
7ᵉ | Hôtel Thoumieux | 79, rue St-Dominique (Invalides/La Tour Maubourg) | 01 47 05 49 75 | fax 01 47 05 36 96 | www.thoumieux.com
"Time travel to the 1920s" at this vet in the 7th, one of "a dying breed: family-owned brasseries"; "the opposite of trendy", it offers bistro and "solid" Southwestern fare, including "a famous cassoulet" and "baseball-size profiteroles"; and if some feel it's "no longer exceptional", that's what makes it "a favorite of families" and "nearby office workers"; P.S. "the servers act grumpy, but it's good-natured fun."

Tierny & Co. 🗷 🅼 *Bistro* — - | - | - | M
(fka Frugier)
16ᵉ | 137, av de Versailles (Exelmans/Mirabeau) | 01 46 47 72 00
The name has changed, thanks to a new chef-owner, but so far all else remains the same at this "lively" "neo-bistro" in the 16th on the way to Versailles; though "small, it's well laid-out", with low lighting, dark-wood tables and a long banquette to create a cozy atmosphere, plus a 30€ prix fixe to please the wallet.

Timbre (Le) 🗷 🅼 *Bistro* — 24 | 16 | 24 | €41
6ᵉ | 3, rue St-Beuve (Vavin) | 01 45 49 10 40 | fax 01 45 78 20 35 | www.restaurantletimbre.com
Wanderers seeking "a wonderful little neighborhood spot" find this bistro near the Luxembourg Gardens offers "just the right combination of food and ambiance" – both provided by "original" English chef-owner Chris Wright, who's a joy to "watch juggling many dishes at once, and making each perfect" (and "surprisingly inexpensive"); yes, the "cramped" space is "absolutely a postage stamp [*timbre*] in size" – "but that's part of the charm."

Timgad (Le) 🗷 *Moroccan* — 20 | 19 | 18 | €49
17ᵉ | 21, rue Brunel (Argentine) | 01 45 74 23 70 | fax 01 40 68 76 46 | www.timgad-paris.com
Couscous critics call this "refined, exotic" table in the 17th "one of the best Moroccans in town", serving the "melt-in-the-mouth" Mahgreb

mainstay and other dishes "of exemplary finesse"; "step into the restaurant and you're right in the heart of Marrakech", thanks to "amazing" decor of hand-carved plaster and service of "authentic warmth"; but the "exceptional meal" does come with an "exceptional price."

Toi ● New French | - | - | - | M |

8e | 27, rue du Colisée (Franklin D. Roosevelt/St-Philippe-du-Roule) | 01 42 56 56 58 | fax 01 42 56 09 60 | www.restaurant-toi.com

Everything old is new again, like the "funky", "flashy, love-it-or-hate-it" 1970s decor at this club near the Champs; it offers "trendy" lounge dining in armchairs or on couches, "creative alcoholic concoctions" "and a young crowd"; but style sentries say the overall experience is already as "dated as the music the DJ spins", and even fans admit it's "more amusing than appetizing", given that the New French menu "isn't very long, in contrast to the service that takes a little too long."

Tokyo Eat ●M New French | 14 | 17 | 13 | €41 |

16e | Palais de Tokyo | 13, av du President Wilson (Iéna) | 01 47 20 00 29 | fax 01 47 20 05 62 | www.palaisdetokyo.com

"Great in summer" – when you can sit on the terrace and enjoy superb views of the Seine and the Eiffel Tower – this "young, funky" New French in the Palais de Tokyo pulls patrons with its futuristic "high design", including "über-cool light fixtures"; but, as with many museum venues, the food and staff "leave less than an imperishable memory."

Tong Yen ● Chinese | 15 | 11 | 13 | €56 |

8e | 1 bis, rue Jean Mermoz (Franklin D. Roosevelt) | 01 42 25 04 23 | fax 01 45 63 51 57

Managing to be "ultra-Parisian and cosmopolitan at the same time", this "well-known Asian" near the Champs offers "all the classics"; but despite its rep as "one of the best Chinese/Vietnamese/Thai in Paris", foes feel "the food and service have deteriorated" – though "delightful owner" Thérèse Luong "makes up for the staff's shortcomings" – and the '60s decor is "too old"; it's also "very dear for the quality of the cuisine, but when you receive Presidents", a premium is perhaps understandable.

Tonnelle Saintongeaise (La) ⊠ Classic French | - | - | - | E |

Neuilly-sur-Seine | 32, bd Vital-Bouhot (Pont-de-Levallois) | 01 46 24 43 15 | fax 01 46 24 36 33 | www.latonnellesaintongeaise.com

With its "charming location", complete with "a terrace right in the middle of Ile de la Jatte", this Classic French is a comfortable hangout (its covered courtyard is agreeable "even in stormy summer weather"); the menu offers "dishes that are simple but always adequate", including specialties from the chef's native Charente and hand-cut steak tartare that's a "must for raw-meat lovers."

Toque (La) ⊠ Classic French | - | - | - | E |

17e | 16, rue de Tocqueville (Villiers) | 01 42 27 97 75 | fax 01 47 63 97 69

"Loyal followers" of chef-owner Jacky Joubert have been coming to his small establishment in the 17th for over a quarter-century to par-

take of "palate-pleasing, if traditional" French cuisine in an alcoved dining room underneath the clouds of a trompe l'oeil ceiling; a "thoughtful staff" completes the "warm", "conservative atmosphere" that's "perfect" "for a business meal" or just an "enjoyable evening."

☑ Tour d'Argent (La) Ⓜ Haute Cuisine | 25 | 28 | 26 | €145 |

5ᵉ | 15-17, quai de la Tournelle (Cardinal Lemoine/Pont-Marie) | 01 43 54 23 31 | fax 01 44 07 12 04 | www.latourdargent.com
Defiant (and dominant) devotees "don't care if it's considered uncool" – this Haute Cuisine table "is still one of the most magical of Parisian places", with its "spectacular views of Notre Dame"; "make sure you ask for a window table when you book, and for heaven's sake order the pressed duck" "with its numbered certificate" – though new chef Stéphane Haissant has "finally updated" the menu with some "excellent" options, served by an initially "haughty", but truly "outstanding staff"; so let the grouches grimace she's "a grande dame in decline" – this tower remains "a reason to sell off your worldly goods for one meal here before you die."

Tournesol (Le) Bistro | ▽ 18 | 17 | 19 | €45 |

16ᵉ | 2, av de Lamballe (Passy) | 01 45 25 95 94 | fax 01 45 25 43 09
"One goes for the terrace and the trendy" scene say patrons of this "nice Passy bistro" – though the cooking is quite "competent" as well; the "quick" servers can "tease you in both French and English."

NEW Toustem (Le) Ⓢ Southwest | - | - | - | E |

5ᵉ | 12, rue de l'Hôtel Colbert (Maubert-Mutualité) | 01 40 51 99 87
The newest entry from chef Hélène Darroze is deemed "delightful" by the few who've discovered it in the 5th; out of "a real historic address, they've made a modern" setting, decorating the 13th-century wood-beamed and stone-walled premises with bright orange and green tones; the homestyle Southwestern fare is "savory" enough, but the staff seems "slightly sleepy."

☑ Train Bleu (Le) Ⓢ Classic French | 19 | 27 | 20 | €62 |

12ᵉ | Gare de Lyon (Gare de Lyon) | 01 43 43 09 06 | fax 01 43 43 97 96 | www.le-train-bleu.com
"Travel in style" at this "belle epoque masterpiece" in the Gare de Lyon, a "grande old dame" of a brasserie with "beautiful" painted scenes of the southern destinations served by the station; "though it's a little more expensive than you want", there's "surprisingly good" Classic French food and "tableside service" (e.g. "lamb from the trolley") – all of which puts you on "the right track to a great evening."

35° Ouest Ⓢ Ⓜ Seafood | 20 | 18 | 21 | €64 |

7ᵉ | 35, rue de Verneuil (Rue du Bac) | 01 42 86 98 88 | fax 01 42 86 00 65
This "little fish that could" recently swam onto the scene with an "intimate", modern "chic" setting near the Rue du Bac and a "small, carefully edited" seafood menu featuring "the freshest ingredients" in "original" preparations; it's "still undiscovered" by tourists, despite an excellent pedigree (the chef is formerly of Magnolias, the

owner from Gaya Rive Gauche), "smiling" service and a "good-value" lunch menu – though dinner prices head rapidly upstream.

Tricotin ● *Asian*

FOOD	DECOR	SERVICE	COST
-	-	-	I

13^e | 15, av de Choisy (Porte de Choisy) | 01 45 84 74 44

Dumpling devotees line up for a table at this "superior" "canteen-style Asian" in Chinatown, where two dining rooms with different menus (but the same "minimal decor") are always "crowded" with "lots of admirers" who dig their chopsticks into "amazingly good" (and "inexpensive") Chinese, Vietnamese or Thai dishes, plus "quality dim sum."

Triporteur (Le) ⑤ *Bistro*

-	-	-	M

15^e | 4, rue de Dantzig (Convention) | 01 45 32 82 40

This neighborhood bistro in the 15th was recently acquired by chef Eric Chauvet, "a young man who's rising rapidly" since his stint at La Tour d'Argent, and his wife, Isabelle, who's replaced the old bric-a-brac decor with soothingly colored taffeta to accompany the "warm welcome"; a chalkboard menu presents a "small but excellent" choice of innovative, market-fresh fare "at fair prices."

Troquet (Le) ⑤Ⓜ *Basque/New French*

24	16	19	€45

15^e | 21, rue François Bonvin (Sèvres-Lecourbe/Volontaire) | 01 45 66 89 00 | fax 01 45 66 89 83

It's worth traveling to an "unassuming" part of the 15th for this "incredible find" of a New French that "distills the best of Paris neighborhood eating", thanks to chef-owner Christian Etchebest's "excellent" Basque-inspired menu that "emphasizes market-fresh" ingredients; despite "nondescript" decor, "locals love it and with good reason" since it offers "incredible value for the money" and the "staff is casual and friendly."

Ⓩ Trou Gascon (Au) ⑤ *Southwest*

26	19	24	€75

12^e | 40, rue Taine (Daumesnil) | 01 43 44 34 26 | fax 01 43 07 80 55 | www.autrougascon.fr

"Let's hear it for the Southwest!" shout supporters of Alain Dutournier's original "off-the-beaten-track" eatery in the 12th that's "worth every travel minute"; "a mixture of classics and innovations", its Gascon cuisine includes "the best confit de canard I've ever had", "transcendent cassoulet" and other "superb heart-attack food" served in "spare but elegant surroundings"; though the wine list's "a little short" of by-the-glass offerings, that's "made up for by a huge selection of Armagnacs", so for most "the real trick is to get up from the table after a meal" here.

Truc Café (Le) Ⓜ *Wine Bar/Bistro*

-	-	-	M

18^e | 58, rue du Poteau (Jules Joffrin) | 01 42 52 64 09

Generously served Classic French dishes and an Italian-oriented wine list have made this *bistrot à vins* in a gentrifying Montmartre neighborhood a hit with a trendy young crowd; changing contemporary art exhibitions and a pretty, quiet little garden out back please as much as the smiling service and modest prices.

	FOOD	DECOR	SERVICE	COST

Truffe Noire (La) 🅰 *Classic French* — | — | — | E

Neuilly-sur-Seine | 2, pl Parmentier (Les Sablons/Porte Maillot) | 01 46 24 94 14 | fax 01 46 24 94 60

Neuilly's nobility and corporate types from La Défense get their dose of decadent eats at this "delightful" denizen that's maintained a "consistently high quality over the years"; within cool, contemporary decor of gray walls and Murano chandeliers, the "very Classic" French fare features the fabulous fungus in all its forms, so "it's expensive – but there's nothing better than a truffle", *n'est-ce pas?*

Truffière (La) 🅰🅼 *Haute Cuisine* 23 | 23 | 23 | €87

5ᵉ | 4, rue Blainville (Cardinal Lemoine/Place Monge) | 01 46 33 29 82 | fax 01 46 33 64 74 | www.latruffiere.com

"Talk about old-fashioned dining": this "romantic" spot, "off the Rue Mouffetard in an alley so narrow you can hardly get out of the taxi", "sets the mood with old stone walls and beamed ceilings" ("be sure to request the cellar"), "extremely courteous servers" and a "sybaritic menu" of Haute Cuisine in which certain "expensive ingredients, as the name indicates, are used with abandon" – "they even put truffles in the dessert soufflé"; yes, it's all "a little dated" and definitely pricey (the wine alone is "highway robbery"), but the latter can be ameliorated at the lunch prix fixe, "a great deal."

Trumilou (Le) *Bistro* 19 | 12 | 18 | €31

4ᵉ | 84, quai de l'Hôtel de Ville (Hôtel-de-Ville/Pont-Marie) | 01 42 77 63 98 | fax 01 48 04 91 89

"Other than its location across from the Seine, there's nothing fancy" here – and that pleases budget eaters who make a beeline for this "boisterous", "friendly", "funky bargain of a place", serving "decent old-style" bistro food in the 4th; sure, the "eclectic decor" is looking "a little tattered", but it's "just the thing to soothe an artist's soul."

Tsé-Yang ⚫ *Chinese* 18 | 17 | 16 | €48

16ᵉ | 25, av Pierre 1er de Serbie (Alma Marceau/Iéna) | 01 47 20 70 22 | fax 01 49 52 03 68

Practically a time zone away from its Chinatown cousins, this "luxurious" 16th-arrondissement Asian draws an upscale clientele who claim it's "the only restaurant where you eat *real* Chinese cuisine" – that is, undiluted by Thai or Vietnamese offerings as is often the case in Paris – served in a "transporting" black-and-gold room; still, some snap it's "a bit too dear, given the quantities served."

Tsukizi 🅰🅼 *Japanese* — | — | — | M

6ᵉ | 2 bis, rue des Ciseaux (Mabillon/St-Germain-des-Prés) | 01 43 54 65 19

"A lot of Japanese" clients and others "who miss real sushi" get a "traditional" taste of Tokyo at this "tiny counter", a Saint-Germain "hideaway" where expats from the old country slice and dice the "fresh products"; zealots even praise the "Zen ambiance" (the critical just call it "cramped").

Uitr *Seafood*

FOOD	DECOR	SERVICE	COST
-	-	-	M

15ᵉ | 1, pl Falguière (Pasteur/Pernety) | 01 47 34 12 24 | fax 01 47 34 12 34

This seafooder in the 15th is "the cheaper version of La Cagouille – and you get what you pay for" say some, citing the "brief menu" and nautical setting that's a bit "beat-up"; but merrier mateys maintain the "cuisine's remarkable", with "very fresh" shellfish; occasional jazz nights also encourage diners to drop anchor here.

Unico 🚫Ⓜ *Argentinean*

FOOD	DECOR	SERVICE	COST
-	-	-	E

11ᵉ | 15, rue Paul Bert (Faidherbe-Chaligny) | 01 43 67 68 08 | www.resto-unico.com

Calling all gauchos: this "trendy Argentine" in the hip Rue Paul Bert tempts with "tender, perfectly prepared pampas-raised beef" and "good Argentinean wines"; with its orange-hued, '70s-vintage decor – so retro it seems "postmodern" – and "bustling, warm" vibe, "this place is indeed *único*."

🆕 Urbane Ⓜ *Bistro*

FOOD	DECOR	SERVICE	COST
-	-	-	M

10ᵉ | 12, rue Arthur Groussier (Belleville/Goncourt) | 01 42 40 74 75

"Tucked away near Belleville", this "little gem", run by a Franco-Irish couple, takes a tasty, transformative approach to bistro classics ("made me realize that I do like boudin noir!"); "everyone loves" "the Sunday brunches, with their generous portions" and acoustic music, but the brown paper–covered tables, colored lights, framed photo-covered walls and "DJs also make it a hip hangout" anytime.

Vagenende ⬤ *Brasserie*

FOOD	DECOR	SERVICE	COST
15	23	16	€48

6ᵉ | 142, bd St-Germain (Mabillon/Odéon) | 01 43 26 68 18 | fax 01 40 51 73 38 | www.vagenende.fr

Commonly called "the poor man's Maxim's", this century-old brasserie in the 6th is "a feast for the eyes" with a "stunningly authentic", "almost edible" art nouveau interior; less mouthwatering is the menu of "acceptable-but-ordinary food", despite an "outstanding" raw bar; nonetheless, the "bustling" ambiance, the "great-for-people-watching" location and the late-night service make it "a fine place for an off-hour meal, just to soak in the decor."

Vaudeville (Le) ⬤ *Brasserie*

FOOD	DECOR	SERVICE	COST
18	21	17	€54

2ᵉ | 29, rue Vivienne (Bourse) | 01 40 20 04 62 | fax 01 40 20 14 35 | www.vaudevilleparis.com

A "stylish clientele" enhances the "sparkling" "marble and mosaic" setting of this art deco spot "across from the Bourse", a "lively late-night brasserie" with a "special-occasion feel"; despite "desultory service", seafood lovers say this is "the best of the Groupe Flo" chain, with the "good", "basic" menu enhanced by "giant platters of *fruits de mer*" that have 'em rolling in the aisles.

Verre Bouteille (Le) ⬤ *Wine Bar/Bistro*

FOOD	DECOR	SERVICE	COST
13	12	14	€37

17ᵉ | 85, av des Ternes (Porte Maillot) | 01 45 74 01 02 | fax 01 47 63 07 02 | www.leverrebouteille.com

"Simple and unpretentious", this wine bar in the 17th is "well-known to noctambules" for its long hours and well-liked by vinophiles for its

"interesting wine list"; bad-mouthing bacchanalians call the "food basic", "the decor faded" and the "welcome not great"; but even if "being open late is its main advantage", it still pours a "good night out."

Verre Volé (Le) *Wine Bar/Bistro*   16 | 15 | 18 | €30
10ᵉ | 67, rue de Lancry (République) | 01 48 03 17 34

Vino-inclined reviewers "run, don't walk" to this "jovial" wine bar on the banks of the Canal Saint-Martin and "while away the afternoon" or evening sampling from a gently priced list of "intelligently and passionately chosen" young varietals alongside "simple" dishes such as oysters or charcuterie; the room is *tout petite* so it can be "hard to find a free table", but at least the cheek-to-jowl ambiance ensures it's always "high-spirited."

Versance (Le) ⊠Ⓜ *Classic/New French*   - | - | - | E
2ᵉ | 16, rue Feydeau (Bourse) | 01 45 08 00 08 | fax 01 45 08 47 99 | www.leversance.fr

A "promising debut" declare disciples of young chef Samuel Cavagnis' "elegant" establishment; his produce-driven French cuisine blends the traditional and the "inventive", as does the white-and-dove-gray decor, which juxtaposes contemporary furniture with 19th-century moldings and stained glass; maybe the staff needs "to be more professional", but most agree that investing in this place near the old Bourse is "already a sure thing" (just make sure your portfolio's liquid).

Viaduc Café (Le) ◐ *Classic/New French*   - | - | - | M
12ᵉ | 43, av Daumesnil (Bastille/Gare de Lyon) | 01 44 74 70 70 | fax 01 44 74 70 71

The trip is "hip" at this "lovely-to-look-at" eatery with stone walls and high ceilings built "under the arches of a former railroad viaduct" in the 12th; it's "understandably popular" for its "original" decor and a "beautiful" large terrace open until the wee hours in summer, despite the "just fair" Classic–New French cuisine; still, it's "not about the food" here – "the whole point of the place is to get a tan and to be seen"; P.S. "great jazz brunch" on Sundays.

Vieille Fontaine Rôtisserie (La) Ⓜ *Classic/New French*   - | - | - | M
Maisons-Laffitte | 8, av Grétry (RER Maisons-Laffitte) | 01 39 62 01 78 | fax 01 39 62 13 43 | www.lesbouchonsdefrancoisclerc.com

With an "agreeable setting in the park of Maisons-Laffitte", this restaurant in a Second Empire mansion attracts locals as well as weekenders to the country with "very fine" Classic and New French cuisine and a staff that's "a delight"; this aristocratic estate is especially "wonderful" "in good weather", when the terrace overlooking the garden is lovely."

Vieux Bistro (Le) *Lyon*   21 | 15 | 18 | €47
4ᵉ | 14, rue du Cloître Notre-Dame (Cité) | 01 43 54 18 95 | fax 01 44 07 35 63 | www.lamaree.fr

"Don't let its location fool you", "on touristy Restaurant Row" "in the shadows of Notre Dame", because "this is the real stuff" – "a quint-

essential bistro" with "homey atmosphere" and "ample portions" of "solid, tasteful, earthy" Lyonnais cuisine; some non-Gallic guests grumble "they push tourists to the rear", but in any case, "the outdoor tables are the best" "for the view" of the cathedral; "if you time it right you can even eat while listening to the choir sing."

Vieux Chêne (Au) 🅂 *Bistro* — — — M

11ᵉ | 7, rue du Dahomey (Faidherbe-Chaligny) | 01 43 71 67 69
Its "simple decor is little changed from its years as a working man's bistro, but the food has a finesse that takes traditional dishes to the next level" at this New French in the 11th; "the owners are always nice", the prices consistently easygoing and be sure to cast your eye over the vintage cognac collection.

Villa Corse (La) 🅂 *Corsica* 20 20 17 €50

15ᵉ | 164, bd de Grenelle (Cambronne/La Motte-Picquet-Grenelle) | 01 53 86 70 81 | fax 01 53 86 90 73 ◑
16ᵉ | 141, av de Malakoff (Porte Maillot) | 01 40 67 18 44 | fax 01 40 67 18 19
The Ile de France meets the Ile de Beauté (as the French call Corsica) at these stylish showcases in the 15th and 16th, both "hot spots that are always busy with pretty young things" sampling the "elaborate", "earthy" eats in "luxurious", "comfortable men's club-like settings"; "service is attentive – but not always accurate", however, and some say the prices would make even a Napoleon retreat.

Village d'Ung et Li Lam ◑ *Chinese/Thai* — — — M

8ᵉ | 10, rue Jean Mermoz (Franklin D. Roosevelt) | 01 42 25 99 79 | fax 01 42 25 12 06
Village people call this original Oriental outpost in the 8th "a must in Paris", as much for the "ultrakitsch decor" (kind of "Asia meets the Champs-Elysées", with a six-ton aquarium on the ceiling) as for the "wholesome" – "if not well-spiced" – Chinese-Thai cuisine and the "smiling welcome."

ⓩ Villaret (Le) ◑🅂 *Bistro* 26 16 23 €53

11ᵉ | 13, rue Ternaux (Oberkampf/Parmentier) | 01 43 57 89 76
It's worth traveling to an "out-of-the-way residential neighborhood" in the 11th to discover this "good example of the bistro-revival phenomenon", whose "inventive" "wonderfully prepared food" is absolutely "amazing"; views vary on the decor – "homey atmosphere, with exposed-stone walls" vs. "nonexistent" – but fans flip for the "friendly, fun service"; and if "prices are becoming a little high", perhaps that befits "one of the best bistros in Paris."

Villa Spicy ◑ *New French* 13 14 13 €47
(fka Spicy)

8ᵉ | 8, av Franklin D. Roosevelt (Franklin D. Roosevelt/St-Philippe-du-Roule) | 01 56 59 62 59 | fax 01 56 59 62 50 | www.spicyrestaurant.com
"Colorful decor" - recently refurbished in cool tones and including a pseudo-veranda (hence, the name change) - beckons the business crowd of the 8th to this "reasonably priced" eatery; the Asian- and

Med-inflected New French fare is "original" enough, but foes fume that "this boring and bland place" belies its name: "there's no spice in the food" or the "characterless service."

Vinci (Le) ⊠ *Classic French/Italian* | - | - | - | E |

16ᵉ | 23, rue Paul Valéry (Victor Hugo) | 01 45 01 68 18 | fax 01 45 01 60 37
Suits in the 16th know this "small" site "on a sleepy side street" as "one of the best deals in the neighborhood", "deserving its loyal clientele" with prix fixes that are "champion for value"; its Joël Robuchon–trained chef cooks up "excellent" dishes that combine "Italian inspiration" and Classic French savoir faire, served amid the "warm" ambiance created by well-spaced tables and reddish tones.

Vin dans les voiles (Le) ⊠ Ⓜ *Wine Bar/Bistro* | - | - | - | I |

16ᵉ | 8, rue Chapu (Exelmans) | 01 46 47 83 98 | fax 01 46 47 83 98 | www.vindaneslesvoiles.com
"If you want just a simple, casual [meal], with a nice selection of wines and an owner who's passionate about them, here's your perfect" place sing supporters of this *bistrot à vins* in the 16th; "charming and cozy", it offers an "often-changing menu and the prices are more than reasonable."

Vin des Pyrenees ❶ *Classic French* | 16 | 15 | 16 | €34 |

4ᵉ | 25, rue Beautrellis (Bastille/St-Paul) | 01 42 72 64 94 | fax 01 42 71 19 62
"Near Bastille", this "unique wine bar" is a "nice neighborhood-type place" with an "at-home feeling" claim converts who concentrate on its "robust, hearty" Classic French fare and a "good vino list at reasonable prices" – dismissing as sour grapes those who find the "food, and especially the service, uneven."

Vinea Café (Le) ❶ *Eclectic* | - | - | - | M |

12ᵉ | 26-28, Cour St-Emilion (Cour St-Emilion) | 01 44 74 09 09 | fax 01 44 74 06 66 | www.vinea-cafe.com
Day-trippers to the shops and cinemas of the "happening scene" of the Cour Saint-Emilion, a renovated district of 19th-century wine storehouses, can grab a noon meal from the "nicely priced lunch menu" or a late dinner of Eclectic eats at this "historic stone building" (an old *cave*) with a "pleasant terrace"; however, critics caution the cuisine's "inconsistent" quality makes prices seem "high."

Vin et Marée *Seafood* | 18 | 14 | 15 | €48 |

1ᵉʳ | 165, rue St-Honoré (Palais Royal-Musée du Louvre) | 01 42 86 06 96 | fax 01 42 86 06 97
7ᵉ | 71, av de Suffren (La Motte-Picquet-Grenelle) | 01 47 83 27 12 | fax 01 43 06 62 35
11ᵉ | 276, bd Voltaire (Nation) | 01 43 72 31 23 | fax 01 40 09 05 24
14ᵉ | 108, av du Maine (Gaîté) | 01 43 20 29 50 | fax 01 43 27 84 11
16ᵉ | 183, bd Murat (Porte de St-Cloud) | 01 46 47 91 39 | fax 01 46 47 69 07
This "chain of simple" seafooders has cast a wide net throughout the city, and its clients trust the "consistent quality" of the "standard

fare" from a "tuna steak big enough for Ahab" to a "gigantesque" baba "with a good bottle of rum generously left at the table"; some carp about the "inattentive" service that leaves them fishing around for a waiter, and the "spacious" settings that seem slightly "sterile" – though entirely smoke-free now.

20 de Bellechasse (Le) ●🅩 Bistro | 19 | 17 | 18 | €58 |

7ᵉ | 20, rue de Bellechasse (Solférino) | 01 47 05 11 11

The owners (two "friendly guys") and a "young crowd" "full of locals" who all "know each other" get this "casual", "hip" bistro "buzzing"; the classic cooking – "enjoyable, fresh" and "well priced" considering the privileged 'hood near the Musée d'Orsay – adds to the appeal, so at times this "happening place" feels like a "crowded shoebox" (don't be surprised if people kick their Pradas off and "dancing ensues").

21 🅩 Seafood | - | - | - | E |

6ᵉ | 21, rue Mazarine (Odéon) | 01 46 33 76 90

Only premier *poissons* gain access to the kitchen of Paul Minchelli, who earned a following at his own eponymous restaurant prior to opening this table with a mysterious black exterior and just a '21' on the awning; it's strategically situated to snag the Saint-Germain elite who slide into black leather booths and order what many consider "the city's best fish, perfectly cooked" from a blackboard menu, at prices that leave some gasping for air; P.S. "reservations mandatory."

🆉 Vin sur Vin 🅩 New French | 26 | 21 | 22 | €82 |

7ᵉ | 20, rue de Monttessuy (Alma Marceau/Ecole Militaire) | 01 47 05 14 20

Its "astonishing wine list" – 600 labels, baby – may be the main attraction at this "small storefront" decorated like "an elegant home" in the 7th; but don't neglect the New French cuisine, which seems like "art"– "interesting", and full of "fine, fresh ingredients"; surveyors are mixed on the service: it possesses "a true passion for food and wine", but "where's the warmth?"; even so, this "out-of-the-way" place is "worth a trip."

🆉 Violon d'Ingres (Le) 🅩🅜 Bistro | 25 | 21 | 23 | €81 |

7ᵉ | 135, rue St-Dominique (Ecole Militaire) | 01 45 55 15 05 | fax 01 45 55 48 42 | www.leviolondingres.com

A while back, chef-owner Christian Constant did a "scaling-down" of his beloved Haute Cuisine table in the 7th, but "the conversion to a bistro hasn't changed the high quality of the food" ("Constant remains constant"); redone to be "sleek and modern, the narrow space obliges tables to be arranged like a railroad dining car, but the lack of intimacy is offset by a warm and informed staff"; though "better now", "prices remain high"; even so, most maintain "you can't visit Paris without dining here."

Vivres (Les) 🅩🅜 Classic French | - | - | - | I |

9ᵉ | 28, rue Pétrelle (Anvers) | 01 42 80 26 10

Chef-owner Jean-Luc André's lower-priced annex to his adjacent Pétrelle in the 9th has the charm of a small country grocery, with

bouquets of flowers and vegetables, a handful of tables and shelves of preserves decorating the small room; eat in or take away the simple Classic French eats like *maman* used to make.

Voltaire (Le) 🛇Ⓜ *Bistro* | 24 | 20 | 22 | €75 |

7ᵉ | 27, quai Voltaire (Rue du Bac) | 01 42 61 17 49

An atmosphere oozing "old-style French charm" and "old-world bistro fare done one better" make this "classic" "along the Seine" in the 7th a major "favorite"; many maintain it's "more of a [private] club than a restaurant", both because of its "elegant dark-wood decor" and its "popularity with celebrities" and a major Paris power crowd – so, you first-timers better "go with a regular or you'll feel like an intruder"; in addition, be sure to "dress chic" and be braced for "definitely pricey" tabs.

Wadja 🛇 *Bistro* | 20 | 12 | 16 | €37 |

6ᵉ | 10, rue de la Grande-Chaumière (Vavin) | 01 46 33 02 02 | fax 01 46 33 02 02

This "unpretentious" neighborhood bistro in Montparnasse "is one of the places where you say, if I lived nearby, I'd eat here at least twice a week", since it has "consistently good" – even occasionally "innovative" – Classic French fare "and a surprising wine list" at prices offering "unbeatable value for the money"; *hélas,* the service can be "cliché French – meaning impatient and haughty."

Waknine 🛇 *New French* | - | - | - | M |

16ᵉ | 9, av Pierre 1er de Serbie (Iéna) | 01 47 23 48 18 | fax 01 47 23 87 33 | www.waknine.fr

The welcoming armchairs "fill up at lunchtime" in this "chic", "charming" 16th-arrondissement address where "always smiling" servers deliver "slightly fusion" New French food; the room can get "noisy" at noon or during impromptu "TGIF wine gatherings", but there's a "softer ambiance at night" and at afternoon tea too.

Wally Le Saharien 🛇Ⓜ *North African* | ▽ 15 | 14 | 14 | €38 |

9ᵉ | 36, rue Rodier (Anvers/Notre-Dame-de-Lorette) | 01 42 85 51 90 | fax 01 42 85 51 90

North African–born Wally is "a true prince of the desert", which partially explains why Parisians steer their caravans toward his longstanding place in the 9th, with its "museum"-like decor of ethnic rugs and objects; converts also call his Algerian eats, including "unique dry couscous", "the best I know"; but malcontents mutter it's all a mirage, slamming "small portions that are nondescript in terms of flavor and presentation" and "prices that are too high for what you get."

Water Bar Colette (Le) 🛇 *Italian/New French* | 14 | 16 | 13 | €36 |

1ᵉʳ | 213, rue St-Honoré (Tuileries) | 01 55 35 33 93 | fax 01 55 35 33 99 | www.colette.fr

"Rich women shopping in the neighborhood" maintain their fashion-friendly figures with "light and fresh" Italian–New French nibbles accompanied by an assortment of "mineral waters with strange

names" at this "spare" cafe in the "super-trendy" store Colette; detractors dismiss it as an "amusing but expensive" "fad" that won't die – "nice bottles, but a bit too much attitude."

Wepler ● *Brasserie* | 14 | 11 | 12 | €44 |

18ᵉ | 14, pl de Clichy (Place de Clichy) | 01 45 22 53 24 | fax 01 44 70 07 50 | www.wepler.com

Overlooking the busy Place de Clichy, this "typical, old-fashioned brasserie", one of the last independents in Paris, serves up "traditional French dishes", including "excellent shellfish platters", to an eclectic crowd of creative artists, shopkeepers, students and tourists; after 100+ years, both the vintage decor and the kitchen unsurprisingly seem "faded" and the staff *"stressé"*, though "speedy" (not so bad, since many patrons are going to a show nearby); but amiable *amis* love it anyway: "it is what it is, even if it's not what it was."

Z Willi's Wine Bar Ⓩ *Wine Bar/Bistro* | 20 | 17 | 19 | €45 |

1ᵉʳ | 13, rue des Petits-Champs (Palais Royal-Musée du Louvre/Pyramides) | 01 42 61 05 09 | fax 01 47 03 36 93 | www.williswinebar.com

"If you're a wine lover, this is the place to go" opine oenophiles of this slightly "cramped" 1st-arrondissement *bar à vins* that stays "true to form after many years" (28, to be exact) under the eye of British expat-owner Mark Williamson; "there are English-speakers in the house", including the staff, "but the food is French", and while it can be either "surprisingly good or so-so", no worries – "Willi's is a state of mind not to be missed."

NEW Winch (Le) *Seafood* | - | - | - | M |

18ᵉ | 44, rue Damremont (Abbesses/Place de Clichy) | 01 42 23 04 63

It's smooth sailing at this seafooder with a laid-back loungelike decor of blue walls and black-and-white photos of Brittany, and "excellent" preparations that range from Breton fish stew to shrimp with basmati rice in a coconut milk sauce; well "worth a visit" if you're touring Montmartre.

Wok Cooking ● *Asian* | - | - | - | M |

11ᵉ | 25, rue des Taillandiers (Bastille) | 01 55 28 88 77 | fax 01 48 10 04 65

"You get to choose your own ingredients and sauces and watch them cook in front of you" at this "affordable" and "always crowded" Asian in the 11th; converts call it a "good concept", but cynics say just wok on by, wondering "why would you do this in Paris?"

W Restaurant (Le) Ⓩ *New French* | - | - | - | E |

8ᵉ | Hôtel Warwick | 5, rue de Berri (George V) | 01 45 61 82 08 | fax 01 45 63 75 81 | www.warwickhotels.com

A few steps off the Champs, this New French could well be "the best business"-lunch destination when quality cuisine can clinch the deal; the kitchen "deserves kudos" for the "fresh" fare prepared with a Mediterranean accent and proffered by "efficient service" – both of which "transcend" the "corporate-chic and cold decor" and the uninspiring "location at the back of an international hotel."

Yen ⊠ Japanese

20 | 15 | 16 | €42

6ᵉ | 22, rue St-Benoît (St-Germain-des-Prés) | 01 45 44 11 18 |
fax 01 45 44 19 48

Gourmands ready for "something other than sushi" nippon over to
this Saint-Germain Japanese for "elaborate", "unconventional" offerings, including "the best soba in Paris", in a coolly "Zen atmosphere"
where "the regulars go upstairs"; but cost-conscious customers
complain that "small" portions and "expensive" tabs mean "you'll
have a yen after eating here . . . for something to eat."

Yugaraj ⓜ Indian

23 | 17 | 18 | €53

6ᵉ | 14, rue Dauphine (Odéon/Pont-Neuf) | 01 43 26 44 91 |
fax 01 46 33 50 77

"It's rare to find good Indian in Paris", but they "rival anything in
London or NYC" at this Saint-Germain subcontinental, whose "gourmet touch means we're not in the mere chicken vindaloo zone
anymore" – in fact, pheasant biryani is more their speed, as are "great
wines"; some feel the decor of Anglo-Indian antiquities "shows
signs of fatigue, but this remains one of the best" of the breed in town.

Zébra Square ◑ Classic French

10 | 15 | 9 | €48

16ᵉ | 3, pl Clément-Ader (Passy/RER Kennedy-Radio France) |
01 44 14 91 91 | fax 01 45 27 18 34 | www.zebrasquare.com

"Très trendy", this "young, noisy" place "across from Le Maison de
la Radio" in the 16th pulls media mavens and the "BCBG crowd" (the
French equivalent of preppie) to its "resolutely modern", Zen-
meets–zebra stripes surrounds; the Classic French "cooking's amateurish" and the staff acts "disillusioned", but "the food and the service
are not the point – the decor, including the patrons, is."

ⓩ Ze Kitchen Galerie ⊠ Eclectic

25 | 20 | 20 | €65

6ᵉ | 4, rue des Grands-Augustins (St-Michel) | 01 44 32 00 32 |
fax 01 44 32 00 33 | www.zekitchengalerie.fr

"Co-chef/owner William Ledeuil has his finger and palate on the
pulse of the modern diner" declare disciples of his seven-year-old,
but still "trendy", Eclectic eatery in Saint-Germain; a "pleasantly
varied" "crowd that's the image of the area" (e.g. affluent, "hip"
gallery-goers) devours "divine repasts" of "intelligent" "quasi
Asian-French" fare, including "fish served à la plancha – on a grill at
your table"; the art-adorned, loftlike space is "sleek, if a little cold",
and so is the staff, some say, "unless they know you"; there's no denying, though, its "title as the best fusion food in Paris."

Zéphyr (Le) ◐ Bistro

- | - | - | M

20ᵉ | 1, rue du Jourdain (Jourdain) | 01 46 36 65 81 | fax 01 40 33 10 89 |
www.lezephyr.com

Its name means gentle breeze, but reviewers blow hot and cold over
this Belleville bistro; the "extremely inventive" fare is "scrumptious"
to some palates, but overpriced to others; still, it's a popular place
"to meet with close friends" and admire the superbly preserved "art
deco setting – a treat for the eyes"; P.S. the tour du chocolat "dessert
sampler is a must for any self-respecting chocolate lover."

	FOOD	DECOR	SERVICE	COST

Zeyer (Le) ◑ *Brasserie*   ▽ 16 | 16 | 19 | €59

14e | 62, rue d'Alésia (Alésia) | 01 45 40 43 88 | fax 01 45 40 64 51
"A monument of the 14th, for over 60 years", this "handsome brasserie" with retro–"art deco atmosphere" has "the same owner as Le
Dôme", and serves much the "same fare – fresh fish, oysters and
fruits de mer"; "a professionally run operation, it's out of the way, but
don't be surprised if you want to come back."

Zinc-Zinc ⌷ *Bistro*   ▽ 16 | 15 | 13 | €34

Neuilly-sur-Seine | 209 ter, av Charles de Gaulle (Pont-de-Neuilly) |
01 40 88 36 06 | fax 01 47 38 16 21 | www.zinczinc.com
Critics may cavil "the cuisine's too greasy and the room too noisy",
but most Neuilly natives find this "lively" bistro "always reliable";
it's especially "nice with the gang after work", when it serves "excellent tapas", and some welcome the weekday breakfast as well.

Zingots (Aux) ◑⌷ *Brasserie*   - | - | - | M

10e | 12, rue de la Fidelité (Château d'Eau/Gare de l'Est) |
01 47 70 19 34 | fax 01 47 70 19 35
Since "good restaurants are scarce in this area" of the 10th, this
sizable brasserie is "a space to check out"; the 1880-vintage decor
with lavish moldings creates a lot of atmosphere in which stylish
young crowds enjoy traditional French dishes like lamb sweetbreads
and Lyonnais sausage with baby cabbages, plus a "quality wine" list
with over 250 different bottles.

Zo ◑⌷ *Eclectic*   - | - | - | M

8e | 13, rue Montalivet (Champs-Elysées-Clémenceau) | 01 42 65 18 18 |
fax 01 42 65 10 91 | www.restaurantzo.com
Fusionistas from the "posh neighborhood" around the Faubourg
Saint-Honoré have made this "happening" table their "local hangout"
with a "contemporary, light" Eclectic menu that meanders from the
Mediterranean to Japan and a bar that specializes in fruity vodkas; for
an eatery *à la mode,* it's "affordable", with surprisingly "nice service."

Zygomates (Les) ⌷Ⓜ *Bistro*   ▽ 20 | 16 | 21 | €44

12e | 7, rue de Capri (Daumesnil/Michel Bizot) | 01 40 19 93 04 |
fax 01 44 73 46 63 | www.leszygomates.fr
The *zygomates* (the muscles used to smile) get a workout at this
"cozy, welcoming" bistro in an "old butcher's shop" in the 12th; as
"it only seats a few dozen people", it's always packed with a "local
crowd" lapping up the "creative" takes on Classic French favorites at
"great prices"; "crossing the city for it might be too much, but if
you're looking for a restaurant in the area, it's very good."

INDEXES

French Cuisines

Includes restaurant names, locations and Food ratings. **Z** indicates places with the highest ratings, popularity and importance.

BISTRO

Abadache	17e	-
Absinthe	1er	20
Accolade	17e	-
Affriolé	7e	22
NEW Alfred	1er	-
Z Allard	6e	21
Z Ami Louis	3e	25
Ami Marcel	15e	17
Ampère	17e	-
AOC	5e	18
Z Ardoise	1er	24
Assiette	14e	-
Astier	11e	21
Atelier Maître Albert	5e	21
Bar des Théâtres	8e	15
Bastide Odéon	6e	22
Z Benoît	4e	24
Beurre Noisette	15e	23
Biche au Bois	12e	20
Bis du Severo	14e	-
Bistral	17e	19
Bistro 121	15e	-
Bistro de Breteuil	7e	16
Bistro/Deux Théâtres	9e	14
Bistro du 17ème	17e	18
Bistro Melrose	17e	-
Bistro Poulbot	18e	-
Bistro St. Ferdinand	17e	14
Bistrot d'à Côté	multi.	21
Bistrot d'André	15e	-
Bistrot de l'Etoile Laur.	16e	-
Z Bistrot de l'Oulette	4e	26
Bistrot de l'Université	7e	18
Bistrot de Paris	7e	16
Bistrot des Dames	17e	14
Bistrot des Vignes	16e	17
Bistrot d'Henri	6e	20
Bistrot du Cap	15e	-
Bistrot du Dôme	multi.	21
Bistrot du Peintre	11e	18
Bistrot du Sommelier	8e	18
Bistrot Niel	17e	-

Bistrot Paul Bert	11e	23
Bistrot Vivienne	2e	18
Z Bon Accueil	7e	24
Boucherie Roulière	6e	-
Bouchons Clerc/P'tit	8e	20
Boulangerie	20e	23
Buisson Ardent	5e	19
Butte Chaillot	16e	21
Café Burq	18e	-
Café Constant	7e	24
Café d'Angel	17e	-
Café de l'Industrie	11e	12
Café de Mars	7e	17
Café du Commerce	15e	16
Café Moderne	2e	21
Café Ruc	1er	15
Caméléon	6e	20
Carte Blanche	9e	-
Cave Gourmande	19e	25
Cerisaie	14e	21
Chardenoux	11e	19
Charpentiers	6e	18
NEW Chéri Bibi	18e	-
Chez André	8e	20
Chez Denise	1er	24
Chez Fred	17e	-
Z Chez Georges	2e	24
Chez Gérard	**Neuilly**	19
Chez Julien	4e	19
Chez L'Ami Jean	7e	24
Chez la Vieille	1er	16
Chez Léna et Mimile	5e	15
Chez Léon	17e	13
Chez Maître Paul	6e	21
Chez Marcel	6e	-
Chez Paul	11e	21
Chez Paul	13e	16
Chez Pauline	1er	20
Chez Ramulaud	11e	16
Chez René	5e	21
Chez Savy	8e	18
Christine	6e	23
NEW Christophe	5e	-

Cinq Mars | 7ᵉ	19
Clou | 17ᵉ	19
Ⓩ Comptoir du Relais | 6ᵉ	26
Coupe Gorge | 4ᵉ	-
Crus de Bourgogne | 2ᵉ	17
NEW Cuisine (11e) | 11ᵉ	-
D'Chez Eux | 7ᵉ	25
2 Pieces Cuisine | 18ᵉ	-
Dos de la Baleine | 4ᵉ	20
Duc de Richelieu | 12ᵉ	-
Ebauchoir | 12ᵉ	-
Entracte | 18ᵉ	-
Entredgeu | 17ᵉ	17
Epi d'Or | 1ᵉʳ	16
Ⓩ Epi Dupin | 6ᵉ	24
NEW Epigramme | 6ᵉ	-
Escargot Montorgueil | 1ᵉʳ	21
Ferrandaise | 6ᵉ	21
NEW Fines Gueules | 1ᵉʳ	-
Fins Gourmets | 7ᵉ	19
Ⓩ Fontaine de Mars | 7ᵉ	21
Fontaines | 5ᵉ	17
Fous d'en Face | 4ᵉ	-
NEW Garance | 10ᵉ	-
Gauloise | 15ᵉ	15
Gavroche | 2ᵉ	17
Georgette | 9ᵉ	22
Gorille Blanc | 7ᵉ	21
Gourmets des Ternes | 8ᵉ	19
NEW Grand Pan | 15ᵉ	-
Grange Batelière | 9ᵉ	-
Grille | 10ᵉ	17
Grille St-Germain | 6ᵉ	17
Jardinier | 9ᵉ	-
Joséphine/Dumonet | 6ᵉ	23
Lescure | 1ᵉʳ	17
Ⓩ Lyonnais | 2ᵉ	21
Maison du Jardin | 6ᵉ	24
Mathusalem | 16ᵉ	-
NEW M Comme Martine | 17ᵉ	-
Mesturet | 2ᵉ	-
Moissonnier | 5ᵉ	19
Ⓩ Mon Vieil Ami | 4ᵉ	24
Moulin à Vent | 5ᵉ	19
Noces de Jeannette | 2ᵉ	-
Oeillade | 7ᵉ	14
Olivades | 7ᵉ	17

Opportun | 14ᵉ	15
Oudino | 7ᵉ	-
Parc aux Cerfs | 6ᵉ	21
Pères et Filles | 6ᵉ	16
Perraudin | 5ᵉ	13
Petit Marguery | 13ᵉ	21
Petit Pascal | 13ᵉ	-
Petit Pergolèse | 16ᵉ	23
Petit Pontoise | 5ᵉ	22
Petit Prince de Paris | 5ᵉ	-
Petit Rétro | 16ᵉ	16
Petit Riche | 9ᵉ	18
Polichinelle Cafe | 11ᵉ	-
Polidor | 6ᵉ	17
Pomponette | 18ᵉ	17
Pouilly Reuilly | St-Gervais	-
Poule au Pot | 1ᵉʳ	23
Press Café | 2ᵉ	-
P'tit Troquet | 7ᵉ	22
Pure Café | 11ᵉ	-
Quincy | 12ᵉ	-
Refectoire | 11ᵉ	-
Ⓩ Régalade | 14ᵉ	25
Rendez-vous/Chauff. | 18ᵉ	-
Repaire de Cartouche | 11ᵉ	16
Rest. du Marché | 15ᵉ	-
Rest. Manufacture | Issy-les-Moul.	21
Rest. Paul | 1ᵉʳ	20
Réveil du 10e (Le) | 10ᵉ	-
Robert et Louise | 3ᵉ	21
Roi du Pot-au-Feu | 9ᵉ	-
Rose de France | 1ᵉʳ	-
Rôtiss. d'en Face | 6ᵉ	21
Rôtiss. du Beaujolais | 5ᵉ	23
Rouge Vif | 7ᵉ	15
NEW Salon du Panthéon | 5ᵉ	-
Saveurs du Marché | Neuilly	-
Scheffer | 16ᵉ	18
Soleil | St-Ouen	-
Soleil | 7ᵉ	19
Sot l'y Laisse | 11ᵉ	-
Spring | 9ᵉ	23
Square Trousseau | 12ᵉ	19
Temps au Temps | 11ᵉ	25
Temps des Cerises | 13ᵉ	-
Terrasse Mirabeau | 16ᵉ	-

Terroir | 13ᵉ	–
Thoumieux | 7ᵉ	19
Tierny & Co. | 16ᵉ	–
Timbre | 6ᵉ	24
Tournesol | 16ᵉ	18
Triporteur | 15ᵉ	–
Trumilou | 4ᵉ	19
NEW Urbane | 10ᵉ	–
Vieux Bistro | 4ᵉ	21
Vieux Chêne | 11ᵉ	–
Z Villaret | 11ᵉ	26
20 de Bellechasse | 7ᵉ	19
Z Violon d'Ingres | 7ᵉ	25
Voltaire | 7ᵉ	24
Wadja | 6ᵉ	20
Zéphyr | 20ᵉ	–
Zinc-Zinc | **Neuilly**	16
Zygomates | 12ᵉ	20

BRASSERIE

Aub. Dab | 16ᵉ	16
Ballon des Ternes | 17ᵉ	15
Boeuf sur le Toit | 8ᵉ	18
Z Bofinger | 4ᵉ	20
Bouillon Racine | 6ᵉ	16
Z Brass. Balzar | 5ᵉ	19
Brass. de l'Ile St. Louis | 4ᵉ	17
Brass. du Louvre | 1ᵉʳ	16
Brass. Flo | 10ᵉ	18
Brass. Julien | 10ᵉ	19
Brass. La Lorraine | 8ᵉ	17
Brass. L'Européen | 12ᵉ	–
Z Brass. Lipp | 6ᵉ	17
Brass. Lutétia | 6ᵉ	18
Brass. Mollard | 8ᵉ	19
Charlot Roi des Coq. | 9ᵉ	15
Chez Francis | 8ᵉ	17
Chez Georges-Maillot | 17ᵉ	18
Chez Jenny | 3ᵉ	19
Chez Les Anges | 7ᵉ	23
Chien qui Fume | 1ᵉʳ	18
Closerie des Lilas | 6ᵉ	18
Z Comptoir du Relais | 6ᵉ	26
Congrès Maillot | 17ᵉ	18
Costes | 1ᵉʳ	18
Z Coupole | 14ᵉ	19
Durand Dupont | **Neuilly**	–

Editeurs | 6ᵉ	14
Flandrin | 16ᵉ	15
Gallopin | 2ᵉ	16
Garnier | 8ᵉ	22
Grand Café | 9ᵉ	13
Grand Colbert | 2ᵉ	19
Marty | 5ᵉ	16
Mascotte | 18ᵉ	–
Petit Bofinger | **multi.**	18
Petit Lutétia | 6ᵉ	19
Petit Zinc | 6ᵉ	18
Pétrus | 17ᵉ	21
Pied de Cochon | 1ᵉʳ	18
Publicis Drugstore | 8ᵉ	11
Relais Plaza | 8ᵉ	23
Rotonde | 6ᵉ	15
Sébillon | **Neuilly**	15
Z Senderens | 8ᵉ	26
Stella | 16ᵉ	20
Suffren | 15ᵉ	14
Tav. de Maître Kanter | 1ᵉʳ	16
Terminus Nord | 10ᵉ	17
Vagenende | 6ᵉ	15
Vaudeville | 2ᵉ	18
Wepler | 18ᵉ	14
Zeyer | 14ᵉ	16
Zingot | 10ᵉ	–

CLASSIC

A. Beauvilliers | 18ᵉ	20
A et M | 16ᵉ	21
NEW Agassin | 7ᵉ	–
Aiguière | 11ᵉ	–
Aimant du Sud | 13ᵉ	–
Z Allard | 6ᵉ	21
Allobroges | 20ᵉ	22
Z Ami Louis | 3ᵉ	25
Arome | 8ᵉ	–
Aub. Bressane | 7ᵉ	20
Aub. de Reine Blanche | 4ᵉ	19
Aub. du Champ/Mars | 7ᵉ	17
Aub. du Clou | 9ᵉ	16
Aub. Nicolas Flamel | 3ᵉ	23
Auguste | 7ᵉ	25
Autobus Imperial | 1ᵉʳ	–
Bacchantes | 9ᵉ	–
Bar Vendôme | 1ᵉʳ	23

Basilic	7e	15	Chez Grisette	18e	–
Beaujolais d'Auteuil	16e	17	Chez Léna et Mimile	5e	15
Biche au Bois	12e	20	Chez Nénesse	3e	–
Bistro de Breteuil	7e	16	Christine	6e	23
Bistro d'Hubert	15e	22	Cigale Récamier	7e	21
Bistro Poulbot	18e	–	Citrus Etoile	8e	20
Bistro St. Ferdinand	17e	14	Closerie des Lilas	6e	18
Bistrot d'à Côté	multi.	21	Comédiens	9e	–
Bistrot d'André	15e	–	Cordonnerie	1er	–
Bistrot d'Henri	6e	20	Coupe-Chou	5e	23
Bistrot Papillon	9e	14	NEW Dali	1er	–
Boeuf Couronné	19e	16	Da Rosa	6e	19
Z Bon Accueil	7e	24	Dauphin	1er	20
Bon Saint Pourçain	6e	18	Deux Canards	10e	18
Bouchons Clerc/P'tit	8e	20	2 Pieces Cuisine	18e	–
Brass. Printemps	9e	11	Drouant	2e	22
Buisson Ardent	5e	19	Ebouillanté	4e	–
Café Beaubourg	4e	16	Ecluse	multi.	16
Café Charbon	11e	15	Z Espadon (L')	1er	26
Z Café de Flore	6e	15	Etoile	16e	24
Café de la Musique	19e	15	Ferme St-Simon	7e	23
Café de la Paix	9e	19	Fermette Marbeuf	8e	18
Café de la Poste	4e	–	Flora Danica	8e	19
Café de l'Esplanade	7e	16	Flore en l'Ile	4e	18
Café Faubourg	8e	22	Florimond	7e	24
Café Guitry	9e	–	Fontaine Gaillon	2e	22
Café Le Petit Pont	5e	14	Fouquet's	8e	18
Z Café Les Deux Magots	6e	16	Gare	16e	14
Z Café Marly	1er	16	Z Gérard Besson	1er	25
Café Terminus	8e	–	Gitane	15e	–
Camille	3e	16	Gourmand (Au)	1er	20
Cap Seguin	Boulogne	–	Grande Armée	16e	15
Caveau du Palais	1er	19	Grand Louvre	1er	18
Cave de l'Os à Moëlle	15e	22	Grange Batelière	9e	–
Caves Pétrissans	17e	19	Gourmand	Neuilly	–
Céladon	2e	21	Guirlande de Julie	3e	15
Chai 33	12e	14	Hangar	3e	18
Chalet (Le)	Neuilly	–	Ile	Issy-les-Moul.	18
Chalet des Iles	16e	14	Ilot Vache	4e	18
Chartier	9e	13	NEW Il Vino	7e	–
NEW Chéri Bibi	18e	–	Jardin des Cygnes	8e	22
Chez Cécile	8e	–	Jardins de Bagatelle	16e	17
Chez Clément	multi.	15	Je Thé . . . Me	15e	–
Chez Denise	1er	24	Joséphine/Dumonet	6e	23
Chez Françoise	7e	17	Z Jules Verne	7e	–
Chez Gégène	Joinville	–	Kiosque	16e	15
Chez Géraud	16e	20	Z Ladurée	multi.	23

Lavinia | 1er	17
Libre Sens | 8e	–
Ma Bourgogne | 4e	18
Macéo | 1er	23
Maison de l'Amér. Latine | 7e	18
Marlotte | 6e	16
Martel | 10e	–
Mathusalem | 16e	–
Maupertu | 7e	21
Maxim's | 8e	18
Méditerranée | 6e	21
☑ Michel Rostang | 17e	27
Monsieur Lapin | 14e	18
Moulin de la Galette | 18e	15
Murat | 16e	13
Natacha | 14e	–
Nos Ancêtres/Gaulois | 4e	13
Obélisque | 8e	23
Oenothèque | 9e	–
Orangerie | 4e	22
Orénoc | 17e	17
☑ Os à Moëlle | 15e	25
Ourcine | 13e	24
Papilles | 5e	23
Passage/Carm. | 11e	–
☑ Passiflore | 16e	26
Paul Chêne | 16e	20
Pavillon Montsouris | 14e	17
Père Claude | 15e	17
Pères et Filles | 6e	16
Petit Châtelet | 5e	–
Petit Colombier | 17e	18
Petite Chaise | 7e	19
Petite Tour | 16e	–
Petit Pascal | 13e	–
Petit Rétro | 16e	16
Petit Riche | 9e	18
Petit St. Benoît | 6e	16
Petit Victor Hugo | 16e	19
Pharamond | 1er	19
Pierre au Palais Royal | 1er	17
Potager du Roy | **Versailles**	19
Procope | 6e	16
Ragueneau | 1er	–
Relais du Parc | 16e	19
Restaurant (Le) | 6e	26
Rest. de la Tour | 15e	21

Rest. du Musée d'Orsay | 7e	17
Rest. du Palais Royal | 1er	19
Rest. Paul | 1er	20
Resto | 8e	–
Ribouldingue | 5e	18
River Café | **Issy-les-Moul.**	14
Robe et le Palais | 1er	19
Rose Bakery | 9e	17
Royal Madeleine | 8e	19
Rubis | 1er	15
Saveurs de Claude | 6e	–
Saveurs du Marché | **Neuilly**	–
Sébillon | **Neuilly**	15
☑ Soufflé | 1er	22
Soupière | 17e	–
Square | 7e	–
Square | 18e	–
☑ Stella Maris | 8e	26
Stéphane Martin | 15e	–
Strapontins | 10e	–
Table d'Anvers | 9e	17
Table Lauriston | 16e	20
Tante Louise | 8e	22
Tante Marguerite | 7e	22
Tastevin | **Maisons-Laff.**	24
Tav. du Sgt. Recruteur | 4e	16
Temps des Cerises | 13e	–
Terres de Truffes | 8e	19
Tonnelle Saintongeaise | **Neuilly**	–
Toque | 17e	–
☑ Train Bleu | 12e	19
Truc Café | 18e	–
Truffe Noire | **Neuilly**	–
Versance | 2e	–
Viaduc Café | 12e	–
Vieille Fontaine | **Maisons-Laff.**	–
☑ Villaret | 11e	26
Vinci | 16e	–
Vin des Pyrenees | 4e	16
Vivres | 9e	–
Wadja | 6e	20
Zébra Square | 16e	10
Zygomates | 12e	20

CONTEMPORARY

Accolade | 17e	–
NEW Afaria | 15e	–

NEW Agassin	7ᵉ	–
Alain Bourgade	16ᵉ	–
Alcazar	6ᵉ	19
Z Ambassadeurs	8ᵉ	28
Amuse Bouche	14ᵉ	17
Angle du Faubourg	8ᵉ	24
Angl'Opéra	2ᵉ	19
Arome	8ᵉ	–
Z Astrance	16ᵉ	28
Atelier Berger	1ᵉʳ	21
Aub. de Reine Blanche	4ᵉ	19
Aub. du Clou	9ᵉ	16
Avant Goût	13ᵉ	23
Avenue	8ᵉ	18
Bamboche	7ᵉ	19
Baptiste	17ᵉ	–
Berkeley	8ᵉ	14
BIOArt	13ᵉ	–
Bistro d'Hubert	15ᵉ	22
Bistrot de l'Etoile Laur.	16ᵉ	–
Bon	16ᵉ	15
Bound	8ᵉ	–
Z Bouquinistes	6ᵉ	23
Z Braisière	17ᵉ	27
Café de l'Esplanade	7ᵉ	16
Café Lenôtre	8ᵉ	18
Café M	8ᵉ	19
Z Café Marly	1ᵉʳ	16
NEW Café Pleyel	8ᵉ	–
Caïus	17ᵉ	19
Camélia	Bougival	20
Cap Seguin	Boulogne	–
Cap Vernet	8ᵉ	17
Carte Blanche	9ᵉ	–
Cartes Postales	1ᵉʳ	24
Cazaudehore	St-Germain-Laye	22
Chateaubriand	11ᵉ	22
Chez Catherine	8ᵉ	23
Chez Michel	10ᵉ	24
Chiberta	8ᵉ	22
Citrus Etoile	8ᵉ	20
Clos des Gourmets	7ᵉ	25
Clos Morillons	15ᵉ	–
Clovis	8ᵉ	–
NEW Cocottes	7ᵉ	21
Cottage Marcadet	18ᵉ	–
Cou de la Girafe	8ᵉ	15
NEW Cristal de Sel	15ᵉ	–
Z Cristal Room	16ᵉ	17
Cuisine (7e)	7ᵉ	25
Dalva	2ᵉ	–
Delicabar	7ᵉ	13
Z 1728	8ᵉ	19
Dôme du Marais	4ᵉ	22
Don Juans	3ᵉ	–
NEW Eclaireur	8ᵉ	–
Famille	18ᵉ	19
First	1ᵉʳ	18
NEW Garance	10ᵉ	–
Gazzetta	12ᵉ	–
Georgette	9ᵉ	22
Gourmand (Au)	1ᵉʳ	20
Z Hélène Darroze	6ᵉ	25
Hier & Aujourd'hui	17ᵉ	–
Z Hiramatsu	16ᵉ	26
Hôtel Amour	9ᵉ	8
Ile	Issy-les-Moul.	18
Jean	9ᵉ	19
NEW Karl et Erich	17ᵉ	–
Macéo	1ᵉʳ	23
Magnolias	Perreux	25
Maison Blanche	8ᵉ	20
Maison du Jardin	6ᵉ	24
Maxan	8ᵉ	–
NEW Mini Palais	8ᵉ	–
Montalembert	7ᵉ	19
Montparnasse 25	14ᵉ	16
Murano	3ᵉ	16
Musichall	8ᵉ	15
NEW Nouvelle Athenes	9ᵉ	–
Z Ombres (Les)	7ᵉ	18
Ourcine	13ᵉ	24
Pershing	8ᵉ	17
Petite Cour	6ᵉ	21
Petit Marché	3ᵉ	22
Petit Pergolèse	16ᵉ	23
Petit Poucet	Levallois	–
Pétrelle	9ᵉ	–
Pinxo	1ᵉʳ	21
Ploum	10ᵉ	–
Point Bar	1ᵉʳ	22
Pomze	8ᵉ	18
Pré Verre	5ᵉ	22
Pur'Grill	2ᵉ	19

Quai | 7e	–
Quinzième | 15e	–
Radis Roses | 9e	–
Réconfort | 3e	–
Relais du Parc | 16e	19
River Café | **Issy-les-Moul.**	14
Rue Balzac | 8e	17
NEW Saut du Loup | 1er	14
Saveurs de Claude | 6e	–
Saveurs de Flora (Les) | 8e	21
16 Haussmann | 9e	18
Z Senderens | 8e	26
Sensing | 6e	24
6 New York | 16e	17
Spoon/Food | 8e	22
Square | 18e	–
Table d'Hédiard | 8e	22
Taïra | 17e	–
Thierry Burlot | 15e	–
Toi | 8e	–
Tokyo Eat | 16e	14
Troquet | 15e	24
Versance | 2e	–
Viaduc Café | 12e	–
Vieille Fontaine | **Maisons-Laff.**	–
Vieux Chêne | 11e	–
Villa Spicy | 8e	13
Z Vin sur Vin | 7e	26
Waknine | 16e	–
Water Bar Colette | 1er	14
W Restaurant | 8e	–

HAUTE CUISINE

Z Alain Ducasse | 8e	28
Z Ambassadeurs | 8e	28
Z Ambroisie | 4e	28
Z Apicius | 8e	26
Z Arpège | 7e	26
Astor | 8e	16
Z Atelier Joël Robuchon | 7e	28
Z Bristol | 8e	27
Z Carré des Feuillants | 1er	26
Cazaudehore | **St-Germain-Laye**	22
Z Cinq (Le) | 8e	28
Z Dominique Bouchet | 8e	27
Elysées (Les) | 8e	23
Z Grand Véfour | 1er	28

Z Guy Savoy | 17e	28
Z Hiramatsu | 16e	26
Z Jacques Cagna | 6e	26
Z Lapérouse | 6e	21
Z Lasserre | 8e	27
Z Laurent | 8e	24
Z Meurice | 1er	27
Muses | 9e	19
Paris | 6e	20
Z Pavillon/Gr. Cascade | 16e	25
Z Pavillon Ledoyen | 8e	26
Z Pierre Gagnaire | 8e	28
Z Pré Catelan | 16e	27
Z Relais d'Auteuil | 16e	27
Relais Louis XIII | 6e	25
Stéphane Gaborieau | 16e	–
Z Table de Joël Robuchon | 16e	26
Table du Baltimore | 16e	–
Table du Lancaster | 8e	23
Z Taillevent | 8e	28
Z Tour d'Argent | 5e	25
Truffière | 5e	23

REGIONAL

ALPINE

Chalet (Le) | **Neuilly**	–
Rest. GR5 | **multi.**	24

ALSACE/JURA

Alsace | 8e	18
Alsaco | 9e	–
Z Bofinger | 4e	20
Chez Jenny | 3e	19
Chez Maître Paul | 6e	21
Epicure 108 | 17e	–
Tav. de Maître Kanter | 1er	16

AUVERGNE

Ambassade/Auvergne | 3e	20
Bath's | 17e	20
Bistrot à Vins Mélac | 11e	14
Chantairelle | 5e	–
Chez Gérard | **Neuilly**	19
Lozère | 6e	18
Mascotte | 18e	–
Nemrod | 6e	16

AVEYRON

Ambassade/Auvergne | 3e	20
Aub. Aveyronnaise | 12e	–
Chez Savy | 8e	18

BASQUE
Bascou | 3e — 20
Basilic | 7e — 15
Casa Alcalde | 15e — ⌐
Chez L'Ami Jean | 7e — 24
Pamphlet | 3e — 23
Z Régalade | 14e — 25
Troquet | 15e — 24

BRITTANY
NEW Breizh Café | 3e — ⌐
Chez Michel | 10e — 24
Crêperie de Josselin | 14e — 22

BURGUNDY
Ma Bourgogne | 4e — 18
Tante Louise | 8e — 22

CORSICA
Alivi | 4e — 16
Casa Olympe | 9e — 24
Cosi (Le) | 5e — 16
Main d'Or | 11e — ⌐
Villa Corse | multi. — 20

GASCONY
Z Braisière | 17e — 27
Comte de Gascogne | Boulogne — ⌐

LYON
Aub. Pyrénées | 11e — 20
Z Benoît | 4e — 24
Chez Fred | 17e — ⌐
Chez Marcel | 6e — ⌐
Chez René | 5e — 21
Duc de Richelieu | 12e — ⌐
Z Lyonnais | 2e — 21
Moissonnier | 5e — 19
Opportun | 14e — 15
Vieux Bistro | 4e — 21

NORTHERN FRANCE
Graindorge | 17e — 22
NEW Petites Sorcières | 14e — ⌐
Pré Salé | 1er — ⌐

PROVENCE
Aimant du Sud | 13e — ⌐
Bastide Odéon | 6e — 22
Bistro de l'Olivier | 8e — 18
Casa Olympe | 9e — 24
Chez Janou | 3e — 23
Z Fish La Boissonnerie | 6e — 22

Olivades | 7e — 17
Petit Niçois | 7e — 16
Sud | 17e — 16

SOUTHWEST
NEW Afaria | 15e — ⌐
Ami Pierre | 11e — 17
Assiette | 14e — ⌐
Aub. Etchégorry | 13e — ⌐
Aub. Pyrénées | 11e — 20
Z Bistrot de l'Oulette | 4e — 26
Café Faubourg | 8e — 22
Cerisaie | 14e — 21
Chez L'Ami Jean | 7e — 24
Chez Papa | multi. — 17
Dauphin | 1er — 20
D'Chez Eux | 7e — 25
Diapason | 18e — ⌐
Domaine de Lintillac | multi. — 18
Fins Gourmets | 7e — 19
Z Fontaine de Mars | 7e — 21
Gamin de Paris | 4e — 21
Z Hélène Darroze | 6e — 25
Il Etait une Oie | 17e — ⌐
J'Go | multi. — 14
Languedoc | 5e — ⌐
Maison Courtine | 14e — 24
Mesturet | 2e — ⌐
Oulette | 12e — 19
Pamphlet | 3e — 23
Pasco | 7e — 22
Rouge Vif | 7e — 15
Salon d'Hélène | 6e — 19
Sarladais | 8e — ⌐
NEW SYDR | 8e — ⌐
Thoumieux | 7e — 19
NEW Toustem | 5e — ⌐
Z Trou Gascon | 12e — 26

SEAFOOD
Autour du Mont | 15e — ⌐
Autour du Saumon | multi. — 17
Ballon et Coquillages | 17e — ⌐
Bar à Huîtres | multi. — 17
Bistrot de Marius | 8e — 21
Bistrot du Cap | 15e — ⌐
Bistrot du Dôme | multi. — 21
Brass. L'Européen | 12e — ⌐

Brass. Lutétia | 6e	18
Cagouille | 14e	25
Cap Vernet | 8e	17
☑ 144 Petrossian | 7e	25
☑ Coupole | 14e	19
Dessirier | 17e	20
Divellec | 7e	24
Dôme | 14e	22
Duc (Le) | 14e	23
Ecailler du Bistrot | 11e	19
Espadon Bleu | 6e	21
Fables de La Fontaine | 7e	24
☑ Fish La Boissonnerie | 6e	22
Fontaine Gaillon | 2e	22
Frégate | 12e	24
Garnier | 8e	22
Gaya | 7e	23
Goumard | 1er	24
Huîtrier | 17e	20
Jarrasse | Neuilly	-
Luna (La) | 8e	17
Maison Prunier | 16e	21
Marée (La) | 8e	23
Marée Denfert/Passy | multi.	-
Marée de Versailles | Versailles	19
Marius | 16e	18
Marius et Janette | 8e	25
Méditerranée | 6e	21
Petit Zinc | 6e	18
Pétrus | 17e	21
Pichet de Paris | 8e	16
Port Alma | 16e	17
NEW P'tit Casier | 15e	-
Rech | 17e	-
Sarladais | 8e	-
35° Ouest | 7e	20
Uitr | 15e	-
Vin et Marée | multi.	18
21 | 6e	-
Wepler | 18e	14
NEW Winch | 18e	-

SHELLFISH

Ballon des Ternes | 17e	15
Ballon et Coquillages | 17e	-
Bar à Huîtres | multi.	17
Charlot Roi des Coq. | 9e	15
Dôme | 14e	22

Ecaille de Fontaine | 2e	-
Ecailler du Bistrot | 11e	19
Garnier | 8e	22
Huîtrerie Régis | 6e	22
Huîtrier | 17e	20
Marée de Versailles | Versailles	19
Marius | 16e	18
Marius et Janette | 8e	25
Pichet de Paris | 8e	16
Rech | 17e	-
Stella | 16e	20
Terminus Nord | 10e	17
Uitr | 15e	-

STEAK

Boeuf Couronné | 19e	16
Boucherie Roulière | 6e	-
Devèz | 8e	16
Gavroche | 2e	17
Gourmets des Ternes | 8e	19
Hippopotamus | multi.	11
Louchebem | 1er	15
☑ Relais/l'Entrecôte | multi.	22
Relais de Venise | 17e	24
Ribouldingue | 5e	18
Severo | 14e	20

WINE BARS/BISTROS

Ami Pierre | 11e	17
Bacchantes | 9e	-
Baratin | 20e	16
Baron Rouge | 12e	-
Bistrot à Vins Mélac | 11e	14
Bistrot du Sommelier | 8e	18
Bons Crus | 1er	-
Bouchons Clerc/P'tit | 8e	20
Bourguignon du Marais | 4e	23
Café Burq | 18e	-
Café du Passage | 11e	-
Cantine de Quentin | 10e	-
Cave de l'Os à Moëlle | 15e	22
Caves Pétrissans | 17e	19
Chai 33 | 12e	14
Chez Grisette | 18e	-
Cloche des Halles | 1er	-
Clown Bar | 11e	17
Coude Fou | 4e	19
Couleurs de Vigne | 15e	-

FRENCH CUISINES

Other Cuisines

Includes restaurant names, locations and Food ratings. ⓩ indicates places with the highest ratings, popularity and importance.

AMERICAN

Breakfast in America | multi.	15
Buffalo Grill | multi.	10
Coffee Parisien | multi.	16
Joe Allen | 1er	13
Meating | 17e	17

ARGENTINEAN

Anahï | 3e	19
El Palenque | 5e	19
Unico | 11e	-

ARMENIAN

Diamantaires | 9e	-

ASIAN

Asian | 8e	16
ⓩ Buddha Bar | 8e	16
Epicure 108 | 17e	-
Orénoc | 17e	17
Passy Mandarin | multi.	20
Tricotin | 13e	-
Wok Cooking | 11e	-

ASIAN FUSION

NEW Mood | 8e	-
Orénoc | 17e	17
ⓩ Passiflore | 16e	26

BAKERIES

BE Boulangépicier | multi.	19
Boulangerie Eric Kayser | 8e	16

BELGIAN

Graindorge | 17e	22
Léon/Bruxelles | multi.	16

BRAZILIAN

Barroco | 6e	-

BRITISH

Rose Bakery | 9e	17

BURGERS

Coffee Parisien | multi.	16
Indiana Café | multi.	7
Joe Allen | 1er	13

CALIFORNIAN

Sept Quinze | 15e	21

CAMBODIAN

Coin/Gourmets | multi.	22
Kambodgia | 16e	-
Mousson | 1er	-
Sinago | 9e	-

CAVIAR

Caviar Kaspia | 8e	25
ⓩ 144 Petrossian | 7e	25
Maison du Caviar | 8e	22
Maison Prunier | 16e	21

CHINESE

(* dim sum specialist)

Chen Soleil d'Est | 15e	-
Chez Ly | 17e	-
Chez Vong | 1er	21
Davé | 1er	18
Diep | 8e	21
Elysées Hong Kong | 16e	-
Lao Tseu | 7e	-
Mirama | 5e	20
New Nioullaville* | 11e	16
Nouveau Village | 13e	18
Tang | 16e	17
Tong Yen | 8e	15
Tsé-Yang | 16e	18
Village d'Ung | 8e	-

CREOLE

Table de Babette | 16e	-

DANISH

Copenhague | 8e	18
Flora Danica | 8e	19
Petite Sirène/Copen. | 9e	-

DESSERT

ⓩ Angelina | 1er	20
A Priori Thé | 2e	16
Café Lenôtre | 8e	18
Dalloyau | multi.	23
Deux Abeilles | 7e	21

Flore en l'Ile | 4e	18
Jean-Paul Hévin | 1er	24
☑ Ladurée | multi.	23
Loir dans/Théière | 4e	16
Mariage Frères | multi.	21
☑ Soufflé | 1er	22

EASTERN EUROPEAN

Chez Marianne | 4e	18

ECLECTIC

Ampère | 17e	-
Apollo | 14e	-
Autour du Saumon | multi.	17
Berkeley | 8e	14
Black Calavados | 8e	-
Café Etienne Marcel | 2e	18
Café Fusion | 13e	-
Café la Jatte | Neuilly	14
Chez Prune | 10e	18
Comptoir | 1er	21
Cook Book | 7e	-
Costes | 1er	18
Durand Dupont | Neuilly	-
Eugène | 8e	-
Fumoir | 1er	17
☑ Georges | 4e	18
Juvéniles | 1er	16
Kong | 1er	14
NEW Lup | 6e	-
Mandalay | Levallois	-
Market | 8e	22
Muscade | 1er	-
No Stress Café | 9e	-
Paradis du Fruit | multi.	14
Pershing | 8e	17
Pure Café | 11e	-
Quai Ouest | St-Cloud	13
Relais Plaza | 8e	23
Rouge St-Honoré | 1er	13
Scoop | 1er	17
Spoon/Food | 8e	22
Vinea Café | 12e	-
☑ Ze Kitchen Galerie | 6e	25
Zo | 8e	-

ETHIOPIAN

Entoto | 13e	-

GREEK

Délices d'Aphrodite | 5e	18
Diamantaires | 9e	-
Mavrommatis | 5e	19

INDIAN

Annapurna | 8e	18
Indra | 8e	-
Maharajah | 5e	17
New Jawad | 7e	18
Ravi | 7e	21
Yugaraj | 6e	23

INDONESIAN

Djakarta | 1er	20

IRISH

Carr's | 1er	-

ISRAELI

☑ As du Fallafel | 4e	24

ITALIAN

(N=Northern; S=Southern)

Amici Miei | 11e	19
Barlotti | 1er	15
Bartolo | 6e	17
Bel Canto | multi.	13
Bellini | 16e	24
Bocconi | 8e	20
Ca d'Oro | N | 1er	18
Café du Passage | 11e	-
Caffé Minotti | 7e	22
Caffé Toscano | 7e	19
Cailloux | 13e	-
Carmine | 7e	-
Carpaccio | 8e	-
Casa Bini | N | 6e	21
Cherche Midi | 6e	19
Chez Livio | Neuilly	13
Chez Vincent | 19e	-
Cibus | 1er	-
Curieux Spaghetti Bar | 4e	-
Da Mimmo | 10e	-
Dell Orto | 9e	-
Emporio Armani | N | 6e	19
Enoteca | 4e	20
Enzo | 14e	-
Fellini | S | multi.	21
Findi | 8e	16

Finzi	8e	13
Fontanarosa	15e	-
Giulio Rebellato	N	16e	20
Gli Angeli	3e	18
Grand Venise	15e	25
I Golosi	9e	17
Il Barone	14e	21
Il Cortile	N	1er	23
Il Viccolo	6e	-
Lei	7e	21
Mori Venice Bar	N	2e	17
Ostéria (L')	4e	22
Osteria Ascolani	18e	-
Paolo Petrini	N	17e	-
Paris Seize	16e	18
Perron	7e	18
Pizzeria d'Auteuil	16e	-
Pizzetta	9e	-
Renoma Café	8e	-
Romantica	Clichy	23
Rucola	17e	-
Rughetta	18e	-
Sale e Pepe	S	18e	-
San	3e	-
Sardegna a Tavola	S	12e	21
Sora Lena	S	17e	-
Sormani	17e	23
Stresa	8e	22
Tav. de Gli Amici	7e	-
Vinci	16e	-
Water Bar Colette	1er	14

JAPANESE

(* sushi specialist)

Aida	7e	23
Azabu	6e	24
Benkay*	15e	24
Bound	8e	-
Foujita*	1er	-
Higuma	1er	15
Inagiku	5e	18
Isami*	4e	25
Issé*	1er	23
Kai	1er	-
Kaïten*	8e	-
Kifune*	17e	-
Kinugawa/Hanawa*	multi.	23
Lô Sushi*	8e	15

Matsuri	multi.	14
Orient-Extrême*	6e	18
Ozu*	16e	23
Ploum	10e	-
Taïra	17e	-
Tsukizi*	6e	-
Yen	6e	20

JEWISH

Pitchi Poï	4e	-

KOREAN

Samiin	7e	-

LEBANESE

Al Dar	multi.	21
Al Diwan	8e	21
Escale du Liban	4e	-
Fakhr el Dine	16e	24
Liza	2e	24
Mont Liban	17e	-
Noura	multi.	19

MEDITERRANEAN

Don Juans	3e	-
Gazzetta	12e	-
NEW Il Vino	7e	-
Pasco	7e	22
Sens	8e	-
7ème Sud	multi.	15
Sept Quinze	15e	21
Soleil	7e	19
Sora Lena	17e	-
Sud	17e	16
Tête Ailleurs	4e	-

MEXICAN

Anahuacalli	5e	21

MIDDLE EASTERN

Chez Marianne	4e	18

MOROCCAN

Al Mounia	16e	17
Andy Wahloo	3e	14
Atlas	5e	20
Chez Omar	3e	21
Comptoir	1er	21
El Mansour	8e	17
Etoile Marocaine	8e	-
Mansouria	11e	22
Martel	10e	-

Oum el Banine	**16ᵉ**	-
Pied de Chameau	**3ᵉ**	-
404	**3ᵉ**	22
Riad	**Neuilly**	-
7ème Sud	**multi.**	15
Timgad	**17ᵉ**	20

NORTH AFRICAN

Boule Rouge	**9ᵉ**	-
Wally Le Saharien	**9ᵉ**	15

PAKISTANI

New Jawad	**7ᵉ**	18

PAN-LATIN

Barrio Latino	**12ᵉ**	12

PIZZA

Amici Miei	**11ᵉ**	19
Bartolo	**6ᵉ**	17
Da Mimmo	**10ᵉ**	-
Enzo	**14ᵉ**	-
Pizzeria d'Auteuil	**16ᵉ**	-
Pizzetta	**9ᵉ**	-
Rughetta	**18ᵉ**	-
Sale e Pepe	**18ᵉ**	-

POLISH

Pitchi Poï	**4ᵉ**	-

PORTUGUESE

Saudade	**1er**	-

RUSSIAN

Caviar Kaspia	**8ᵉ**	25
Daru	**8ᵉ**	-
Maison du Caviar	**8ᵉ**	22

SANDWICHES

BE Boulangépicier	**multi.**	19
Boulangerie Eric Kayser	**8ᵉ**	16
Cosi	**6ᵉ**	19
Dame Tartine	**4ᵉ**	14
Ferme	**1er**	-
Lina's	**multi.**	16
Sauvignon	**7ᵉ**	14

SEAFOOD

Autour du Saumon	**multi.**	17
Copenhague	**8ᵉ**	18
Sens	**8ᵉ**	-

SEYCHELLES

Coco de Mer	**5ᵉ**	-

SOUTHEAST ASIAN

Baan-Boran	**1er**	20
Banyan	**15ᵉ**	19
Blue Elephant	**11ᵉ**	20
Chez Ly	**17ᵉ**	-
Chieng Mai	**5ᵉ**	16
Davé	**1er**	18
Diep	**8ᵉ**	21
Erawan	**15ᵉ**	17
Khun Akorn	**11ᵉ**	-
Kim Anh	**15ᵉ**	-
Lac-Hong	**16ᵉ**	20
Lao Siam	**19ᵉ**	15
Nouveau Village	**13ᵉ**	18
Palanquin	**6ᵉ**	18
Paradis Thai	**13ᵉ**	15
Reuan Thai	**11ᵉ**	-
Sawadee	**15ᵉ**	-
Suave	**13ᵉ**	-
Tan Dinh	**7ᵉ**	23
Thiou/Petit Thiou	**multi.**	21
Tong Yen	**8ᵉ**	15
Village d'Ung	**8ᵉ**	-

SPANISH

(* tapas specialist)	
Bellota-Bellota	**7ᵉ**	19
Casa Alcalde	**15ᵉ**	-
Casa Tina*	**16ᵉ**	-
Chez Ramona*	**20ᵉ**	-
Fogón*	**6ᵉ**	21
Rosimar	**16ᵉ**	-

STEAKHOUSES

Buffalo Grill	**multi.**	10
Meating	**17ᵉ**	17
Unico	**11ᵉ**	-

TEX-MEX

Indiana Café	**multi.**	7
Studio	**4ᵉ**	-

THAI

Baan-Boran	**1er**	20
Banyan	**15ᵉ**	19
Blue Elephant	**11ᵉ**	20
Chez Ly	**17ᵉ**	-
Chieng Mai	**5ᵉ**	16
Erawan	**15ᵉ**	17

OTHER CUISINES

Khun Akorn	11^e	-	**VIETNAMESE**	
Lao Siam	19^e	15	Coin/Gourmets	**multi.**	22
Nouveau Village	13^e	18	Davé	1er	18
Paradis Thai	13^e	15	Kambodgia	16^e	-
Reuan Thai	11^e	-	Kim Anh	15^e	-
Sawadee	15^e	-	Lac-Hong	16^e	20
Thiou/Petit Thiou	**multi.**	21	Palanquin	6^e	18
Village d'Ung	8^e	-	Suave	13^e	-
			Tan Dinh	7^e	23

TURKISH

Sizin | 9e -

Locations

Includes restaurant names, cuisines and Food ratings. ☑ indicates places with the highest ratings, popularity and importance.

Paris

1ST ARRONDISSEMENT

Absinthe	*Bistro*	20
NEW Alfred	*Bistro*	-
☑ Angelina	*Tea*	20
☑ Ardoise	*Bistro*	24
Atelier Berger	*New Fr.*	21
Autobus Imperial	*Classic Fr.*	-
Baan-Boran	*Thai*	20
Barlotti	*Italian*	15
Bar Vendôme	*Classic Fr.*	23
Bons Crus	*Wine*	-
Brass. du Louvre	*Brass.*	16
Ca d'Oro	*Italian*	18
☑ Café Marly	*Classic/New Fr.*	16
Café Ruc	*Bistro*	15
☑ Carré des Feuillants	*Haute*	26
Carr's	*Irish*	-
Cartes Postales	*New Fr.*	24
Caveau du Palais	*Classic Fr.*	19
Chez Denise	*Bistro*	24
Chez la Vieille	*Bistro*	16
Chez Pauline	*Bistro*	20
Chez Vong	*Chinese*	21
Chien qui Fume	*Brass.*	18
Cibus	*Italian*	-
Cloche des Halles	*Wine*	-
Coin/Gourmets	*Cambodian/Viet.*	22
Comptoir	*Eclectic/Moroccan*	21
Cordonnerie	*Classic Fr.*	-
Costes	*Eclectic*	18
NEW Dali	*Classic Fr.*	-
Dauphin	*Southwest*	20
Davé	*Chinese/Viet.*	18
Djakarta	*Indonesian*	20
Ecluse	*Wine*	16
Epi d'Or	*Bistro*	16
Escargot Montorgueil	*Bistro*	21
☑ Espadon (L')	*Classic Fr.*	26
Fellini	*Italian*	21
Ferme	*Sandwiches*	-
NEW Fines Gueules	*Wine*	-
First	*New Fr.*	18
Foujita	*Japanese*	-
Fumoir	*Eclectic*	17
☑ Gérard Besson	*Classic Fr.*	25
Goumard	*Seafood*	24
Gourmand (Au)	*Classic/New Fr.*	20
Grand Louvre	*Classic Fr.*	18
☑ Grand Véfour	*Haute*	28
Higuma	*Japanese*	15
Hippopotamus	*Steak*	11
Il Cortile	*Italian*	23
Issé	*Japanese*	23
Jean-Paul Hévin	*Dessert/Tea*	24
Joe Allen	*Amer.*	13
Juvéniles	*Wine*	16
Kai	*Japanese*	-
Kinugawa/Hanawa	*Japanese*	23
Kong	*Eclectic*	14
Lavinia	*Classic Fr.*	17
Léon/Bruxelles	*Belgian*	16
Lescure	*Bistro*	17
Louchebem	*Steak*	15
Macéo	*Classic/New Fr.*	23
Matsuri	*Japanese*	14
☑ Meurice	*Haute*	27
Mousson	*Cambodian*	-
Muscade	*Eclectic/Tea*	-
Paradis du Fruit	*Eclectic*	14
Pharamond	*Classic Fr.*	19
Pied de Cochon	*Brass.*	18
Pierre au Palais Royal	*Classic Fr.*	17
Pinxo	*New Fr.*	21
Point Bar	*New Fr.*	22
Poule au Pot	*Bistro*	23
Pré Salé	*N France*	-
Ragueneau	*Classic Fr./Tea*	-
Rest. du Palais Royal	*Classic Fr.*	19
Rest. Paul	*Bistro*	20
Robe et le Palais	*Wine*	19
Rose de France	*Bistro*	-
Rouge St-Honoré	*Eclectic*	13
Rubis	*Wine*	15
Saudade	*Portugese*	-

LOCATIONS

NEW Saut du Loup	*New Fr.*	14
Scoop	*Eclectic*	17
Z Soufflé	*Classic Fr.*	22
Tav. de Maître Kanter	*Brass.*	16
Tav. Henri IV	*Wine*	16
Vin et Marée	*Seafood*	18
Water Bar Colette	*Italian/New Fr.*	14
Z Willi's Wine Bar	*Wine*	20

2ND ARRONDISSEMENT

Angl'Opéra	*New Fr.*	19
A Priori Thé	*Tea*	16
Bistrot Vivienne	*Bistro*	18
Café Etienne Marcel	*Eclectic*	18
Café Moderne	*Bistro*	21
Céladon	*Classic Fr.*	21
Chez Clément	*Classic Fr.*	15
Z Chez Georges	*Bistro*	24
Crus de Bourgogne	*Bistro*	17
Dalva	*New Fr.*	-
Domaine de Lintillac	*Southwest*	18
Drouant	*Classic Fr.*	22
Ecaille de Fontaine	*Shellfish*	-
Fontaine Gaillon	*Classic Fr.*	22
Gallopin	*Brass.*	16
Gavroche	*Bistro*	17
Grand Colbert	*Brass.*	19
Hippopotamus	*Steak*	11
Legrand Filles et Fils	*Wine*	-
Lina's	*Sandwiches*	16
Liza	*Lebanese*	24
Z Lyonnais	*Lyon*	21
Mesturet	*Southwest*	-
Mori Venice Bar	*Italian*	17
Noces de Jeannette	*Bistro*	-
Noura	*Lebanese*	19
Paradis du Fruit	*Eclectic*	14
Passy Mandarin	*Asian*	20
Press Café	*Bistro*	-
Pur'Grill	*New Fr.*	19
NEW Racines	*Wine Bar/Bistro*	-
Vaudeville	*Brass.*	18
Versance	*Classic/New Fr.*	-

3RD ARRONDISSEMENT

Ambassade/Auvergne	*Auvergne*	20
Z Ami Louis	*Bistro*	25

Anahï	*Argent.*	19
Andy Wahloo	*Moroccan*	14
Aub. Nicolas Flamel	*Classic Fr.*	23
Bar à Huîtres	*Seafood*	17
Bascou	*Basque*	20
NEW Breizh Café	*Brittany*	-
Buffalo Grill	*Steak*	10
Camille	*Bistro*	16
Chez Janou	*Provence*	23
Chez Jenny	*Alsace*	19
Chez Nénesse	*Classic Fr.*	-
Chez Omar	*Moroccan*	21
Don Juans	*Med./New Fr.*	-
Gli Angeli	*Italian*	18
Guirlande de Julie	*Classic Fr.*	15
Hangar	*Classic Fr.*	18
Indiana Café	*Tex-Mex*	7
Murano	*New Fr.*	16
Pamphlet	*Basque/Southwest*	23
Petit Marché	*New Fr.*	22
Pied de Chameau	*Moroccan*	-
404	*Moroccan*	22
Réconfort	*New Fr.*	-
Robert et Louise	*Bistro*	21
San	*Italian*	-

4TH ARRONDISSEMENT

Alivi	*Corsica*	16
Z Ambroisie	*Haute*	28
Z As du Fallafel	*Israeli*	24
Aub. de Reine Blanche	*Classic/New Fr.*	19
Autour du Saumon	*Seafood*	17
Bel Canto	*Italian*	13
Z Benoît	*Lyon*	24
Z Bistrot de l'Oulette	*Southwest*	26
Bistrot du Dôme	*Seafood*	21
Z Bofinger	*Brass.*	20
Bourguignon du Marais	*Wine*	23
Brass. de l'Ile St. Louis	*Brass.*	17
Breakfast in America	*Amer.*	15
Café Beaubourg	*Classic Fr.*	16
Café de la Poste	*Classic Fr.*	-
Chez Clément	*Classic Fr.*	15
Chez Julien	*Bistro*	19
Chez Marianne	*Mideast.*	18
Coude Fou	*Wine*	19

Coupe Gorge	*Bistro*	–
Curieux Spaghetti Bar	*Italian*	–
Dalloyau	*Dessert/Tea*	23
Dame Tartine	*Sandwiches*	14
Dôme du Marais	*New Fr.*	22
Dos de la Baleine	*Bistro*	20
Ebouillanté	*Classic Fr./Tea*	–
Enoteca	*Italian*	20
Escale du Liban	*Lebanese*	–
Flore en l'Ile	*Classic Fr.*	18
Fous d'en Face	*Bistro*	–
Gamin de Paris	*Southwest*	21
🄉 Georges	*Eclectic*	18
Hippopotamus	*Steak*	11
Ilot Vache	*Classic Fr.*	18
Isami	*Japanese*	25
Léon/Bruxelles	*Belgian*	16
Loir dans/Théière	*Dessert/Tea*	16
Ma Bourgogne	*Burgundy*	18
Mariage Frères	*Dessert/Tea*	21
🄉 Mon Vieil Ami	*Bistro*	24
Nos Ancêtres/Gaulois	*Classic Fr.*	13
Orangerie	*Classic Fr.*	22
Ostéria (L')	*Italian*	22
Petit Bofinger	*Brass.*	18
Pitchi Poï	*Jewish/Polsih*	–
Studio	*Tex-Mex*	–
Tav. du Sgt. Recruteur	*Classic Fr.*	16
Tête Ailleurs	*Med.*	–
Trumilou	*Bistro*	19
Vieux Bistro	*Lyon*	21
Vin des Pyrenees	*Classic Fr.*	16

5TH ARRONDISSEMENT

Al Dar	*Lebanese*	21
Anahuacalli	*Mex.*	21
AOC	*Bistro*	18
Atelier Maître Albert	*Bistro*	21
Atlas	*Moroccan*	20
Bar à Huîtres	*Seafood*	17
🄉 Brass. Balzar	*Brass.*	19
Breakfast in America	*Amer.*	15
Buffalo Grill	*Steak*	10
Buisson Ardent	*Bistro*	19
Café Le Petit Pont	*Classic Fr.*	14
Chantairelle	*Auvergne*	–

Chez Léna et Mimile	*Bistro*	15
Chez René	*Lyon*	21
Chieng Mai	*Thai*	16
NEW Christophe	*Bistro*	–
Coco de Mer	*Seychelles*	–
Coin/Gourmets	*Cambodían/Viet.*	22
Cosi (Le)	*Corsica*	16
Coupe-Chou	*Classic Fr.*	23
Délices d'Aphrodite	*Greek*	18
El Palenque	*Argent.*	19
Fontaines	*Bistro*	17
Hippopotamus	*Steak*	11
Inagiku	*Japanese*	18
Languedoc	*Southwest*	–
Louis Vin	*Wine*	19
Maharajah	*Indian*	17
Marty	*Brass.*	16
Mauzac	*Wine*	–
Mavrommatis	*Greek*	19
Mirama	*Chinese*	20
Moissonnier	*Lyon*	19
Moulin à Vent	*Bistro*	19
Papilles	*Classic Fr.*	23
Paradis du Fruit	*Eclectic*	14
Perraudin	*Bistro*	13
Petit Châtelet	*Classic Fr.*	–
Petit Pontoise	*Bistro*	22
Petit Prince de Paris	*Bistro*	–
Pré Verre	*New Fr.*	22
Ribouldingue	*Classic Fr.*	18
Rôtiss. du Beaujolais	*Bistro*	23
NEW Salon du Panthéon	*Bistro*	–
🄉 Tour d'Argent	*Haute*	25
NEW Toustem	*Southwest*	–
Truffière	*Haute*	23

6TH ARRONDISSEMENT

Alcazar	*New Fr.*	19
🄉 Allard	*Bistro*	21
Azabu	*Japanese*	24
Barroco	*Brazilian*	–
Bartolo	*Italian*	17
Bastide Odéon	*Provence*	22
Bistrot d'Henri	*Bistro*	20
Bon Saint Pourçain	*Classic Fr.*	18
Boucherie Roulière	*Bistro*	–
Bouillon Racine	*Brass.*	16

🆉 Bouquinistes	*New Fr.*	23
🆉 Brass. Lipp	*Brass.*	17
Brass. Lutétia	*Brass.*	18
🆉 Café de Flore	*Classic Fr.*	15
🆉 Café Les Deux Magots	*Classic Fr.*	16
Caméléon	*Bistro*	20
Casa Bini	*Italian*	21
Charpentiers	*Bistro*	18
Cherche Midi	*Italian*	19
Chez Clément	*Classic Fr.*	15
Chez Maître Paul	*Alsace*	21
Chez Marcel	*Lyon*	-
Christine	*Bistro*	23
Closerie des Lilas	*Classic Fr.*	18
Coffee Parisien	*Amer.*	16
🆉 Comptoir du Relais	*Bistro/Brass.*	26
Cosi	*Sandwiches*	19
🆕 Crémerie	*Wine*	-
Dalloyau	*Dessert/Tea*	23
Da Rosa	*Classic Fr.*	19
Ecluse	*Wine*	16
Editeurs	*Brass.*	14
Emporio Armani	*Italian*	19
🆉 Epi Dupin	*Bistro*	24
🆕 Epigramme	*Bistro*	-
Espadon Bleu	*Seafood*	21
Ferrandaise	*Bistro*	21
🆉 Fish La Boissonnerie	*Provence*	22
Fogón	*Spanish*	21
Grille St-Germain	*Bistro*	17
🆉 Hélène Darroze	*New Fr./Southwest*	25
Hippopotamus	*Steak*	11
Huîtrerie Régis	*Shellfish*	22
Il Viccolo	*Italian*	-
Indiana Café	*Tex-Mex*	7
🆉 Jacques Cagna	*Haute*	26
J'Go	*Southwest*	14
Joséphine/Dumonet	*Bistro*	23
🆉 Ladurée	*Classic Fr./Tea*	23
🆉 Lapérouse	*Haute*	21
Léon/Bruxelles	*Belgian*	16
Lozère	*Auvergne*	18
🆕 Lup	*Eclectic*	-
Maison du Jardin	*Bistro*	24
Mariage Frères	*Dessert/Tea*	21
Marlotte	*Classic Fr.*	16
Méditerranée	*Seafood*	21
Nemrod	*Auvergne*	16
Noura	*Lebanese*	19
Orient-Extrême	*Japanese*	18
Palanquin	*Viet.*	18
Paradis du Fruit	*Eclectic*	14
Parc aux Cerfs	*Bistro*	21
Paris	*Haute*	20
Pères et Filles	*Bistro*	16
Petite Cour	*New Fr.*	21
Petit Lutétia	*Brass.*	19
Petit St. Benoît	*Classic Fr.*	16
Petit Zinc	*Brass.*	18
Polidor	*Bistro*	17
Procope	*Classic Fr.*	16
🆉 Relais/l'Entrecôte	*Steak*	22
Relais Louis XIII	*Haute*	25
Restaurant (Le)	*Classic Fr.*	26
Rôtiss. d'en Face	*Bistro*	21
Rotonde	*Brass.*	15
Salon d'Hélène	*Southwest*	19
Saveurs de Claude	*Classic/New Fr.*	-
Sensing	*New Fr.*	24
Timbre	*Bistro*	24
Tsukizi	*Japanese*	-
Vagenende	*Brass.*	15
21	*Seafood*	-
Wadja	*Bistro*	20
Yen	*Japanese*	20
Yugaraj	*Indian*	23
🆉 Ze Kitchen Galerie	*Eclectic*	25

7TH ARRONDISSEMENT

Affriolé	*Bistro*	22
🆕 Agassin	*Classic/New Fr.*	-
Aida	*Japanese*	23
🆉 Arpège	*Haute*	26
🆉 Atelier Joël Robuchon	*Haute*	28
Aub. Bressane	*Classic Fr.*	20
Aub. du Champ/Mars	*Classic Fr.*	17
Auguste	*Classic Fr.*	25
Bamboche	*New Fr.*	19
Basilic	*Basque*	15
Bellota-Bellota	*Spanish*	19

Bistro de Breteuil	*Bistro*	16
Bistrot de l'Université	*Bistro*	18
Bistrot de Paris	*Bistro*	16
☑ Bon Accueil	*Bistro*	24
Café Constant	*Bistro*	24
Café de l'Esplanade	*Classic/New Fr.*	16
Café de Mars	*Bistro*	17
Caffé Minotti	*Italian*	22
Caffé Toscano	*Italian*	19
Carmine	*Italian*	-
☑ 144 Petrossian	*Seafood*	25
Chez Françoise	*Classic Fr.*	17
Chez L'Ami Jean	*Basque/Bistro*	24
Chez Les Anges	*Brass.*	23
Cigale Récamier	*Classic Fr.*	21
Cinq Mars	*Bistro*	19
Clos des Gourmets	*New Fr.*	25
NEW Cocottes	*New Fr.*	21
Cook Book	*Eclectic*	-
Cuisine (7e)	*New Fr.*	25
D'Chez Eux	*Bistro/Southwest*	25
Delicabar	*New Fr.*	13
Deux Abeilles	*Dessert/Tea*	21
Divellec	*Seafood*	24
Domaine de Lintillac	*Southwest*	18
Fables de La Fontaine	*Seafood*	24
Ferme St-Simon	*Classic Fr.*	23
Fins Gourmets	*Southwest*	19
Florimond	*Classic Fr.*	24
☑ Fontaine de Mars	*Southwest*	21
Gaya	*Seafood*	23
Gorille Blanc	*Bistro*	21
NEW Il Vino	*Classic Fr./Med.*	-
☑ Jules Verne	*Classic Fr.*	-
Lao Tseu	*Chinese*	-
Lei	*Italian*	21
Lina's	*Sandwiches*	16
Maison de l'Amér. Latine	*Classic Fr.*	18
Maupertu	*Classic Fr.*	21
Montalembert	*New Fr.*	19
New Jawad	*Indian/Pakistani*	18
Oeillade	*Bistro*	14
Olivades	*Provence*	17
☑ Ombres (Les)	*New Fr.*	18
Oudino	*Bistro*	-

Pasco	*Med./Southwest*	22
Perron	*Italian*	18
Petite Chaise	*Classic Fr.*	19
Petit Niçois	*Provence*	16
P'tit Troquet	*Bistro*	22
Quai	*New Fr.*	-
Ravi	*Indian*	21
Rest. du Musée d'Orsay	*Classic Fr.*	17
Rouge Vif	*Southwest*	15
Samiin	*Korean*	-
Sauvignon	*Sandwiches/Wine*	14
7ème Sud	*Med./Moroccan*	15
Soleil	*Med.*	19
Square	*Classic Fr.*	-
Tan Dinh	*Viet.*	23
Tante Marguerite	*Classic Fr.*	22
Tav. de Gli Amici	*Italian*	-
Thiou/Petit Thiou	*Thai*	21
Thoumieux	*Bistro/Southwest*	19
35° Ouest	*Seafood*	20
Vin et Marée	*Seafood*	18
20 de Bellechasse	*Bistro*	19
☑ Vin sur Vin	*New Fr.*	26
☑ Violon d'Ingres	*Bistro*	25
Voltaire	*Bistro*	24

8TH ARRONDISSEMENT

☑ Alain Ducasse	*Haute*	28
Al Diwan	*Lebanese*	21
Alsace	*Alsace*	18
☑ Ambassadeurs	*Haute/New Fr.*	28
Angle du Faubourg	*New Fr.*	24
Annapurna	*Indian*	18
☑ Apicius	*Haute*	26
Arome	*Classic/New Fr.*	-
Asian	*Asian*	16
Astor	*Haute*	16
Avenue	*New Fr.*	18
Bar des Théâtres	*Bistro*	15
BE Boulangépicier	*Sandwiches*	19
Berkeley	*Eclectic*	14
Bistro de l'Olivier	*Provence*	18
Bistrot de Marius	*Seafood*	21
Bistrot du Sommelier	*Wine*	18
Black Calavados	*Eclectic*	-
Bocconi	*Italian*	20
Boeuf sur le Toit	*Brass.*	18

Bouchons Clerc/P'tit | *Classic Fr.*	20
Boulangerie Eric Kayser | *Bakery/Sandwiches*	16
Bound | *Japanese/New Fr.*	-
Brass. La Lorraine | *Brass.*	17
Brass. Mollard | *Brass.*	19
Z Bristol | *Haute*	27
Z Buddha Bar | *Asian*	16
Café Faubourg | *Classic Fr.*	22
Café Lenôtre | *New Fr.*	18
Café M | *New Fr.*	19
NEW Café Pleyel | *New Fr.*	-
Café Terminus | *Classic Fr.*	-
Cap Vernet | *New Fr.*	17
Carpaccio | *Italian*	-
Caviar Kaspia | *Russian*	25
Chez André | *Bistro*	20
Chez Catherine | *New Fr.*	23
Chez Cécile | *Classic Fr.*	-
Chez Clément | *Classic Fr.*	15
Chez Francis | *Brass.*	17
Chez Papa | *Southwest*	17
Chez Savy | *Aveyron*	18
Chiberta | *New Fr.*	22
Z Cinq (Le) | *Haute*	28
Citrus Etoile | *Classic/New Fr.*	20
Clovis | *New Fr.*	-
Copenhague | *Danish*	18
Cou de la Girafe | *New Fr.*	15
Dalloyau | *Dessert/Tea*	23
Daru | *Russian*	-
Devèz | *Steak*	16
Diep | *Asian*	21
Z 1728 | *New Fr.*	19
Z Dominique Bouchet | *Haute*	27
NEW Eclaireur | *New Fr.*	-
Ecluse | *Wine*	16
El Mansour | *Moroccan*	17
Elysées (Les) | *Haute*	23
Etoile Marocaine | *Moroccan*	-
Eugène | *Eclectic*	-
Fermette Marbeuf | *Classic Fr.*	18
Findi | *Italian*	16
Finzi | *Italian*	13
Flora Danica | *Classic Fr./Danish*	19
Fouquet's | *Classic Fr.*	18
Garnier | *Brass.*	22
Gourmets des Ternes | *Bistro*	19
Hippopotamus | *Steak*	11
Indiana Café | *Tex-Mex*	7
Indra | *Indian*	-
Jardin des Cygnes | *Classic Fr.*	22
Kaïten | *Japanese*	-
Kinugawa/Hanawa | *Japanese*	23
Z Ladurée | *Classic Fr./Tea*	23
Z Lasserre | *Haute*	27
Z Laurent | *Haute*	24
Léon/Bruxelles | *Belgian*	16
Libre Sens | *Classic Fr.*	-
Lina's | *Sandwiches*	16
Lô Sushi | *Japanese*	15
Luna (La) | *Seafood*	17
Maison Blanche | *New Fr.*	20
Maison du Caviar | *Russian*	22
Marée (La) | *Seafood*	23
Mariage Frères | *Dessert/Tea*	21
Marius et Janette | *Seafood*	25
Market | *Eclectic*	22
Maxan | *New Fr.*	-
Maxim's | *Classic Fr.*	18
NEW Mini Palais | *New Fr.*	-
NEW Mood | *Asian Fusion*	-
Musichall | *New Fr.*	15
Obélisque | *Classic Fr.*	23
Paradis du Fruit | *Eclectic*	14
Z Pavillon Ledoyen | *Haute*	26
Pershing | *Eclectic/New Fr.*	17
Pichet de Paris | *Seafood*	16
Z Pierre Gagnaire | *Haute*	28
Pomze | *New Fr.*	18
Publicis Drugstore | *Brass.*	11
Z Relais/l'Entrecôte | *Steak*	22
Relais Plaza | *Brass./Eclectic*	23
Renoma Café | *Italian*	-
Resto | *Classic Fr.*	-
Royal Madeleine | *Classic Fr.*	19
Rue Balzac | *New Fr.*	17
Sarladais | *Southwest*	-
Saveurs de Flora (Les) | *New Fr.*	21
Z Senderens | *Brass./New Fr.*	26
Sens | *Med.*	-
Spoon/Food | *Eclectic/New Fr.*	22
Z Stella Maris | *Classic Fr.*	26

Stresa | *Italian*	22
NEW SYDR | *Southwest*	-
Table d'Hédiard | *New Fr.*	22
Table du Lancaster | *Haute*	23
Z Taillevent | *Haute*	28
Tante Louise |	22
Burgundy/Classic Fr.	
Terres de Truffes | *Classic Fr.*	19
Thiou/Petit Thiou | *Thai*	21
Toi | *New Fr.*	-
Tong Yen | *Chinese*	15
Village d'Ung | *Chinese/Thai*	-
Villa Spicy | *New Fr.*	13
W Restaurant | *New Fr.*	-
Zo | *Eclectic*	-

9TH ARRONDISSEMENT

Alsaco | *Alsace*	-
Aub. du Clou | *Classic Fr.*	16
Bacchantes | *Wine*	-
BE Boulangépicier | *Sandwiches*	19
Bistro/Deux Théâtres | *Bistro*	14
Bistrot Papillon | *Bistro*	14
Boule Rouge | *African*	-
Brass. Printemps | *Classic Fr.*	11
Buffalo Grill | *Steak*	10
Café de la Paix | *Classic Fr.*	19
Café Guitry | *Classic Fr.*	-
Carte Blanche | *Bistro/New Fr.*	-
Casa Olympe | *Corsica/Provence*	24
Charlot Roi des Coq. | *Brass.*	15
Chartier | *Classic Fr.*	13
Comédiens | *Classic Fr.*	-
Dell Orto | *Italian*	-
Diamantaires | *Armenian/Greek*	-
Domaine de Lintillac | *Southwest*	18
Georgette | *Bistro*	22
Grand Café | *Brass.*	13
Grange Batelière | *Classic Fr.*	-
Hôtel Amour | *New Fr.*	8
I Golosi | *Italian*	17
Indiana Café | *Tex-Mex*	7
Jardinier | *Bistro*	-
Jean | *New Fr.*	19
J'Go | *Southwest*	14
Z Ladurée | *Classic Fr./Tea*	23
Léon/Bruxelles | *Belgian*	16
Lina's | *Sandwiches*	16

Muses | *Haute*	19
No Stress Café | *Eclectic*	-
NEW Nouvelle Athenes | *New Fr.*	-
Oenothèque | *Wine*	-
Petite Sirène/Copen. | *Danish*	-
Petit Riche | *Bistro*	18
Pétrelle | *New Fr.*	-
Pizzetta | *Italian*	-
Radis Roses | *New Fr.*	-
Roi du Pot-au-Feu | *Bistro*	-
Rose Bakery | *British/Fr.*	17
16 Haussmann | *New Fr.*	18
Sinago | *Cambodian*	-
Sizin | *Turkish*	-
Spring | *Bistro*	23
Table d'Anvers | *Classic Fr.*	17
Vivres | *Classic Fr.*	-
Wally Le Saharien | *N African*	15

10TH ARRONDISSEMENT

Brass. Flo | *Brass.*	18
Brass. Julien | *Brass.*	19
Buffalo Grill | *Steak*	10
Cantine de Quentin | *Wine*	-
Chez Michel | *Brittany/New Fr.*	24
Chez Papa | *Southwest*	17
Chez Prune | *Eclectic*	18
Da Mimmo | *Italian*	-
Deux Canards | *Classic Fr.*	18
NEW Garance | *Bistro/New Fr.*	-
Grille | *Bistro*	17
Hippopotamus | *Steak*	11
Indiana Café | *Tex-Mex*	7
Martel | *Classic Fr./Moroccan*	-
Ploum | *Japanese/New Fr.*	-
Réveil du 10e (Le) | *Bistro*	-
Strapontins | *Classic Fr.*	-
Terminus Nord | *Brass.*	17
NEW Urbane | *Bistro*	-
Verre Volé | *Wine*	16
Zingot | *Brass.*	-

11TH ARRONDISSEMENT

Aiguière | *Classic Fr.*	-
Amici Miei | *Italian*	19
Ami Pierre | *Southwest*	17
Astier | *Bistro*	21
Aub. Pyrénées | *Southwest*	20

Bistrot à Vins Mélac	*Wine*	14
Bistrot du Peintre	*Bistro*	18
Bistrot Paul Bert	*Bistro*	23
Blue Elephant	*Thai*	20
Café Charbon	*Classic Fr.*	15
Café de l'Industrie	*Bistro*	12
Café du Passage	*Wine*	-
Chardenoux	*Bistro*	19
Chateaubriand	*New Fr.*	22
Chez Paul	*Bistro*	21
Chez Ramulaud	*Bistro*	16
Clown Bar	*Wine*	17
NEW Cuisine (11e)	*Bistro*	-
Ecailler du Bistrot	*Seafood*	19
Indiana Café	*Tex-Mex*	7
Khun Akorn	*Thai*	-
Léon/Bruxelles	*Belgian*	16
Main d'Or	*Corsica*	-
Mansouria	*Moroccan*	22
New Nioullaville	*Chinese*	16
Paradis du Fruit	*Eclectic*	14
Passage/Carm.	*Wine*	-
Polichinelle Cafe	*Bistro*	-
Pure Café	*Eclectic*	-
Refectoire	*Bistro*	-
Repaire de Cartouche	*Bistro*	16
Reuan Thai	*Thai*	-
Sot l'y Laisse	*Bistro*	-
Temps au Temps	*Bistro*	25
Unico	*Argent.*	-
Vieux Chêne	*Bistro*	-
Z Villaret	*Bistro*	26
Vin et Marée	*Seafood*	18
Wok Cooking	*Asian*	-

12TH ARRONDISSEMENT

Aub. Aveyronnaise	*Aveyron*	-
Baron Rouge	*Wine*	-
Barrio Latino	*Pan-Latin*	12
Biche au Bois	*Bistro*	20
Brass. L'Européen	*Brass.*	-
Chai 33	*Wine*	14
Duc de Richelieu	*Lyon*	-
Ebauchoir	*Bistro*	-
Frégate	*Seafood*	24
Gazzetta	*Med./New Fr.*	-
Hippopotamus	*Steak*	11

Lina's	*Sandwiches*	16
Oulette	*Southwest*	19
Quincy	*Bistro*	-
Sardegna a Tavola	*Italian*	21
Square Trousseau	*Bistro*	19
Z Train Bleu	*Classic Fr.*	19
Z Trou Gascon	*Southwest*	26
Viaduc Café	*Classic/New Fr.*	-
Vinea Café	*Eclectic*	-
Zygomates	*Bistro*	20

13TH ARRONDISSEMENT

Aimant du Sud	*Classic Fr.*	-
Aub. Etchégorry	*Southwest*	-
Avant Goût	*New Fr.*	23
BIOArt	*New Fr.*	-
Buffalo Grill	*Steak*	10
Café Fusion	*Eclectic*	-
Cailloux	*Italian*	-
Chez Paul	*Bistro*	16
Entoto	*Ethiopian*	-
Nouveau Village	*Chinese/Thai*	18
Ourcine	*Classic/New Fr.*	24
Paradis Thai	*Thai*	15
Petit Marguery	*Bistro*	21
Petit Pascal	*Bistro*	-
Suave	*Viet.*	-
Temps des Cerises	*Bistro*	-
Terroir	*Bistro*	-
Tricotin	*Asian*	-

14TH ARRONDISSEMENT

Amuse Bouche	*New Fr.*	17
Apollo	*Eclectic*	-
Assiette	*Bistro*	-
Bar à Huîtres	*Seafood*	17
Bis du Severo	*Bistro*	-
Bistrot du Dôme	*Seafood*	21
Buffalo Grill	*Steak*	10
Cagouille	*Seafood*	25
Cerisaie	*Southwest*	21
Chez Clément	*Classic Fr.*	15
Chez Papa	*Southwest*	17
Z Coupole	*Brass.*	19
Crêperie de Josselin	*Brittany*	22
Dôme	*Seafood*	22
Duc (Le)	*Seafood*	23
Enzo	*Italian*	-

Hippopotamus | *Steak*	11
Il Barone | *Italian*	21
Indiana Café | *Tex-Mex*	7
Léon/Bruxelles | *Belgian*	16
Maison Courtine | *Southwest*	24
Marée Denfert/Passy | *Seafood*	-
Monsieur Lapin | *Classic Fr.*	18
Montparnasse 25 | *New Fr.*	16
Natacha | *Classic Fr.*	-
Opportun | *Lyon*	15
Paradis du Fruit | *Eclectic*	14
Pavillon Montsouris | *Classic Fr.*	17
NEW Petites Sorcières | *North. Fr.*	-
Z Régalade | *Basque/Bistro*	25
Severo | *Steak*	20
Vin et Marée | *Seafood*	18
Zeyer | *Brass.*	16

15TH ARRONDISSEMENT

NEW Afaria | *New Fr./Southwest*	-
Ami Marcel | *Bistro*	17
Autour du Mont | *Seafood*	-
Autour du Saumon | *Seafood*	17
Banyan | *Thai*	19
Benkay | *Japanese*	24
Beurre Noisette | *Bistro*	23
Bistro 121 | *Bistro*	-
Bistro d'Hubert |	22
Bistrot d'André | *Bistro*	-
Bistrot du Cap | *Seafood*	-
Buffalo Grill | *Steak*	10
Café du Commerce | *Bistro*	16
Casa Alcalde | *Basque/Spanish*	-
Cave de l'Os à Moëlle | *Wine*	22
Chen Soleil d'Est | *Chinese*	-
Chez Clément | *Classic Fr.*	15
Chez Papa | *Southwest*	17
Clos Morillons | *New Fr.*	-
Couleurs de Vigne | *Wine*	-
NEW Cristal de Sel | *New Fr.*	-
Dix Vins | *Wine*	-
Erawan | *Thai*	17
Fellini | *Italian*	21
Fontanarosa | *Italian*	-
Gauloise | *Bistro*	15
Gitane | *Classic Fr.*	-
NEW Grand Pan | *Bistro*	-

Grand Venise | *Italian*	25
Hippopotamus | *Steak*	11
Je Thé . . . Me | *Classic Fr.*	-
Kim Anh | *Viet.*	-
Z Os à Moëlle | *Classic Fr.*	25
Père Claude | *Classic Fr.*	17
NEW P'tit Casier | *Seafood*	-
Quinzième | *New Fr.*	-
Rest. de la Tour | *Classic Fr.*	21
Rest. du Marché | *Bistro*	-
Sawadee | *Thai*	-
Sept Quinze | *Cal./Med.*	21
Stéphane Martin | *Classic Fr.*	-
Suffren | *Brass.*	14
Thierry Burlot | *New Fr.*	-
Triporteur | *Bistro*	-
Troquet | *Basque/New Fr.*	24
Uitr | *Seafood*	-
Villa Corse | *Corsica*	20

16TH ARRONDISSEMENT

A et M | *Classic Fr.*	21
Alain Bourgade | *New Fr.*	-
Al Dar | *Lebanese*	21
Al Mounia | *Moroccan*	17
Z Astrance | *New Fr.*	28
Aub. Dab | *Brass.*	16
Beaujolais d'Auteuil | *Classic Fr.*	17
Bellini | *Italian*	24
Bistrot de l'Etoile Laur. | *Bistro*	-
Bistrot des Vignes | *Bistro*	17
Bon | *New Fr.*	15
Butte Chaillot | *Bistro*	21
Casa Tina | *Spanish*	-
Chalet des Iles | *Classic Fr.*	14
Chez Géraud | *Classic Fr.*	20
Coffee Parisien | *Amer.*	16
Z Cristal Room | *New Fr.*	17
Elysées Hong Kong | *Chinese*	-
Etoile | *Classic Fr.*	24
Fakhr el Dine | *Lebanese*	24
Flandrin | *Brass.*	15
Gare | *Classic Fr.*	14
Giulio Rebellato | *Italian*	20
Grande Armée | *Classic Fr.*	15
Z Hiramatsu | *Haute/New French*	26
Jardins de Bagatelle | *Classic Fr.*	17

LOCATIONS

Kambodgia | *SE Asian*	–
Kiosque | *Classic Fr.*	15
Lac-Hong | *Viet.*	20
Lina's | *Sandwiches*	16
Maison Prunier | *Seafood*	21
Marée Denfert/Passy | *Seafood*	–
Marius | *Seafood*	18
Mathusalem | *Bistro*	–
Matsuri | *Japanese*	14
Murat | *Classic Fr.*	13
Noura | *Lebanese*	19
Oum el Banine | *Moroccan*	–
Ozu | *Japanese*	23
Paris Seize | *Italian*	18
☑ Passiflore | *Asian/Classic Fr.*	26
Passy Mandarin | *Asian*	20
Paul Chêne | *Classic Fr.*	20
☑ Pavillon/Gr. Cascade | *Haute*	25
Petite Tour | *Classic Fr.*	–
Petit Pergolèse | *Bistro*	23
Petit Rétro | *Bistro*	16
Petit Victor Hugo | *Classic Fr.*	19
Pizzeria d'Auteuil | *Italian*	–
Port Alma | *Seafood*	17
☑ Pré Catelan | *Haute*	27
☑ Relais d'Auteuil | *Haute*	27
Relais du Parc | *Classic/New Fr.*	19
Rest. GR5 | *Alpine*	24
Rosimar | *Spanish*	–
Scheffer | *Bistro*	18
7ème Sud | *Med./Moroccan*	15
6 New York | *New Fr.*	17
Stella | *Brass.*	20
Stéphane Gaborieau | *Haute*	–
Table de Babette | *Creole*	–
☑ Table de Joël Robuchon | *Haute*	26
Table du Baltimore | *Haute*	–
Table Lauriston | *Classic Fr.*	20
Tang | *Chinese*	17
Terrasse Mirabeau | *Bistro*	–
Tierny & Co. | *Bistro*	–
Tokyo Eat | *New Fr.*	14
Tournesol | *Bistro*	18
Tsé-Yang | *Chinese*	18
Villa Corse | *Corsica*	20
Vinci | *Classic Fr./Italian*	–
Vin dans les voiles | *Wine*	–

Vin et Marée | *Seafood*	18
Waknine | *New Fr.*	–
Zébra Square | *Classic Fr.*	10

17TH ARRONDISSEMENT

Abadache | *Bistro*	–
Accolade | *Bistro*	–
Ampère | *Bistro/Eclectic*	–
Autour du Saumon | *Seafood*	17
Ballon des Ternes | *Brass.*	15
Ballon et Coquillages | *Seafood*	–
Baptiste | *New Fr.*	–
Bath's | *Auvergne/New Fr.*	20
Bistral | *Bistro*	19
Bistro du 17ème | *Bistro*	18
Bistro Melrose | *Bistro*	–
Bistro St. Ferdinand | *Bistro*	14
Bistrot d'à Côté | *Bistro*	21
Bistrot des Dames | *Bistro*	14
Bistrot Niel | *Bistro*	–
☑ Braisière | *Gascony*	27
Buffalo Grill | *Steak*	10
Café d'Angel | *Bistro*	–
Caïus | *New Fr.*	19
Caves Pétrissans | *Wine*	19
Chez Clément | *Classic Fr.*	15
Chez Fred | *Lyon*	–
Chez Georges-Maillot | *Brass.*	18
Chez Léon | *Bistro*	13
Chez Ly | *Chinese/Thai*	–
Clou | *Bistro*	19
Congrès Maillot | *Brass.*	18
Dessirier | *Seafood*	20
Ecluse | *Wine*	16
Entredgeu | *Bistro*	17
Epicure 108 | *Alsace/Asian*	–
Graindorge | *N France*	22
☑ Guy Savoy | *Haute*	28
Hier & Aujourd'hui | *New Fr.*	–
Huîtrier | *Seafood*	20
Il Etait une Oie | *Southwest*	–
⚠NEW Karl et Erich | *New Fr.*	–
Kifune | *Japanese*	–
Léon/Bruxelles | *Belgian*	16
Lina's | *Sandwiches*	16
⚠NEW M Comme Martine | *Bistro*	–
Meating | *Steak*	17

Z Michel Rostang | *Classic Fr.* | 27

Mont Liban | *Lebanese* | -

Orénoc | *Asian/Classic Fr.* | 17

Paolo Petrini | *Italian* | -

Paradis du Fruit | *Eclectic* | 14

Petit Bofinger | *Brass.* | 18

Petit Colombier | *Classic Fr.* | 18

Pétrus | *Brass.* | 21

Rech | *Seafood* | -

Relais de Venise | *Steak* | 24

Rest. GR5 | *Alpine* | 24

Rucola | *Italian* | -

Sora Lena | *Italian/Med.* | -

Sormani | *Italian* | 23

Soupière | *Classic Fr.* | -

Sud | *Med./Provence* | 16

Taïra | *Japanese/New Fr.* | -

Timgad | *Moroccan* | 20

Toque | *Classic Fr.* | -

Verre Bouteille | *Wine* | 13

18TH ARRONDISSEMENT

A. Beauvilliers | *Classic Fr.* | 20

Bistro Poulbot | *Bistro* | -

Café Burq | *Wine* | -

NEW Chéri Bibi | *Bistro* | -

Chez Grisette | *Wine* | -

Cottage Marcadet | *New Fr.* | -

2 Pieces Cuisine | *Bistro* | -

Diapason | *Southwest* | -

Entracte | *Bistro* | -

Famille | *New Fr.* | 19

Mascotte | *Auvergne* | -

Moulin de la Galette | *Classic Fr.* | 15

Osteria Ascolani | *Italian* | -

Pomponette | *Bistro* | 17

Rendez-vous/Chauff. | *Bistro* | -

Rughetta | *Italian* | -

Sale e Pepe | *Italian* | -

Square | *Classic/New Fr.* | -

Truc Café | *Wine* | -

Wepler | *Brass.* | 14

NEW Winch | *Seafood* | -

19TH ARRONDISSEMENT

Boeuf Couronné | *Classic Fr.* | 16

Buffalo Grill | *Steak* | 10

Café de la Musique | *Classic Fr.* | 15

Cave Gourmande | *Bistro* | 25

Chez Vincent | *Italian* | -

Lao Siam | *Thai* | 15

20TH ARRONDISSEMENT

Allobroges | *Classic Fr.* | 22

Baratin | *Wine* | 16

Boulangerie | *Bistro* | 23

Chez Ramona | *Spanish* | -

Zéphyr | *Bistro* | -

Outlying Areas

BOUGIVAL

Camélia | *New Fr.* | 20

BOULOGNE-BILLANCOURT

Cap Seguin | *Classic Fr.* | -

Chez Clément | *Classic Fr.* | 15

Comte de Gascogne | *Gascony* | -

Dalloyau | *Dessert/Tea* | 23

CLICHY

Romantica | *Italian* | 23

ISSY-LES-MOULINEAUX

Ile | *Classic/New Fr.* | 18

Rest. Manufacture | *Bistro* | 21

River Café | *Classic/New Fr.* | 14

JOINVILLE-LE-PONT

Chez Gégène | *Classic Fr.* | -

LA DÉFENSE

Matsuri | *Japanese* | 14

Petit Bofinger | *Brass.* | 18

LE PRÉ-ST-GERVAIS

Pouilly Reuilly | *Bistro* | -

LEVALLOIS-PERRET

Mandalay | *Eclectic* | -

Petit Poucet | *New Fr.* | -

MAISONS-LAFFITTE

Tastevin | *Classic Fr.* | 24

Vieille Fontaine | *Classic/New Fr.* | -

NEUILLY-SUR-SEINE

Bel Canto | *Italian* | 13

Bistrot d'à Côté | *Bistro* | 21

Café la Jatte | *Eclectic* | 14

Chalet (Le) | *Alpine/Classic Fr.*   -

Chez Gérard | *Auvergne*   19

Chez Livio | *Italian*   13

Coffee Parisien | *Amer.*   16

Durand Dupont | *Eclectic*   -

Gourmand | *Classic Fr.*   -

Jarrasse | *Seafood*   -

Lina's | *Sandwiches*   16

Paradis du Fruit | *Eclectic*   14

Riad | *Moroccan*   -

Saveurs du Marché | *Bistro*   -

Sébillon | *Brass.*   15

Tonnelle Saintongeaise | -
   Classic Fr.

Truffe Noire | *Classic Fr.*   -

Zinc-Zinc | *Bistro*   16

PERREUX-SUR-MARNE

Magnolias | *New Fr.*   25

SAINT-CLOUD

Quai Ouest | *Eclectic*   13

SAINT-GERMAIN-EN-LAYE

Cazaudehore | *Haute*   22

SAINT-OUEN

Soleil | *Bistro*   -

VERSAILLES

Marée de Versailles | *Seafood*   19

Potager du Roy | *Classic Fr.*   19

VINCENNES

Petit Bofinger | *Brass.*   18

Special Features

Listings cover the best in each category and include names, locations and Food ratings. Multi-location restaurants' features may vary by branch. ☒ indicates places with the highest ratings, popularity and importance.

BREAKFAST

(See also Hotel Dining)

Alsace	8ᵉ	18
☒ Angelina	1ᵉʳ	20
A Priori Thé	2ᵉ	16
Autour du Saumon	**multi.**	17
Avenue	8ᵉ	18
Bar des Théâtres	8ᵉ	15
Berkeley	8ᵉ	14
☒ Brass. Balzar	5ᵉ	19
Brass. La Lorraine	8ᵉ	17
Brass. Printemps	9ᵉ	11
Breakfast in America	**multi.**	15
Café Beaubourg	4ᵉ	16
☒ Café de Flore	6ᵉ	15
Café de la Musique	19ᵉ	15
Café de l'Esplanade	7ᵉ	16
Café Lenôtre	8ᵉ	18
Café Le Petit Pont	5ᵉ	14
☒ Café Les Deux Magots	6ᵉ	16
☒ Café Marly	1ᵉʳ	16
Café Ruc	1ᵉʳ	15
Camille	3ᵉ	16
Cazaudehore	**St-Germain-Laye**	22
Chez Clément	**multi.**	15
Chez Prune	10ᵉ	18
Cloche des Halles	1ᵉʳ	-
Congrès Maillot	17ᵉ	18
Couleurs de Vigne	15ᵉ	-
☒ Coupole	14ᵉ	19
Dalloyau	**multi.**	23
Deux Abeilles	7ᵉ	21
Dôme	14ᵉ	22
Duc de Richelieu	12ᵉ	-
Editeurs	6ᵉ	14
Ferme	1ᵉʳ	-
Flandrin	16ᵉ	15
Flore en l'Ile	4ᵉ	18
Fontaines	5ᵉ	17
Fouquet's	8ᵉ	18
Gavroche	2ᵉ	17
Grand Café	9ᵉ	13

Grande Armée	16ᵉ	15
Grille St-Germain	6ᵉ	17
☒ Ladurée	**multi.**	23
Lina's	**multi.**	16
Loir dans/Théière	4ᵉ	16
Ma Bourgogne	4ᵉ	18
Main d'Or	11ᵉ	-
Mascotte	18ᵉ	-
Murat	16ᵉ	13
Nemrod	6ᵉ	16
Noura	16ᵉ	19
Point Bar	1ᵉʳ	22
Pomze	8ᵉ	18
Procope	6ᵉ	16
Publicis Drugstore	8ᵉ	11
Rest. Paul	1ᵉʳ	20
Rotonde	6ᵉ	15
Rue Balzac	8ᵉ	17
Sauvignon	7ᵉ	14
Suffren	15ᵉ	14
Table d'Hédiard	8ᵉ	22
Tav. de Maître Kanter	1ᵉʳ	16
Terminus Nord	10ᵉ	17
Tricotin	13ᵉ	-
Vaudeville	2ᵉ	18
Viaduc Café	12ᵉ	-
Wepler	18ᵉ	14
Zèbra Square	16ᵉ	10
Zeyer	14ᵉ	16
Zinc-Zinc	**Neuilly**	16

BRUNCH

Alcazar	6ᵉ	19
☒ Angelina	1ᵉʳ	20
A Priori Thé	2ᵉ	16
Asian	8ᵉ	16
Barlotti	1ᵉʳ	15
Barrio Latino	12ᵉ	12
Berkeley	8ᵉ	14
Blue Elephant	11ᵉ	20
Bon	16ᵉ	15
Breakfast in America	**multi.**	15

Café Beaubourg	4e	16	BUSINESS DINING	
Café Charbon	11e	15	NEW Alfred	1er	-
Café de la Musique	19e	15	Z Ami Louis	3e	25
Café de l'Industrie	11e	12	Angle du Faubourg	8e	24
Café Etienne Marcel	2e	18	Angl'Opéra	2e	19
Café la Jatte	Neuilly	14	Z Astrance	16e	28
Café Le Petit Pont	5e	14	Auguste	7e	25
Carr's	1er	-	Bistro St. Ferdinand	17e	14
Chai 33	12e	14	Bistrot de l'Etoile Laur.	16e	-
Chez Prune	10e	18	Bistrot Niel	17e	-
Curieux Spaghetti Bar	4e	-	Boeuf Couronné	19e	16
Delicabar	7e	13	Boeuf sur le Toit	8e	18
Durand Dupont	Neuilly	-	Buisson Ardent	5e	19
Editeurs	6e	14	Café de l'Esplanade	7e	16
Ferme	1er	-	Café Faubourg	8e	22
Findi	8e	16	Caffé Minotti	7e	22
Flora Danica	8e	19	Cap Vernet	8e	17
Flore en l'Ile	4e	18	Caves Pétrissans	17e	19
Fumoir	1er	17	Céladon	2e	21
Gare	16e	14	Z 144 Petrossian	7e	25
Jardin des Cygnes	8e	22	Chez André	8e	20
Joe Allen	1er	13	Chez Les Anges	7e	23
Lina's	multi.	16	Chez Pauline	1er	20
Liza	2e	24	Chez Savy	8e	18
Loir dans/Théière	4e	16	Chiberta	8e	22
Mariage Frères	6e	21	Clos des Gourmets	7e	25
Market	8e	22	Copenhague	8e	18
Murano	3e	16	Costes	1er	18
No Stress Café	9e	-	Cuisine (7e)	7e	25
Paradis du Fruit	multi.	14	NEW Dali	1er	-
Pershing	8e	17	Dessirier	17e	20
Pitchi Poï	4e	-	Divellec	7e	24
Publicis Drugstore	8e	11	Dôme	14e	22
Quai	7e	-	Dôme du Marais	4e	22
404	3e	22	Z Dominique Bouchet	8e	27
Refectoire	11e	-	Drouant	2e	22
Renoma Café	8e	-	Duc (Le)	14e	23
Rouge St-Honoré	1er	13	Flora Danica	8e	19
Scoop	1er	17	Fouquet's	8e	18
Studio	4e	-	Gaya	7e	23
Viaduc Café	12e	-	Georgette	9e	22
Villa Spicy	8e	13	Z Gérard Besson	1er	25
Vinea Café	12e	-	Goumard	1er	24
Wepler	18e	14	Graindorge	17e	22
W Restaurant	8e	-	Z Guy Savoy	17e	28
Zébra Square	16e	10	Z Hélène Darroze	6e	25
			Il Cortile	1er	23

subscribe to ZAGAT.com

NEW Il Vino | **7e**	–
Issé | **1er**	23
Z Jules Verne | **7e**	–
Z Lapérouse | **6e**	21
Macéo | **1er**	23
Maison Blanche | **8e**	20
Mansouria | **11e**	22
Marée (La) | **8e**	23
Marius | **16e**	18
Marty | **5e**	16
Maxan | **8e**	–
Meating | **17e**	17
Z Meurice | **1er**	27
Montalembert | **7e**	19
Mori Venice Bar | **2e**	17
Paris | **6e**	20
Paris Seize | **16e**	18
Pasco | **7e**	22
Petit Bofinger | **4e**	18
Petit Marguery | **13e**	21
Petit Pergolèse | **16e**	23
Pétrus | **17e**	21
Pichet de Paris | **8e**	16
Pierre au Palais Royal | **1er**	17
Z Pierre Gagnaire | **8e**	28
Pomze | **8e**	18
Pré Salé | **1er**	–
Pur'Grill | **2e**	19
Relais Louis XIII | **6e**	25
Salon d'Hélène | **6e**	19
Saveurs de Flora (Les) | **8e**	21
Sébillon | **Neuilly**	15
16 Haussmann | **9e**	18
Sormani | **17e**	23
Z Stella Maris | **8e**	26
Stresa | **8e**	22
Z Table de Joël Robuchon | **16e**	26
Table du Lancaster | **8e**	23
Table Lauriston | **16e**	20
Tan Dinh | **7e**	23
Tante Louise | **8e**	22
Terrasse Mirabeau | **16e**	–
Thierry Burlot | **15e**	–
Tierny & Co. | **16e**	–
Z Train Bleu | **12e**	19
35° Ouest | **7e**	20
Z Trou Gascon | **12e**	26
Vagenende | **6e**	15
Vaudeville | **2e**	18
Versance | **2e**	–
Villa Spicy | **8e**	13
Vin et Marée | **multi.**	18
Voltaire | **7e**	24
W Restaurant | **8e**	–

CELEBRITY CHEFS

Z Alain Ducasse | *Alain Ducasse* | **8e**	28
Z Ambroisie | *Bernard Pacaud* | **4e**	28
Z Apicius | *Jean-Pierre Vigato* | **8e**	26
Z Arpège | *Alain Passard* | **7e**	26
Z Astrance | *Pascal Barbot* | **16e**	28
Z Atelier Joël Robuchon | *Joël Robuchon* | **7e**	28
Z Benoît | *Alain Ducasse* | **4e**	24
Bistrot d'à Côté | *Michel Rostang* | **multi.**	21
Boulangerie Eric Kayser | *Eric Kayser* | **8e**	16
Z Bouquinistes | *Guy Savoy* | **6e**	23
Z Bristol | *Eric Frechon* | **8e**	27
Butte Chaillot | *Guy Savoy* | **16e**	21
Z Carré des Feuillants | *Alain Dutournier* | **1er**	26
Chiberta | *Guy Savoy* | **8e**	22
Z Cinq (Le) | *Philippe Legendre* | **8e**	28
NEW Cocottes | *Christian Constant* | **7e**	21
Z Comptoir du Relais | *Yves Camdeborde* | **6e**	26
NEW Dali | *Yannick Alleno* | **1er**	–
Drouant | *Antoine Westermann* | **2e**	22
Elysées (Les) | *Eric Briffard* | **8e**	23
Z Espadon (L') | *Michel Roth* | **1er**	26
Fables de La Fontaine | *Christian Constant* | **7e**	24
Gaya | *Pierre Gagnaire* | **7e**	23
Z Grand Véfour | *Guy Martin* | **1er**	28
Z Guy Savoy | *Guy Savoy* | **17e**	28
Z Hélène Darroze | *Hélène Darroze* | **6e**	25
Z Hiramatsu | *Hiroyuki Hiramatsu* | **16e**	26
Z Jacques Cagna | *Jacques Cagna* | **6e**	26
Z Jules Verne | *Alain Ducasse* | **7e**	–

Restaurant	Rating
Z Lasserre | *Jean-Louis Nomicos* | 8e	27
Z Lyonnais | *Alain Ducasse* | 2e	21
Market | *Jean-Georges Vongerichten* | 8e	22
Z Michel Rostang | *Michel Rostang* | 17e	27
Z Mon Vieil Ami | *Antoine Westermann* | 4e	24
Z Pavillon Ledoyen | *Christian Le Squer* | 8e	26
NEW Petites Sorcières | *Ghislaine Arabian* | 14e	-
Z Pierre Gagnaire | *Pierre Gagnaire* | 8e	28
Pinxo | *Alain Dutournier* | 1er	21
Rech | *Alain Ducasse* | 17e	-
Relais Plaza | *Alain Ducasse* | 8e	23
Salon d'Hélène | *Hélène Darroze* | 6e	19
Z Senderens | *Alain Senderens* | 8e	26
Sensing | *Guy Martin* | 6e	24
Spoon/Food | *Alain Ducasse* | 8e	22
NEW SYDR | *Alain Dutournier* | 8e	-
Z Table de Joël Robuchon | *Joël Robuchon* | 16e	26
Table du Lancaster | *Michel Troisgros* | 8e	23
Z Taillevent | *Alain Solivérès* | 8e	28
NEW Toustem | *Hélène Darroze* | 5e	-
Z Trou Gascon | *Alain Dutournier* | 12e	26
21 | *Paul Minchelli* | 6e	-
Z Violon d'Ingres | *Christian Constant* | 7e	25
Z Ze Kitchen Galerie | *William Ledeuil* | 6e	25

CHEESE TRAYS

Restaurant	Rating
A. Beauvilliers | 18e	20
NEW Agassin | 7e	-
Aiguière | 11e	-
Aimant du Sud | 13e	-
Alain Bourgade | 16e	-
Z Alain Ducasse | 8e	28
Alivi | 4e	16
Z Ambroisie | 4e	28
Ami Marcel | 15e	17
Ampère | 17e	-
Z Apicius | 8e	26
Arome | 8e	-
Z Arpège | 7e	26
Astier | 11e	21
Astor | 8e	16
Atelier Berger | 1er	21
Z Atelier Joël Robuchon | 7e	28
Aub. Dab | 16e	16
Bacchantes | 9e	-
Ballon des Ternes | 17e	15
Ballon et Coquillages | 17e	-
Bar Vendôme | 1er	23
Bath's | 17e	20
Beaujolais d'Auteuil | 16e	17
Bel Canto | 4e	13
Bistral | 17e	19
Bistro 121 | 15e	-
Bistrot à Vins Mélac | 11e	14
Bistrot du Sommelier | 8e	18
Boeuf Couronné | 19e	16
Z Bon Accueil | 7e	24
Bons Crus | 1er	-
Bouchons Clerc/P'tit | 8e	20
Bouillon Racine | 6e	16
Bound | 8e	-
Bourguignon du Marais | 4e	23
Z Braisière | 17e	27
Brass. du Louvre | 1er	16
Brass. Flo | 10e	18
Brass. Lutétia | 6e	18
Café de l'Industrie | 11e	12
Café du Passage | 11e	-
Café Faubourg | 8e	22
Café Fusion | 13e	-
Café Terminus | 8e	-
Camélia | **Bougival**	20
Carmine | 7e	-
Z Carré des Feuillants | 1er	26
Caveau du Palais | 1er	19
Cave de l'Os à Moëlle | 15e	22
Caves Pétrissans | 17e	19
Caviar Kaspia | 8e	25
Cazaudehore | **St-Germain-Laye**	22
Céladon | 2e	21
Chantairelle | 5e	-
Chez André | 8e	20
Chez Catherine | 8e	23

Chez Françoise | 7e	17	Giulio Rebellato | 16e	20
Chez Fred | 17e	-	Goumard | 1er	24
Z Chez Georges | 2e	24	Gourmand (Au) | 1er	20
Chez Léon | 17e	13	Graindorge | 17e	22
Chez Les Anges | 7e	23	Grand Café | 9e	13
Chez Maître Paul | 6e	21	Z Grand Véfour | 1er	28
Chez Nénesse | 3e	-	Grille | 10e	17
Chez Ramulaud | 11e	16	Z Guy Savoy | 17e	28
Chez René | 5e	21	Z Hélène Darroze | 6e	25
Chiberta | 8e	22	Huîtrerie Régis | 6e	22
Z Cinq (Le) | 8e	28	I Golosi | 9e	17
Citrus Etoile | 8e	20	Il Cortile | 1er	23
Cloche des Halles | 1er	-	NEW Il Vino | 7e	-
Closerie des Lilas | 6e	18	Z Jacques Cagna | 6e	26
Clou | 17e	19	Jardin des Cygnes | 8e	22
Clovis | 8e	-	Jarrasse | Neuilly	-
Comédiens | 9e	-	Jean | 9e	19
Congrès Maillot | 17e	18	J'Go | 6e	14
Cook Book | 7e	-	Joséphine/Dumonet | 6e	23
Copenhague | 8e	18	Z Jules Verne | 7e	-
Cordonnerie | 1er	-	NEW Karl et Erich | 17e	-
Cosi (Le) | 5e	16	Z Lasserre | 8e	27
Cottage Marcadet | 18e	-	Z Laurent | 8e	24
NEW Crémerie | 6e	-	Lavinia | 1er	17
NEW Cuisine (11e) | 11e	-	Louchebem | 1er	15
NEW Dali | 1er	-	Macéo | 1er	23
Dalloyau | 8e	23	Magnolias | Perreux	25
Diapason | 18e	-	Main d'Or | 11e	-
Divellec | 7e	24	Maison Blanche | 8e	20
Dôme | 14e	22	Maison du Jardin | 6e	24
Dôme du Marais | 4e	22	Marée (La) | 8e	23
Drouant | 2e	22	Marlotte | 6e	16
Duc de Richelieu | 12e	-	Mascotte | 18e	-
Ecailler du Bistrot | 11e	19	Maupertu | 7e	21
NEW Eclaireur | 8e	-	NEW M Comme Martine | 17e	-
Elysées (Les) | 8e	23	Meating | 17e	17
Epicure 108 | 17e	-	Mesturet | 2e	-
Epi d'Or | 1er	16	Z Meurice | 1er	27
NEW Epigramme | 6e	-	Z Michel Rostang | 17e	27
Z Espadon (L') | 1er	26	Moissonnier | 5e	19
Ferme St-Simon | 7e	23	Montparnasse 25 | 14e	16
Fermette Marbeuf | 8e	18	Murano | 3e	16
Fins Gourmets | 7e	19	Muses | 9e	19
Fontaine Gaillon | 2e	22	Nos Ancêtres/Gaulois | 4e	13
Fontaines | 5e	17	No Stress Café | 9e	-
Fouquet's | 8e	18	Oenothèque | 9e	-
Garnier | 8e	22	Oudino | 7e	-

SPECIAL FEATURES

Paolo Petrini | 17ᵉ	_⌋	Stéphane Gaborieau | 16ᵉ	_⌋
Papilles | 5ᵉ	23⌋	**Z** Table de Joël Robuchon | 16ᵉ	26⌋
Paris | 6ᵉ	20⌋	Table du Baltimore | 16ᵉ	_⌋
Passage/Carm. | 11ᵉ	_⌋	Table du Lancaster | 8ᵉ	23⌋
Z Passiflore | 16ᵉ	26⌋	Table Lauriston | 16ᵉ	20⌋
Paul Chêne | 16ᵉ	20⌋	Tante Louise | 8ᵉ	22⌋
Z Pavillon/Gr. Cascade | 16ᵉ	25⌋	Tastevin | **Maisons-Laff.**	24⌋
Z Pavillon Ledoyen | 8ᵉ	26⌋	Tav. de Gli Amici | 7ᵉ	_⌋
Pavillon Montsouris | 14ᵉ	17⌋	Tav. Henri IV | 1ᵉʳ	16⌋
Petit Colombier | 17ᵉ	18⌋	Tête Ailleurs | 4ᵉ	_⌋
Petite Sirène/Copen. | 9ᵉ	_⌋	Thoumieux | 7ᵉ	19⌋
NEW Petites Sorcières | 14ᵉ	_⌋	Tierny & Co. | 16ᵉ	_⌋
Petit Pascal | 13ᵉ	_⌋	Timbre | 6ᵉ	24⌋
Pétrelle | 9ᵉ	_⌋	Tokyo Eat | 16ᵉ	14⌋
Pichet de Paris | 8ᵉ	16⌋	**Z** Tour d'Argent | 5ᵉ	25⌋
Z Pierre Gagnaire | 8ᵉ	28⌋	**Z** Train Bleu | 12ᵉ	19⌋
Point Bar | 1ᵉʳ	22⌋	**Z** Trou Gascon | 12ᵉ	26⌋
Polichinelle Cafe | 11ᵉ	_⌋	Truffe Noire | **Neuilly**	_⌋
Pomze | 8ᵉ	18⌋	Truffière | 5ᵉ	23⌋
Port Alma | 16ᵉ	17⌋	Vaudeville | 2ᵉ	18⌋
Poule au Pot | 1ᵉʳ	23⌋	Versance | 2ᵉ	_⌋
Press Café | 2ᵉ	_⌋	Vieux Chêne | 11ᵉ	_⌋
Procope | 6ᵉ	16⌋	**Z** Villaret | 11ᵉ	26⌋
Pure Café | 11ᵉ	_⌋	Vin dans les voiles | 16ᵉ	_⌋
Quinzième | 15ᵉ	_⌋	Vin des Pyrenees | 4ᵉ	16⌋
NEW Racines | 2ᵉ	_⌋	**Z** Violon d'Ingres | 7ᵉ	25⌋
Ragueneau | 1ᵉʳ	_⌋	Vivres | 9ᵉ	_⌋
Z Relais d'Auteuil | 16ᵉ	27⌋	Waknine | 16ᵉ	_⌋
Relais de Venise | 17ᵉ	24⌋	Wepler | 18ᵉ	14⌋
Relais du Parc | 16ᵉ	19⌋	**Z** Willi's Wine Bar | 1ᵉʳ	20⌋
Relais Louis XIII | 6ᵉ	25⌋	**NEW** Winch | 18ᵉ	_⌋
Rendez-vous/Chauff. | 18ᵉ	_⌋	W Restaurant | 8ᵉ	_⌋
Romantica | **Clichy**	23⌋	Zéphyr | 20ᵉ	_⌋
Rose Bakery | 9ᵉ	17⌋	Zingot | 10ᵉ	_⌋
Rôtiss. du Beaujolais | 5ᵉ	23⌋	Zo | 8ᵉ	_⌋
Royal Madeleine | 8ᵉ	19⌋		

CHILD-FRIENDLY

(Alternatives to the usual fast-food places; * children's menu available)

Salon d'Hélène | 6ᵉ	19⌋	Aiguière* | 11ᵉ	_⌋
NEW Salon du Panthéon | 5ᵉ	_⌋	Alcazar* | 6ᵉ	19⌋
Sardegna a Tavola | 12ᵉ	21⌋	Ampère | 17ᵉ	_⌋
Sauvignon | 7ᵉ	14⌋	Amuse Bouche | 14ᵉ	17⌋
Saveurs de Flora (Les) | 8ᵉ	21⌋	Anahuacalli* | 5ᵉ	21⌋
Sébillon | **Neuilly**	15⌋	A Priori Thé* | 2ᵉ	16⌋
16 Haussmann | 9ᵉ	18⌋	Asian* | 8ᵉ	16⌋
Sot l'y Laisse | 11ᵉ	_⌋	**Z** Atelier Joël Robuchon | 7ᵉ	28⌋
Z Soufflé | 1ᵉʳ	22⌋	Atlas* | 5ᵉ	20⌋
Soupière | 17ᵉ	_⌋		
Stella | 16ᵉ	20⌋		

Aub. Dab*	16e	16	Petite Sirène/Copen.	9e	-
Autour du Saumon*	multi.	17	Petite Tour*	16e	-
Bar à Huîtres*	multi.	17	Petit Poucet*	Levallois	-
Bar Vendôme*	1er	23	Pied de Cochon	1er	18
BE Boulangépicier	8e	19	Point Bar*	1er	22
BIOArt*	13e	-	Port Alma	16e	17
Bistro 121	15e	-	Procope	6e	16
Bistro de Breteuil*	7e	16	Quai Ouest	St-Cloud	13
Bistrot d'André*	15e	-	⊠ Relais/l'Entrecôte	multi.	22
Bistrot du Dôme	14e	21	Rest. du Musée d'Orsay*	7e	17
Boeuf sur le Toit*	8e	18	Rest. du Palais Royal	1er	19
⊠ Bofinger*	4e	20	River Café	Issy-les-Moul.	14
Brass. du Louvre*	1er	16	Rôtiss. d'en Face	6e	21
Brass. Julien*	10e	19	Rôtiss. du Beaujolais	5e	23
Brass. Lutétia*	6e	18	Rotonde*	6e	15
Brass. Mollard*	8e	19	Sardegna a Tavola	12e	21
Breakfast in America	multi.	15	Sébillon*	Neuilly	15
Buffalo Grill*	multi.	10	Studio*	4e	-
Café de la Musique	19e	15	Tang	16e	17
Café de la Paix*	9e	19	Tav. de Maître Kanter*	1er	16
Chai 33*	12e	14	Terminus Nord*	10e	17
Chalet (Le)*	Neuilly	-	⊠ Train Bleu*	12e	19
Chalet des Iles*	16e	14	Trumilou	4e	19
Chez Clément*	multi.	15	Vagenende*	6e	15
Chez Jenny*	3e	19	Vaudeville*	2e	18
Chez Livio*	Neuilly	13	Viaduc Café*	12e	-
Congrès Maillot*	17e	18	Vieux Bistro	4e	21
Cook Book*	7e	-	Village d'Ung*	8e	-
⊠ Coupole*	14e	19	Villa Spicy*	8e	13
Dame Tartine*	4e	14	Wepler*	18e	14
Fouquet's*	8e	18	**CLOSED JULY/AUGUST**	
Gare*	16e	14	(Varies; call ahead to confirm dates)	
Gauloise*	15e	15	Abadache	17e	-
Gitane	15e	-	Accolade	17e	-
Hippopotamus*	multi.	11	A et M	16e	21
Indiana Café*	multi.	7	Affriolé	7e	22
J'Go*	9e	14	Aida	7e	23
Kiosque*	16e	15	NEW Alfred	1er	-
⊠ Ladurée	8e	23	Allobroges	20e	22
Languedoc	5e	-	⊠ Ambassadeurs	8e	28
Léon/Bruxelles*	multi.	16	⊠ Ami Louis	3e	25
Monsieur Lapin	14e	18	Ami Marcel	15e	17
Orénoc*	17e	17	Ami Pierre	11e	17
Paradis Thai	13e	15	Anahï	3e	19
Pavillon Montsouris*	14e	17	Angle du Faubourg	8e	24
Petit Bofinger*	multi.	18	Angl'Opéra	2e	19
Petite Cour	6e	21	AOC	5e	18

Restaurant	Rating	Restaurant	Rating
Z Apicius | 8ᵉ	26	Chez Grisette | 18ᵉ	-
Z Astrance | 16ᵉ	28	Chez L'Ami Jean | 7ᵉ	24
Aub. Aveyronnaise | 12ᵉ	-	Chez la Vieille | 1ᵉʳ	16
Aub. du Champ/Mars | 7ᵉ	17	Chez Marcel | 6ᵉ	-
Aub. Pyrénées | 11ᵉ	20	Chez Nénesse | 3ᵉ	-
Auguste | 7ᵉ	25	Chez René | 5ᵉ	21
Autour du Mont | 15ᵉ	-	Chez Savy | 8ᵉ	18
Autour du Saumon | 15ᵉ	17	Chieng Mai | 5ᵉ	16
Baptiste | 17ᵉ	-	Cibus | 1ᵉʳ	-
Baratin | 20ᵉ	16	Cinq Mars | 7ᵉ	19
Bar des Théâtres | 8ᵉ	15	Clos des Gourmets | 7ᵉ	25
Bascou | 3ᵉ	20	Clou | 17ᵉ	19
Bel Canto | multi.	13	Clovis | 8ᵉ	-
Bellini | 16ᵉ	24	Cook Book | 7ᵉ	-
Z Benoît | 4ᵉ	24	Copenhague | 8ᵉ	18
Bistral | 17ᵉ	19	Cordonnerie | 1ᵉʳ	-
Bistro de l'Olivier | 8ᵉ	18	Cottage Marcadet | 18ᵉ	-
Bistro Poulbot | 18ᵉ	-	Cou de la Girafe | 8ᵉ	15
Bistrot à Vins Mélac | 11ᵉ	14	Couleurs de Vigne | 15ᵉ	-
Bistrot d'à Côté | 17ᵉ	21	NEW Crémerie | 6ᵉ	-
Bistrot de l'Université | 7ᵉ	18	Crêperie de Josselin | 14ᵉ	22
Bistrot de Paris | 7ᵉ	16	Cuisine (7e) | 7ᵉ	25
Bistrot des Vignes | 16ᵉ	17	NEW Cuisine (11e) | 11ᵉ	-
Bistrot du Dôme | 4ᵉ	21	Daru | 8ᵉ	-
Bistrot du Sommelier | 8ᵉ	18	Dell Orto | 9ᵉ	-
Bistrot Papillon | 9ᵉ	14	2 Pieces Cuisine | 18ᵉ	-
Bistrot Paul Bert | 11ᵉ	23	Z 1728 | 8ᵉ	19
Boucherie Roulière | 6ᵉ	-	Ecaille de Fontaine | 2ᵉ	-
Boulangerie | 20ᵉ	23	Ecailler du Bistrot | 11ᵉ	19
Boule Rouge | 9ᵉ	-	Enzo | 14ᵉ	-
Bourguignon du Marais | 4ᵉ	23	Z Epi Dupin | 6ᵉ	24
Butte Chaillot | 16ᵉ	21	Escargot Montorgueil | 1ᵉʳ	21
Café Lenôtre | 8ᵉ	18	Ferme St-Simon | 7ᵉ	23
Café Moderne | 2ᵉ	21	Florimond | 7ᵉ	24
Caffé Minotti | 7ᵉ	22	Fontaine Gaillon | 2ᵉ	22
Caffé Toscano | 7ᵉ	19	Frégate | 12ᵉ	24
Camélia | Bougival	20	Gaya | 7ᵉ	23
Cantine de Quentin | 10ᵉ	-	Gazzetta | 12ᵉ	-
Carpaccio | 8ᵉ	-	Georgette | 9ᵉ	22
Z Carré des Feuillants | 1ᵉʳ	26	Z Gérard Besson | 1ᵉʳ	25
Carte Blanche | 9ᵉ	-	Giulio Rebellato | 16ᵉ	20
Casa Olympe | 9ᵉ	24	Gourmand (Au) | 1ᵉʳ	20
Caves Pétrissans | 17ᵉ	19	Z Grand Véfour | 1ᵉʳ	28
Caviar Kaspia | 8ᵉ	25	Grand Venise | 15ᵉ	25
Cerisaie | 14ᵉ	21	Grange Batelière | 9ᵉ	-
Chen Soleil d'Est | 15ᵉ	-	Grille | 10ᵉ	17
Chez Gérard | Neuilly	19	Hangar | 3ᵉ	18

Hier & Aujourd'hui	17e	-	
Z Hiramatsu	16e	26	
Huîtrerie Régis	6e	22	
Il Cortile	1er	23	
Inagiku	5e	18	
Jardinier	9e	-	
J'Go	9e	14	
Kai	1er	-	
NEW Karl et Erich	17e	-	
Maison du Jardin	6e	24	
Mori Venice Bar	2e	17	
Mousson	1er	-	
Muses	9e	19	
Oudino	7e	-	
Ourcine	13e	24	
Papilles	5e	23	
Paris	6e	20	
Passy Mandarin	16e	20	
Paul Chêne	16e	20	
Petit Pascal	13e	-	
Pétrelle	9e	-	
Pétrus	17e	21	
Ploum	10e	-	
Pré Salé	1er	-	
P'tit Troquet	7e	22	
Radis Roses	9e	-	
Relais de Venise	17e	24	
Resto	8e	-	
Ribouldingue	5e	18	
Royal Madeleine	8e	19	
Sensing	6e	24	
7ème Sud	16e	15	
Severo	14e	20	
6 New York	16e	17	
Soleil	7e	19	
Sot l'y Laisse	11e	-	
Z Soufflé	1er	22	
Stéphane Gaborieau	16e	-	
Suave	13e	-	
Table du Lancaster	8e	23	
Table Lauriston	16e	20	
Tang	16e	17	
Tav. de Gli Amici	7e	-	
Tav. Henri IV	1er	16	
Temps au Temps	11e	25	
Tête Ailleurs	4e	-	
Tierny & Co.	16e	-	

35° Ouest	7e	20	
Z Trou Gascon	12e	26	
Versance	2e	-	
Vin dans les voiles	16e	-	
21	6e	-	
Vivres	9e	-	
Yugaraj	6e	23	

DANCING

Barrio Latino	12e	12	
Bound	8e	-	
Café de Mars	7e	17	
Chez Clément	17e	15	
Chez Gégène	Joinville	-	
Z Coupole	14e	19	
Etoile	16e	24	
Musichall	8e	15	
Vinea Café	12e	-	

DELIVERY

Affriolé	7e	22	
Aiguière	11e	-	
Anahuacalli	5e	21	
Atlas	5e	20	
Autour du Saumon	multi.	17	
Bistro 121	15e	-	
Caffé Toscano	7e	19	
Chez Vincent	19e	-	
Coco de Mer	5e	-	
Cook Book	7e	-	
Dalloyau	6e	23	
Delicabar	7e	13	
Escale du Liban	4e	-	
Findi	8e	16	
NEW Fines Gueules	1er	-	
Issé	1er	23	
Jarrasse	Neuilly	-	
Kifune	17e	-	
Z Ladurée	6e	23	
Lina's	multi.	16	
Maharajah	5e	17	
Maison du Caviar	8e	22	
Matsuri	16e	14	
Mavrommatis	5e	19	
Mont Liban	17e	-	
Mousson	1er	-	
Pamphlet	3e	23	
Petite Tour	16e	-	

SPECIAL FEATURES

Point Bar	1er	22
Polichinelle Cafe	11e	–
Pomze	8e	18
Relais Louis XIII	6e	25
Suffren	15e	14
NEW Urbane	10e	–
Wally Le Saharien	9e	15
Zingot	10e	–

DINING ALONE

(Other than hotels and places with counter service)

NEW Agassin	7e	–
Aimant du Sud	13e	–
Alcazar	6e	19
NEW Alfred	1er	–
Alsace	8e	18
Ami Marcel	15e	17
Ampère	17e	–
Amuse Bouche	14e	17
Z As du Fallafel	4e	24
Assiette	14e	–
Aub. Bressane	7e	20
Azabu	6e	24
Ballon des Ternes	17e	15
Bar à Huîtres	**multi.**	17
Bar des Théâtres	8e	15
Bistrot à Vins Mélac	11e	14
Bistrot de Marius	8e	21
Bistrot du Peintre	11e	18
Boeuf sur le Toit	8e	18
Bouchons Clerc/P'tit	8e	20
Bouillon Racine	6e	16
Boulangerie Eric Kayser	8e	16
Bourguignon du Marais	4e	23
Brass. de l'Ile St. Louis	4e	17
Breakfast in America	**multi.**	15
Buisson Ardent	5e	19
Ca d'Oro	1er	18
Café Beaubourg	4e	16
Z Café de Flore	6e	15
Café de la Poste	4e	–
Café de l'Industrie	11e	12
Café du Commerce	15e	16
Café du Passage	11e	–
Café Lenôtre	8e	18
Z Café Les Deux Magots	6e	16
Z Café Marly	1er	16

NEW Café Pleyel	8e	–
Caméléon	6e	20
Camille	3e	16
Cap Vernet	8e	17
Carr's	1er	–
Charlot Roi des Coq.	9e	15
Charpentiers	6e	18
Chartier	9e	13
Chez Catherine	8e	23
Z Chez Georges	2e	24
Chez Jenny	3e	19
Chez la Vieille	1er	16
Chez Maître Paul	6e	21
Chez Marcel	6e	–
Chez Marianne	4e	18
Closerie des Lilas	6e	18
NEW Cocottes	7e	21
Coffee Parisien	**multi.**	16
Congrès Maillot	17e	18
Cosi	6e	19
Z Coupole	14e	19
Curieux Spaghetti Bar	4e	–
Delicabar	7e	13
Deux Canards	10e	18
Duc de Richelieu	12e	–
Durand Dupont	**Neuilly**	–
Ecluse	**multi.**	16
Emporio Armani	6e	19
Entracte	18e	–
Epi d'Or	1er	16
Escargot Montorgueil	1er	21
Fakhr el Dine	16e	24
Ferme	1er	–
NEW Fines Gueules	1er	–
Fins Gourmets	7e	19
Z Fish La Boissonnerie	6e	22
Fous d'en Face	4e	–
Fumoir	1er	17
Gauloise	15e	15
Georgette	9e	22
Gourmand (Au)	1er	20
Isami	4e	25
Jarrasse	**Neuilly**	–
Jean	9e	19
Je Thé . . . Me	15e	–
Joe Allen	1er	13
Joséphine/Dumonet	6e	23

NEW Karl et Erich | 17e	-
Kinugawa/Hanawa | 8e	23
Z Ladurée | **multi.**	23
Languedoc | 5e	-
Lao Tseu | 7e	-
Legrand Filles et Fils | 2e	-
Lina's | **multi.**	16
Lô Sushi | 8e	15
Ma Bourgogne | 4e	18
Marée Denfert/Passy | 14e	-
Marty | 5e	16
Maupertu | 7e	21
Mauzac | 5e	-
Maxan | 8e	-
Moulin à Vent | 5e	19
Mousson | 1er	-
Nemrod | 6e	16
No Stress Café | 9e	-
Oenothèque | 9e	-
Pamphlet | 3e	23
Papilles | 5e	23
Paradis Thai | 13e	15
Pasco | 7e	22
Pères et Filles | 6e	16
Perraudin | 5e	13
Petit Bofinger | 4e	18
Petit Colombier | 17e	18
Petite Chaise | 7e	19
Petite Sirène/Copen. | 9e	-
NEW Petites Sorcières | 14e	-
Petit Lutétia | 6e	19
Petit Marguery | 13e	21
Petit Pergolèse | 16e	23
Petit Rétro | 16e	16
Petit Riche | 9e	18
Polidor | 6e	17
Poule au Pot | 1er	23
P'tit Troquet | 7e	22
NEW Racines | 2e	-
Repaire de Cartouche | 11e	16
Rest. du Marché | 15e	-
Roi du Pot-au-Feu | 9e	-
Rose Bakery | 9e	17
Rose de France | 1er	-
Rubis | 1er	15
Suffren | 15e	14
Table d'Hédiard | 8e	22

Tan Dinh | 7e	23
Tav. Henri IV | 1er	16
Terminus Nord | 10e	17
Vagenende | 6e	15
Viaduc Café | 12e	-
Vieux Bistro | 4e	21
Vieux Chêne | 11e	-
Vin et Marée | **multi.**	18
Z Vin sur Vin | 7e	26
Wepler | 18e	14
Wok Cooking | 11e	-
Zéphyr | 20e	-

ENTERTAINMENT

(Call for days and times of performances)

Alivi | Corsican | 4e	16
Annapurna | sitar | 8e	18
Asian | DJ | 8e	16
Avenue | DJ | 8e	18
Barlotti | DJ | 1er	15
Barrio Latino | salsa | 12e	12
Barroco | live music | 6e	-
Bar Vendôme | piano | 1er	23
Bel Canto | opera | **multi.**	13
Berkeley | DJ | 8e	14
Café Charbon | concerts | 11e	15
Café Faubourg | piano | 8e	22
Café Le Petit Pont | jazz | 5e	14
Carr's | Irish | 1er	-
Chez Cécile | jazz | 8e	-
Chez Françoise | live music | 7e	17
Chez Gégène | dancing | Joinville	-
Diamantaires | orchestra | 9e	-
Djakarta | Balinese | 1er	20
Jardin des Cygnes | piano | 8e	22
Z Lasserre | piano | 8e	27
Maxim's | piano | 8e	18
Musichall | varies | 8e	15
Nos Ancêtres/Gaulois | guitar | 4e	13
Passage/Carm. | debates | 11e	-
Pied de Chameau | snake charmer/dancers | 3e	-
Polichinelle Cafe | concerts | 11e	-
Quai Ouest | clown | **St-Cloud**	13
Relais Plaza | jazz | 8e	23
Saudade | Fado | 1er	-

Viaduc Café | jazz | 12ᵉ	–
Zébra Square | DJ | 16ᵉ	10
Zo | DJ | 8ᵉ	–

FAMILY-STYLE

Aimant du Sud | 13ᵉ	–
Z Allard | 6ᵉ	21
Allobroges | 20ᵉ	22
Ampère | 17ᵉ	–
Z Ardoise | 1ᵉʳ	24
Bartolo | 6ᵉ	17
Café du Passage | 11ᵉ	–
Chez Papa | multi.	17
Closerie des Lilas | 6ᵉ	18
Flore en l'Île | 4ᵉ	18
Z Fontaine de Mars | 7ᵉ	21
Fous d'en Face | 4ᵉ	–
Joséphine/Dumonet | 6ᵉ	23
Marty | 5ᵉ	16
Z Mon Vieil Ami | 4ᵉ	24
Repaire de Cartouche | 11ᵉ	16
Wok Cooking | 11ᵉ	–

FIREPLACES

Atelier Maître Albert | 5ᵉ	21
Aub. du Clou | 9ᵉ	16
Bon | 16ᵉ	15
Brass. L'Européen | 12ᵉ	–
Carr's | 1ᵉʳ	–
Cazaudehore | St-Germain-Laye	22
Chalet des Îles | 16ᵉ	14
Costes | 1ᵉʳ	18
Coupe-Chou | 5ᵉ	23
Z Cristal Room | 16ᵉ	17
Diamantaires | 9ᵉ	–
Z 1728 | 8ᵉ	19
Fontaine Gaillon | 2ᵉ	22
Je Thé . . . Me | 15ᵉ	–
Montalembert | 7ᵉ	19
Murano | 3ᵉ	16
Nos Ancêtres/Gaulois | 4ᵉ	13
Paradis Thai | 13ᵉ	15
Z Pavillon/Gr. Cascade | 16ᵉ	25
Pavillon Montsouris | 14ᵉ	17
Petit Châtelet | 5ᵉ	–
Petit Colombier | 17ᵉ	18
Petit Poucet | Levallois	–
Petit Victor Hugo | 16ᵉ	19

Pétrelle | 9ᵉ	–
Z Pré Catelan | 16ᵉ	27
NEW P'tit Casier | 15ᵉ	–
Quai Ouest | St-Cloud	13
Relais du Parc | 16ᵉ	19
River Café | Issy-les-Moul.	14
Robert et Louise | 3ᵉ	21
Romantica | Clichy	23
Sud | 17ᵉ	16
Tastevin | Maisons-Laff.	24
Truffière | 5ᵉ	23
Villa Corse | 16ᵉ	20
Yugaraj | 6ᵉ	23

HISTORIC PLACES

(Year opened; * building)

1407 | Aub. Nicolas Flamel* | 3ᵉ	–
1582 | Tour d'Argent | 5ᵉ	25
1608 | Ragueneau | 1ᵉʳ	–
1640 | Cordonnerie* | 1ᵉʳ	–
1650 | Aiguière* | 11ᵉ	–
1680 | Petite Chaise | 7ᵉ	19
1686 | Procope | 6ᵉ	16
1728 | 1728* | 8ᵉ	19
1758 | Ambassadeurs* | 8ᵉ	28
1760 | Grand Véfour | 1ᵉʳ	28
1766 | Lapérouse | 6ᵉ	21
1800 | Andy Wahloo* | 3ᵉ	14
1800 | Black Calavados* | 8ᵉ	–
1823 | A Priori Thé* | 2ᵉ	16
1832 | Escargot Montorgueil | 1ᵉʳ	21
1845 | Polidor | 6ᵉ	17
1854 | Petit Riche | 9ᵉ	18
1855 | Brass. du Louvre | 1ᵉʳ	16
1856 | Charpentiers | 6ᵉ	18
1862 | Café de la Paix | 9ᵉ	19
1862 | Ladurée | 8ᵉ	23
1864 | Bofinger | 4ᵉ	20
1867 | Brass. Mollard | 8ᵉ	19
1870 | Boeuf Couronné | 19ᵉ	16
1872 | Goumard | 1ᵉʳ	24
1876 | Gallopin | 2ᵉ	16
1876 | Grange Batelière | 9ᵉ	–
1880 | Aub. du Clou* | 9ᵉ	16
1880 | Brass. Lipp | 6ᵉ	17
1881 | Café Terminus | 8ᵉ	–
1885 | Café Les Deux Magots | 6ᵉ	16
1886 | Brass. Balzar | 5ᵉ	19

Year	Name	Location	Rating
1890	Bouillon Racine	6e	16
1890	Brass. Julien	10e	19
1890	Passage/Carm.	11e	-
1892	Wepler	18e	14
1893	Maxim's	8e	18
1895	Caves Pétrissans	17e	19
1896	Chartier	9e	13
1897	Ladurée	9e	23
1897	Pouilly Reuilly	**St-Gervais**	-
1899	Fouquet's	8e	18
1900	Brass. de l'Ile St. Louis	4e	17
1900	Café Lenôtre*	8e	18
1900	Chez Gégène	**Joinville**	-
1900	Chez Pauline	1er	20
1900	Gauloise	15e	15
1900	Noces de Jeannette	2e	-
1900	Pavillon/Gr. Cascade	16e	25
1900	Pavillon Ledoyen	8e	26
1900	Pré Catelan	16e	27
1900	Rest. Paul	1er	20
1900	Vieux Chêne*	11e	-
1901	Petit St. Benoît	6e	16
1901	Train Bleu	12e	19
1903	Angelina	1er	20
1903	Bistrot de Paris	7e	16
1903	Perraudin	5e	13
1903	Rotonde	6e	15
1904	Vagenende	6e	15
1905	Bons Crus	1er	-
1906	Rendez-vous/Chauff.	18e	-
1908	Chardenoux	11e	19
1909	Bistrot d'André	15e	-
1909	Pomponette	18e	17
1910	Brass. Lutétia	6e	18
1910	Fontaine de Mars	7e	21
1912	Benoît	4e	24
1913	Marty	5e	16
1913	Zeyer	14e	16
1914	Sébillon	**Neuilly**	15
1918	Daru	8e	-
1919	Chez Marcel	6e	-
1919	Lescure	1er	17
1920	Chez Julien	4e	19
1920	Closerie des Lilas	6e	18
1920	Hôtel Amour*	9e	8
1920	Maison Prunier	16e	21
1920	Petit Niçois	7e	16
1920	Tournesol	16e	18
1922	Boeuf sur le Toit	8e	18
1922	Café du Commerce	15e	16
1923	Chez Savy	8e	18
1923	Thoumieux	7e	19
1924	Ami Louis	3e	25
1924	Bristol	8e	27
1925	Biche au Bois	12e	20
1925	Gourmand	**Neuilly**	-
1925	Grand Venise	15e	25
1925	Petit Lutétia	6e	19
1925	Rech	17e	-
1925	Terminus Nord	10e	17
1926	Chez Georges-Maillot	17e	18
1927	Caviar Kaspia	8e	25
1927	Coupole	14e	19
1928	Cazaudehore	**St-Germain-Laye**	22
1929	Diamantaires	9e	-
1929	Jardin des Cygnes	8e	22
1929	Petit Colombier	17e	18
1929	Tante Louise	8e	22
1929	Zéphyr	20e	-
1930	Allard	6e	21
1930	Garnier	8e	22
1930	Trumilou	4e	19
1931	Chez L'Ami Jean	7e	24
1932	Chiberta	8e	22
1932	Crus de Bourgogne	2e	17
1935	Epi d'Or	1er	16
1935	Poule au Pot	1er	23
1935	Truffe Noire	**Neuilly**	-
1936	Relais Plaza	8e	23
1937	Chez André	8e	20
1937	Chez Léna et Mimile	5e	15
1939	Voltaire	7e	24
1940	Flandrin	16e	15
1942	Lasserre	8e	27
1942	Méditerranée	6e	21
1943	Royal Madeleine	8e	19
1945	Aub. Bressane	7e	20
1945	Chez Fred	17e	-
1945	Chez Paul	11e	21
1945	Pied de Cochon	1er	18
1946	Chez Maître Paul	6e	21
1946	Taillevent	8e	28
1947	Moulin à Vent	5e	19

1948 | Rubis | 1er	15	
1949 | Chez Françoise | 7^e	17	
1950 | Diapason | 18^e	-	
1950 | Terrasse Mirabeau* | 16^e	-	
1951 | Bartolo | 6^e	17	
1951 | Deux Canards | 10^e	18	
1951 | Petit Châtelet | 5^e	-	
1952 | Bistro 121 | 15^e	-	
1954 | Sauvignon | 7^e	14	
1955 | Copenhague | 8^e	18	
1956 | Maison du Caviar | 8^e	22	
1956 | Robert et Louise | 3^e	21	
1957 | Chez René | 5^e	21	
1958 | Publicis Drugstore | 8^e	11	

HOLIDAY MEALS

(Special prix fixe meals offered at major holidays)

Z Ambassadeurs | 8^e	28
Z Ambroisie | 4^e	28
Z Apicius | 8^e	26
Z Arpège | 7^e	26
Astor | 8^e	16
Z Atelier Joël Robuchon | 7^e	28
Z Benoît | 4^e	24
Z Bristol | 8^e	27
Z Café Les Deux Magots | 6^e	16
Z 144 Petrossian | 7^e	25
Chen Soleil d'Est | 15^e	-
Chiberta | 8^e	22
Z Cinq (Le) | 8^e	28
Z Coupole | 14^e	19
Daru | 8^e	-
Diapason | 18^e	-
Divellec | 7^e	24
Z Espadon (L') | 1er	26
Goumard | 1er	24
Z Guy Savoy | 17^e	28
Huîtrier | 17^e	20
Jardins de Bagatelle | 16^e	17
Z Jules Verne | 7^e	-
Z Lapérouse | 6^e	21
Z Lasserre | 8^e	27
Marée (La) | 8^e	23
Maxim's | 8^e	18
Montparnasse 25 | 14^e	16
Paris | 6^e	20
Z Pavillon/Gr. Cascade | 16^e	25

Z Pavillon Ledoyen | 8^e	26
Z Pierre Gagnaire | 8^e	28
Potager du Roy | **Versailles**	19
Z Pré Catelan | 16^e	27
Relais Louis XIII | 6^e	25
Romantica | **Clichy**	23
Rue Balzac | 8^e	17
Salon d'Hélène | 6^e	19
Z Senderens | 8^e	26
Sormani | 17^e	23
Table d'Anvers | 9^e	17
Z Taillevent | 8^e	28
Tan Dinh | 7^e	23
Z Tour d'Argent | 5^e	25
Z Trou Gascon | 12^e	26
Wally Le Saharien | 9^e	15

HOTEL DINING

Ambassador, Hôtel	
16 Haussmann | 9^e	18
Amour, Hôtel	
Hôtel Amour | 9^e	8
Astor, Hôtel	
Astor | 8^e	16
Balzac, Hôtel	
Z Pierre Gagnaire | 8^e	28
Castille Paris, Hôtel	
Il Cortile | 1er	23
Concorde St-Lazare, Hôtel	
Café Terminus | 8^e	-
Costes, Hôtel	
Costes | 1er	18
Crillon, Hôtel de	
Z Ambassadeurs | 8^e	28
Obélisque | 8^e	23
du Louvre, Hôtel	
Brass. du Louvre | 1er	16
Edouard VII, Hôtel	
Angl'Opéra | 2^e	19
El Dorado, Hôtel	
Bistrot des Dames | 17^e	14
Four Seasons George V	
Z Cinq (Le) | 8^e	28
Hôtel Le Parc	
Relais du Parc | 16^e	19
Hôtel Meurice	
NEW Dali | 1er	-

Hôtel Relais Saint-Germain
Ζ Comptoir du Relais | 6ᵉ   26

Hyatt, Hôtel
Café M | 8ᵉ   19

InterContinental Le Grand
Hôtel
Café de la Paix | 9ᵉ   19

Lancaster, Hôtel
Table du Lancaster | 8ᵉ   23

Le Bristol, Hôtel
Ζ Bristol | 8ᵉ   27

Le Méridien Etoile
Orénoc | 17ᵉ   17

Le Méridien Montparnasse
Montparnasse 25 | 14ᵉ   16

L'Hôtel
Restaurant (Le) | 6ᵉ   26

Lutétia, Hôtel
Brass. Lutétia | 6ᵉ   18
Paris | 6ᵉ   20

Marignan, Hôtel
Spoon/Food | 8ᵉ   22

Meurice, Hôtel
Ζ Meurice | 1ᵉʳ   27

Montalembert, Hôtel
Montalembert | 7ᵉ   19

Murano Urban Resort
Murano | 3ᵉ   16

Novotel Tour Eiffel, Hôtel
Benkay | 15ᵉ   24

Park Hyatt Paris-Vendôme
Pur'Grill | 2ᵉ   19

Pershing Hall, Hôtel
Pershing | 8ᵉ   17

Plaza-Athénée
Ζ Alain Ducasse | 8ᵉ   28
Relais Plaza | 8ᵉ   23

Pont Royal
Ζ Atelier Joël Robuchon | 7ᵉ   28

Prince de Galles, Hôtel
Jardin des Cygnes | 8ᵉ   22

Renaissance Paris Vendôme
Pinxo | 1ᵉʳ   21

Ritz, Hôtel
Bar Vendôme | 1ᵉʳ   23
Ζ Espadon (L') | 1ᵉʳ   26

Royal Monceau, Hôtel
Carpaccio | 8ᵉ   -

Scribe, Hôtel
Muses | 9ᵉ   19

Sofitel Arc de Triomphe
Clovis | 8ᵉ   -

Sofitel Demeure Hôtel
Baltimore
Table du Baltimore | 16ᵉ   -

Sofitel Le Faubourg
Café Faubourg | 8ᵉ   22

Terrass Hôtel
Diapason | 18ᵉ   -

Thoumieux, Hôtel
Thoumieux | 7ᵉ   19

Vernet, Hôtel
Elysées (Les) | 8ᵉ   23

Ville, Hôtel de
Ζ Benoît | 4ᵉ   24

Warwick, Hôtel
W Restaurant | 8ᵉ   -

Westin Hotel
First | 1ᵉʳ   18

Westminster, Hôtel
Céladon | 2ᵉ   21

JACKET REQUIRED

(* Tie also required)

Ζ Alain Ducasse* | 8ᵉ   28
Ζ Ambroisie* | 4ᵉ   28
Ζ Arpège* | 7ᵉ   26
Ζ Astrance | 16ᵉ   28
Ζ Carré des Feuillants* | 1ᵉʳ   26
Ζ Cinq (Le) | 8ᵉ   28
Ζ Espadon (L')* | 1ᵉʳ   26
Ζ Grand Véfour | 1ᵉʳ   28
Ζ Jules Verne | 7ᵉ   -
Ζ Lasserre | 8ᵉ   27
Maxim's* | 8ᵉ   18
Ζ Meurice | 1ᵉʳ   27
Ζ Michel Rostang* | 17ᵉ   27
Orangerie | 4ᵉ   22
Ζ Pavillon/Gr. Cascade | 16ᵉ   25
Ζ Pavillon Ledoyen | 8ᵉ   26
Ζ Pré Catelan* | 16ᵉ   27
Relais Plaza | 8ᵉ   23
Ζ Taillevent* | 8ᵉ   28
Ζ Tour d'Argent* | 5ᵉ   25

LATE DINING

(Weekday closing hour)

Al Dar | 12 AM | **multi.**	21
Al Diwan | 12 AM | 8ᵉ	21
Alsace | 24 hrs. | 8ᵉ	18
Ami Pierre | 12 AM | 11ᵉ	17
Anahï | 12 AM | 3ᵉ	19
Andy Wahloo | 12 AM | 3ᵉ	14
Asian | 12 AM | 8ᵉ	16
☑ Atelier Joël Robuchon | 12 AM | 7ᵉ	28
Aub. Dab | 2 AM | 16ᵉ	16
Avenue | 1 AM | 8ᵉ	18
Bacchantes | 12:30 AM | 9ᵉ	-
Ballon des Ternes | 12 AM | 17ᵉ	15
Bar à Huîtres | varies | **multi.**	17
Bar des Théâtres | 1 AM | 8ᵉ	15
Barlotti | 12:30 AM | 1ᵉʳ	15
Barrio Latino | 12:45 AM | 12ᵉ	12
Barroco | 12 AM | 6ᵉ	-
Berkeley | 1 AM | 8ᵉ	14
Bistro/Deux Théâtres | 12:30 AM | 9ᵉ	14
Bistro Melrose | 1 AM | 17ᵉ	-
☑ Bistrot de l'Oulette | 12 AM | 4ᵉ	26
Bistrot du Peintre | 12 AM | 11ᵉ	18
Black Calavados | 12 AM | 8ᵉ	-
Blue Elephant | 12 AM | 11ᵉ	20
Bœuf Couronné | 12 AM | 19ᵉ	16
Bœuf sur le Toit | 1 AM | 8ᵉ	18
☑ Bofinger | 12:30 AM | 4ᵉ	20
Bound | 1 AM | 8ᵉ	-
☑ Brass. Balzar | 12 AM | 5ᵉ	19
Brass. Flo | 12:30 AM | 10ᵉ	18
Brass. Julien | 1 AM | 10ᵉ	19
Brass. La Lorraine | 1 AM | 8ᵉ	17
Brass. L'Européen | 1 AM | 12ᵉ	-
☑ Brass. Lipp | 1 AM | 6ᵉ	17
Brass. Mollard | 12:30 AM | 8ᵉ	19
☑ Buddha Bar | 12:30 AM | 8ᵉ	16
Café Beaubourg | 12 AM | 4ᵉ	16
Café Burq | 12 AM | 18ᵉ	-
☑ Café de Flore | 1:30 AM | 6ᵉ	15
Café de la Musique | varies | 19ᵉ	15
Café de l'Esplanade | 12:45 AM | 7ᵉ	16
Café de l'Industrie | 12 AM | 11ᵉ	12
Café du Commerce | 12 AM | 15ᵉ	16
Café du Passage | 1 AM | 11ᵉ	-
Café Etienne Marcel | 12 AM | 2ᵉ	18
Café Le Petit Pont | varies | 5ᵉ	14
☑ Café Les Deux Magots | 1 AM | 6ᵉ	16
☑ Café Marly | 2 AM | 1ᵉʳ	16
Café Ruc | 1 AM | 1ᵉʳ	15
Camille | 12 AM | 3ᵉ	16
Caviar Kaspia | 1 AM | 8ᵉ	25
Chai 33 | 12 AM | 12ᵉ	14
Charlot Roi des Coq. | varies | 9ᵉ	15
NEW Chéri Bibi | 12 AM | 18ᵉ	-
Chez André | 1 AM | 8ᵉ	20
Chez Clément | 1 AM | **multi.**	15
Chez Denise | 6:30 AM | 1ᵉʳ	24
Chez Francis | 12:30 AM | 8ᵉ	17
Chez Françoise | 12 AM | 7ᵉ	17
Chez Janou | 12 AM | 3ᵉ	23
Chez Jenny | 12 AM | 3ᵉ	19
Chez L'Ami Jean | 12 AM | 7ᵉ	24
Chez Michel | 12 AM | 10ᵉ	24
Chez Papa | 1 AM | **multi.**	17
Chez Paul | 12 AM | 11ᵉ	21
Chez Paul | 12 AM | 13ᵉ	16
Chez Prune | 1 AM | 10ᵉ	18
Chez Vincent | 12 AM | 19ᵉ	-
Chien qui Fume | 1 AM | 1ᵉʳ	18
Christine | 12 AM | 6ᵉ	23
Clown Bar | 12 AM | 11ᵉ	17
Coco de Mer | 12 AM | 5ᵉ	-
Coffee Parisien | varies | **multi.**	16
Congrès Maillot | 2 AM | 17ᵉ	18
Costes | 24 hrs. | 1ᵉʳ	18
Coude Fou | 12 AM | 4ᵉ	19
Coupe Gorge | 12 AM | 4ᵉ	-
☑ Coupole | 1:30 AM | 14ᵉ	19
Curieux Spaghetti Bar | 12 AM | 4ᵉ	-
Dell Orto | 12 AM | 9ᵉ	-
Devèz | 12:30 AM | 8ᵉ	16
Diep | 12:30 AM | 8ᵉ	21
Dôme | 12:30 AM | 14ᵉ	22
Duc de Richelieu | 1 AM | 12ᵉ	-
Durand Dupont | 12 AM | **Neuilly**	-
Ecluse | 1 AM | **multi.**	16
Editeurs | 2 AM | 6ᵉ	14

Escale du Liban | 12 AM | 4e —
Etoile | 1 AM | 16e — 24
Fakhr el Dine | 12 AM | 16e — 24
NEW Fines Gueules | 2 AM | 1er —
Flore en l'Ile | 2 AM | 4e — 18
Fogón | 12 AM | 6e — 21
Fouquet's | 12 AM | 8e — 18
Fous d'en Face | 12 AM | 4e —
Gallopin | 12 AM | 2e — 16
Gamin de Paris | 2 AM | 4e — 21
Gavroche | 1 AM | 2e — 17
Grand Café | 24 hrs. | 9e — 13
Grand Colbert | 1 AM | 2e — 19
Grande Armée | 1 AM | 16e — 15
Grille St-Germain | 12:30 AM | 6e — 17
Hippopotamus | varies | **multi.** — 11
Hôtel Amour | 11:30 PM | 9e — 8
Huîtrerie Régis | 12 AM | 6e — 22
NEW Il Vino | 12 AM | 7e —
Indiana Café | 1 AM | **multi.** — 7
J'Go | 12 AM, 2 AM | **multi.** — 14
Joe Allen | 12:30 AM | 1er — 13
Kaïten | 12 AM | 8e —
Kong | 12:30 AM | 1er — 14
Z Ladurée | 12 AM | 8e — 23
Léon/Bruxelles | varies | **multi.** — 16
Libre Sens | 12 AM | 8e —
Lô Sushi | 12 AM | 8e — 15
NEW Lup | 5 AM | 6e —
Ma Bourgogne | 1 AM | 4e — 18
Main d'Or | 12 AM | 11e —
Maison du Caviar | 1 AM | 8e — 22
Martel | 12 AM | 10e —
NEW Mood | 12 AM | 8e —
Murano | 12 AM | 3e — 16
Murat | 12 AM | 16e — 13
Musichall | 5 AM | 8e — 15
New Jawad | 12 AM | 7e — 18
New Nioullaville | 12:30 AM | 11e — 16
Noura | 12 AM | **multi.** — 19
Opportun | 12 AM | 14e — 15
Orangerie | 12 AM | 4e — 22
Osteria Ascolani | 2 AM | 18e —
Paradis du Fruit | 1 AM | **multi.** — 14
Paul Chêne | 12 AM | 16e — 20
Pershing | 12 AM | 8e — 17
Petit Bofinger | varies | 4e — 18

Petit Marché | 12 AM | 3e — 22
Petit Prince de Paris | 12 AM | 5e —
Petit Riche | 12:15 AM | 9e — 18
Petit Zinc | 12 AM | 6e — 18
Pied de Chameau | 1 AM | 3e —
Pied de Cochon | 24 hrs. | 1er — 18
Pierre au Palais Royal | 12 AM | 1er — 17
Polidor | 12:30 AM | 6e — 17
Pomponette | 12 AM | 18e — 17
Poule au Pot | 5 AM | 1er — 23
Procope | 1 AM | 6e — 16
Publicis Drugstore | 2 AM | 8e — 11
404 | 12 AM | 3e — 22
Renoma Café | varies | 8e —
Rotonde | 1 AM | 6e — 15
Sébillon | 12 AM | **Neuilly** — 15
Sens | 11:30 PM | 8e —
Stella | 1 AM | 16e — 20
Studio | 12:30 AM | 4e —
Suffren | 12 AM | 15e — 14
Tav. de Maître Kanter | 24 hrs. | 1er — 16
Terminus Nord | 1 AM | 10e — 17
Tong Yen | 12:15 AM | 8e — 15
Tricotin | 12 AM | 13e —
Vagenende | 1 AM | 6e — 15
Vaudeville | 1 AM | 2e — 18
Verre Bouteille | varies | 17e — 13
Viaduc Café | 3 AM | 12e —
Village d'Ung | 12 AM | 8e —
Villa Spicy | 12 AM | 8e — 13
Vinea Café | 12 AM | 12e —
Wepler | 1 AM | 18e — 14
Zéphyr | 12 AM | 20e —
Zeyer | 12:30 AM | 14e — 16
Zingot | 12 AM | 10e —
Zo | 12 AM | 8e —

MEET FOR A DRINK

Alcazar | 6e — 19
Z Angelina | 1er — 20
Autobus Imperial | 1er —
Bar des Théâtres | 8e — 15
Baron Rouge | 12e —
Bistrot à Vins Mélac | 11e — 14
Bistrot du Peintre | 11e — 18
Bistrot Paul Bert | 11e — 23

Black Calavados | 8ᵉ	—	Gavroche | 2ᵉ	17
Bons Crus | 1ᵉʳ	—	Grande Armée | 16ᵉ	15
Bourguignon du Marais | 4ᵉ	23	Indiana Café | multi.	7
Z Brass. Balzar | 5ᵉ	19	Juvéniles | 1ᵉʳ	16
Breakfast in America | 5ᵉ	15	Z Ladurée | multi.	23
Z Buddha Bar | 8ᵉ	16	Legrand Filles et Fils | 2ᵉ	—
Café Beaubourg | 4ᵉ	16	Lina's | multi.	16
Café Burq | 18ᵉ	—	Loir dans/Théière | 4ᵉ	16
Café Charbon | 11ᵉ	15	Ma Bourgogne | 4ᵉ	18
Z Café de Flore | 6ᵉ	15	Mauzac | 5ᵉ	—
Café de la Musique | 19ᵉ	15	NEW Mini Palais | 8ᵉ	—
Café de l'Esplanade | 7ᵉ	16	Murano | 3ᵉ	16
Café de l'Industrie | 11ᵉ	12	Musichall | 8ᵉ	15
Café du Passage | 11ᵉ	—	Nemrod | 6ᵉ	16
Café la Jatte | Neuilly	14	No Stress Café | 9ᵉ	—
Café Lenôtre | 8ᵉ	18	NEW Nouvelle Athenes | 9ᵉ	—
Z Café Les Deux Magots | 6ᵉ	16	Oenothèque | 9ᵉ	—
Z Café Marly | 1ᵉʳ	16	Publicis Drugstore | 8ᵉ	11
Café Ruc | 1ᵉʳ	15	NEW Racines | 2ᵉ	—
Carr's | 1ᵉʳ	—	Rest. du Palais Royal | 1ᵉʳ	19
Cave de l'Os à Moëlle | 15ᵉ	22	River Café | Issy-les-Moul.	14
Cloche des Halles | 1ᵉʳ	—	Rubis | 1ᵉʳ	15
Closerie des Lilas | 6ᵉ	18	NEW Salon du Panthéon | 5ᵉ	—
Clown Bar | 11ᵉ	17	Sauvignon | 7ᵉ	14
Comptoir | 1ᵉʳ	21	Suffren | 15ᵉ	14
Cosi | 6ᵉ	19	NEW SYDR | 8ᵉ	—
Coude Fou | 4ᵉ	19	Viaduc Café | 12ᵉ	—
Z Coupole | 14ᵉ	19	Vinea Café | 12ᵉ	—
Curieux Spaghetti Bar | 4ᵉ	—	Z Vin sur Vin | 7ᵉ	26
Dalloyau | multi.	23	Wepler | 18ᵉ	14
Dame Tartine | 4ᵉ	14	Z Willi's Wine Bar | 1ᵉʳ	20
Deux Abeilles | 7ᵉ	21	Zébra Square | 16ᵉ	10
Dix Vins | 15ᵉ	—	Zo | 8ᵉ	—
Dôme | 14ᵉ	22		

NO AIR-CONDITIONING

NEW Eclaireur | 8ᵉ	—	Abadache | 17ᵉ	—
Ecluse | multi.	16	Accolade | 17ᵉ	—
Enoteca | 4ᵉ	20	A et M | 16ᵉ	21
Etoile | 16ᵉ	24	NEW Afaria | 15ᵉ	—
Ferme | 1ᵉʳ	—	Aimant du Sud | 13ᵉ	—
NEW Fines Gueules | 1ᵉʳ	—	NEW Alfred | 1ᵉʳ	—
First | 1ᵉʳ	18	Alivi | 4ᵉ	16
Z Fish La Boissonnerie | 6ᵉ	22	Alsaco | 9ᵉ	—
Fontaines | 5ᵉ	17	Z Ami Louis | 3ᵉ	25
Fouquet's | 8ᵉ	18	Ami Pierre | 11ᵉ	17
Fous d'en Face | 4ᵉ	—	Amuse Bouche | 14ᵉ	17
Fumoir | 1ᵉʳ	17	Anahuacalli | 5ᵉ	21
NEW Garance | 10ᵉ	—		

Name	Rating	Name	Rating
Z Angelina	1er	20	Chez Françoise	7e	17
AOC	5e	18	Chez Georges-Maillot	17e	18
Apollo	14e	-	Chez Géraud	16e	20
A Priori Thé	2e	16	Chez Grisette	18e	-
Assiette	14e	-	Chez Julien	4e	19
Atelier Berger	1er	21	Chez Léon	17e	13
Aub. du Champ/Mars	7e	17	Chez Marcel	6e	-
Aub. Nicolas Flamel	3e	23	Chez Marianne	4e	18
Autour du Mont	15e	-	Chez Michel	10e	24
Autour du Saumon	multi.	17	Chez Nénesse	3e	-
Baratin	20e	16	Chez Omar	3e	21
Bascou	3e	20	Chez Paul	11e	21
Biche au Bois	12e	20	Chez Paul	13e	16
BIOArt	13e	-	Chez Pauline	1er	20
Bistro d'Hubert	15e	22	Chez Prune	10e	18
Bistrot d'à Côté	multi.	21	Chez Ramona	20e	-
Bistrot d'André	15e	-	Chez René	5e	21
Z Bistrot de l'Oulette	4e	26	NEW Christophe	5e	-
Bistrot de l'Université	7e	18	Cibus	1er	-
Bistrot de Marius	8e	21	Cloche des Halles	1er	-
Bistrot de Paris	7e	16	Closerie des Lilas	6e	18
Bistrot des Dames	17e	14	Clou	17e	19
Bistrot d'Henri	6e	20	Clown Bar	11e	17
Bistrot Vivienne	2e	18	Coco de Mer	5e	-
Bon Saint Pourçain	6e	18	Coin/Gourmets	5e	22
Bouchons Clerc/P'tit	8e	20	Cordonnerie	1er	-
Brass. de l'Ile St. Louis	4e	17	Cosi	6e	-
Breakfast in America	5e	15	Coupe Gorge	4e	19
NEW Breizh Café	3e	-	NEW Crémerie	6e	-
Ca d'Oro	1er	18	NEW Cristal de Sel	15e	-
Café Beaubourg	4e	16	Crus de Bourgogne	2e	17
Café Burq	18e	-	Dalva	2e	-
Café Charbon	11e	15	Dame Tartine	4e	14
Café de Mars	7e	17	Dauphin	1er	20
Café Le Petit Pont	5e	14	Dell Orto	9e	-
Cagouille	14e	25	Deux Abeilles	7e	21
Cailloux	13e	-	2 Pieces Cuisine	18e	-
Caméléon	6e	20	Devèz	8e	16
Cap Seguin	Boulogne	-	Dix Vins	15e	-
Carr's	1er	-	Djakarta	1er	20
Caves Pétrissans	17e	19	Dôme du Marais	4e	22
Cerisaie	14e	21	Duc de Richelieu	12e	-
Chalet (Le)	Neuilly	-	Durand Dupont	Neuilly	-
Chalet des Iles	16e	14	Ebouillanté	4e	-
Chantairelle	5e	-	Ecluse	8e	16
Chardenoux	11e	19	Entoto	13e	-
NEW Chéri Bibi	18e	-	Entracte	18e	-

SPECIAL FEATURES

Epi d'Or | 1er	16	Petit Bofinger | 17e	18
🄩 Epi Dupin | 6e	24	Petit Châtelet | 5e	-
NEW Epigramme | 6e	-	Petite Sirène/Copen. | 9e	-
NEW Fines Gueules | 1er	-	NEW Petites Sorcières | 14e	-
Fins Gourmets | 7e	19	Petit Lutétia | 6e	19
Flandrin | 16e	15	Petit Marché | 3e	22
Flore en l'Ile | 4e	18	Petit Marguery | 13e	21
Fouquet's | 8e	18	Petit Niçois | 7e	16
NEW Garance | 10e	-	Petit Pascal | 13e	-
Gauloise | 15e	15	Petit Poucet | Levallois	-
Gavroche | 2e	17	Pétrelle | 9e	-
Georgette | 9e	22	Pharamond | 1er	19
Gorille Blanc | 7e	21	Pitchi Poï | 4e	-
Gourmets des Ternes | 8e	19	Pomponette | 18e	17
Graindorge | 17e	22	🄩 Pré Catelan | 16e	27
NEW Grand Pan | 15e	-	Pré Salé | 1er	-
Grange Batelière | 9e	-	Procope | 6e	16
Gourmand | Neuilly	-	P'tit Troquet | 7e	22
Hier & Aujourd'hui | 17e	-	Pure Café | 11e	-
Huîtrerie Régis | 6e	22	Quinzième | 15e	-
Il Barone | 14e	21	NEW Racines | 2e	-
Il Etait une Oie | 17e	-	Réconfort | 3e	-
Jardins de Bagatelle | 16e	17	Relais de Venise | 17e	24
Jean | 9e	19	Rendez-vous/Chauff. | 18e	-
Khun Akorn | 11e	-	Repaire de Cartouche | 11e	16
Louchebem | 1er	15	Rest. du Marché | 15e	-
🄩 Lyonnais | 2e	21	Rest. du Palais Royal | 1er	19
Ma Bourgogne | 4e	18	Rest. GR5 | 16e	24
Marée Denfert/Passy | multi.	-	Rest. Paul | 1er	20
Marius | 16e	18	Réveil du 10e (Le) | 10e	-
Martel | 10e	-	River Café | Issy-les-Moul.	14
Mascotte | 18e	-	Robert et Louise | 3e	21
Maupertu | 7e	21	Roi du Pot-au-Feu | 9e	-
NEW Mini Palais | 8e	-	Romantica | Clichy	23
Moissonnier | 5e	19	Rose de France | 1er	-
🄩 Mon Vieil Ami | 4e	24	Rughetta | 18e	-
Moulin à Vent | 5e	19	Sale e Pepe | 18e	-
Mousson | 1er	-	Sardegna a Tavola | 12e	21
No Stress Café | 9e	-	Sauvignon | 7e	14
🄩 Os à Moëlle | 15e	25	Scheffer | 16e	18
Osteria Ascolani | 18e	-	Sept Quinze | 15e	21
Ourcine | 13e	24	Sinago | 9e	-
Pasco | 7e	22	Soleil | St-Ouen	-
🄩 Pavillon/Gr. Cascade | 16e	25	Sot l'y Laisse | 11e	-
Pavillon Montsouris | 14e	17	Square | 18e	-
Pères et Filles | 6e	16	Square Trousseau | 12e	19
Perraudin | 5e	13	Strapontins | 10e	-

Tastevin | **Maisons-Laff.**	24
Tav. Henri IV | **1er**	16
Temps au Temps | **11e**	25
Temps des Cerises | **13e**	-
Terrasse Mirabeau | **16e**	-
Terroir | **13e**	-
Timbre | **6e**	24
Tokyo Eat | **16e**	14
Tonnelle Saintongeaise | **Neuilly**	-
Tournesol | **16e**	18
Z Train Bleu | **12e**	19
Triporteur | **15e**	-
Troquet | **15e**	24
Truc Café | **18e**	-
Truffe Noire | **Neuilly**	-
Tsukizi | **6e**	-
Uitr | **15e**	-
Vaudeville | **2e**	18
Verre Volé | **10e**	16
Vieille Fontaine | **Maisons-Laff.**	-
Vieux Chêne | **11e**	-
Vin et Marée | **16e**	18
Wadja | **6e**	20
Waknine | **16e**	-
Z Willi's Wine Bar | **1er**	20
NEW Winch | **18e**	-
Zéphyr | **20e**	-
Zinc-Zinc | **Neuilly**	16
Zygomates | **12e**	20

NOTEWORTHY NEWCOMERS

Afaria | **15e**	-
Agassin | **7e**	-
Alfred | **1er**	-
Breizh Café | **3e**	-
Café Pleyel | **8e**	-
Chéri Bibi | **18e**	-
Christophe | **5e**	-
Cocottes | **7e**	21
Crémerie | **6e**	-
Cristal de Sel | **15e**	-
Cuisine (11e) | **11e**	-
Dali | **1er**	-
Eclaireur | **8e**	-
Epigramme | **6e**	-
Fines Gueules | **1er**	-
Garance | **10e**	-

Grand Pan | **15e**	-
Il Vino | **7e**	-
Karl et Erich | **17e**	-
Lup | **6e**	-
Marée Denfert/Passy | **14e**	-
M Comme Martine | **17e**	-
Mini Palais | **8e**	-
Mood | **8e**	-
Nouvelle Athenes | **9e**	-
Petites Sorcières | **14e**	-
P'tit Casier | **15e**	-
Racines | **2e**	-
Salon du Panthéon | **5e**	-
Saut du Loup | **1er**	14
SYDR | **8e**	-
Toustem | **5e**	-
Urbane | **10e**	-
Winch | **18e**	-

OPEN SUNDAY

Alcazar | **6e**	19
Al Dar | **16e**	21
Al Diwan | **8e**	21
Alivi | **4e**	16
Allobroges | **20e**	22
Alsace | **8e**	18
Ambassade/Auvergne | **3e**	20
Z Ambassadeurs | **8e**	28
Z Ami Louis | **3e**	25
Anahï | **3e**	19
Anahuacalli | **5e**	21
Apollo | **14e**	-
A Priori Thé | **2e**	16
Z Ardoise | **1er**	24
Z As du Fallafel | **4e**	24
Asian | **8e**	16
Assiette | **14e**	-
Astier | **11e**	21
Z Atelier Joël Robuchon | **7e**	28
Atelier Maître Albert | **5e**	21
Atlas | **5e**	20
Aub. Aveyronnaise | **12e**	-
Aub. de Reine Blanche | **4e**	19
Aub. du Clou | **9e**	16
Avenue | **8e**	18
Azabu | **6e**	24
Ballon des Ternes | **17e**	15

SPECIAL FEATURES

Ballon et Coquillages	17e	-	Café Beaubourg	4e	16
Bamboche	7e	19	Café Charbon	11e	15
Banyan	15e	19	Café de la Musique	19e	15
Bar à Huîtres	**multi.**	17	Café de la Paix	9e	19
Bar des Théâtres	8e	15	Café de l'Industrie	11e	12
Barlotti	1er	15	Café de Mars	7e	17
Baron Rouge	12e	-	Café du Commerce	15e	16
Barrio Latino	12e	12	Café du Passage	11e	-
Barroco	6e	-	Café Etienne Marcel	2e	18
Bar Vendôme	1er	23	Café Faubourg	8e	22
Basilic	7e	15	Café la Jatte	**Neuilly**	14
Beaujolais d'Auteuil	16e	17	Café Lenôtre	8e	18
Bel Canto	4e	13	Café Le Petit Pont	5e	14
Benkay	15e	24	Ⓩ Café Les Deux Magots	6e	16
Ⓩ Benoît	4e	24	Café Ruc	1er	15
Berkeley	8e	14	Café Terminus	8e	-
Bis du Severo	14e	-	Cagouille	14e	25
Bistro 121	15e	-	Camille	3e	16
Bistro de Breteuil	7e	16	Cantine de Quentin	10e	-
Bistro du 17ème	17e	18	Carmine	7e	-
Bistro St. Ferdinand	17e	14	Carpaccio	8e	-
Bistrot de Marius	8e	21	Carr's	1er	-
Bistrot des Vignes	16e	17	Casa Alcalde	15e	-
Bistrot d'Henri	6e	20	Casa Bini	6e	21
Bistrot du Cap	15e	-	Casa Tina	16e	-
Bistrot du Dôme	**multi.**	21	Caveau du Palais	1er	19
Bistrot du Peintre	11e	18	Cave de l'Os à Moëlle	15e	22
Blue Elephant	11e	20	Cazaudehore	**St-Germain-Laye**	22
Boeuf Couronné	19e	16	Céladon	2e	21
Ⓩ Bofinger	4e	20	Chai 33	12e	14
Bon	16e	15	Chalet (Le)	**Neuilly**	-
Boucherie Roulière	6e	-	Chalet des Iles	16e	14
Bound	8e	-	Chardenoux	11e	19
Ⓩ Brass. Balzar	5e	19	Charlot Roi des Coq.	9e	15
Brass. de l'Ile St. Louis	4e	17	Charpentiers	6e	18
Brass. du Louvre	1er	16	Chartier	9e	13
Brass. Flo	10e	18	Cherche Midi	6e	19
Brass. Julien	10e	19	**NEW** Chéri Bibi	18e	-
Brass. La Lorraine	8e	17	Chez André	8e	20
Brass. L'Européen	12e	-	Chez Clément	**multi.**	15
Brass. Printemps	9e	11	Chez Francis	8e	17
Breakfast in America	**multi.**	15	Chez Françoise	7e	17
NEW Breizh Café	3e	-	Chez Gégène	**Joinville**	-
Ⓩ Bristol	8e	27	Chez Georges-Maillot	17e	18
Ⓩ Buddha Bar	8e	16	Chez Janou	3e	23
Buffalo Grill	**multi.**	10	Chez Jenny	3e	19
Ca d'Oro	1er	18	Chez Julien	4e	19

Chez Livio	Neuilly	13	
Chez Ly	17e	-	
Chez Maître Paul	6e	21	
Chez Marianne	4e	18	
Chez Omar	3e	21	
Chez Papa	multi.	17	
Chez Paul	11e	21	
Chez Paul	13e	16	
Chez Prune	10e	18	
Chez Ramona	20e	-	
Chien qui Fume	1er	18	
Christine	6e	23	
Z Cinq (Le)	8e	28	
Closerie des Lilas	6e	18	
Coin/Gourmets	5e	22	
Z Comptoir du Relais	6e	26	
Congrès Maillot	17e	18	
Cosi	6e	19	
Costes	1er	18	
Coude Fou	4e	19	
Coupe-Chou	5e	23	
Coupe Gorge	4e	-	
Z Coupole	14e	19	
Cuisine (7e)	7e	25	
Curieux Spaghetti Bar	4e	-	
NEW Dali	1er	-	
Dalloyau	multi.	23	
Dalva	2e	-	
Dame Tartine	4e	14	
Da Rosa	6e	19	
Davé	1er	18	
Délices d'Aphrodite	5e	18	
Dessirier	17e	20	
Devèz	8e	16	
Dôme	14e	22	
Drouant	2e	22	
Durand Dupont	Neuilly	-	
Ebouillanté	4e	-	
Ecluse	multi.	16	
Editeurs	6e	14	
Elysées Hong Kong	16e	-	
Enoteca	4e	20	
Entracte	18e	-	
Escale du Liban	4e	-	
Escargot Montorgueil	1er	21	
Z Espadon (L')	1er	26	
Espadon Bleu	6e	21	

Etoile Marocaine	8e	-	
Fables de La Fontaine	7e	24	
Fakhr el Dine	16e	24	
Fellini	1er	21	
Ferme	1er	-	
Findi	8e	16	
NEW Fines Gueules	1er	-	
Finzi	8e	13	
First	1er	18	
Z Fish La Boissonnerie	6e	22	
Flandrin	16e	15	
Flora Danica	8e	19	
Flore en l'Ile	4e	18	
Fogón	6e	21	
Z Fontaine de Mars	7e	21	
Fontaines	5e	17	
Fontanarosa	15e	-	
Foujita	1er	-	
Fous d'en Face	4e	-	
Fumoir	1er	17	
NEW Garance	10e	-	
Gare	16e	14	
Garnier	8e	22	
Z Georges	4e	18	
Giulio Rebellato	16e	20	
Graindorge	17e	22	
Grand Café	9e	13	
Grande Armée	16e	15	
Grand Louvre	1er	18	
Grille St-Germain	6e	17	
Gourmand	Neuilly	-	
Guirlande de Julie	3e	15	
Higuma	1er	15	
Hippopotamus	multi.	11	
Hôtel Amour	9e	8	
Huîtrerie Régis	6e	22	
Huîtrier	17e	20	
Ile	Issy-les-Moul.	18	
Ilot Vache	4e	18	
NEW Il Vino	7e	-	
Indiana Café	multi.	7	
Jardin des Cygnes	8e	22	
Jardins de Bagatelle	16e	17	
Jarrasse	Neuilly	-	
J'Go	6e	14	
Joe Allen	1er	13	
Z Jules Verne	7e	-	

SPECIAL FEATURES

Kai | 1er	–	Nouveau Village | 13e	18
Khun Akorn | 11e	–	Obélisque | 8e	23
Kim Anh | 15e	–	Z Ombres (Les) | 7e	18
Kong | 1er	14	Orangerie | 4e	22
Z Ladurée | multi.	23	Osteria Ascolani | 18e	–
Languedoc | 5e	–	Ozu | 16e	23
Lao Siam | 19e	15	Pamphlet | 3e	23
Lao Tseu | 7e	–	Paradis du Fruit | multi.	14
Lei | 7e	21	Paradis Thai | 13e	15
Léon/Bruxelles | multi.	16	Parc aux Cerfs | 6e	21
Lina's | 16e	16	Pasco | 7e	22
Liza | 2e	24	Passy Mandarin | multi.	20
Loir dans/Théière | 4e	16	Z Pavillon/Gr. Cascade | 16e	25
Lô Sushi | 8e	15	Pavillon Montsouris | 14e	17
Louis Vin | 5e	19	Pères et Filles | 6e	16
Ma Bourgogne | 4e	18	Perraudin | 5e	13
Maharajah | 5e	17	Pershing | 8e	17
Main d'Or | 11e	–	Petit Bofinger | multi.	18
Maison Blanche | 8e	20	Petit Châtelet | 5e	–
Maison du Caviar | 8e	22	Petite Chaise | 7e	19
Marée Denfert/Passy | multi.	–	Petite Cour | 6e	21
Mariage Frères | multi.	21	NEW Petites Sorcières | 14e	–
Marius et Janette | 8e	25	Petit Lutétia | 6e	19
Market | 8e	22	Petit Marché | 3e	22
Marty | 5e	16	Petit Niçois | 7e	16
Mascotte | 18e	–	Petit Pontoise | 5e	22
Matsuri | multi.	14	Petit Poucet | Levallois	–
Mauzac | 5e	–	Petit Zinc | 6e	18
Meating | 17e	17	Pétrus | 17e	21
Méditerranée | 6e	21	Pied de Cochon | 1er	18
NEW Mini Palais | 8e	–	Pinxo | 1er	21
Mirama | 5e	20	Pitchi Poï | 4e	–
Monsieur Lapin | 14e	18	Pizzeria d'Auteuil | 16e	–
Montalembert | 7e	19	Polichinelle Cafe | 11e	–
Mont Liban | 17e	–	Polidor | 6e	17
Z Mon Vieil Ami | 4e	24	Procope | 6e	16
NEW Mood | 8e	–	Publicis Drugstore | 8e	11
Moulin de la Galette | 18e	15	Pure Café | 11e	–
Murano | 3e	16	Pur'Grill | 2e	19
Murat | 16e	13	Quai | 7e	–
Muscade | 1er	–	Quai Ouest | St-Cloud	13
New Jawad | 7e	18	404 | 3e	22
New Nioullaville | 11e	16	Ragueneau | 1er	–
Noces de Jeannette | 2e	–	Réconfort | 3e	–
Nos Ancêtres/Gaulois | 4e	13	Refectoire | 11e	–
No Stress Café | 9e	–	Z Relais/l'Entrecôte | multi.	22
Noura | multi.	19	Relais de Venise | 17e	24

Relais Plaza | 8ᵉ	23
Renoma Café | 8ᵉ	-
Rest. du Musée d'Orsay | 7ᵉ	17
Rest. Paul | 1ᵉʳ	20
Reuan Thai | 11ᵉ	-
River Café | Issy-les-Moul.	14
Robert et Louise | 3ᵉ	21
Rose Bakery | 9ᵉ	17
Rose de France | 1ᵉʳ	-
Rôtiss. du Beaujolais | 5ᵉ	23
Rotonde | 6ᵉ	15
Rouge St-Honoré | 1ᵉʳ	13
Royal Madeleine | 8ᵉ	19
Samiin | 7ᵉ	-
San | 3ᵉ	-
NEW Saut du Loup | 1ᵉʳ	14
Sauvignon | 7ᵉ	14
Scoop | 1ᵉʳ	17
Sébillon | Neuilly	15
Z Senderens | 8ᵉ	26
7ème Sud | 16ᵉ	15
Soleil | St-Ouen	-
Stella | 16ᵉ	20
Strapontins | 10ᵉ	-
Studio | 4ᵉ	-
Suffren | 15ᵉ	14
Table d'Anvers | 9ᵉ	17
Z Table de Joël Robuchon | 16ᵉ	26
Table du Lancaster | 8ᵉ	23
Tastevin | Maisons-Laff.	24
Tav. de Maître Kanter | 1ᵉʳ	16
Tav. du Sgt. Recruteur | 4ᵉ	16
Terminus Nord | 10ᵉ	17
Thiou/Petit Thiou | 8ᵉ	21
Thoumieux | 7ᵉ	19
Toi | 8ᵉ	-
Tokyo Eat | 16ᵉ	14
Tong Yen | 8ᵉ	15
Z Tour d'Argent | 5ᵉ	25
Tournesol | 16ᵉ	18
Tricotin | 13ᵉ	-
Truc Café | 18ᵉ	-
Trumilou | 4ᵉ	19
Tsé-Yang | 16ᵉ	18
Uitr | 15ᵉ	-
NEW Urbane | 10ᵉ	-
Vagenende | 6ᵉ	15

Vaudeville | 2ᵉ	18
Verre Bouteille | 17ᵉ	13
Verre Volé | 10ᵉ	16
Viaduc Café | 12ᵉ	-
Vieille Fontaine | Maisons-Laff.	-
Vieux Bistro | 4ᵉ	21
Village d'Ung | 8ᵉ	-
Villa Spicy | 8ᵉ	13
Vin des Pyrenees | 4ᵉ	16
Vinea Café | 12ᵉ	-
Vin et Marée | multi.	18
Wepler | 18ᵉ	14
NEW Winch | 18ᵉ	-
Wok Cooking | 11ᵉ	-
Yugaraj | 6ᵉ	23
Zébra Square | 16ᵉ	10
Zéphyr | 20ᵉ	-
Zeyer | 14ᵉ	16

OUTDOOR DINING

(G=garden; P=patio; S=sidewalk; T=terrace)

Absinthe | S, T | 1ᵉʳ	20
A et M | S | 16ᵉ	21
Aimant du Sud | S, T | 13ᵉ	-
Alain Bourgade | G | 16ᵉ	-
Z Alain Ducasse | P | 8ᵉ	28
Al Dar | S, T | multi.	21
Alivi | T | 4ᵉ	16
Alsace | S | 8ᵉ	18
Amici Miei | S | 11ᵉ	19
Ampère | S | 17ᵉ	-
AOC | T | 5ᵉ	18
A Priori Thé | P | 2ᵉ	16
Asian | S | 8ᵉ	16
Astier | S | 11ᵉ	21
Atlas | S | 5ᵉ	20
Aub. Aveyronnaise | P, S, T | 12ᵉ	-
Aub. Dab | S | 16ᵉ	16
Aub. du Clou | S, T | 9ᵉ	16
Aub. Etchégorry | S | 13ᵉ	-
Avenue | T | 8ᵉ	18
Ballon des Ternes | S, T | 17ᵉ	15
Barlotti | P, S | 1ᵉʳ	15
Bartolo | S, T | 6ᵉ	17
Bar Vendôme | P | 1ᵉʳ	23
Basilic | G, T | 7ᵉ	15
Beaujolais d'Auteuil | S | 16ᵉ	17

SPECIAL FEATURES

BE Boulangépicier | S | 8ᵉ	19
Berkeley | T | 8ᵉ	14
BIOArt | T | 13ᵉ	-
Bistro de Breteuil | T | 7ᵉ	16
Bistro d'Hubert | T | 15ᵉ	22
Bistro du 17ème | S | 17ᵉ	18
Bistro Melrose | S | 17ᵉ	-
Bistrot à Vins Mélac | S | 11ᵉ	14
Bistrot d'à Côté | S, T | multi.	21
Bistrot de Marius | S | 8ᵉ	21
Bistrot des Dames | G | 17ᵉ	14
Bistrot du Cap | T | 15ᵉ	-
Bistrot du Peintre | T | 11ᵉ	18
Bistrot Niel | S, T | 17ᵉ	-
Bistrot Vivienne | T | 2ᵉ	18
Bocconi | S | 8ᵉ	20
⚡ Bon Accueil | S | 7ᵉ	24
Bon Saint Pourçain | S | 6ᵉ	18
Bouchons Clerc/P'tit | S | 8ᵉ	20
Bourguignon du Marais | T | 4ᵉ	23
Brass. de l'Ile St. Louis | T | 4ᵉ	17
Brass. du Louvre | T | 1ᵉʳ	16
⚡ Bristol | G | 8ᵉ	27
Buisson Ardent | S | 5ᵉ	19
Café Beaubourg | T | 4ᵉ	16
Café Charbon | S | 11ᵉ	15
⚡ Café de Flore | S, T | 6ᵉ	15
Café de la Musique | T | 19ᵉ	15
Café de la Paix | S | 9ᵉ	19
Café de l'Esplanade | S | 7ᵉ	16
Café de l'Industrie | S | 11ᵉ	12
Café de Mars | S | 7ᵉ	17
Café du Passage | S | 11ᵉ	-
Café Etienne Marcel | S | 2ᵉ	18
Café Fusion | S | 13ᵉ	-
Café Guitry | T | 9ᵉ	-
Café la Jatte | G, T | Neuilly	14
Café Lenôtre | G, P | 8ᵉ	18
Café Le Petit Pont | T | 5ᵉ	14
⚡ Café Les Deux Magots | G, T | 6ᵉ	16
⚡ Café Marly | T | 1ᵉʳ	16
Café Ruc | S | 1ᵉʳ	15
Cagouille | T | 14ᵉ	25
Cailloux | S | 13ᵉ	-
Camille | S | 3ᵉ	16
Cap Seguin | T | Boulogne	-

Cap Vernet | T | 8ᵉ	17
Carpaccio | T | 8ᵉ	-
Casa Alcalde | S | 15ᵉ	-
Casa Tina | S | 16ᵉ	-
Caves Pétrissans | T | 17ᵉ	19
Cazaudehore | G, T | St-Germain-Laye	22
Chai 33 | T | 12ᵉ	14
Chalet des Iles | G, T | 16ᵉ	14
Chantairelle | G | 5ᵉ	-
Charpentiers | S | 6ᵉ	18
Cherche Midi | S | 6ᵉ	19
Chez André | S | 8ᵉ	20
Chez Francis | S | 8ᵉ	17
Chez Gégène | S, T | Joinville	-
Chez Gérard | S | Neuilly	19
Chez Janou | T | 3ᵉ	23
Chez Léna et Mimile | T | 5ᵉ	15
Chez Les Anges | S | 7ᵉ	23
Chez Livio | T | Neuilly	13
Chez Ly | S | 17ᵉ	-
Chez Marcel | S | 6ᵉ	-
Chez Marianne | S, T | 4ᵉ	18
Chez Michel | S | 10ᵉ	24
Chez Omar | T | 3ᵉ	21
Chez Papa | S | multi.	17
Chez Paul | S | 11ᵉ	21
Chez Paul | S | 13ᵉ	16
Chez Prune | S | 10ᵉ	18
Chez Ramulaud | S | 11ᵉ	16
Chez René | T | 5ᵉ	21
Chez Savy | S | 8ᵉ	18
Chez Vong | T | 1ᵉʳ	21
Chien qui Fume | S, T | 1ᵉʳ	18
Cigale Récamier | T | 7ᵉ	21
⚡ Cinq (Le) | T | 8ᵉ	28
Cloche des Halles | S, T | 1ᵉʳ	-
Clos des Gourmets | T | 7ᵉ	25
Closerie des Lilas | T | 6ᵉ	18
Clown Bar | S | 11ᵉ	17
Comptoir | S | 1ᵉʳ	21
Copenhague | T | 8ᵉ	18
Cordonnerie | S | 1ᵉʳ	-
Costes | G, P | 1ᵉʳ	18
Coupe-Chou | T | 5ᵉ	23
Crus de Bourgogne | S | 2ᵉ	17
Dalloyau | S, T | multi.	23

Name	Score
Dame Tartine | T | 4^e	14
Da Mimmo | S | 10^e	-
Da Rosa | T | 6^e	19
Daru | S | 8^e	-
Dauphin | S | 1er	20
Délices d'Aphrodite | S | 5^e	18
Deux Abeilles | S | 7^e	21
Devèz | S | 8^e	16
Diapason | T | 18^e	-
Duc de Richelieu | T | 12^e	-
Durand Dupont | G | **Neuilly**	-
Ebauchoir | S | 12^e	-
Editeurs | S | 6^e	14
El Mansour | S | 8^e	17
Entracte | T | 18^e	-
Z Epi Dupin | S | 6^e	24
Z Espadon (L') | G, T | 1er	26
Eugène | S | 8^e	-
Fables de La Fontaine | T | 7^e	24
Findi | S | 8^e	16
Fins Gourmets | S | 7^e	19
Flandrin | S, T | 16^e	15
Flora Danica | G, T | 8^e	19
Flore en l'Ile | S, T | 4^e	18
Florimond | S | 7^e	24
Z Fontaine de Mars | S, T | 7^e	21
Fontaine Gaillon | T | 2^e	22
Fontaines | S, T | 5^e	17
Fontanarosa | T | 15^e	-
Fouquet's | S, T | 8^e	18
Fous d'en Face | S | 4^e	-
Fumoir | S | 1er	17
Gallopin | S | 2^e	16
Gare | G, T | 16^e	14
Gauloise | S, T | 15^e	15
Z Georges | T | 4^e	18
Gitane | S | 15^e	-
Gorille Blanc | S | 7^e	21
Gourmets des Ternes | S | 8^e	19
Grand Café | S | 9^e	13
Grande Armée | S | 16^e	15
Grille St-Germain | S | 6^e	17
Gourmand | T | **Neuilly**	-
Guirlande de Julie | S, T | 3^e	15
Hangar | S | 3^e	18
Hippopotamus | T | 6^e	11
Il Cortile | P | 1er	23
Ile | G, T | **Issy-les-Moul.**	18
Issé | S | 1er	23
Jardin des Cygnes | T | 8^e	22
Jardins de Bagatelle | G, T | 16^e	17
Jarrasse | S, T | **Neuilly**	-
Je Thé . . . Me | S, T | 15^e	-
Joe Allen | S, T | 1er	13
Joséphine/Dumonet | S | 6^e	23
Kaïten | S, T | 8^e	-
Khun Akorn | T | 11^e	-
Kim Anh | T | 15^e	-
Kiosque | S, T | 16^e	15
Z Laurent | G, T | 8^e	24
Legrand Filles et Fils | P | 2^e	-
Lei | S | 7^e	21
Lescure | S, T | 1er	17
Ma Bourgogne | S, T | 4^e	18
Main d'Or | S | 11^e	-
Maison Courtine | S | 14^e	24
Maison de l'Amér. Latine | G | 7^e	18
Marée de Versailles | T | **Versailles**	19
Marius | S, T | 16^e	18
Marius et Janette | S, T | 8^e	25
Market | S | 8^e	22
Marlotte | S, T | 6^e	16
Martel | S, T | 10^e	-
Marty | S, T | 5^e	16
Mathusalem | S, T | 16^e	-
Maupertu | S, T | 7^e	21
Mauzac | S | 5^e	-
Mavrommatis | S, T | 5^e	19
Méditerranée | S, T | 6^e	21
Montalembert | S, T | 7^e	19
Moulin à Vent | S, T | 5^e	19
Moulin de la Galette | P | 18^e	15
Murat | S | 16^e	13
Muscade | G | 1er	-
Natacha | S | 14^e	-
Nemrod | S, T | 6^e	16
New Nioullaville | S | 11^e	16
No Stress Café | S, T | 9^e	-
Noura | G | 6^e	19
Opportun | S | 14^e	15
Oulette | S, T | 12^e	19
Papilles | S, T | 5^e	23
Parc aux Cerfs | P | 6^e	21

SPECIAL FEATURES

Paris Seize | S | 16e	18
Pasco | T | 7e	22
☑ Pavillon/Gr. Cascade | T | 16e	25
Pavillon Montsouris | G, T | 14e	17
Père Claude | S | 15e	17
Pères et Filles | S, T | 6e	16
Perraudin | P | 5e	13
Pershing | P | 8e	17
Petite Chaise | S | 7e	19
Petite Cour | T | 6e	21
Petit Marché | S | 3e	22
Petit Marguery | T | 13e	21
Petit Pontoise | S | 5e	22
Petit Poucet | G, P, T | Levallois	-
Petit Victor Hugo | S, T | 16e	19
Pharamond | S, T | 1er	19
Pichet de Paris | 8e	16
Pitchi Poï | T | 4e	-
Point Bar | S, T | 1er	22
Polichinelle Cafe | S | 11e	-
Pomze | S, T | 8e	18
☑ Pré Catelan | G, T | 16e	27
Publicis Drugstore | S, T | 8e	11
Pure Café | S, T | 11e	-
Pur'Grill | T | 2e	19
Quai Ouest | T | St-Cloud	13
Rech | T | 17e	-
☑ Relais/l'Entrecôte | S, T | multi.	22
Relais de Venise | S, T | 17e	24
Restaurant (Le) | P | 6e	26
Rest. de la Tour | S | 15e	21
Rest. du Marché | S, T | 15e	-
Rest. du Palais Royal | G | 1er	19
Rest. GR5 | S, T | multi.	24
Rest. Manufacture | T | Issy-les-Moul.	21
Rest. Paul | S, T | 1er	20
Resto | S, T | 8e	-
Riad | S | Neuilly	-
River Café | T | Issy-les-Moul.	14
Romantica | P, T | Clichy	23
Rotonde | S, T | 6e	15
Rouge St-Honoré | T | 1er	13
Rughetta | T | 18e	-
Sauvignon | S | 7e	14
Saveurs de Claude | S | 6e	-
Saveurs de Flora (Les) | S | 8e	21

Sawadee | S, T | 15e	-
Scoop | S | 1er	17
16 Haussmann | T | 9e	18
7ème Sud | S, T | multi.	15
Sept Quinze | S, T | 15e	21
Soupière | S, T | 17e	-
Square | S | 7e	-
Square | G | 18e	-
Square Trousseau | S | 12e	19
Stella | S | 16e	20
Strapontins | S, T | 10e	-
Stresa | S | 8e	22
Studio | P | 4e	-
Sud | P | 17e	16
Suffren | S, T | 15e	14
Table d'Anvers | S, T | 9e	17
Tastevin | G | Maisons-Laff.	24
Temps au Temps | S, T | 11e	25
Terrasse Mirabeau | T | 16e	-
Terroir | S | 13e	-
Thiou/Petit Thiou | S | 7e	21
Tokyo Eat | T | 16e	14
Tonnelle Saintongeaise | G | Neuilly	-
Tournesol | S | 16e	18
Triporteur | S | 15e	-
Troquet | S | 15e	24
Trumilou | S | 4e	19
Vagenende | S, T | 6e	15
Vaudeville | S | 2e	18
Viaduc Café | S, T | 12e	-
Vieille Fontaine | G | Maisons-Laff.	-
Vieux Bistro | S | 4e	21
Vieux Chêne | S | 11e	-
Villa Spicy | S | 8e	13
Vinea Café | T | 12e	-
20 de Bellechasse | S | 7e	19
Wepler | S | 18e	14
Zébra Square | S, T | 16e	10
Zéphyr | T | 20e	-
Zo | S | 8e	-

PARKING

(V=valet, *=validated)

A et M | V | 16e	21
☑ Alain Ducasse | V | 8e	28
Al Dar | V | 5e	21

Al Diwan | V | 8^e	21	Céladon | V | 2^e	21
Z Ambassadeurs | V | 8^e	28	Chalet des Iles | V | 16^e	14
Z Ambroisie | V | 4^e	28	Chen Soleil d'Est | V | 15^e	-
Z Apicius | V | 8^e	26	Chez Françoise | V | 7^e	17
Arome | V | 8^e	-	Chez Fred | V | 17^e	-
Asian | V | 8^e	16	Chez Georges-Maillot | V | 17^e	18
Astor | V | 8^e	16	Chez Jenny | V | 3^e	19
Aub. Bressane | V | 7^e	20	Chez Les Anges | V | 7^e	23
Avenue | V | 8^e	18	Chez Livio | V | **Neuilly**	13
Barlotti | V | 1er	15	Chez Vong | V | 1er	21
Barrio Latino | V | 12^e	12	Chiberta | V | 8^e	22
Bar Vendôme | V | 1er	23	Closerie des Lilas | V | 6^e	18
Bastide Odéon | V | 6^e	22	Clou | V | 17^e	19
Bath's | V | 17^e	20	Clovis | V | 8^e	-
Benkay | V | 15^e	24	Comte de Gascogne | V |	-
Berkeley | V | 8^e	14	**Boulogne**	
BIOArt | V | 13^e	-	Congrès Maillot | V | 17^e	18
Bistro 121 | V | 15^e	-	Copenhague | V | 8^e	18
Bistrot d'à Côté | V | **multi.**	21	Costes | V | 1er	18
Bistrot de Marius | V | 8^e	21	Cou de la Girafe | V | 8^e	15
Bistrot de Paris | V | 7^e	16	**Z** Cristal Room | V | 16^e	17
Bistrot Niel | V | 17^e	-	Dalloyau | V | 8^e	23
Blue Elephant* | 11^e	20	Delicabar | V | 7^e	13
Bocconi | V | 8^e	20	Dessirier | V | 17^e	20
Boeuf Couronné | V | 19^e	16	Diep | V | 8^e	21
Boeuf sur le Toit | V | 8^e	18	Divellec | V | 7^e	24
Bon | V | 16^e	15	**Z** 1728 | V | 8^e	19
Bouchons Clerc/P'tit | V | 8^e	20	Drouant | V | 2^e	22
Z Bouquinistes | V | 6^e	23	Duc (Le) | V | 14^e	23
Brass. Flo | V | 10^e	18	El Mansour | V | 8^e	17
Brass. Julien | V | 10^e	19	Elysées (Les) | V | 8^e	23
Brass. La Lorraine | V | 8^e	17	Escargot Montorgueil | V | 1er	21
Z Bristol | V | 8^e	27	**Z** Espadon (L') | V | 1er	26
Z Buddha Bar | V | 8^e	16	Etoile | V | 16^e	24
Café de l'Esplanade | V | 7^e	16	Findi | V | 8^e	16
Café du Commerce | V | 15^e	16	First | V | 1er	18
Café Faubourg | V | 8^e	22	Flandrin | V | 16^e	15
Café la Jatte | V | **Neuilly**	14	Flora Danica | V | 8^e	19
Café Lenôtre | V | 8^e	18	Fontaine Gaillon | V | 2^e	22
Café M | V | 8^e	19	Fouquet's | V | 8^e	18
Café Terminus | V | 8^e	-	Gare | V | 16^e	14
Caffè Minotti | V | 7^e	22	Garnier | V | 8^e	22
Cap Seguin | V | **Boulogne**	-	**Z** Georges | V | 4^e	18
Carpaccio | V | 8^e	-	**Z** Gérard Besson | V | 1er	25
Z Carré des Feuillants | V | 1er	26	Goumard | V | 1er	24
Caves Pétrissans | V | 17^e	19	Grand Colbert | V | 2^e	19
Caviar Kaspia | V | 8^e	25	Grande Armée | V | 16^e	15

SPECIAL FEATURES

☑ Grand Véfour | V | 1er	28
Grand Venise | V | 15e	25
☑ Guy Savoy | V | 17e	28
☑ Hélène Darroze | V | 6e	25
Huîtrier | V | 17e	20
Il Cortile | V | 1er	23
Ile | V | **Issy-les-Moul.**	18
☑ Jacques Cagna | V | 6e	26
Jardin des Cygnes | V | 8e	22
Jarrasse | V | **Neuilly**	–
Kinugawa/Hanawa | V | 8e	23
Kiosque | V | 16e	15
Kong | V | 1er	14
☑ Lapérouse | V | 6e	21
☑ Lasserre | V | 8e	27
☑ Laurent | V | 8e	24
Lei | V | 7e	21
Liza | V | 2e	24
NEW Lup | V | 6e	–
☑ Lyonnais | V | 2e	21
Maison Blanche | V | 8e	20
Maison du Caviar | V | 8e	22
Maison Prunier | V | 16e	21
Marée (La) | V | 8e	23
Marée Denfert/Passy | V | **multi.**	–
Marius | V | 16e	18
Marius et Janette | V | 8e	25
Market | V | 8e	22
Marty | V | 5e	16
Mathusalem | V | 16e	–
Maxan | V | 8e	–
Maxim's | V | 8e	18
Meating | V | 17e	17
Méditerranée | V | 6e	21
☑ Meurice | V | 1er	27
☑ Michel Rostang | V | 17e	27
Montalembert | V | 7e	19
Mori Venice Bar | V | 2e	17
Moulin à Vent | V | 5e	19
Murano | V | 3e	16
Murat | V | 16e	13
Muses | V | 9e	19
Musichall | V | 8e	15
Obélisque | V | 8e	23
Orangerie | V | 4e	22
Ozu | V | 16e	23

Paris | V | 6e	20
Pasco* | 7e	22
☑ Passiflore | V | 16e	26
Paul Chêne | V | 16e	20
☑ Pavillon/Gr. Cascade | V | 16e	25
☑ Pavillon Ledoyen | V | 8e	26
Pavillon Montsouris | V | 14e	17
Pershing | V | 8e	17
Petit Pergolèse | V | 16e	23
Petit Poucet | V | **Levallois**	–
Pétrus | V | 17e	21
☑ Pierre Gagnaire | V | 8e	28
Pinxo | V | 1er	21
☑ Pré Catelan | V | 16e	27
Pur'Grill | V | 2e	19
Quai Ouest | V | **St-Cloud**	13
Quinzième | V | 15e	–
☑ Relais d'Auteuil | V | 16e	27
Relais Plaza | V | 8e	23
River Café | V | **Issy-les-Moul.**	14
Romantica | V | **Clichy**	23
Rôtiss. d'en Face | V | 6e	21
Rue Balzac | V | 8e	17
Salon d'Hélène | V | 6e	19
San | V | 3e	–
NEW Saut du Loup | V | 1er	14
Sébillon | V | **Neuilly**	15
16 Haussmann | V | 9e	18
☑ Senderens | V | 8e	26
Sensing | V | 6e	24
6 New York | V | 16e	17
Sora Lena | V | 17e	–
Sormani | V | 17e	23
Spoon/Food | V | 8e	22
Stella | V | 16e	20
Sud | V | 17e	16
Table de Babette | V | 16e	–
☑ Table de Joël Robuchon | V | 16e	26
Table d'Hédiard | V | 8e	22
Table du Baltimore | V | 16e	–
Table du Lancaster | V | 8e	23
☑ Taillevent | V | 8e	28
Tang | V | 16e	17
Terrasse Mirabeau | V | 16e	–
Thiou/Petit Thiou | V | 7e	21
Timgad | V | 17e	20

Toi | V | 8ᵉ	–
Tong Yen | V | 8ᵉ	15
Z Tour d'Argent | V | 5ᵉ	25
NEW Toustem | V | 5ᵉ	–
Truffe Noire | V | Neuilly	–
Villa Corse | V | 15ᵉ	20
Village d'Ung | V | 8ᵉ	–
Villa Spicy | V | 8ᵉ	13
Vin et Marée | V | multi.	18
NEW Winch | V | 18ᵉ	–
W Restaurant | V | 8ᵉ	–
Zébra Square | V | 16ᵉ	10

PEOPLE-WATCHING

A. Beauvilliers | 18ᵉ	20
Absinthe | 1ᵉʳ	20
Z Alain Ducasse | 8ᵉ	28
Z Ami Louis | 3ᵉ	25
Anahï | 3ᵉ	19
Angle du Faubourg | 8ᵉ	24
Z Arpège | 7ᵉ	26
Astor | 8ᵉ	16
Z Astrance | 16ᵉ	28
Z Atelier Joël Robuchon | 7ᵉ	28
Avenue | 8ᵉ	18
Barlotti | 1ᵉʳ	15
Z Benoît | 4ᵉ	24
Berkeley | 8ᵉ	14
Black Calavados | 8ᵉ	–
Z Brass. Balzar | 5ᵉ	19
Z Brass. Lipp | 6ᵉ	17
Z Bristol | 8ᵉ	27
Café Beaubourg | 4ᵉ	16
Z Café de Flore | 6ᵉ	15
Café de l'Esplanade | 7ᵉ	16
Café Etienne Marcel | 2ᵉ	18
Café Guitry | 9ᵉ	–
Z Café Les Deux Magots | 6ᵉ	16
Caffé Minotti | 7ᵉ	22
Z 144 Petrossian | 7ᵉ	25
Chateaubriand | 11ᵉ	22
Chez Les Anges | 7ᵉ	23
Chez Omar | 3ᵉ	21
Z Cinq (Le) | 8ᵉ	28
Cinq Mars | 7ᵉ	19
Copenhague | 8ᵉ	18
Costes | 1ᵉʳ	18

NEW Dali | 1ᵉʳ	–
Divellec | 7ᵉ	24
Dôme | 14ᵉ	22
Drouant | 2ᵉ	22
Duc (Le) | 14ᵉ	23
NEW Eclaireur | 8ᵉ	–
Elysées (Les) | 8ᵉ	23
Z Epi Dupin | 6ᵉ	24
Z Espadon (L') | 1ᵉʳ	26
Ferme St-Simon | 7ᵉ	23
Flandrin | 16ᵉ	15
Fouquet's | 8ᵉ	18
Gare | 16ᵉ	14
Gauloise | 15ᵉ	15
Z Georges | 4ᵉ	18
Grande Armée | 16ᵉ	15
Z Grand Véfour | 1ᵉʳ	28
Z Guy Savoy | 17ᵉ	28
Z Hélène Darroze | 6ᵉ	25
Il Cortile | 1ᵉʳ	23
Jarrasse | Neuilly	–
Joséphine/Dumonet | 6ᵉ	23
Kong | 1ᵉʳ	14
Z Lasserre | 8ᵉ	27
NEW Lup | 6ᵉ	–
Maison Blanche | 8ᵉ	20
Maison de l'Amér. Latine | 7ᵉ	18
Maison Prunier | 16ᵉ	21
Market | 8ᵉ	22
Méditerranée | 6ᵉ	21
NEW Mini Palais | 8ᵉ	–
Murano | 3ᵉ	16
Musichall | 8ᵉ	15
Z Ombres (Les) | 7ᵉ	18
Orangerie | 4ᵉ	22
Z Pavillon Ledoyen | 8ᵉ	26
Pétrelle | 9ᵉ	–
Z Pierre Gagnaire | 8ᵉ	28
Z Pré Catelan | 16ᵉ	27
Publicis Drugstore | 8ᵉ	11
Quinzième | 15ᵉ	–
Relais Plaza | 8ᵉ	23
Renoma Café | 8ᵉ	–
Restaurant (Le) | 6ᵉ	26
Salon d'Hélène | 6ᵉ	19
NEW Salon du Panthéon | 5ᵉ	–
NEW Saut du Loup | 1ᵉʳ	14

SPECIAL FEATURES

🅩 Senderens | 8ᵉ	26
Sensing | 6ᵉ	24
6 New York | 16ᵉ	17
Sormani | 17ᵉ	23
Spoon/Food | 8ᵉ	22
Square Trousseau | 12ᵉ	19
Stresa | 8ᵉ	22
🅩 Table de Joël Robuchon | 16ᵉ	26
Table du Lancaster | 8ᵉ	23
🅩 Taillevent | 8ᵉ	28
Tan Dinh | 7ᵉ	23
Terrasse Mirabeau | 16ᵉ	-
Thiou/Petit Thiou | 7ᵉ	21
Tong Yen | 8ᵉ	15
🅩 Tour d'Argent | 5ᵉ	25
Voltaire | 7ᵉ	24

POWER SCENES

A. Beauvilliers | 18ᵉ	20
🅩 Alain Ducasse | 8ᵉ	28
🅩 Ambassadeurs | 8ᵉ	28
🅩 Ambroisie | 4ᵉ	28
🅩 Apicius | 8ᵉ	26
🅩 Arpège | 7ᵉ	26
Assiette | 14ᵉ	-
🅩 Atelier Joël Robuchon | 7ᵉ	28
Aub. Bressane | 7ᵉ	20
Bar des Théâtres | 8ᵉ	15
Bastide Odéon | 6ᵉ	22
🅩 Benoît | 4ᵉ	24
Bistrot de l'Etoile Laur. | 16ᵉ	-
Bistrot de l'Université | 7ᵉ	18
Bistrot de Marius | 8ᵉ	21
Bistrot de Paris | 7ᵉ	16
Bistrot d'Henri | 6ᵉ	20
Bistrot Niel | 17ᵉ	-
Bon Saint Pourçain | 6ᵉ	18
🅩 Brass. Balzar | 5ᵉ	19
🅩 Brass. Lipp | 6ᵉ	17
🅩 Bristol | 8ᵉ	27
🅩 Café de Flore | 6ᵉ	15
Café Faubourg | 8ᵉ	22
Caffè Minotti | 7ᵉ	22
Cagouille | 14ᵉ	25
Cap Vernet | 8ᵉ	17
Carpaccio | 8ᵉ	-
🅩 Carré des Feuillants | 1ᵉʳ	26

Caves Pétrissans | 17ᵉ	19
Caviar Kaspia | 8ᵉ	25
Cazaudehore | St-Germain-Laye	22
Céladon | 2ᵉ	21
Chen Soleil d'Est | 15ᵉ	-
Cherche Midi | 6ᵉ	19
Chez Les Anges | 7ᵉ	23
Chiberta | 8ᵉ	22
Cigale Récamier | 7ᵉ	21
Clos des Gourmets | 7ᵉ	25
Closerie des Lilas | 6ᵉ	18
Comte de Gascogne | Boulogne	-
Copenhague | 8ᵉ	18
Costes | 1ᵉʳ	18
🅩 Cristal Room | 16ᵉ	17
Dessirier | 17ᵉ	20
Divellec | 7ᵉ	24
Dôme | 14ᵉ	22
Duc (Le) | 14ᵉ	23
Elysées (Les) | 8ᵉ	23
🅩 Espadon (L') | 1ᵉʳ	26
Etoile | 16ᵉ	24
Ferme St-Simon | 7ᵉ	23
Flandrin | 16ᵉ	15
Fouquet's | 8ᵉ	18
Gare | 16ᵉ	14
Gaya | 7ᵉ	23
🅩 Georges | 4ᵉ	18
Goumard | 1ᵉʳ	24
Grande Armée | 16ᵉ	15
🅩 Grand Véfour | 1ᵉʳ	28
🅩 Guy Savoy | 17ᵉ	28
🅩 Hiramatsu | 16ᵉ	26
NEW Il Vino | 7ᵉ	-
Issé | 1ᵉʳ	23
Jarrasse | Neuilly	-
Joséphine/Dumonet | 6ᵉ	23
🅩 Jules Verne | 7ᵉ	-
🅩 Ladurée | 8ᵉ	23
🅩 Lasserre | 8ᵉ	27
🅩 Laurent | 8ᵉ	24
Maison Blanche | 8ᵉ	20
Maison Prunier | 16ᵉ	21
Marée (La) | 8ᵉ	23
Marius | 16ᵉ	18
Marius et Janette | 8ᵉ	25
Market | 8ᵉ	22

Marlotte | 6ᵉ	16
Marty | 5ᵉ	16
Mathusalem | 16ᵉ	-
Meating | 17ᵉ	17
🅩 Meurice | 1ᵉʳ	27
🅩 Michel Rostang | 17ᵉ	27
Montalembert | 7ᵉ	19
Montparnasse 25 | 14ᵉ	16
Mori Venice Bar | 2ᵉ	17
Obélisque | 8ᵉ	23
Oenothèque | 9ᵉ	-
Oulette | 12ᵉ	19
Paris | 6ᵉ	20
Paul Chêne | 16ᵉ	20
🅩 Pavillon/Gr. Cascade | 16ᵉ	25
🅩 Pavillon Ledoyen | 8ᵉ	26
Pavillon Montsouris | 14ᵉ	17
Perron | 7ᵉ	18
Petit Colombier | 17ᵉ	18
Petit Marguery | 13ᵉ	21
Petit Poucet | **Levallois**	-
Petit Rétro | 16ᵉ	16
Pétrus | 17ᵉ	21
Pichet de Paris | 8ᵉ	16
Pierre au Palais Royal | 1ᵉʳ	17
🅩 Pierre Gagnaire | 8ᵉ	28
Port Alma | 16ᵉ	17
🅩 Pré Catelan | 16ᵉ	27
Quincy | 12ᵉ	-
🅩 Relais d'Auteuil | 16ᵉ	27
Relais Plaza | 8ᵉ	23
Sébillon | **Neuilly**	15
🅩 Senderens | 8ᵉ	26
Sormani | 17ᵉ	23
🅩 Stella Maris | 8ᵉ	26
Stresa | 8ᵉ	22
Table d'Anvers | 9ᵉ	17
🅩 Table de Joël Robuchon | 16ᵉ	26
Table du Lancaster | 8ᵉ	23
🅩 Taillevent | 8ᵉ	28
Tan Dinh | 7ᵉ	23
Tante Marguerite | 7ᵉ	22
Terrasse Mirabeau | 16ᵉ	-
Tong Yen | 8ᵉ	15
Tonnelle Saintongeaise | **Neuilly**	-
🅩 Tour d'Argent | 5ᵉ	25
Tsé-Yang | 16ᵉ	18

Vieux Bistro | 4ᵉ	21
🅩 Violon d'Ingres | 7ᵉ	25
Voltaire | 7ᵉ	24

QUICK BITES

🅩 Angelina | 1ᵉʳ	20
A Priori Thé | 2ᵉ	16
🅩 As du Fallafel | 4ᵉ	24
Bar des Théâtres | 8ᵉ	15
Baron Rouge | 12ᵉ	-
Barrio Latino | 12ᵉ	12
BE Boulangépicier | 8ᵉ	19
BIOArt | 13ᵉ	-
Bistrot à Vins Mélac | 11ᵉ	14
Bons Crus | 1ᵉʳ	-
Boulangerie Eric Kayser | 8ᵉ	16
Brass. Printemps | 9ᵉ	11
Breakfast in America | **multi.**	15
NEW Breizh Café | 3ᵉ	-
🅩 Buddha Bar | 8ᵉ	16
Buffalo Grill | **multi.**	10
Café Beaubourg | 4ᵉ	16
🅩 Café de Flore | 6ᵉ	15
Café du Commerce | 15ᵉ	16
🅩 Café Les Deux Magots | 6ᵉ	16
🅩 Café Marly | 1ᵉʳ	16
Cave de l'Os à Moëlle | 15ᵉ	22
Chez Marianne | 4ᵉ	18
Chez Papa | **multi.**	17
Cloche des Halles | 1ᵉʳ	-
Clown Bar | 11ᵉ	17
NEW Cocottes | 7ᵉ	21
Coffee Parisien | **multi.**	16
Congrès Maillot | 17ᵉ	18
Cosi | 6ᵉ	19
NEW Crémerie | 6ᵉ	-
Crêperie de Josselin | 14ᵉ	22
Dalloyau | **multi.**	23
Dame Tartine | 4ᵉ	14
Da Rosa | 6ᵉ	19
Duc de Richelieu | 12ᵉ	-
Ebouillanté | 4ᵉ	-
Ecluse | **multi.**	16
Emporio Armani | 6ᵉ	19
Escale du Liban | 4ᵉ	-
Ferme | 1ᵉʳ	-
NEW Fines Gueules | 1ᵉʳ	-
Fous d'en Face | 4ᵉ	-

Fumoir | **1ᵉʳ**	17
NEW Garance | **10ᵉ**	-
Garnier | **8ᵉ**	22
Indiana Café | **multi.**	7
Je Thé . . . Me | **15ᵉ**	-
Joe Allen | **1ᵉʳ**	13
Juvéniles | **1ᵉʳ**	16
Léon/Bruxelles | **multi.**	16
Lina's | **multi.**	16
Loir dans/Théière | **4ᵉ**	16
Lô Sushi | **8ᵉ**	15
Ma Bourgogne | **4ᵉ**	18
Maison du Caviar | **8ᵉ**	22
Mariage Frères | **multi.**	21
Mauzac | **5ᵉ**	-
Mesturet | **2ᵉ**	-
Mirama | **5ᵉ**	20
Murat | **16ᵉ**	13
Nemrod | **6ᵉ**	16
Noura | **multi.**	19
Papilles | **5ᵉ**	23
Paradis du Fruit | **5ᵉ**	14
Petite Sirène/Copen. | **9ᵉ**	-
Pinxo | **1ᵉʳ**	21
Press Café | **2ᵉ**	-
Publicis Drugstore | **8ᵉ**	11
Ragueneau | **1ᵉʳ**	-
Rest. du Musée d'Orsay | **7ᵉ**	17
Rose Bakery | **9ᵉ**	17
Rubis | **1ᵉʳ**	15
NEW Salon du Panthéon | **5ᵉ**	-
Sauvignon | **7ᵉ**	14
Scoop | **1ᵉʳ**	17
NEW SYDR | **8ᵉ**	-
Table d'Hédiard | **8ᵉ**	22
Tav. Henri IV | **1ᵉʳ**	16
Tsukizi | **6ᵉ**	-
Viaduc Café | **12ᵉ**	-
Vinea Café | **12ᵉ**	-
✓ Vin sur Vin | **7ᵉ**	26
Wok Cooking | **11ᵉ**	-

QUIET CONVERSATION

A. Beauvilliers | **18ᵉ**	20
NEW Agassin | **7ᵉ**	-
Aiguière | **11ᵉ**	-
Aimant du Sud | **13ᵉ**	-

NEW Alfred | **1ᵉʳ**	-
Alivi | **4ᵉ**	16
Allobroges | **20ᵉ**	22
Ambassade/Auvergne | **3ᵉ**	20
Ami Marcel | **15ᵉ**	17
Ampère | **17ᵉ**	-
Amuse Bouche | **14ᵉ**	17
Angl'Opéra | **2ᵉ**	19
A Priori Thé | **2ᵉ**	16
Assiette | **14ᵉ**	-
✓ Astrance | **16ᵉ**	28
Atelier Berger | **1ᵉʳ**	21
✓ Atelier Joël Robuchon | **7ᵉ**	28
Aub. du Clou | **9ᵉ**	16
Aub. Pyrénées | **11ᵉ**	20
Bamboche | **7ᵉ**	19
Basilic | **7ᵉ**	15
Bellini | **16ᵉ**	24
✓ Benoît | **4ᵉ**	24
Bistro d'Hubert | **15ᵉ**	22
Bistro Poulbot | **18ᵉ**	-
Bistrot d'à Côté | **multi.**	21
Bistrot d'Henri | **6ᵉ**	20
Bistrot du Peintre | **11ᵉ**	18
Boeuf sur le Toit | **8ᵉ**	18
Bon Saint Pourçain | **6ᵉ**	18
Bouillon Racine | **6ᵉ**	16
✓ Bouquinistes | **6ᵉ**	23
Brass. Flo | **10ᵉ**	18
Brass. Julien | **10ᵉ**	19
✓ Brass. Lipp | **6ᵉ**	17
Brass. Mollard | **8ᵉ**	19
Buisson Ardent | **5ᵉ**	19
Butte Chaillot | **16ᵉ**	21
Ca d'Oro | **1ᵉʳ**	18
Café de l'Industrie | **11ᵉ**	12
Café du Passage | **11ᵉ**	-
Café Faubourg | **8ᵉ**	22
Café Lenôtre | **8ᵉ**	18
✓ Café Les Deux Magots | **6ᵉ**	16
Café M | **8ᵉ**	19
✓ Café Marly | **1ᵉʳ**	16
Caffé Minotti | **7ᵉ**	22
Caméléon | **6ᵉ**	20
Camélia | **Bougival**	20
Cap Vernet | **8ᵉ**	17
Carpaccio | **8ᵉ**	-

Cartes Postales	1er	24	Gallopin	2e	16
Cave Gourmande	19e	25	NEW Garance	10e	-
Caviar Kaspia	8e	25	Garnier	8e	22
Z 144 Petrossian	7e	25	Gaya	7e	23
Chardenoux	11e	19	Georgette	9e	22
Charpentiers	6e	18	Z Gérard Besson	1er	25
Chez Géraud	16e	20	Gli Angeli	3e	18
Chez Les Anges	7e	23	Goumard	1er	24
Chez Maître Paul	6e	21	Gourmand (Au)	1er	20
Chez Pauline	1er	20	Graindorge	17e	22
Chez René	5e	21	Guirlande de Julie	3e	15
Chiberta	8e	22	Huîtrier	17e	20
Cigale Récamier	7e	21	Il Cortile	1er	23
Clos des Gourmets	7e	25	Isami	4e	25
Closerie des Lilas	6e	18	Jean	9e	19
Copenhague	8e	18	Joséphine/Dumonet	6e	23
Costes	1er	18	Z Jules Verne	7e	-
Coupe-Chou	5e	23	NEW Karl et Erich	17e	-
Z Coupole	14e	19	Kiosque	16e	15
Crus de Bourgogne	2e	17	Z Ladurée	multi.	23
Cuisine (7e)	7e	25	Z Lapérouse	6e	21
NEW Cuisine (11e)	11e	-	Legrand Filles et Fils	2e	-
NEW Dali	1er	-	Macéo	1er	23
Dalva	2e	-	Magnolias	Perreux	25
Da Rosa	6e	19	Maison Blanche	8e	20
Daru	8e	-	Mansouria	11e	22
Dauphin	1er	20	Marée (La)	8e	23
Délices d'Aphrodite	5e	18	Mariage Frères	multi.	21
Dessirier	17e	20	Marlotte	6e	16
Diapason	18e	-	Marty	5e	16
Dix Vins	15e	-	Maupertu	7e	21
Djakarta	1er	20	Maxan	8e	-
Ebouillanté	4e	-	NEW M Comme Martine	17e	-
Ecaille de Fontaine	2e	-	Meating	17e	17
El Mansour	8e	17	Méditerranée	6e	21
Entoto	13e	-	Montalembert	7e	19
Entracte	18e	-	Moulin de la Galette	18e	15
Epi d'Or	1er	16	Murano	3e	16
NEW Epigramme	6e	-	Muscade	1er	-
Erawan	15e	17	No Stress Café	9e	-
Escargot Montorgueil	1er	21	Obélisque	8e	23
NEW Fines Gueules	1er	-	Orangerie	4e	22
Fins Gourmets	7e	19	Orénoc	17e	17
Flora Danica	8e	19	Oulette	12e	19
Flore en l'Ile	4e	18	Pamphlet	3e	23
Z Fontaine de Mars	7e	21	Pasco	7e	22
Fontanarosa	15e	-	Pères et Filles	6e	16

Restaurant	Score		Restaurant	Score
Petit Colombier	17e	18	Z Allard	6e	21
Petite Chaise	7e	19	Z Ambassadeurs	8e	28
Petite Sirène/Copen.	9e	-	Z Ambroisie	4e	28
Petit Lutétia	6e	19	Z Arpège	7e	26
Petit Marguery	13e	21	Astor	8e	16
Petit Prince de Paris	5e	-	Z Astrance	16e	28
Petit Rétro	16e	16	Bambocke	7e	19
Pierre au Palais Royal	1er	17	Bistro Poulbot	18e	-
Z Pierre Gagnaire	8e	28	Blue Elephant	11e	20
Point Bar	1er	22	Bouillon Racine	6e	16
Polidor	6e	17	Z Bouquinistes	6e	23
Potager du Roy	Versailles	19	Brass. Flo	10e	18
NEW P'tit Casier	15e	-	Brass. Julien	10e	19
P'tit Troquet	7e	22	Z Bristol	8e	27
Repaire de Cartouche	11e	16	Buisson Ardent	5e	19
Restaurant (Le)	6e	26	Z Café de Flore	6e	15
Rest. du Marché	15e	-	Café Lenôtre	8e	18
Rest. du Palais Royal	1er	19	Z Café Les Deux Magots	6e	16
Roi du Pot-au-Feu	9e	-	Z Café Marly	1er	16
Rose de France	1er	-	Casa Olympe	9e	24
Rue Balzac	8e	17	Caviar Kaspia	8e	25
NEW Salon du Panthéon	5e	-	Z 144 Petrossian	7e	25
Sarladais	8e	-	Chalet des Iles	16e	14
Saudade	1er	-	Chardenoux	11e	19
NEW Saut du Loup	1er	14	Chez Julien	4e	19
Sébillon	Neuilly	15	Chez Pauline	1er	20
16 Haussmann	9e	18	Closerie des Lilas	6e	18
Sot l'y Laisse	11e	-	Copenhague	8e	18
Z Soufflé	1er	22	Costes	1er	18
Z Stella Maris	8e	26	Coupe-Chou	5e	23
Stresa	8e	22	Z Coupole	14e	19
Table du Lancaster	8e	23	Z Cristal Room	16e	17
Taïra	17e	-	Crus de Bourgogne	2e	17
Tan Dinh	7e	23	Délices d'Aphrodite	5e	18
Tante Louise	8e	22	Dôme	14e	22
Tête Ailleurs	4e	-	El Mansour	8e	17
Thiou/Petit Thiou	7e	21	Elysées (Les)	8e	23
Z Trou Gascon	12e	26	Epi d'Or	1er	16
Tsé-Yang	16e	18	Z Espadon (L')	1er	26
Viaduc Café	12e	-	Fakhr el Dine	16e	24
Vieux Bistro	4e	21	First	1er	18
Vin dans les voiles	16e	-	Flora Danica	8e	19
Z Vin sur Vin	7e	26	Z Fontaine de Mars	7e	21
NEW Winch	18e	-	Gavroche	2e	17
			Z Georges	4e	18
ROMANTIC PLACES			Z Grand Véfour	1er	28
A. Beauvilliers	18e	20	Guirlande de Julie	3e	15
Z Alain Ducasse	8e	28			

☑ Guy Savoy | 17e | 28
Il Cortile | 1er | 23
☑ Jacques Cagna | 6e | 26
Jardins de Bagatelle | 16e | 17
Joséphine/Dumonet | 6e | 23
☑ Jules Verne | 7e | -
☑ Ladurée | **multi.** | 23
☑ Lapérouse | 6e | 21
☑ Lasserre | 8e | 27
☑ Laurent | 8e | 24
Ma Bourgogne | 4e | 18
Macéo | 1er | 23
Maison Blanche | 8e | 20
Maison de l'Amér. Latine | 7e | 18
Mansouria | 11e | 22
Marty | 5e | 16
Maxim's | 8e | 18
Méditerranée | 6e | 21
☑ Meurice | 1er | 27
Moulin de la Galette | 18e | 15
Muscade | 1er | -
Orangerie | 4e | 22
☑ Pavillon/Gr. Cascade | 16e | 25
☑ Pavillon Ledoyen | 8e | 26
Pavillon Montsouris | 14e | 17
Petit Prince de Paris | 5e | -
Potager du Roy | **Versailles** | 19
☑ Pré Catelan | 16e | 27
Relais Louis XIII | 6e | 25
Restaurant (Le) | 6e | 26
Rest. Paul | 1er | 20
Romantica | **Clichy** | 23
Rughetta | 18e | -
Sormani | 17e | 23
Square Trousseau | 12e | 19
☑ Stella Maris | 8e | 26
Tan Dinh | 7e | 23
Tête Ailleurs | 4e | -
Timgad | 17e | 20
☑ Tour d'Argent | 5e | 25
☑ Train Bleu | 12e | 19
☑ Trou Gascon | 12e | 26
Versance | 2e | -
Zingot | 10e | -

SINGLES SCENES

Absinthe | 1er | 20
A et M | 16e | 21

Alsace | 8e | 18
Alsaco | 9e | -
Amici Miei | 11e | 19
Angle du Faubourg | 8e | 24
Apollo | 14e | -
Astor | 8e | 16
Aub. du Clou | 9e | 16
Autobus Imperial | 1er | -
Bar des Théâtres | 8e | 15
Barlotti | 1er | 15
Baron Rouge | 12e | -
Barrio Latino | 12e | 12
Berkeley | 8e | 14
Bistro/Deux Théâtres | 9e | 14
Bistrot à Vins Mélac | 11e | 14
Bistrot d'à Côté | 17e | 21
Black Calavados | 8e | -
Bon | 16e | 15
☑ Brass. Balzar | 5e | 19
☑ Buddha Bar | 8e | 16
Café Beaubourg | 4e | 16
Café Burq | 18e | -
☑ Café de Flore | 6e | 15
Café de la Paix | 9e | 19
Café de l'Esplanade | 7e | 16
Café du Passage | 11e | -
Café Etienne Marcel | 2e | 18
Café la Jatte | **Neuilly** | 14
Café Lenôtre | 8e | 18
☑ Café Les Deux Magots | 6e | 16
Café M | 8e | 19
☑ Café Marly | 1er | 16
Café Ruc | 1er | 15
Carr's | 1er | -
Cave de l'Os à Moëlle | 15e | 22
Chateaubriand | 11e | 22
Cherche Midi | 6e | 19
Chez Gégène | **Joinville** | -
Cinq Mars | 7e | 19
Closerie des Lilas | 6e | 18
Clown Bar | 11e | 17
Comédiens | 9e | -
Costes | 1er | 18
Curieux Spaghetti Bar | 4e | -
Delicabar | 7e | 13
NEW Eclaireur | 8e | -
Emporio Armani | 6e | 19

SPECIAL FEATURES

Enoteca | 4ᵉ	20	Chez Catherine | 8ᵉ	23
Etoile | 16ᵉ	24	Chez Les Anges | 7ᵉ	23
Fumoir | 1ᵉʳ	17	Coin/Gourmets | multi.	22
NEW Garance | 10ᵉ	–	Cuisine (7e) | 7ᵉ	25
Grille St-Germain | 6ᵉ	17	Dôme du Marais | 4ᵉ	22
Joe Allen | 1ᵉʳ	13	Duc (Le) | 14ᵉ	23
Kiosque | 16ᵉ	15	Elysées (Les) | 8ᵉ	23
Kong | 1ᵉʳ	14	Etoile | 16ᵉ	24
Loir dans/Théière | 4ᵉ	16	Fakhr el Dine | 16ᵉ	24
Lô Sushi | 8ᵉ	15	Fontaine Gaillon | 2ᵉ	22
NEW Lup | 6ᵉ	–	Frégate | 12ᵉ	24
NEW Mini Palais | 8ᵉ	–	Garnier | 8ᵉ	22
Murano | 3ᵉ	16	Georgette | 9ᵉ	22
Murat | 16ᵉ	13	Graindorge | 17ᵉ	22
Musichall | 8ᵉ	15	Grand Venise | 15ᵉ	25
NEW Nouvelle Athenes | 9ᵉ	–	Huîtrerie Régis | 6ᵉ	22
Pinxo | 1ᵉʳ	21	Il Cortile | 1ᵉʳ	23
Press Café | 2ᵉ	–	Isami | 4ᵉ	25
Restaurant (Le) | 6ᵉ	26	Issé | 1ᵉʳ	23
Rubis | 1ᵉʳ	15	Jardin des Cygnes | 8ᵉ	22
Sauvignon | 7ᵉ	14	Jean-Paul Hévin | 1ᵉʳ	24
Vinea Café | 12ᵉ	–	Kinugawa/Hanawa | multi.	23
Zo | 8ᵉ	–	Liza | 2ᵉ	24

SLEEPERS

(Good to excellent food, but little known)

		Macéo | 1ᵉʳ	23
Affriolé | 7ᵉ	22	Magnolias | **Perreux**	25
Allobroges | 20ᵉ	22	Maison Courtine | 14ᵉ	24
Aub. Nicolas Flamel | 3ᵉ	23	Maison du Caviar | 8ᵉ	22
Auguste | 7ᵉ	25	Mansouria | 11ᵉ	22
Avant Goût | 13ᵉ	23	Marée (La) | 8ᵉ	23
Azabu | 6ᵉ	24	Obélisque | 8ᵉ	23
Bellini | 16ᵉ	24	Ostéria (L') | 4ᵉ	22
Benkay | 15ᵉ	24	Ourcine | 13ᵉ	24
Beurre Noisette | 15ᵉ	23	Ozu | 16ᵉ	22
Bistro d'Hubert | 15ᵉ	22	Pamphlet | 3ᵉ	23
Bistrot Paul Bert | 11ᵉ	23	Papilles | 5ᵉ	23
Boulangerie | 20ᵉ	23	Pasco | 7ᵉ	22
Bourguignon du Marais | 4ᵉ	23	Petit Marché | 3ᵉ	22
Café Faubourg | 8ᵉ	22	Petit Pergolèse | 16ᵉ	23
Caffé Minotti | 7ᵉ	22	Point Bar | 1ᵉʳ	22
Cagouille | 14ᵉ	25	Poule au Pot | 1ᵉʳ	23
Cartes Postales | 1ᵉʳ	24	Restaurant (Le) | 6ᵉ	26
Casa Olympe | 9ᵉ	24	Rest. GR5 | **multi.**	24
Cave de l'Os à Moëlle | 15ᵉ	22	Romantica | **Clichy**	23
Cave Gourmande | 19ᵉ	25	Sensing | 6ᵉ	24
Cazaudehore | **St-Germain-Laye**	22	Sormani | 17ᵉ	23
		Spring | 9ᵉ	23
		Stresa | 8ᵉ	22

Table d'Hédiard	8e	22	Chez Marianne	4e	18
Table du Lancaster	8e	23	Chez Michel	10e	24
Tante Louise	8e	22	Chez Vincent	19e	-
Tante Marguerite	7e	22	Chiberta	8e	22
Tastevin	**Maisons-Laff.**	24	Chieng Mai	5e	16
Temps au Temps	11e	25	☑ Cinq (Le)	8e	28
Timbre	6e	24	Clovis	8e	-
Troquet	15e	24	Coco de Mer	5e	-
Truffière	5e	23	Comte de Gascogne	**Boulogne**	-
Yugaraj	6e	23	Copenhague	8e	18

TASTING MENUS

			☑ Cristal Room	16e	17
Aida	7e	23	Cuisine (7e)	7e	25
Aiguière	11e	-	D'Chez Eux	7e	25
Alain Bourgade	16e	-	Diapason	18e	-
☑ Alain Ducasse	8e	28	☑ Dominique Bouchet	8e	27
Allobroges	20e	22	Elysées (Les)	8e	23
Al Mounia	16e	17	☑ Espadon (L')	1er	26
Angle du Faubourg	8e	24	Ferrandaise	6e	21
☑ Apicius	8e	26	Fogón	6e	21
Arome	8e	-	Fouquet's	8e	18
☑ Arpège	7e	26	Gazzetta	12e	-
Asian	8e	16	☑ Gérard Besson	1er	25
Astor	8e	16	Graindorge	17e	22
☑ Astrance	16e	28	Grand Colbert	2e	19
Atelier Berger	1er	21	☑ Grand Véfour	1er	28
Aub. Nicolas Flamel	3e	23	☑ Guy Savoy	17e	28
Avant Goût	13e	23	☑ Hélène Darroze	6e	25
Baan-Boran	1er	20	☑ Hiramatsu	16e	26
Bamboche	7e	19	**NEW** Il Vino	7e	-
Bar à Huîtres	3e	17	Inagiku	5e	18
Bistrot d'à Côté	17e	21	Issé	1er	23
Bistrot du Sommelier	8e	18	☑ Jacques Cagna	6e	26
Blue Elephant	11e	20	Jean	9e	19
☑ Bristol	8e	27	☑ Jules Verne	7e	-
☑ Buddha Bar	8e	16	Kinugawa/Hanawa	**multi.**	23
Café de la Paix	9e	19	☑ Lapérouse	6e	21
Camélia	**Bougival**	20	☑ Lasserre	8e	27
Carpaccio	8e	-	☑ Laurent	8e	24
☑ Carré des Feuillants	1er	26	Magnolias	**Perreux**	25
Cartes Postales	1er	24	Maharajah	5e	17
Casa Tina	16e	-	Mansouria	11e	22
Céladon	2e	21	Marée (La)	8e	23
☑ 144 Petrossian	7e	25	Mavrommatis	5e	19
Chen Soleil d'Est	15e	-	Maxan	8e	-
Chez Catherine	8e	23	☑ Meurice	1er	27
Chez Cécile	8e	-	☑ Michel Rostang	17e	27
Chez L'Ami Jean	7e	24	Mont Liban	17e	-

Montparnasse 25	14ᵉ	16
Moulin de la Galette	18ᵉ	15
Muses	9ᵉ	19
Noura	16ᵉ	19
Olivades	7ᵉ	17
Orangerie	4ᵉ	22
Orient-Extrême	6ᵉ	18
🄩 Os à Moëlle	15ᵉ	25
Ozu	16ᵉ	23
Paris	6ᵉ	20
Passy Mandarin	16ᵉ	20
Paul Chêne	16ᵉ	20
🄩 Pavillon/Gr. Cascade	16ᵉ	25
🄩 Pavillon Ledoyen	8ᵉ	26
Petit Colombier	17ᵉ	18
Petit Marguery	13ᵉ	21
🄩 Pierre Gagnaire	8ᵉ	28
Potager du Roy	Versailles	19
🄩 Pré Catelan	16ᵉ	27
Pur'Grill	2ᵉ	19
Quinzième	15ᵉ	-
🄩 Relais d'Auteuil	16ᵉ	27
Relais Louis XIII	6ᵉ	25
Restaurant (Le)	6ᵉ	26
Romantica	Clichy	23
Salon d'Hélène	6ᵉ	19
San	3ᵉ	-
Saveurs de Flora (Les)	8ᵉ	21
Sawadee	15ᵉ	-
16 Haussmann	9ᵉ	18
Sensing	6ᵉ	24
Spring	9ᵉ	23
🄩 Stella Maris	8ᵉ	26
Stéphane Gaborieau	16ᵉ	-
Table d'Anvers	9ᵉ	17
Table de Babette	16ᵉ	-
🄩 Table de Joël Robuchon	16ᵉ	26
Table du Baltimore	16ᵉ	-
Table du Lancaster	8ᵉ	23
🄩 Taillevent	8ᵉ	28
Taïra	17ᵉ	-
Tang	16ᵉ	17
Terrasse Mirabeau	16ᵉ	-
Thierry Burlot	15ᵉ	-
🄩 Train Bleu	12ᵉ	19
Troquet	15ᵉ	24
Truffe Noire	Neuilly	-

Truffière	5ᵉ	23
🄩 Villaret	11ᵉ	26
🄩 Violon d'Ingres	7ᵉ	25
Wally Le Saharien	9ᵉ	15
W Restaurant	8ᵉ	-

TEEN APPEAL

Absinthe	1ᵉʳ	20
Alcazar	6ᵉ	19
Al Dar	multi.	21
Anahï	3ᵉ	19
Anahuacalli	5ᵉ	21
🄩 Angelina	1ᵉʳ	20
Annapurna	8ᵉ	18
Apollo	14ᵉ	-
🄩 As du Fallafel	4ᵉ	24
Asian	8ᵉ	16
Aub. du Clou	9ᵉ	16
Autobus Imperial	1ᵉʳ	-
Avant Goût	13ᵉ	23
Avenue	8ᵉ	18
Bar des Théâtres	8ᵉ	15
Baron Rouge	12ᵉ	-
Barrio Latino	12ᵉ	12
Bartolo	6ᵉ	17
Bascou	3ᵉ	20
Berkeley	8ᵉ	14
BIOArt	13ᵉ	-
Bistrot à Vins Mélac	11ᵉ	14
Bistrot d'André	15ᵉ	-
🄩 Bistrot de l'Oulette	4ᵉ	26
Bistrot des Dames	17ᵉ	14
Bistrot du Peintre	11ᵉ	18
Blue Elephant	11ᵉ	20
Bon	16ᵉ	15
Boulangerie	20ᵉ	23
Breakfast in America	multi.	15
NEW Breizh Café	3ᵉ	-
🄩 Buddha Bar	8ᵉ	16
Buffalo Grill	multi.	10
Café Beaubourg	4ᵉ	16
Café Burq	18ᵉ	-
Café Charbon	11ᵉ	15
Café de la Musique	19ᵉ	15
Café de la Poste	4ᵉ	-
Café de l'Esplanade	7ᵉ	16
Café de l'Industrie	11ᵉ	12
Café de Mars	7ᵉ	17

Café du Commerce | 15e	16	Fous d'en Face | 4e	-
Café du Passage | 11e	-	Fumoir | 1er	17
Café la Jatte | Neuilly	14	Gamin de Paris | 4e	21
Café Lenôtre | 8e	18	NEW Garance | 10e	-
Z Café Marly | 1er	16	Z Georges | 4e	18
Café Ruc | 1er	15	Gli Angeli | 3e	18
Cailloux | 13e	-	Grande Armée | 16e	15
Carr's | 1er	-	Grille St-Germain | 6e	17
Chalet des Iles | 16e	14	Hangar | 3e	18
Chartier | 9e	13	Hippopotamus | multi.	11
Chez Clément | multi.	15	Ile | Issy-les-Moul.	18
Chez L'Ami Jean | 7e	24	Indiana Café | multi.	7
Chez Marianne | 4e	18	Isami | 4e	25
Chez Omar | 3e	21	Joe Allen | 1er	13
Chez Papa | multi.	17	Kiosque | 16e	15
Chez Paul | 11e	21	Kong | 1er	14
Chez Prune | 10e	18	Lao Siam | 19e	15
Chez Vong | 1er	21	Léon/Bruxelles | multi.	16
Clown Bar | 11e	17	Lina's | multi.	16
Coco de Mer | 5e	-	Loir dans/Théière | 4e	16
NEW Cocottes | 7e	21	Lô Sushi | 8e	15
Coffee Parisien | multi.	16	NEW Lup | 6e	-
Coin/Gourmets | 5e	22	Ma Bourgogne | 4e	18
Comptoir | 1er	21	Mauzac | 5e	-
Cosi | 6e	19	Mavrommatis | 5e	19
Costes | 1er	18	NEW Mini Palais | 8e	-
Coude Fou | 4e	19	Mirama | 5e	20
Z Coupole | 14e	19	Murat | 16e	13
Crêperie de Josselin | 14e	22	No Stress Café | 9e	-
Curieux Spaghetti Bar | 4e	-	NEW Nouvelle Athenes | 9e	-
Dame Tartine | 4e	14	Ostéria (L') | 4e	22
Delicabar | 7e	13	Paradis du Fruit | 5e	14
Délices d'Aphrodite | 5e	18	Paradis Thai | 13e	15
Dix Vins | 15e	-	Petite Sirène/Copen. | 9e	-
Durand Dupont | Neuilly	-	Pied de Cochon | 1er	18
Ebouillanté | 4e	-	Polidor | 6e	17
Emporio Armani | 6e	19	Press Café | 2e	-
Enoteca | 4e	20	Quai Ouest | St-Cloud	13
Entoto | 13e	-	404 | 3e	22
Entracte | 18e	-	Refectoire | 11e	-
Erawan | 15e	17	Rendez-vous/Chauff. | 18e	-
Etoile | 16e	24	Renoma Café | 8e	-
Ferme | 1er	-	River Café | Issy-les-Moul.	14
Z Fish La Boissonnerie | 6e	22	Rose Bakery | 9e	17
Fogón | 6e	21	Rubis | 1er	15
Z Fontaine de Mars | 7e	21	San | 3e	-
Fontaines | 5e	17	Sardegna a Tavola | 12e	21

SPECIAL FEATURES

Sauvignon	7e	14	Annapurna	8e	18
16 Haussmann	9e	18	Asian	8e	16
Sept Quinze	15e	21	Atlas	5e	20
Spoon/Food	8e	22	Benkay	15e	24
Square Trousseau	12e	19	Blue Elephant	11e	20
Tav. de Maître Kanter	1er	16	NEW Breizh Café	3e	-
Thiou/Petit Thiou	7e	21	Z Buddha Bar	8e	16
Tricotin	13e	-	Café la Jatte	Neuilly	14
Trumilou	4e	19	Cerisaie	14e	21
Vagenende	6e	15	Chalet des Iles	16e	14
Vaudeville	2e	18	Chen Soleil d'Est	15e	-
Viaduc Café	12e	-	Chez Gégène	Joinville	-
Villa Spicy	8e	13	Chez Vong	1er	21
Vinea Café	12e	-	Coco de Mer	5e	-
Water Bar Colette	1er	14	Délices d'Aphrodite	5e	18
Wok Cooking	11e	-	Djakarta	1er	20
Yen	6e	20	Enoteca	4e	20
Zébra Square	16e	10	Entoto	13e	-
Zéphyr	20e	-	Erawan	15e	17
Zo	8e	-	Etoile Marocaine	8e	-

THEME RESTAURANTS

Aub. Nicolas Flamel	3e	23	Fakhr el Dine	16e	24
Bar à Huîtres	multi.	17	Fogón	6e	21
Barrio Latino	12e	12	NEW Il Vino	7e	-
Bel Canto	multi.	13	Isami	4e	25
Bellota-Bellota	7e	19	Jardins de Bagatelle	16e	17
Bistrot d'André	15e	-	Mansouria	11e	22
Breakfast in America	multi.	15	Mavrommatis	5e	19
NEW Breizh Café	3e	-	Monsieur Lapin	14e	18
Z Buddha Bar	8e	16	Saudade	1er	-
Café de la Musique	19e	15	Z Soufflé	1er	22
Chez Clément	multi.	15	Z Stella Maris	8e	26
Coco de Mer	5e	-	Taïra	17e	-
NEW Cocottes	7e	21	Tan Dinh	7e	23
NEW Il Vino	7e	-	Timgad	17e	20
Léon/Bruxelles	multi.	16	Tricotin	13e	-
Lina's	multi.	16	Tsé-Yang	16e	18
Monsieur Lapin	14e	18	Wally Le Saharien	9e	15
Nos Ancêtres/Gaulois	4e	13	Yen	6e	20
Paradis du Fruit	5e	14		
Pomze	8e	18		

TRENDY

Rouge St-Honoré	1er	13	NEW Afaria	15e	-
Wok Cooking	11e	-	Aida	7e	23
		Alcazar	6e	19

TRANSPORTING EXPERIENCES

		Z Ami Louis	3e	25
Alsaco	9e	-	Anahï	3e	19
Anahï	3e	19	Andy Wahloo	3e	14
		Angle du Faubourg	8e	24

Restaurant	Score
Angl'Opéra	2e	19

Restaurant	Score
Angl'Opéra | 2e	19
Z Astrance | 16e	28
Z Atelier Joël Robuchon | 7e	28
Aub. du Clou | 9e	16
Autobus Imperial | 1er	-
Avenue | 8e	18
Barlotti | 1er	15
Barrio Latino | 12e	12
Black Calavados | 8e	-
Bon | 16e	15
Bound | 8e	-
Z Buddha Bar | 8e	16
Butte Chaillot | 16e	21
Café Beaubourg | 4e	16
Café Burq | 18e	-
Café Charbon | 11e	15
Z Café de Flore | 6e	15
Café de l'Esplanade | 7e	16
Café du Passage | 11e	-
Café Etienne Marcel | 2e	18
Café Guitry | 9e	-
Cailloux | 13e	-
Caméléon | 6e	20
Cantine de Quentin | 10e	-
Z 144 Petrossian | 7e	25
Chateaubriand | 11e	22
Cherche Midi | 6e	19
NEW Chéri Bibi | 18e	-
Chez Julien | 4e	19
Chez Les Anges | 7e	23
Chez Omar | 3e	21
Chez Paul | 11e	21
Chez Prune | 10e	18
Chez Ramona | 20e	-
Chez Ramulaud | 11e	16
Chez Vong | 1er	21
Chieng Mai | 5e	16
NEW Cocottes | 7e	21
Z Comptoir du Relais | 6e	26
Costes | 1er	18
Z Cristal Room | 16e	17
Curieux Spaghetti Bar | 4e	-
Dalva | 2e	-
Delicabar | 7e	13
Dix Vins | 15e	-
Don Juans | 3e	-
Durand Dupont | Neuilly	-

Restaurant	Score
NEW Eclaireur | 8e	-
Etoile | 16e	24
Famille | 18e	19
Z Fish La Boissonnerie | 6e	22
Z Fontaine de Mars | 7e	21
Fouquet's | 8e	18
Fumoir | 1er	17
NEW Garance | 10e	-
Gare | 16e	14
Gazzetta | 12e	-
Z Georges | 4e	18
Gli Angeli | 3e	18
Grande Armée | 16e	15
NEW Grand Pan | 15e	-
Hangar | 3e	18
Ile | Issy-les-Moul.	18
Il Viccolo | 6e	-
Kong | 1er	14
Legrand Filles et Fils | 2e	-
NEW Lup | 6e	-
Maison Blanche | 8e	20
Market | 8e	22
Martel | 10e	-
NEW Mini Palais | 8e	-
Murano | 3e	16
Musichall | 8e	15
NEW Nouvelle Athenes | 9e	-
Ozu | 16e	23
Point Bar | 1er	22
404 | 3e	22
Quinzième | 15e	-
NEW Racines | 2e	-
Refectoire | 11e	-
Relais Plaza | 8e	23
Renoma Café | 8e	-
Restaurant (Le) | 6e	26
Rest. Manufacture | Issy-les-Moul.	21
Ribouldingue | 5e	18
River Café | Issy-les-Moul.	14
Rose Bakery | 9e	17
Rughetta | 18e	-
NEW Salon du Panthéon | 5e	-
San | 3e	-
NEW Saut du Loup | 1er	14
Sensing | 6e	24
Sormani | 17e	23

SPECIAL FEATURES

Spoon/Food | 8ᵉ	22
Stresa | 8ᵉ	22
NEW SYDR | 8ᵉ	-
Table du Lancaster | 8ᵉ	23
Tong Yen | 8ᵉ	15
Truc Café | 18ᵉ	-
Unico | 11ᵉ	-
Voltaire | 7ᵉ	24
Water Bar Colette | 1ᵉʳ	14
Z Ze Kitchen Galerie | 6ᵉ	25

VIEWS

Absinthe | 1ᵉʳ	20
Alain Bourgade | 16ᵉ	-
NEW Alfred | 1ᵉʳ	-
Alivi | 4ᵉ	16
Alsace | 8ᵉ	18
Z Angelina | 1ᵉʳ	20
Aub. de Reine Blanche | 4ᵉ	19
Aub. Etchégorry | 13ᵉ	-
Autobus Imperial | 1ᵉʳ	-
Avenue | 8ᵉ	18
Bar Vendôme | 1ᵉʳ	23
Basilic | 7ᵉ	15
Bel Canto | 4ᵉ	13
Benkay | 15ᵉ	24
BIOArt | 13ᵉ	-
Bistro de Breteuil | 7ᵉ	16
Bistrot du Cap | 15ᵉ	-
Bistrot Vivienne | 2ᵉ	18
Z Bon Accueil | 7ᵉ	24
Z Bouquinistes | 6ᵉ	23
Bourguignon du Marais | 4ᵉ	23
Brass. de l'Ile St. Louis | 4ᵉ	17
Brass. du Louvre | 1ᵉʳ	16
Brass. L'Européen | 12ᵉ	-
Café Beaubourg | 4ᵉ	16
Z Café de Flore | 6ᵉ	15
Café de la Musique | 19ᵉ	15
Café de la Poste | 4ᵉ	-
Café de l'Esplanade | 7ᵉ	16
Café Faubourg | 8ᵉ	22
Café la Jatte | Neuilly	14
Café Lenôtre | 8ᵉ	18
Café Le Petit Pont | 5ᵉ	14
Z Café Marly | 1ᵉʳ	16
Cagouille | 14ᵉ	25

Cantine de Quentin | 10ᵉ	-
Cap Seguin | Boulogne	-
Cap Vernet | 8ᵉ	17
Carpaccio | 8ᵉ	-
Caveau du Palais | 1ᵉʳ	19
Caviar Kaspia | 8ᵉ	25
Cazaudehore | St-Germain-Laye	22
Chalet des Iles | 16ᵉ	14
Chantairelle | 5ᵉ	-
Charlot Roi des Coq. | 9ᵉ	15
Chez Clément | 8ᵉ	15
Chez Francis | 8ᵉ	17
Chez Fred | 17ᵉ	-
Chez Gégène | Joinville	-
Chez Julien | 4ᵉ	19
Chez Léna et Mimile | 5ᵉ	15
Chez Paul | 13ᵉ	16
Chez Prune | 10ᵉ	18
Chien qui Fume | 1ᵉʳ	18
Z Cinq (Le) | 8ᵉ	28
Cloche des Halles | 1ᵉʳ	-
Clos des Gourmets | 7ᵉ	25
Comptoir | 1ᵉʳ	21
Copenhague | 8ᵉ	18
Dalloyau | 6ᵉ	23
Dame Tartine | 4ᵉ	14
Dauphin | 1ᵉʳ	20
D'Chez Eux | 7ᵉ	25
Diapason | 18ᵉ	-
Divellec | 7ᵉ	24
Duc de Richelieu | 12ᵉ	-
Durand Dupont | Neuilly	-
Z Espadon (L') | 1ᵉʳ	26
Etoile | 16ᵉ	24
Fables de La Fontaine | 7ᵉ	24
First | 1ᵉʳ	18
Flora Danica | 8ᵉ	19
Flore en l'Ile | 4ᵉ	18
Z Fontaine de Mars | 7ᵉ	21
Fontaine Gaillon | 2ᵉ	22
Fontaines | 5ᵉ	17
Fouquet's | 8ᵉ	18
Fous d'en Face | 4ᵉ	-
Fumoir | 1ᵉʳ	17
NEW Garance | 10ᵉ	-
Z Georges | 4ᵉ	18
Gli Angeli | 3ᵉ	18

Restaurant	Score
Grand Café | 9ᵉ	13
Grande Armée | 16ᵉ	15
☒ Grand Véfour | 1ᵉʳ	28
Guirlande de Julie | 3ᵉ	15
Il Cortile | 1ᵉʳ	23
Ile | **Issy-les-Moul.**	18
NEW Il Vino | 7ᵉ	-
Isami | 4ᵉ	25
Jardins de Bagatelle | 16ᵉ	17
☒ Jules Verne | 7ᵉ	-
Khun Akorn | 11ᵉ	-
Kinugawa/Hanawa | 8ᵉ	23
Kiosque | 16ᵉ	15
Kong | 1ᵉʳ	14
☒ Ladurée | 8ᵉ	23
☒ Lapérouse | 6ᵉ	21
☒ Lasserre | 8ᵉ	27
Lavinia | 1ᵉʳ	17
Legrand Filles et Fils | 2ᵉ	-
Léon/Bruxelles | **multi.**	16
Maison Blanche | 8ᵉ	20
Maison de l'Amér. Latine | 7ᵉ	18
Marius | 16ᵉ	18
Market | 8ᵉ	22
Marty | 5ᵉ	16
Maupertu | 7ᵉ	21
Mavrommatis | 5ᵉ	19
Méditerranée | 6ᵉ	21
Moissonnier | 5ᵉ	19
Montalembert | 7ᵉ	19
Moulin de la Galette | 18ᵉ	15
Muscade | 1ᵉʳ	-
NEW Nouvelle Athenes | 9ᵉ	-
☒ Ombres (Les) | 7ᵉ	18
Ozu | 16ᵉ	23
Papilles | 5ᵉ	23
Parc aux Cerfs | 6ᵉ	21
Pasco | 7ᵉ	22
☒ Pavillon/Gr. Cascade | 16ᵉ	25
☒ Pavillon Ledoyen | 8ᵉ	26
Pershing | 8ᵉ	17
Petit Bofinger | 17ᵉ	18
Petit Châtelet | 5ᵉ	-
Petite Cour | 6ᵉ	21
Petit Marché | 3ᵉ	22
Petit Pergolèse | 16ᵉ	23
Petit Poucet | **Levallois**	-

Restaurant	Score
Petit Zinc | 6ᵉ	18
Pied de Cochon | 1ᵉʳ	18
Pitchi Poï | 4ᵉ	-
Point Bar | 1ᵉʳ	22
Port Alma | 16ᵉ	17
Pouilly Reuilly | **St-Gervais**	-
Poule au Pot | 1ᵉʳ	23
Procope | 6ᵉ	16
Pure Café | 11ᵉ	-
Quai | 7ᵉ	-
Quai Ouest | **St-Cloud**	13
Rech | 17ᵉ	-
☒ Relais/l'Entrecôte | 6ᵉ	22
Relais de Venise | 17ᵉ	24
Rest. de la Tour | 15ᵉ	21
Rest. du Musée d'Orsay | 7ᵉ	17
Rest. du Palais Royal | 1ᵉʳ	19
Rest. Paul | 1ᵉʳ	20
Resto | 8ᵉ	-
River Café | **Issy-les-Moul.**	14
Romantica | **Clichy**	23
Rose de France | 1ᵉʳ	-
Rotonde | 6ᵉ	15
Rouge St-Honoré | 1ᵉʳ	13
NEW Saut du Loup | 1ᵉʳ	14
Sawadee | 15ᵉ	-
Sébillon | **Neuilly**	15
Square | 7ᵉ	-
Square | 18ᵉ	-
Square Trousseau | 12ᵉ	19
Suffren | 15ᵉ	14
Table d'Anvers | 9ᵉ	17
Table d'Hédiard | 8ᵉ	22
Table du Lancaster | 8ᵉ	23
Tastevin | **Maisons-Laff.**	24
Tav. Henri IV | 1ᵉʳ	16
Terrasse Mirabeau | 16ᵉ	-
Terres de Truffes | 8ᵉ	19
Thiou/Petit Thiou | 7ᵉ	21
Tonnelle Saintongeaise | **Neuilly**	-
☒ Tour d'Argent | 5ᵉ	25
Tournesol | 16ᵉ	18
☒ Train Bleu | 12ᵉ	19
Truc Café | 18ᵉ	-
Trumilou | 4ᵉ	19
Vaudeville | 2ᵉ	18
Vieille Fontaine | **Maisons-Laff.**	-

SPECIAL FEATURES

Vinea Café | 12ᵉ	-
Vin et Marée | 1ᵉʳ	18
Voltaire | 7ᵉ	24
Waknine | 16ᵉ	-
Wepler | 18ᵉ	14
Ⓩ Willi's Wine Bar | 1ᵉʳ	20

VISITORS ON EXPENSE ACCOUNT

A. Beauvilliers | 18ᵉ	20
Ⓩ Ambroisie | 4ᵉ	28
Ⓩ Ami Louis | 3ᵉ	25
Ⓩ Arpège | 7ᵉ	26
Assiette | 14ᵉ	-
Ⓩ Atelier Joël Robuchon | 7ᵉ	28
Auguste | 7ᵉ	25
Ⓩ Benoît | 4ᵉ	24
Café Faubourg | 8ᵉ	22
Caffè Minotti | 7ᵉ	22
Carpaccio | 8ᵉ	-
Ⓩ Carré des Feuillants | 1ᵉʳ	26
Caviar Kaspia | 8ᵉ	25
Chen Soleil d'Est | 15ᵉ	-
Chez Les Anges | 7ᵉ	23
Chez Pauline | 1ᵉʳ	20
Chiberta | 8ᵉ	22
Clovis | 8ᵉ	-
Copenhague | 8ᵉ	18
Cuisine (7e) | 7ᵉ	25
Dessirier | 17ᵉ	20
Divellec | 7ᵉ	24
Dôme | 14ᵉ	22
Ⓩ Dominique Bouchet | 8ᵉ	27
Drouant | 2ᵉ	22
Duc (Le) | 14ᵉ	23
NEW Eclaireur | 8ᵉ	-
Ferme St-Simon | 7ᵉ	23
Flora Danica | 8ᵉ	19
Fouquet's | 8ᵉ	18
Frégate | 12ᵉ	24
Garnier | 8ᵉ	22
Gaya | 7ᵉ	23
Ⓩ Gérard Besson | 1ᵉʳ	25
Goumard | 1ᵉʳ	24
Ⓩ Grand Véfour | 1ᵉʳ	28
Ⓩ Guy Savoy | 17ᵉ	28
Ⓩ Hélène Darroze | 6ᵉ	25
Il Cortile | 1ᵉʳ	23

NEW Il Vino | 7ᵉ	-
Ⓩ Jacques Cagna | 6ᵉ	26
Jarrasse | Neuilly	-
Joséphine/Dumonet | 6ᵉ	23
Ⓩ Jules Verne | 7ᵉ	-
Kifune | 17ᵉ	-
Ⓩ Lasserre | 8ᵉ	27
Ⓩ Laurent | 8ᵉ	24
Maison Blanche | 8ᵉ	20
Mansouria | 11ᵉ	22
Marée (La) | 8ᵉ	23
Marius | 16ᵉ	18
Maxim's | 8ᵉ	18
Meating | 17ᵉ	17
Ⓩ Michel Rostang | 17ᵉ	27
Muses | 9ᵉ	19
Obélisque | 8ᵉ	23
Orangerie | 4ᵉ	22
Orénoc | 17ᵉ	17
Oulette | 12ᵉ	19
Ⓩ Pavillon Ledoyen | 8ᵉ	26
Petit Colombier | 17ᵉ	18
Pétrus | 17ᵉ	21
Pierre au Palais Royal | 1ᵉʳ	17
Ⓩ Pierre Gagnaire | 8ᵉ	28
Pomze | 8ᵉ	18
Ⓩ Pré Catelan | 16ᵉ	27
Relais Louis XIII | 6ᵉ	25
Relais Plaza | 8ᵉ	23
Ⓩ Senderens | 8ᵉ	26
Ⓩ Stella Maris | 8ᵉ	26
Table d'Anvers | 9ᵉ	17
Ⓩ Table de Joël Robuchon | 16ᵉ	26
Table du Lancaster | 8ᵉ	23
Ⓩ Taillevent | 8ᵉ	28
Taïra | 17ᵉ	-
Tante Marguerite | 7ᵉ	22
Terrasse Mirabeau | 16ᵉ	-
Ⓩ Tour d'Argent | 5ᵉ	25
Ⓩ Trou Gascon | 12ᵉ	26
W Restaurant | 8ᵉ	-

WATERSIDE

BIOArt | 13ᵉ	-
Brass. de l'Ile St. Louis | 4ᵉ	17
Buffalo Grill | 13ᵉ	10
Cap Seguin | Boulogne	-

Chalet des Iles | 16^e	14
Chez Gégène | **Joinville**	-
Chez Prune | 10^e	18
Gourmand | **Neuilly**	-
Petit Poucet | **Levallois**	-
Quai | 7^e	-
Quai Ouest | **St-Cloud**	13
River Café | **Issy-les-Moul.**	14

WINNING WINE LISTS

Z Alain Ducasse | 8^e	28
Z Ambassadeurs | 8^e	28
Z Ambroisie | 4^e	28
Z Atelier Joël Robuchon | 7^e	28
Bistrot du Sommelier | 8^e	18
Bistrot Paul Bert | 11^e	23
Bouchons Clerc/P'tit | 8^e	20
Bourguignon du Marais | 4^e	23
Z Bristol | 8^e	27
Café Burq | 18^e	-
Café Lenôtre | 8^e	18
Cagouille | 14^e	25
Z Carré des Feuillants | 1er	26
Cave de l'Os à Moëlle | 15^e	22
Caves Pétrissans | 17^e	19
Z 144 Petrossian | 7^e	25
Chai 33 | 12^e	14
Chez Géraud | 16^e	20
Z Cinq (Le) | 8^e	28
Coupe Gorge | 4^e	-
NEW Crémerie | 6^e	-
Dessirier | 17^e	20
Divellec | 7^e	24
Drouant | 2^e	22
Ecluse | **multi.**	16
Elysées (Les) | 8^e	23
Enoteca | 4^e	20
Ferme St-Simon | 7^e	23
NEW Fines Gueules | 1er	-
Z Fish La Boissonnerie | 6^e	22
Fogón | 6^e	21
Z Gérard Besson | 1er	25
Z Grand Véfour | 1er	28

Z Guy Savoy | 17^e	28
Z Hélène Darroze | 6^e	25
Il Cortile | 1er	23
NEW Il Vino | 7^e	-
Z Jacques Cagna | 6^e	26
Joséphine/Dumonet | 6^e	23
Z Jules Verne | 7^e	-
Z Lasserre | 8^e	27
Z Laurent | 8^e	24
Lavinia | 1er	17
Legrand Filles et Fils | 2^e	-
Macéo | 1er	23
Marée (La) | 8^e	23
Maxim's | 8^e	18
Z Meurice | 1er	27
Z Michel Rostang | 17^e	27
Montparnasse 25 | 14^e	16
Muses | 9^e	19
Oenothèque | 9^e	-
Oulette | 12^e	19
Paris | 6^e	20
Z Pavillon/Gr. Cascade | 16^e	25
Z Pavillon Ledoyen | 8^e	26
Petit Marguery | 13^e	21
Pierre au Palais Royal | 1er	17
Z Pierre Gagnaire | 8^e	28
NEW Racines | 2^e	-
Relais Louis XIII | 6^e	25
Saudade | 1er	-
Z Senderens | 8^e	26
Spoon/Food | 8^e	22
Z Stella Maris | 8^e	26
Table d'Anvers | 9^e	17
Z Taillevent | 8^e	28
Tante Marguerite | 7^e	22
Tav. Henri IV | 1er	16
Z Tour d'Argent | 5^e	25
Z Trou Gascon | 12^e	26
Vieux Chêne | 11^e	-
Vin dans les voiles | 16^e	-
Z Vin sur Vin | 7^e	26
Yugaraj | 6^e	23

Wine Vintage Chart

This chart, based on our 0 to 30 scale, is designed to help you select wine. The ratings (by **Howard Stravitz**, a law professor at the University of South Carolina) reflect the vintage quality and the wine's readiness to drink. We exclude the 1991–1993 vintages because they are not that good. A dash indicates the wine is either past its peak or too young to rate. Loire ratings are for dry white wines.

Whites

	88	89	90	94	95	96	97	98	99	00	01	02	03	04	05	06
French:																
Alsace	-	25	25	24	23	23	22	25	23	25	27	25	22	24	25	-
Burgundy	-	23	22	-	28	27	24	22	26	25	24	27	23	27	26	24
Loire Valley	-	-	-	-	-	-	-	-	-	24	25	26	23	24	27	24
Champagne	24	26	29	-	26	27	24	23	24	24	22	26	-	-	-	-
Sauternes	29	25	28	-	21	23	25	23	24	24	28	25	26	21	26	23
California:																
Chardonnay	-	-	-	-	-	-	-	-	24	23	26	26	25	27	29	25
Sauvignon Blanc	-	-	-	-	-	-	-	-	-	-	27	28	26	27	26	27
Austrian:																
Grüner Velt./ Riesling	-	-	-	-	25	21	26	26	25	22	23	25	26	25	26	-
German:	25	26	27	24	23	26	25	26	23	21	29	27	24	26	28	-

Reds

	88	89	90	94	95	96	97	98	99	00	01	02	03	04	05	06
French:																
Bordeaux	23	25	29	22	26	25	23	25	24	29	26	24	25	24	27	25
Burgundy	-	24	26	-	26	27	25	22	27	22	24	27	25	25	27	25
Rhône	26	28	28	24	26	22	25	27	26	27	26	-	25	24	25	-
Beaujolais	-	-	-	-	-	-	-	-	24	-	23	25	22	28	26	-
California:																
Cab./Merlot	-	-	28	29	27	25	28	23	26	22	27	26	25	24	24	23
Pinot Noir	-	-	-	-	-	-	24	23	24	23	27	28	26	25	24	-
Zinfandel	-	-	-	-	-	-	-	-	-	25	23	27	24	23	-	-
Oregon:																
Pinot Noir	-	-	-	-	-	-	-	-	-	-	27	25	26	27	-	-
Italian:																
Tuscany	-	-	25	22	24	20	29	24	27	24	27	20	25	25	22	24
Piedmont	-	27	27	-	23	26	27	26	25	28	27	20	24	25	26	-
Spanish:																
Rioja	-	-	-	26	26	24	25	22	25	24	27	20	24	25	26	24
Ribera del Duero/Priorat	-	-	-	26	26	27	25	24	25	24	27	20	24	26	26	24
Australian:																
Shiraz/Cab.	-	-	-	24	26	23	26	28	24	24	27	27	25	26	24	-
Chilean:	-	-	-	-	-	24	-	25	23	26	24	25	24	26	-	-

ON THE GO.
IN THE KNOW.

ZAGAT TO GO℠

Unlimited access to Zagat dining & travel content in hundreds of major cities.

Search by name, location, ratings, cuisine, special features and Top Lists.

For BlackBerry,® Palm,® Windows Mobile® and mobile phones.

Zagat ▼ New York City				
▼ View All		1562 Choice		
Name	F	D	S	C
A	22	11	19	23
Abboccato	23	20	21	61
Abigael's	20	16	18	45
Above	18	19	18	50
Aburiya Kinnosuke	25	21	21	51
Acappella	24	21	24	67
Acqua Pazza	21	19	20	51
Lookup	Advanced Searc			

Get it now at **mobile.zagat.com** or text* **ZAGAT** to **78247**

Zagat Products

RESTAURANTS & MAPS

America's Top Restaurants
Atlanta
Beijing
Boston
Brooklyn
California Wine Country
Cape Cod & The Islands
Chicago
Connecticut
Europe's Top Restaurants
Hamptons (incl. wineries)
Hong Kong
Las Vegas
London
Long Island (incl. wineries)
Los Angeles I So. California
(guide & map)
Miami Beach
Miami I So. Florida
Montréal
New Jersey
New Jersey Shore
New Orleans
New York City (guide & map)
Palm Beach
Paris
Philadelphia
San Diego
San Francisco (guide & map)
Seattle
Shanghai
Texas
Tokyo
Toronto
Vancouver
Washington, DC I Baltimore
Westchester I Hudson Valley
World's Top Restaurants

LIFESTYLE GUIDES

America's Top Golf Courses
Movie Guide
Music Guide
NYC Gourmet Shop./Entertaining
NYC Shopping

NIGHTLIFE GUIDES

Los Angeles
New York City
San Francisco

HOTEL & TRAVEL GUIDES

Beijing
Hong Kong
Las Vegas
London
New Orleans
Montréal
Shanghai
Toronto
U.S. Family Travel
U.S. Top Hotels, Resorts & Spas
Vancouver
Walt Disney World Insider's Guide
World's Top Hotels, Resorts & Spas

WEB & WIRELESS SERVICES

ZAGAT TO GO[SM] for handhelds
ZAGAT.com[SM] • ZAGAT.mobi[SM]

**Available wherever books are sold or at ZAGAT.com. To customize
Zagat guides as gifts or marketing tools, call 800-540-9609.**